FINDING INDIANA ANCESTORS

A Guide to Historical Research

THE DAILY GRAPHIC

AN ILLUSTRATED EVENING NEWSPAPER

39 & 41 PARK PLACE

VOL. XXII. | All the News. Four Editions Daily. | NEW YORK, THURSDAY, APRIL 8, 1880—TEN PAGES. | $12 Per Year in Advance. Single Copies, Five Cents. | NO. 2191.

WHY THEY EMIGRATE.

This cartoon signed "Thos. Worth" illustrates several of the reasons why people immigrated to the United States at the end of the nineteenth century. The top section shows crowds of people fleeing military oppression. The bottom section depicts the promises of America: agricultural abundance, common schools, religious freedom, ample factory work, and a warm welcome from Uncle Sam. Worth also highlights the fact that entire families were immigrating. (Contributed by Douglas E. Clanin)

FINDING INDIANA ANCESTORS
A Guide to Historical Research

EDITED BY

M. Teresa Baer and Geneil Breeze

CONTRIBUTING EDITORS
Judith Q. McMullen and Kathleen M. Breen

EDITORIAL INTERNS
Bethany Natali, Doria Lynch, Evan M. Gaughan, and Amanda C. Jones

INDIANA HISTORICAL SOCIETY PRESS   INDIANAPOLIS 2007

Printed in the United States of America

This book is a publication of the
Indiana Historical Society Press
450 West Ohio Street
Indianapolis, Indiana 46202-3269 USA
www.indianahistory.org
Telephone orders 1-800-447-1830
Fax orders 317-234-0562
Online orders @ shop.indianahistory.org

Photo credits for front cover: Indiana Historical Society

The paper in this publication meets the minimum requirements of American National Standard for Information Sciences—Permanence of Paper for Printed Library materials, ANSI Z39.48-1984.

Library of Congress Cataloging-in-Publication Data

Finding Indiana ancestors : a guide to historical research / edited by M. Teresa Baer and Geneil Breeze ; contributing editors, Judith Q. McMullen and Kathleen M. Breen.

  p. cm.
 Includes bibliographical references and index.
 ISBN-13: 978-0-87195-203-5 (alk. paper)
 1. Indiana—genealogy—Handbooks, manuals, etc. I. Baer, M. Teresa, 1956- II. Breeze, Geneil, 1965- III. McMullen, Judith Q., 1945- IV. Breen, Kathleen M.
 F525.F56 2007
 929'.107207—dc22

                                                2006048810

The editors of *Finding Indiana Ancestors: A Guide to Historical Research*
dedicate this book to the editors of *The Hoosier Genealogist*
who helped to build the foundations for family history research in Indiana.

Guest Editors
JANUARY TO DECEMBER 1961

Nell W. Reeser
JANUARY 1962 TO FEBRUARY 1965

Dorothy Riker
MARCH 1965 TO SEPTEMBER 1978

Rebah M. Fraustein
OCTOBER 1978 TO DECEMBER 1988

Ruth Dorrel
JANUARY 1989 TO DECEMBER 1999

Contents

PART 3: RESEARCHING RECORDS

PART 4: RESEARCHING WITH MAPS

Preface

Genealogy is history on the most personal level, a quest to discover and share stories about one's forebears. The journey begins with the researcher's life, covers the stories of the researcher's parents, and quickly moves back in time to grandparents, great-grandparents, and generations the researcher could never have known in life. As the search deepens into the past, it also widens outward in the present, encompassing aunts, uncles, cousins, distant relatives, and other people who have some knowledge of the lives the researcher is reconstructing.

All this branching backward and outward can be confusing and lead to roadblocks. First-time researchers may wonder where to go to find information and how to go about compiling it. Intrigued with the family legends and photos that they have found or that relatives have shared with them, they wonder where they can find other material containing knowledge of their ancestors. Places like archives and courthouses sound intimidating at first, and as a new researcher begins to dig around in the books and documents in these places, the sheer number of sources available appears daunting. What is in all those boxes, folders, and books? Which sources would be most helpful? What do you look for first? Where do you go from there? And then later, what do you do with all of the stuff you have gathered? How do you make sense of it? How do you keep track of it all? The mind of the beginning researcher is filled with how-to questions.

In reality, the initial questions of researchers into historical materials are the same whether they are seeking information about an individual in their bloodline or about a broader historical topic such as the history of a community or the story behind a particular subject. Many of the sources that will help to tell these stories overlap. After all, the history of a person is part of the larger history of a community, which is a puzzle piece of the history of the state, which is integral to the history of the country, and so forth. Family history is history.

So, how do researchers get started? Beyond the basics taught in schools and colleges—go to libraries, find trustworthy Web sites on the Internet, visit a local historical society's archives, and use printed sources for background and a few firsthand documents for interesting details—what does a researcher do? Many states publish guides to historical research to help genealogists, historians, and others know where to go for particular types of information. Most recently, George K. Schweitzer provided such a guide for Indiana, titled *Indiana Genealogical Research*, in 1996. *Finding Indiana Ancestors: A Guide to Historical Research* moves beyond Schweitzer's useful reference source and two guides written earlier than Schweitzer's by showing how to conduct research in the various facilities and on the Internet, how to draw out the most complete and accurate data from old documents, and how to piece together all the data into a cohesive picture of an ancestor or a topic. *Finding Indiana Ancestors: A Guide to Historical Research* provides a good overview of research in general while focusing on sources that deal specifically with Indiana. So, county courthouses will be discussed alongside state archives and national repositories.

The idea for this book had its seed in the often-reprinted pamphlet by the Indiana Historical Society, *Finding Indiana Ancestors*. Since 1967 this small tool has helped Hoosiers from fourth graders to adults start the process of family history research. With a bare-bones explanation, it tells what genealogy is, gives an outline of how genealogical research is conducted, and provides contact information for the state's major repositories. The last time it was updated and reprinted, in 2000, the Indiana Historical Society decided that it was time to compile a comprehensive guide that would delve with insight and detail into all the topics addressed by the pamphlet and add a lot of other basic research subjects to the mix. With its excellent connections to many professionals who work in the state's major libraries and archives and to many professional genealogists and historians, the Society was readily able to contract experts on each facility or research subject to write articles about their areas of expertise. Originally, all these valuable and interesting essays appeared in the Society's quarterly family history journal, *The Hoosier Genealogist* (*THG*), or the upgraded version, *The Hoosier Genealogist: CONNECTIONS*. In this book, they finally come together to form a complete guide for historical research in Indiana.

The main thrust of the *Finding Indiana Ancestors* book is on beginning the research process. The book is divided into six parts. Parts 1–3 focus on getting started, working with family stories and pictures, moving on to document sources in libraries and archives, and understanding what different manuscript sources can offer. Parts 4 and 5 discuss researching with maps and researching different ethnic groups, using German Americans, African Americans, and Native Americans as examples. Part 6 concludes the book with pieces that introduce lesser known manuscript items and artifact research, give background on nineteenth-century medicinal and industrial history, and discuss verification of data. Two appendixes present a sample family group sheet and a sample pedigree chart, and a brief index cross-references subject matter that appears in multiple segments of the book.

The individual chapters within the six parts of the guide often move beyond the how-to mode and provide short examples to help researchers turn data into stories. On a larger scale, special articles, called models, are inserted between the parts of the book to inspire readers with the possibilities that loom from conducting genealogical and

historical research. The authors of the models have dug deeply into hitherto unknown resources, stumbled upon particularly engaging material in a manuscript collection, chosen an original topic for research, or found a compelling angle to an old subject. Through their research and analysis of data new facts emerged, vivid stories arose, and new windows opened onto the past. Their pieces provide meaningful context into which researchers can place the information they find. Randy Mills tells how to write family history to bring an ancestor to life in his or her time and place. Judy McMullen relates the story of the little-known African American pioneers of Harrison County. Ernie Moore digs deeply into Civil War history to discover if his ancestor truly was wounded in battle as family legend insists. Richard Bland paints a picture of Indiana in 1848 using an eyewitness's account. Dan Carpenter depicts the poignant story of Indiana's Chinese Americans. The final essay portrays the loneliness and anxiety experienced by the World War I soldiers of Henry County as they expressed it in their letters back home.

The editors of *Finding Indiana Ancestors: A Guide to Historical Research* welcome readers to the growing community of historical researchers in Indiana. Having worked for seven years to compile this reference tool for beginning and intermediate researchers, we hope to see many dog-eared copies in satchels and book bags, on library shelves and in classrooms, passing from one hand to another. Our goal is to help students and family history researchers delve deeply and widely into the sources that bear witness to the lives of their forebears. We also invite our readers to join the Indiana Historical Society and read its family history journal *The Hoosier Genealogist: CONNECTIONS*. In future years, this periodical will continue its mission to help researchers at all levels learn where to go for the next piece of information, how to interpret the data, and how to incorporate each new fact into the stories of our ancestors—the people of Indiana.

M. TERESA BAER
Editor, Family History Publications
Indiana Historical Society Press

Part 1
Getting Started

Collage created by Susan S. Sutton, design coordinator, and Kim C. Ferrill, photographer, for cover of *Finding Indiana Ancestors*, pamphlet, fourth ed. (Indianapolis: Indiana Historical Society, 2000). Images and documents from IHS collections.

Beginning and Organizing Your Family History

BETTY L. WARREN

If you are just starting your family history research, you have a major advantage because you can organize your materials from the very beginning instead of having to deal with piles of paper and stacks of stuff. For the more experienced researcher, the following suggestions and techniques may help as well.

By definition, genealogy is the study of a family's bloodline pedigree with the accompanying dates and places for each pair of parental names. Family history is all the rest of the information about siblings, heritage traditions, and adopted lineage. Most people start with themselves. If you are doing this for posterity, my suggestion would be to start with your children and research your line as well as your spouse's line. Five basic questions guide family history research:

1) What do you know about your family? Some of us know more details of our family history than others. What you do know should be verified.
2) What are you seeking to learn? This must be specific.
3) What record is extant? Try to determine if a record exists that will tell you what you want to learn. Remember that very few records were officially established for use specifically by genealogists.
4) Where is that record? Consider jurisdictional levels of document creation to determine a possible location; then go find it!
5) Now what? If that document answered the question, it probably opened up a few more as well. So, you start the research cycle again using what you now know about the family. If it did not answer the question, try another record source.

Before searching for information at the library, the courthouse, or on the computer, you must determine what you already know. This eliminates wasting time looking for something you may already have! Compile an inventory of home and family sources. Read and then sort all of the photographs, letters, mementos, newspaper clippings, funeral cards, Bibles, and anything else the family has accumulated. Next, visit other family members who might have information to contribute. Interview the older family members about their memories of weddings, reunions, funerals, and other family gatherings. This is often easier said than done, as some family members do not want to discuss certain aspects of the family history.

Next, check the possibility of any publication that has already been distributed about your family. A major compiled source is the set of *Genealogies in the Library of Congress* edited by Marion J. Kaminkow (1972–1987). Another valuable source is the several-volume *Genealogical and Local History Books in Print* (1956–1992) by Netti Schreiner-Yantis. Keep in mind that some family histories were edited and published, while other manuscripts were just taken to a printer and copied. You will find a wide variety of books on the shelf, many well documented and some with errors. There is also an abundance of compiled data "published" on computer disc and the Internet—again, some well documented but many with errors.

Another guide that might set you on the right course is the International Genealogical Index (IGI), which is available online at www.familysearch.org or on CD. Some older versions may still be available on microfiche. As the name implies, this is a worldwide index of deceased persons abstracted primarily from vital records. Most entries refer researchers to microfilm of original records in regard to an event such as a birth, marriage, or death. Some entries are from submitted material, and this information should be used only as a guide to verify your existing data. It might be just what you need to lead you into the right geographic area. Of course, the IGI is not all-inclusive. In addition, check every possible spelling of the names you are researching.

A valuable source for research is the census. A federal census has been taken every ten years since 1790. Although the population schedules are the ones most frequently used by genealogists, other portions of the census are also useful: the mortality schedules, the agricultural and manufacturing schedules, statistical compilations, slave enumerations, state and territorial census records, and the military census. The records are primarily available on microfilm, and some are now on the Internet. Most years of the population schedules are indexed, some using the phonetic Soundex Code. Statistical data of a census is often available within a year following the completion of the record taking. Because of privacy laws, the actual population schedules are only made public after seventy-two years; so the 1930 census is the most recent release for genealogical research.

Vital records provide the foundation for genealogical research. The verification of the birth, marriage, and death dates on a family tree is required for a documented search. The date that births and deaths began to be recorded varies from state to state. The recording of marriages often began with the formation of a county, but marriage records contain little application information until just before 1900. Access to vital records is becoming increasingly difficult across the nation. Several states are passing legislation in the name of security to inhibit searching. Some vital records are more available at a county-level public health office rather than at the state level. Many early records have been abstracted and are available in libraries or online. If you have a question or concern about obtaining access to Indiana's public records, you may want to contact the Public Access Counselor's office of the state of Indiana at 800-228-6013 or through the www.IN.gov Web site. Other states may have similar agencies.

Viable options for vital records from the era prior to their official recording are cemetery and church records. These are considered private records, but many have been abstracted and indexed. Most dedicated genealogists will want to make the trip to the burial location of an ancestor just to stand by the grave as relatives did years before—and to photograph the tombstone, of course! Church histories, often including membership and confirmation lists, baptismal dates, burial dates, sextons' records, ministers' names, and/or excommunications, are often part of a local library collection.

Court records for both civil and criminal actions provide a great deal of insight into the community activities of ancestors. A paper trail is always nice to find, even if it involves a murder trial. If an ancestor's name appears on a jury list or elsewhere in a court record, this proves the person was in a certain place at a certain time.

Remember that courts exist on different levels of jurisdiction: city, county, district, state, and federal. The Order Books usually give the instructions the judge ordered, which will guide you in your search.

Records in chancery, orphan, and equity courts usually name the heirs. Divorce proceedings, guardianship receipts, affidavits, depositions, commissioner reports, and apprentice papers are also possibilities for enhancing research findings. Land deeds, tract books, mortgages, and property transfer records are in the courthouse as are wills and probate records. Often, voter registrations, citizenship papers, tax records, and newspapers are stored somewhere in the building, too.

Plan on taking some time to go through the Miscellaneous Records books. Most information in these books should have been entered in more appropriately labeled books, such as those for probates, indentures, guardianships, and so forth. You might also come across such items as partition books, quit titles, farm registries, oaths of allegiance, longevity lists, petitions for name change, insane records, and coroner reports. Each courthouse is arranged differently, and you can only hope it never caught fire! Approach with patience and caution—many courthouse employees are much more concerned about today's records than those from the past. Be prepared to be scanned upon entering the building; also no smoking, food, beverages, or weapons are allowed.

Military record files can provide a wealth of information regarding an ancestor. Most records of military service from the Revolutionary War through the Spanish-American War are stored at the National Archives and Records Administration (NARA) in Washington, DC. Records for the First and Second World Wars and other modern conflicts are at the National Personnel Records Center in Saint Louis, Missouri. Information about accessing these records

IMMIGRANT ANCESTOR

Betty L. Warren

FAMILY SURNAME	IMMIGRANT ANCESTOR	AGE	DATE OF ARRIVAL	PORT OF ARRIVAL	SHIP NAME	DATE OF DEPARTURE	PORT OF DEPARTURE	COUNTRY OF ORIGIN	VILLAGE NAME
WILLIAMS	unknown		prior to 1801					England?	
ERDMAYER/ADMIRE	George	c23	1748	New York	Edinburgh		Rotterdam	Germany	
MACKEY	David	c20	c1812/15					Ireland	
FRAß/FROSS	unknown		prior to 1798					Germany	
HENDRICKSON	unknown		prior to 1827					Germany?	
DANNREUTHER	Lawrence	38	1852	New Orleans	Bark Eberhard		Bremen	Germany	Donndorf
BOPP	Catherine	28	1852	New Orleans	Bark Eberhard		Bremen	Germany	Lindenhardt
ISTERLING	unknown		prior to 1854					Germany	
HAHN	unknown		prior to 1854					Germany	
UNGAR/UNGER	Michael	23	1748	New York	Judith		Rotterdam	Germany	Wollmesheim
WILLET	unknown		prior to 1790					Germany?	
RIEDESEL/RITTASE	John	27	c1815					Germany	Wunderthausen
BART/BARDT	unknown		prior to 1787					Germany?	
ALVEY	uncertain Joseph		1657	Maryland				England	
SPENCER	unknown		prior to 1828					England?	
KENDALL	uncertain Thomas		1660's	Virginia				England	
GILMORE	John	c18	c1718	Philadelphia				Scotland via Ireland	

Sample of record-keeping form to organize immigrant ancestor data. Use this type of list for each family line to determine what time periods need to be researched for your ancestors' immigration records. (Courtesy of Betty L. Warren)

can be found at the NARA Web site (www.archives. gov). Keep in mind that these are federal level records. State or local militia records are usually stored within a state's archives or with its adjutant general's office.

Passenger lists abound for certain time periods. Some are indexed, but the spellings of the names are not always as you expect them to be. There are several series of indexed volumes to assist with particular ethnic groups, for example: *Germans to America* in sixty-seven volumes (1988–2002) and *Italians to America* in sixteen volumes (1992–2002), both by Ira A. Glazier and P. William Filby. Be aware that not all passengers were listed, and cargo was often considered more important than names. Not everyone came through Ellis Island because it was only open from 1892 until 1954. The other major ports of entry were New York, Boston, Philadelphia, Baltimore, and New Orleans; but do not overlook the smaller ports.

RECORDS INVENTORY

Ancestor's Name	Relationship to Researcher	Type of Document	Location

RESEARCH LOG

Family surname_____

Objective _____

Date of Search	call #	description of source	comments	locality

CORRESPONDENCE CALENDAR

Family surname_____
Dates from _____ to _____

Date of letter	addressee	summary purpose	SASE	date rcvd	Thank You	again?

Samples of forms that document the genealogical research process (Courtesy of Betty L. Warren)

Passenger lists were not required by federal law until 1819. Many of those lists have been microfilmed and are available through the NARA and library research facilities such as the Indiana State Library, the Allen County Public Library, and Family History Centers maintained by the Church of Jesus Christ of Latter-day Saints.

Naturalization is a multistep process. Declarations of Intention, Petitions for Naturalization, and Final Papers were often recorded as the immigrants moved across the country. Residency requirements varied at different time periods, and early state laws were not uniform. Therefore, immigration records are not always in the same court or even the same state. Other sources can provide data as well: school records, occupational files, biographies, scrapbooks, telephone books, newspapers, letters, Bible records, diaries, journals, city directories, photographs, personal address books, autograph books, club and society records, and genealogical society periodicals.

Maps can provide geographic details and clues to a family's migration routes. Early pioneer settlements were usually on the rivers and canal systems and then later along the railroad lines. Remember that street names and house numbers can change, and the possibility even exists that a house could be picked up and moved!

Once you begin accumulating data, try to arrange it in a usable and organized way. Unfortunately, there is no perfect system, or we would all be using it. There are, however, three characteristics to maintaining a good system. The first is to keep it simple so that others can understand the information and so that it can be shared with relatives. The second characteristic is to keep the system expandable. Do not use numbering or filing procedures that would exclude the possibility of adding family members or other information. The third characteristic is to keep the material retrievable. If you cannot find something that you know you have when you want it, it is as good as not having it at all. Being able to retrieve an item also reduces the possibility of unnecessary duplication of data.

There are computer programs that will organize your information once you enter all of the data. However, you will still have piles of paper and stacks of stuff to organize because computer storage is not archival quality storage. A hard drive can crash, disc data can disappear in proximity to magnets, and an electrical power surge can erase everything in a flash of lightning. Acid-free paper, file folders, and boxes are available for storage of your family history data. Original documents in fragile condition may require special care. Paperwork can be filed alphabetically, by assigned number, or by family surname group. Using colors to code within your chosen system will help, too.

Taking notes as the research progresses will be of valuable assistance in organizing your materials. Be aware of person, place, and time as you record data. The format of your notes will need to be consistent for later reading. What made sense the day the notes were written may not be easily recognizable several days or years later. When writing down a name, select a format that fits the type of record you are creating. You may wish to use one type for charts, another for narrative details, and possibly another on forms. You could list the surname first and separate it with a comma, such as: Warren, Betty L., but that style is very awkward in a narrative format. One of the best formats is to capitalize the surname to avoid any possibility of confusion: Betty L. WARREN. Maiden names can be indicated with parentheses: Betty L. (WILLIAMS) WARREN. Italics are nice in a typescript, but difficult in notes or on a handwritten chart.

When documenting a date, keep in mind that genealogists deal with a time frame that crosses centuries, so be sure to use all four numerals for the year. Using only the numerals for the day and month could cause confusion. Many systems now utilize the international or military style, which puts the day first and then the month, so that "06/09/1776" would correctly read as the sixth of September in the year 1776, rather than the ninth of June that same year. Always remember to use two digits for the day and the month to avoid mistakes. Some people prefer to use abbreviations for the months, which further reduces the possibility of error, but be careful with "Jan." and "Jun."!

When writing down a location, start with the smallest geographic unit, such as the town or village

TIPS AND PRECAUTIONS

- Always work from the known to the unknown. Do not make generational leaps without documenting the linkage. Just because Richard Warren came over on the *Mayflower*, you are not necessarily related because you have that name in your lineage.

- Family traditions are leads. They are often embellished but usually have a grain of truth embedded within them. Try not to burst too many bubbles with your documented research!

- Your pedigree chart is your guide. Some research organizations will permit very little paperwork to accompany you into their facilities. Always travel with a copy of your chart to work to fill in the blanks.

- Do not overlook the obvious. It is quite impossible for five-year-old women to give birth, as well as those who are dead and buried. Be careful of the parents who name their children after themselves and their aunts and uncles. Two different people can have the same name; cousins with the same name can be born in the same year.

- Check and recheck. Do not copy down and pass on other people's mistakes. Cite your sources; know where your information is coming from to determine its credibility.

- Create timelines for your ancestors. Placing them in historical context will give clues for finding missing data and will help you understand their lives.

- Do not be ashamed of what you find. If you start digging under the family tree to find your roots, you are going to turn over some dirt!

name, then list the township or district. Next comes the county, the state, and finally the country. This is usually fairly simple to do when an atlas is available. Remember to label the townships "Twp." and the counties "Co." It is not so easy when using foreign names, because you will not always know if a name is for a village or a state. Sometimes it may be necessary to start with the name of the country and work back to a farm or estate name. Do the homework: study gazetteers and atlases to learn the area.

Plan your research. Create a notebook with specific ideas of what family documents need to be researched. Include a chart that indicates your immigrant ancestors' dates of arrival. Use the library card catalogs online ahead of time to select what items you will need.

Log your research. Keep a record of what materials you have researched and where you were so that time will not be wasted looking at the same thing twice and so that something that might be of interest later can be easily retrieved.

Keep a correspondence calendar to track inquiries and requests. Do not rely just on your computer e-mail. When writing an actual letter, remember to include a self-addressed, stamped envelope (SASE) to facilitate a prompt reply. That SASE can be a #9 envelope to avoid having to fold up a #10 envelope.

The two basic forms to use in your research are the pedigree or ancestor chart and the family group sheet. The ancestor chart is the direct lineage going back from you or your child through biological sets of parents. These charts can have as many as five or more generations on a page and contain just the bare essentials. Remember that no matter how many mar-

riages a person has had, the descendant child can have only two biological parents. The family group sheet is where the siblings and all the details are recorded for every marriage on the ancestor chart. Extra pages can be used to accommodate narrative information in addition to the essential facts. Many commercial forms are available, or you can create your own.

Before selecting a genealogical numbering system, determine if you are going to number all ancestors or only the descendants of one pair of ancestors. It does make a difference. It usually makes more sense to number all the ancestors beginning with yourself or your child as number one if you are preparing to do all collateral lines and go back as far as possible. However, if you are planning to publish a book on just one particular line of a family, you may want to start with the earliest known ancestor and number forward from him or her. Either way, there are several numbering systems, and none are perfect. Several published works and computer programs are available that may help you determine which numbering system will fit your needs best and be the most understandable.

As your research proceeds, it may be beneficial to join a genealogical and/or a historical organization. Membership benefits often include query insertions in newsletters, discounts at bookstores and conferences, as well as more reading material than you can possibly imagine!

Remember that your ancestors have had centuries to leave a trail. You cannot trace that trail with one visit to a research facility, nor can you find it in an evening at the computer. Much like your ancestors when they left their homeland, you are embarking upon a *lifelong* journey.

Internet Research

AMY JOHNSON CROW

———————————————— • ————————————————

Genealogy, at its essence, is about making connections. In our research, we strive to make connections to our ancestors. Along the way, we inevitably make connections with other researchers.

Making connections is easy on the Internet, which has quickly become an important part of everyday life. With e-mail, online banking, news, instant weather forecasts, and even ordering pizza—all facets of life seem to be touched by the Internet.

A pursuit entirely about connections and a new way of exchanging information made the marriage of genealogy and the Internet inevitable. Genealogists embraced the Internet from the beginning. Bulletin boards and subscriber services in the 1980s gave way to the burgeoning World Wide Web in the early 1990s. Today, a search for the word *genealogy* on the Google search engine (www.google.com) yields more than fifty million hits. That's more than *stamp collecting* or *coin collecting* or even *Indiana basketball.*

General Research Strategies

The Internet has been referred to as the "information superhighway." The analogy to a highway is a strong one. People use the Internet to get from point A to point B; the Internet has many access points; and there are occasional traffic jams on the Internet. You can traverse both a highway and the Internet with no particular plan on how to get from here to there. Although that might be a good idea for a Sunday drive in the country, it often ends in frustration when applied to the Internet.

The ease of use of the Internet (technological connector) and the World Wide Web (collection of informational sites) is both an asset and a liability for genealogists. It is easy to click on links taking you from one site to another and possibly to the discovery of new information. However, it is just as easy to start clicking on links only to discover that several hours have passed, you have found nothing meaningful, and you have no idea where you are or how you got there.

Just like research at a library or courthouse, effective Internet research begins with a plan. A good plan contains a goal and an inventory. Determining what you want to find will focus the search. There is a difference between "surfing" and "researching." Sitting down at the computer "to find something on the family" is surfing. When surfing, you may find some interesting tidbits, but they are unlikely to be meaningful. Research, on the other hand, has a stated purpose. What is the goal of the research? Is it to find Susan's parents, William's death, or information on Henry's Civil War unit?

Taking inventory is a necessity, which begins with an assessment of what is known about the problem at hand. If the goal is to find William's date and place of death, take clues about his life before looking for his death. For example, if William has been found consistently in the census in Dubois County, Indiana, the logical place to begin looking for information about his death would be Dubois County, Indiana.

Evaluating What You Find

It has been said that genealogy without documentation is mythology. As in offline research, it is imperative to evaluate information found online. A Web site or a family file may lay out ten generations of ancestors, but if just one of those generations is wrong, everything past that point may belong on someone else's family tree.

Reviewing the documentation of online family compilations allows the researcher to evaluate the accuracy of the conclusions presented. A family tree with citations to sources such as original vital records, wills, and pension records can more reliably be evaluated for its accuracy than one that cites nothing but other family files—and certainly more than a family tree that has no source citations at all.

Genealogists must also evaluate abstracted and transcribed sources. A key concept to keep in mind is the difference between original and derivative sources. Original sources are those that are the first, earliest record of a fact. A marriage record at the county courthouse is an example of an original source. Derivative sources are sources that are not original. They may have been compiled from other sources, rewritten, transferred to another format, and so forth. Abstracts or transcriptions of those courthouse marriage records are derivative sources. The importance in this becomes clear when you consider the errors that can occur at every step of compilation or reformatting. People make errors—they misread handwriting, type the wrong letter, leave out words, or insert words that were not in the original.

The closest that a researcher can get to original sources on the Internet are digitized images of original sources. Everything else is derivative. This does not mean that genealogists should not use the Internet. It means that researchers must remember that the vast majority of materials found on the Internet are derivative sources and that, when possible, it is best to look at the original sources.

Before Beginning Research

Web sites can sometimes be misleading. The title may say "Pretzel County Deaths, 1880–1902," when only a few death records for one particular family in that county are actually listed. If researchers do not realize this, they may search the database, and when they do not find their ancestors listed, they may conclude that their ancestors did not die in Pretzel County between 1880 and 1902. This conclusion may not be correct as that particular Web site does not include all Pretzel County deaths for the time period.

Before plugging names into a Web site's "Search" function, read all prefatory matter. Often a site will feature a "Frequently Asked Questions" (FAQ) page, explaining more about the site. Careful researchers should follow all links to "About This Site," "What This Site Includes," and similar pages. Knowing what is and is not included in the site is vital to accurately evaluating any search results.

A Template of Sites

It can be overwhelming to decide where to start with millions of Web sites devoted to genealogy and millions more of interest that are not specifically about genealogy. Just as it is a good research practice to cover the major records for each ancestor—vital records, censuses, and a literature search—it is a good practice to cover the major types of Web sites. I call it "a template of sites," which should be examined for all ancestors, regardless of where and when they lived.

Many sites are devoted to specific areas, usually a county or state. Which sites should you visit for your ancestor who was born in Adams County, Pennsylvania, married in Perry County, Ohio, lived for a time in Allegan County, Michigan, and died in Jay

County, Indiana? The answer: the sites appropriate to each of these four places.

This template of sites is obviously not an exhaustive list of all the sites that have useful information. It is merely the beginning of the exciting process of online research. Thorough researchers use tools such as Internet search engines (Yahoo, Google, AltaVista, and so on), constructing good search phrases to find sites and family files of interest. Using *genealogy* by itself is not productive, unless you have the time to look at fifty million sites. A search on *19th century Indiana migration* will yield fewer results, but it is more likely to contain links to sites with information on migration into and out of Indiana in the 1800s, if that is what you are trying to find.

USGenWeb Project

The USGenWeb Project (www.usgenweb.org) is an all-volunteer effort to make genealogical data for every county in the United States available on the Internet. (A similar project for foreign countries is WorldGenWeb, which can be found at www.world genweb.org.) USGenWeb is arranged by state and then broken down by county.

The strength of the USGenWeb Project is its various county GenWeb sites. To find a specific county, first go to the project's site and click on "The Project's State Pages." From there you can choose between a map of the United States or a listing of states in alpha-

betical order. Click on the state you want, and you will be taken to the state GenWeb site. Each state site is arranged differently. The Indiana GenWeb site (www. ingenweb.org) allows visitors to choose a county from a map or an alphabetical listing.

Each county GenWeb site is different, but the majority feature abstracted data sources, queries, sur-

name listings, and a brief history of the county. Many offer links to related sites, such as libraries, genealogical and historical societies, and families from the area. An excellent example of a county GenWeb site is that for Orange County, Indiana (www.usgennet. org/usa/in/county/orange/). It clearly lays out its contents, along with information about each group of records. The breadth and depth of the materials that this site covers are outstanding.

RootsWeb

RootsWeb (www.rootsweb.com) is another volunteer-led effort. Although it is now owned by Ancestry.com, a pay-subscription service, all of the data on RootsWeb is provided by volunteers and is available at no charge.

RootsWeb has many facets: databases, Web sites, mail lists, and WorldConnect, which is a collection of online family files. The easiest way to search these vast files is through the search engine at the top of the main page. Be certain to enter the name into the RootsWeb search, rather than the Ancestry. com search. The Ancestry.com search will show the hits from Ancestry.com, but you cannot view them unless you are an Ancestry.com subscriber or at a library with Ancestry.com access.

The RootsWeb mail lists are an invaluable resource not only for finding information but also for connecting with others researching the same ancestors. Researchers can subscribe to the lists of interest free of charge. The messages are delivered directly to the subscribers' e-mail addresses. Most of the RootsWeb mail lists are also archived so that everyone can search and read past messages. There are mail lists for specific surnames, states, counties, and topics, such as computer programs and ethnic groups.

The mail-list archives are not included in the RootsWeb search, and each mail-list archive must be searched separately. When searching the archives, consider all possible lists. If your ancestor was Alvy Henderson, who was born in Fairfield County, Ohio, lived in Huntington County, Indiana, and served in the Civil War in the Forty-seventh Indiana Infantry, there are several appropriate mail lists to examine. These include the Henderson surname list, the statewide Ohio and Indiana lists, as well as those specific to Fairfield County and Huntington County. There is also a list for those interested in Indiana in the Civil War.

WorldConnect features family files called GEDCOM files. GEDCOM, short for GEnealogical Data COMmunication, allows people with different genealogical software to view the same database. While not all of the files on WorldConnect are documented, it is too large of a collection to ignore. At the very least, genealogists can make contact with others researching the same lines and get clues for furthering their own research.

State Historical Societies

State historical societies have not ignored the digital revolution. Their Web sites are growing with databases, scanned images, finding aids, and online catalogs. The Indiana Historical Society's (IHS) Web site (www.indianahistory.org) features a "Quicklink"

called "Family History Research" for its genealogical publications and programs as well as an online catalog of its collections and digital images, including Indiana postcards, a great resource for images of towns across the state. In addition, every-name indexes for the Society's family history journal, *The Hoosier Genealogist*, from the 2000 volume on are being published online.

Even the sites that do not have extensive databases can be of use to the genealogist. The search for "family history" must include the history of the area where the family lived. Many state historical society Web sites feature online essays and exhibits about the areas they represent. It is an excellent way to begin placing families in context with their surroundings. Societies can be found by entering the name of the

state and the words "historical society" into almost any Internet search engine. A Web page that has links to state historical societies is "U.S. State Historical Societies and State Archives Directory," compiled by Joe Ryan, on the Syracuse University Web site (http://web.syr.edu/~jryan/infopro/hs.html).

State Archives and Libraries

As the official repository for older state records and documents, state archives and libraries have always been popular destinations for genealogical road trips. Now their Web sites are becoming popular destinations on the information superhighway.

Like those for state historical societies, many state archives' and libraries' Web sites feature databases, scanned images, and online catalogs. The Indiana State Library Web site at www.statelib.lib.in.us has numerous databases, including "Indiana Marriages through 1850."

The Georgia Secretary of State's office maintains a page of links to all fifty state archives at www.sos. state.ga.us/archives/what_do_we_have/other_state_ archives/default.htm. A similar page with links to all fifty state libraries, sponsored by the Library of Congress, can be found at www.loc.gov/global/library/ statelib.html.

Local Genealogical and Historical Societies

The Internet is not exclusive to large organizations. Many worthwhile sites are sponsored by small groups. For example, the Monroe County (Indiana) Historical Society's Web site at www.monroehistory. org/librarymain.htm features news about the organization, databases such as Revolutionary War patriots in the county and grantor/grantee indexes, and links to related sites.

Many local organizations can be found through the Federation of Genealogical Societies' "Society Hall" at www.familyhistory.com/societyhall/main. asp. A search on an Internet search engine such as Google, using a phrase such as *Allen County Indiana genealogical society*, is another way of finding these valuable resources.

To find contact information for Indiana's county historians and county genealogical and historical societies, visit the IHS Web site, click on "Quick-links," and choose "Local History Services."

Local Libraries

Most libraries do not allow their genealogical collections to circulate, which may be why their Web sites are often overlooked by genealogists. Even if you are not planning a research trip to the public library in the county where your ancestor lived, a "virtual visit" is often productive.

An increasing number of public libraries—large and small, urban and rural—feature information about local history and databases, such as obituary indexes. The Crawfordsville District Public Library in Indiana has an outstanding Web site for genealogists at www.cdpl.lib.in.us. Under the link to "Local History," researchers find Montgomery County cemetery readings, the Montgomery County Clerk of the Circuit Court Register of Negroes and Mulattoes, Crawfordsville High School yearbooks, and many more databases. There are also digitized photos of the area. This is an excellent example of a public library making information available via the Internet.

The easiest way to find a public library in the United States is through Public Libraries.com at www.publiclibraries.com. It is arranged by state and then by library name. Although the word "genealogy" does not always appear on public library Web sites, look for links such as "Local History," "Digital Archives," and "About the Area."

FamilySearch

FamilySearch (www.familysearch.org), sponsored by the Church of Jesus Christ of Latter-day Saints, is a site deserving of its own category. If all it contained was the catalog of the LDS Family History Library, it would be worthwhile, but it includes so much more. FamilySearch also has abstracts of the 1880 federal census, the 1881 British and Canadian censuses, online versions of the International Genealogical Index (IGI), Ancestral File (a collection of family files), and several other databases.

Often overlooked at FamilySearch is a resource called "Research Helps," which consists of guides for every state in the United States, as well as for countless foreign countries. The guides range in topic from what records are available for a state to lists of words that genealogists should know when working with documents in a foreign language. They are invaluable resources, and all of them are free to view online. "Research Helps" can be found under the "Search" tab on the FamilySearch main page.

Conclusion

The Internet is filled with millions of sites that are useful to genealogists. It is easy to become overwhelmed at the sheer volume of data available. However, this wonderful means of exchanging information must be viewed as a tool, not as an end by itself. The Internet may have changed the way genealogists obtain some data, but it did not change the fundamentals of genealogical research, such as evaluating what is found. With a specific goal, an inventory of what is known about the problem, an eye toward evaluation, and a basic template of sites to examine, time spent online can be productive genealogical research time, not merely surfing time.

A group of Native Americans listening avidly to one of their storytellers (Drawing by Angela M. Gouge)

Oral History

BARBARA TRUESDELL

"The universe is composed of stories, not atoms."
—Muriel Rukeyser

———————————————•———————————————

People love stories. At any family gathering—holidays, family reunions, weddings, or funerals—an important part of the event for everyone is the time spent telling stories about family members. These stories can be funny, sad, exciting, or scary. The stories that a family tells and retells are part of that family's "oral tradition." The stories may be about cousins or grandparents who are known to all the family, or the stories may be about ancestors who are remembered by only a few of the oldest relatives or by only the stories still told about them.

The Indiana Historical Society's first children's book, *Casper and Catherine Move to America: An Immigrant Family's Adventures, 1849–1850,* is about one family's ancestors and their adventures migrating from Europe to America. It is a special form of oral tradition, called a family "legend" or "oral history." This legend is part of the family's story of itself, told in author Brian Hasler's family for generations. By writing it down, Hasler is preserving it for future generations, even if the family forgets to tell the story anymore. Writing it down also makes it possible to share the story with more people. This is important because many families share the experience of migrating from Europe to the United States. By hearing the oral histories of many of these families, we can begin to imagine the larger story of how Europeans became Americans.

Oral history is an old way of remembering the past. For thousands of years groups of people passed down their history through storytellers—individuals who memorized stories about their ancestors and created stories about present-day events to tell at gatherings throughout the year. Older storytellers taught younger storytellers so that the group's history would not be lost. Native American groups passed down their histories this way. Their stories told how the tribes came to America, about the connections between people and nature, about their warriors' brave deeds, and many other things. Today many Native American stories can be found in books, so that we can all learn from them, but most important, so that the history of Native Americans will continue to be passed down.

During the twentieth century oral history became important to American historians as they tried to discover more about our past. They came to realize that oral history often tells about the lives of ordinary people. The stories help historians write history that is about all of us, not just a few "important" people. Today many historians worldwide use both written records and oral traditions, if they are available, to create and pass down more complete histories about people. Oral history is especially useful for studying groups that have no written history and for writing biographies and family histories.

As a method of studying the past, collecting oral history is at least as old as recorded history itself. Donald Ritchie, in his 1995 book *Doing Oral History*, touches on some examples of oral history's early uses. Three thousand years ago scribes of the Zhou dynasty in China collected the sayings of the people for the use of court historians. In the fifth century BCE (before the Christian era), the Greek historian Herodotus gathered information from Persians and Phoenicians for his account of the Persian Wars. Later historians used written histories along with oral sources to capture stories about people and events in the past. This practice was followed for centuries. For example, Jules Michelet wrote a history of the French Revolution (1789–1799) fifty years after it took place by contrasting official government documents with the recollections of people who had lived through the era.

However, as Ritchie explains, with the rise of the German school of scientific history in the nineteenth century, oral sources fell out of favor with historians. History moved from a literary form to an academic discipline based on the rigorous testing of evidence. Oral sources were dismissed as less objective than written sources, seen by historians as subjective memories hopelessly biased by the individual's point of view. The reemergence of oral sources in historical research in the United States developed after World War II with the work of Allan Nevins at Columbia University, who was concerned that modern communication and transportation were making letter writing and diary keeping obsolete. Nevins, recognizing the importance of audiotape recording as a means to capture a verbatim record of an interview and preserve it for future reference, founded the Columbia Oral History Research Office in 1948.

While oral history's initial focus in America was on the recollections of famous people, scholars soon began to recognize that oral history could illuminate the lives of ordinary people and give new insights into past events. Oral history projects and centers developed on every continent as oral historians began collecting historical stories from people telling about their lives or their families by recording them on audio- or videotape. The history field discovered that it had many voices, and oral history became recognized as another research tool that could be applied to a wide variety of historical subjects.

Some historians still question the usefulness of oral history as a source of information for what happened in the past, arguing that memory is unreliable. It is true that people do not always remember things exactly as they happened. A living person is not a computer, after all. People have feelings, opinions, and circumstances in their lives that can affect their ideas of their family history and how it should be presented and interpreted. A person's gender, ethnicity, generation, religion, friends, and enemies help them decide how to tell their stories—what details to share and what details to change. For instance, if an ancestor was a Civil War hero who later turned into a thief, the descendant might be proud to tell other people about his war adventures, but might not want to tell how he was later sent to jail.

People forget details, too. Anyone who has heard the same family story told many times knows that it is never told exactly the same way. Stories tend to change over time as a storyteller's memory fades and as a story is repeated by different people. The words change, and parts of the story can be added or left out. Sometimes relatives even argue about parts of the story! This does not mean that the story is untrue or that it has lost its value—just that some parts may not be entirely correct. This is part of the storytelling process, however, and while it can change a story, it can also make that story remarkably stable. For example, when the author Alex Haley began to study an oral history narrative told in his family about his ancestor who had been brought to the United States from Africa as a slave, he found that even though the story had changed with different tellings, many of its details had been carefully preserved, even to the pronunciation of certain African words. With that story as his starting place, Haley was able to find where his

European emigrants swapping stories aboard a ship bound for the United States, mid-nineteenth century (Drawing by Angela M. Gouge)

ancestor had originally lived and return to Africa to visit his ancestor's village.

So, oral narratives are not as stable as written documents. Instead, oral narratives are dynamic—they grow and change with the people who tell them. In fact, this is an important part of what keeps a story alive—it can be shaped to the needs of the person telling it and the audience listening to it, so that it remains fresh and relevant. If a story does not continue to "speak" to its audience, making people feel that something important and valuable is being shared with them, narrators will stop telling it, and the story will die.

An audience's experiences partly determine which stories are considered relevant, but, of course, experiences are only part of our lives. Our experiences—*and* the thoughts and feelings we have about those experiences—help to shape who we are, how we think about ourselves, and how we remember the past. The people around us in our families, neighborhoods, cities, and nation also help to shape who we are, what we think and feel, and how we remember the past. The stories that we share come from what we remember and from what the people around us remember. Our stories are a way of taking compass readings in the flow of time, helping us to see the roads that our own lives have taken and showing us the paths that our families and communities have traveled. Collecting oral history helps to capture those compass readings, allowing interested people to learn useful facts about the past and to see the world and human events from multiple points of view—a difficult goal when research is limited to official documents. This goal is an important one, though, because ultimately, oral history shows how different individuals and groups use the past to shape the present and the future.

Thus, oral history is important to the field of history because it has opened history to interpretations of the past other than that of the professional historian. Where once history was written from a third-person viewpoint that lumped individuals into a faceless mass of people, we now have eyewitness accounts of modern events, and the stories of numerous groups are part of historical discourse.

Casper & Charles

Charles & Jasper

Jasper & Kenneth

Brian & Hugh

Kenneth & Brian

Depiction of five generations of Hasler fathers passing down their family's immigration story to their sons, beginning with Casper and Charles and ending with Brian and Hugh (Drawing by Angela M. Gouge)

With that multiplicity of voices, the past is more alive, more complex, more contentious, more multilayered, and more enriching. Furthermore, in acknowledging multiple voices, historians have had to acknowledge their own voices and to consider critically their role in the construction of historical narratives. Oral history has also been instrumental in developing the study of memory—not only how individuals remember the past but also how collective memory, the shared past of a group of people, is constructed and used.

Everybody has stories to tell. Stories like *Casper and Catherine Move to America* tell about a family's history. They also tell what the storyteller or the family considers important enough to pass on to future generations—what they value and what they want people to remember about them. You see, oral history is a way to capture a piece of a person's life in his or her own words. This gives us a glimpse into the human heart that we can preserve and pass down for the future.

Family Reunions

WILLIAM DUBOIS JR.

⎯⎯⎯⎯⎯⎯⎯⎯⎯⎯ • ⎯⎯⎯⎯⎯⎯⎯⎯⎯⎯

As the American frontier moved west, families became geographically dispersed and lost day-to-day contact. By the early twentieth century, reunions became important as a way for family members to return to familiar places, see and talk with relatives, socialize with each other, catch up on family and hometown events, and reminisce about the past. Even when families were separated by long distances, readily available passenger train service and the advent of the automobile made it relatively easy for family members to travel home for these annual gatherings.

An outgrowth of such family get-togethers was a record, usually labeled "Minutes," in which an elected secretary entered reunion dates and locations, business items (usually an election of officers, a financial report, and other reunion matters), entertainment "programs" including the names of the entertainers and what they presented or performed, names of attendees, and other information.

Not surprisingly, reunion minutes can make dull reading. That said, it is also true that the minutes often include important genealogical information and provide clues to other data. Minutes of one eastern Indiana family reunion still being held today illustrate this.

The Cline-Davis reunion draws its name from Alexander Henderson Cline (1832–1885) and his second wife, Lucinda (Davis) Pinney (1837–1920), of Jay and Randolph counties. The first Cline-Davis reunion was held on September 12, 1908, and except for wartime interruptions or cancellations during public health crises (the 1949 polio epidemic, for example), the reunion has been held continuously ever since. The first reunions took place on family farms, including the home place of Alexander Cline's father, William, in Madison Township, Jay County. Later, the reunion was held at the Jackson Township School in Randolph County and at a Grange hall in Darke County, Ohio, northeast of Union City. Today's reunions are held at a Greenville, Ohio, park. In the early years, reunion attendance often topped one hundred, and once reached nearly two hundred.

For reunion purposes, the definition of family was elastic. Over multiple generations, Clines and Davises participated in family reunions because they were one of—or a descendant of one of—the following:

• Children of Alexander Cline, a Union army veteran who had six children each by his two wives, Elizabeth F. Cochran (ca. 1832–1864), and Lucinda.

- Hiram Pinney (1861–1947), Lucinda Cline's son by her first husband, Wilson Pinney, who died in the Civil War.
- Siblings of Lucinda Cline, who had three sisters and seven brothers.
- Siblings of Alexander Cline, who had a full brother, four full sisters, two half brothers, and five half sisters. (Four others died young or as infants.)

Alexander Henderson Cline and his second wife, Lucinda (Davis) Pinney Cline (Courtesy of William DuBois Jr.)

The Clines, Davises, and related families were among Jay and Randolph counties' earliest settlers. Ziba Davis (1798–1875) and his wife, Loruhama Badgley (1799–1864), parents of Lucinda Cline, came to Jackson Township, Randolph County, in 1836. William Cline (1746–1853) and his second wife, Jane Woten (1801–1865), parents of Alexander Cline, came to Madison Township, Jay County, in 1847. Some of William Cline's children by his first wife, Susannah Lance (ca. 1762–ca. 1823), settled in what became Jay County as early as 1833. The parents of Jane Cline, Bell Woten (1765–1856) and Jane Gilliland (1776–1864), and some of their other children were also early settlers in the part of Randolph County organized in 1836 as Jay County.

There are several useful types of information embedded in the minutes of the Cline-Davis reunion that are likely to be found in the records of other families' gatherings as well. These include the following:

Actual Genealogical Data. The record of the eighth (1915) Cline-Davis reunion was the first to include listings of "those . . . who passed away since last year" and births. No dates were recorded for either category, and the list of births did not give parents' names. Over the years, the recorded data became more specific, although not nearly as complete as genealogists might wish. Marriages also were reported. (Reporting and recording errors were common, so skepticism about this data is wise. Nonetheless, the information provides a good starting point for further investigation.) Other data with genealogical value was also recorded; for example, the minutes of the thirty-seventh (1944) Cline-Davis reunion show twenty-nine family members in the armed forces and, in some cases, the places where they were thought to be serving.

Genealogies or Clues to Their Existence. Family-compiled genealogies are not always published or widely disseminated. As early as 1912, Cline-Davis reunion participants named a family member to chair an historical committee. At the seventh (1914) and ninth (1916) reunions, Lydia (Cline) Simmons—sister of Alexander Cline—presented a Cline history. Hannah Mae (Cline) Matchett, daughter of Alexander Cline, once presented a Davis history. At the thirty-fourth (1941) reunion, participants decided to do a family tree for all of Alexander Cline's twelve children and assigned a person in each line to collect information. The forty-fourth (1951) reunion minutes note receipt of family trees for six children and indicate that "others promised to send them to the secretary later."

Reunion minutes contain an outline genealogy of the family of Joe Cline (1877–1971). One of the six children of Alexander and Lucinda Cline, Joe, married Vesta Annette Kemp (1888–1951). Genealogies of the families of Alexander Cline's eleven other children did not make it into the reunion minutes or did not survive as part of that record, but the family's interest in its heritage may account for the fact that sound information on the Clines and Davises is not difficult to find today.

Early principals in Cline-Davis reunions included (front) Anna Lucidia (Cline) Peden (1868–1960); second row: John Cline (1875–1970), Hannah Mae (Cline) Matchett (1871–1961), Lydia Ann (Cline) Simmons (1836–1923), and Joe Cline (1877–1971); and, third row: William Henderson "Will" Cline (1856–1945), Hiram Pinney (1861–1947), and Fred Cline (1873–1957). Anna Peden, Mae Matchett, and John, Joe, and Fred Cline are Alexander and Lucinda Cline's children. Lydia Simmons is Alexander's sister. Will Cline is Alexander's son by Elizabeth F. Cochran. Hiram Pinney is Lucinda Cline's son by her first husband, Wilson Pinney. (Courtesy of William DuBois Jr.)

Information Showing Relationships. Genealogical researchers take a giant step forward once relationships are known or understood. This is especially true of women, who acquire new surnames with marriage. Without the names of spouses, fact-finding grinds to a halt. Some reunion minutes not only show who was born, married, or died but also indicate how one individual relates to another person—as wife, husband, daughter, son, niece, nephew, grandchild, or in-law. These indicators aid researchers in identifying relationships and sorting out families.

Information Showing Places of Residence. Searching for data on individuals whose places of residence are unknown is the genealogical equivalent of hunting a needle in a very large haystack. For 1924 and 1932, the Cline-Davis reunion minutes contain mailing lists of individuals to whom reunion "notices" were sent. Such lists and lists of attendees, which may include towns or counties of residence, narrow the geographic focus in which a researcher needs to find meaningful information.

In short, reunion minutes can be an important source of genealogical data. Often, this data provides clues for further research that may lead to information of greater significance.

———————————•———————————

Bibliographic Note: Copies of Cline-Davis reunion minutes through the late 1970s, made by the author from the originals, were analyzed for this chapter. Relationships cited here are based on the research and personal knowledge of the author, a lifelong researcher into the history of his Cline, Davis, and DuBois ancestors.

Mary Deter

Photographs and Family History

ELAINE G. ROSA

—————————————— • ——————————————

As I began organizing my family's genealogical charts, correspondence, reference books, and research notes, I realized I had very few photographs of family ancestors, their homes, or the communities in which they lived and worked. Despite these shortcomings, I was determined to collect photographic images related to my family in order to answer questions that intrigued my children and me. Did our ancestors pass any family traits down to us? How did they earn a living? What was it like where they lived? Luckily, resources are available to help create visual records of families and their hometowns.

If you are as fortunate as the residents of Brookville, Indiana, a local photographer may have documented area residents and their homes, community life, and special celebrations. In 1902 Benjamin Franklin Winans, a local printer, bought a camera and began to photograph the Brookville community and the surrounding Franklin County area. Winans had the foresight to write captions and dates for thousands of his glass-plate negatives, many of which survive, to visually record community members, everyday life, and special events in his small Hoosier town.

While studio portraits make up the major portion of many family photo collections, less formal poses provide informative details about our ancestors' daily lives. Winans's photograph of Mary Deter is a fine example. The photograph of Deter combines a stoic central figure with rich textures of worn boards, a woolen blanket, and a pristine linen scarf to capture Deter's rural environment.[1] This photo projects an image of a woman who, though frail in old age, endured the passage of time with strength and dignity.

Winans also documented the working lives of Brookville residents. Local blacksmiths, Mike, Adam, and Ed Williams, showed how they forged iron into wheel rims and horseshoes for the community's horse-drawn carriages and wagons. "Doc" Stout traveled the countryside selling Watkins medicinal products from a wagon during the heyday of patent medicines and tonics. These photographs depict livelihoods that our ancestors practiced one hundred years ago and more that have been transformed through modern technology.

Winans captured notable area homesteads on film for future generations as well. In 1914 William Wolber and his wife posed for Winans on the front porch of their family home. According to a local newspaper, the Wolbers won a $100 prize for having the best-kept farm. Winans's photograph documented the Wolbers' hard work and pride of place. Schoonover descendants also have a Winans photographic record of their family's homestead. This photo offers a visual image of a sturdy log cabin that is rustic but functional—an integral part of a pioneer's life. Photographs such as these add rich details to family stories and records. Images can provide missing information for a family member, clarify a controversial family story, or illuminate the background of an ancestor's life.

Gather the family photographs you have and study them closely. These photos are more than a random collection of people and places; they are a composite timeline of your family's lives. From informal vacation photos and birthday parties to weddings and formal family portraits, these scenes provide perspectives that may have never been captured elsewhere.

A critical first step in the process of studying photos is to create a worksheet for each one. Document the details of individuals, objects, and background elements in each photograph on a worksheet and attach a photocopy or digital image of each photograph to its worksheet (store the original photographs in archival-quality photo sleeves and storage boxes). On the worksheets give each photograph a title or caption and record identifying marks, photographer's name and/or imprint (if available), a physical description of each person in the photograph including the person's clothing, and background details. Write a general description of the photograph (type of image, condition, size, thickness, and mounting style) and, if the image is borrowed, include contact information about the photograph's owner (name, address, and telephone number) or citation information about its source (manuscript or book author, title, publisher, and date).

With basic worksheets and copies of your photographs, the detective work can begin. Relatives may help fill in gaps on photo worksheets and provide photographs that you do not have in your collection. Take copies of photographs and worksheets to family gatherings and see who can provide missing information and family stories related to the people and places in the photos.

Manuscript conservation consultants and reference books and articles about photography history and photographic preservation can assist in dating photos and identifying their origins and types. If you have an extensive photo collection, you may consider purchasing a set of basic photograph reference books for use at home.

Your local public library, state library and archives, local and state genealogical libraries, and special collections libraries house materials that can help identify people and places in your photos, resolve questions concerning them, and place them in their historic contexts. Family manuscript collections, census records, and city directories may help identify persons or places in photos. Local history collections with photographs and maps and published histories of communities and counties can be especially useful for resolving questions about photographs. Local newspapers, centennial celebration publications, and special library collections contain firsthand accounts of community happenings that may shed light on the scenes in your family photos. In addition, library staff can assist in locating and obtaining materials from other libraries and furnish access to online resources available through libraries only.

Be thorough in gathering information; even small details can provide important clues. A Winans photograph of the Brookville Fire Department (opposite) is a good example. Look carefully at the background. Although partially obscured, the letters on the structure provide enough details to inform viewers that the men in the foreground may have been associated with the Brookville Fire Department—as in fact they were. Winans shot this photo of the firefighters on October 23, 1910.

After you have researched the photographs in your personal collection, extend your search to identify other ancestors who may have had their photographs taken (that would include anyone who may have been living in 1839 when daguerreotypes were introduced to the present) and where they lived and worked. Look for photos in genealogy research documents such as immigration and naturalization papers, marriage certificates, court records, military and

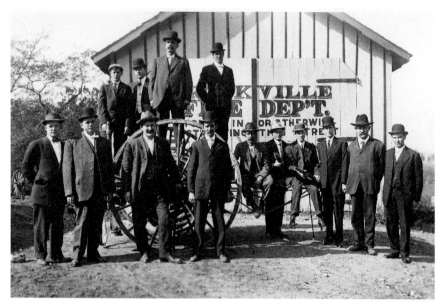

(Clockwise from top left) Mike, Adam, and Ed Williams; "Doc" Stout; Brookville Fire Department

police records, passports, licenses, school yearbooks, and manuscript collections. Ask other relatives and close family friends to check their family papers for photographs. Biographical encyclopedias and community histories highlighting the accomplishments of a community often contain photographs or engravings of area residents, businesses, churches, and local landmarks. Church and organizational directories may provide members' photographs. Newspapers are also excellent sources of photographs, especially sections containing engagements, wedding announcements, obituaries, and major news events.

Photographs greatly enhance the narratives and lineage charts in family histories. Images offer visual depictions of family and community life, business enterprises, and special events. By collecting and documenting images of our ancestors, their homes, work, and locales, we can breathe life into our genealogical records. It is a rewarding task and well worth the effort.

———————————— • ————————————

1. All images in this chapter come from Donald L. Dunaway, *The Photography of Ben Winans of Brookville, Indiana, 1902–1926* (Indianapolis: Indiana Historical Society Press, 2001).

Selected Bibliography: Sturdevant, Katherine Scott. *Bringing Your Family History to Life Through Social History.* Cincinnati: Betterway Books, 2000. Taylor, Maureen A. *Uncovering Your Ancestry Through Family Photographs.* Cincinnati: Betterway Books, 2000.

Labeling and Preserving Family Photographs

CAROLYN M. BRADY

If you spend much time in antique malls or flea markets, you've seen them: boxes of anonymous photos, someone else's ancestors for sale. I collect old photographs, and the majority I own are unlabeled or have cryptic labels, which is probably how they ended up on the market. A picture may be worth a thousand words, but a photograph cannot tell as complete a story if basic information is not recorded for posterity. This chapter will offer advice on labeling family photos based on my experience working in museums and researching my own family's history.

Before I continue, I should make a confession. I have been an avid photographer since childhood and have boxes of photos waiting to be properly labeled and placed in archival storage. Since the development of relatively inexpensive, easy-to-use cameras starting in the late 1800s, many families have accumulated cupboards full of photos. Almost all of us have limited time and funds, and we have to set priorities. I suggest starting with the older family photos first, especially those for which no negatives survive, but don't neglect important photos from your own lifetime.

I was recently given responsibility for my grandparents' photos, a wonderful collection dating from the early 1900s to the 1970s, many of them either unlabeled or labeled in Japanese. Right now these have priority over my personal photos, but I did take the time to organize the rolls of photos taken at a recent family reunion. I put the negatives in archival quality plastic sleeves so they wouldn't get scratched and transferred the prints to acid-free envelopes with pockets for both photos and negatives. Eventually I plan to store these negatives separately for safekeeping, but I must admit that I've found it very useful to have them on hand every time I need to make yet another reprint.

The envelopes have space on front and back to write basic descriptions of the contents, so even when I do not have time to label every single print, I can at least record that photos 14 through 20, for example, show my nieces at the beach. I write in pencil on the empty envelope so that I won't accidentally make any indentations on the photographs or negatives. The first time I list a person on the roll (including myself), I use his or her first and last name (including maiden names) and then refer to them by their first names for the rest of the roll. If you keep a copy of the family tree stored with your photos, you might not have to spend as much time writing who's related to whom, but you should mention other relationships (friends and neighbors) that might not otherwise be recorded. I also note locations, sometimes including street addresses, and I try to list the names in such a way that it's obvious even to strangers who's who.

After I have new prints developed, I write dates and general descriptions of events and locations on the envelope before I guiltily throw them in a box to deal with later. If you can at least keep your photos in rough chronological order, this will help you when the time comes to organize them. If I'm on a trip where I take many rolls of film that I won't develop until I get home, I number my rolls and note the dates and places on a piece of paper that I put in the film canister with each roll as soon as I take it out of the camera. When traveling I keep a letter size piece of paper with my name, address, and e-mail, which I photograph with each new roll of film so that there is some record of whose pictures these are if the canister drops out of my bag and some kind stranger develops it.

If you take a lot of photos, you might consider keeping a logbook in which to write down what you are photographing as you take the pictures. I kept one while working as a curator at a historic site, assigning a number to each roll of film and photo. For example, photo #1996-3-24 was negative #24

File # ___ Box # ___	Oregon trip roll #1 – Travel – Smithville Reunion Aug 11-12 2000	
	Description	Date

Date	Subject	Place
Aug. 11 #2	Katherine (SMITH) PETERS & Kids Nina & Susan PETERS	waiting for our flight out of Chicago O'Hare airport
#3	Wildfire smoke seen from air	over Montana or Idaho?
#4	Uncle Bob (Robert THOMPSON), cousin Janet TURNER, Mom (Margaret [THOMPSON] SMITH), Dad (James R. SMITH) Katherine & Susan	meeting at the airport, Portland OR
#5	Mom's childhood friends Mary SANDERS & Mitzi (ANDERSON) LAWRENCE	#5-12 Smithville Reunion
#6	Mitzi's brother Gene ANDERSON & Uncle Bob	Mixer at Doubletree
#7	Mom, Uncle Harry THOMPSON & Janet	Hotel, Portland, OR

PHOTO ARCHIVE ◆ LIGHT IMPRESSIONS Acid & Lignin free. #4281

on the third roll of film shot in 1996. Note that depending on how your camera loads film, the first exposure on the roll may not be negative #1. You may have to reconcile numbers at a later date. I would write down dates, names, location, or inventory numbers of whatever I was photographing, so that months later when I had time to label the photographs, I had all that information already recorded (especially helpful since I had usually forgotten the details by then). In fact, I generally just wrote the photo number and date on the back of each photo and put them in archival sleeves in a binder with a photocopy of the appropriate pages

A fictionalized example of the storage envelopes the author used for photos from a reunion. There is more space for information on the reverse side of the envelope. (Courtesy of Carolyn M. Brady)

The author photographed each page of her grandparents' album before removing the contents. Using a pencil, she numbered the photos, paper captions, and the blank spaces left on the album pages. The numbered slip of paper indicates this was page A16. Following is a sample of preliminary notes made for photo #A16-2:

- Six men seated at tables with Go game boards
- 4 5/8" x 2 7/8" real photo postcard, edges trimmed
- Japanese caption on back and side paper Ken Takara's translation: "1917—men playing Go" L–R: unknown, Motoji [Mototsugu] MORITA, Taichi INUKAI, Kiyoshi KAWAHARA or KAWABARA?, George TAKAGI, unknown
- Same men, clothing, and scalloped border picture format as photo #L8-4, probably taken same time in Hood River, OR
 (Courtesy of Carolyn M. Brady)

(Left) Outline charts are especially useful for labeling photos of large groups. This photo from the author's grandparents' album shows only a third of a much larger photo of a picnic in Hood River, Oregon, in 1928. Because the figures in the back were so small, the author numbered everyone and found there were at least 265 people! (Courtesy of Carolyn M. Brady)

(Above) Outline chart of photo (Courtesy of Carolyn M. Brady)

from the log. Then it was easy to see which negative was needed for a reprint. I also stored the negatives separately in a fireproof cabinet. If you can afford it, spend the extra money to get an index print when you develop your film because it makes a very useful reference, especially when you give all your photos away to family and friends, leaving you with just the negatives.

While digital cameras make sharing photos online much quicker and easier, I am not convinced of their effectiveness in long-term preservation of a family's photo history. A few decades ago archivists hoped new technology would help solve storage space problems, but now data recorded on magnetic tapes and obsolete floppy disks provide a different set of challenges. Given the speed with which technology evolves, it is uncertain whether fifty years from now it will be easier for people to see the photos stored in a box or the images burned on a compact disc. If you use a digital camera, consider making high-quality prints of the important images. Ironically, "old-fashioned" black-and-white photographs are expected to hold their image quality longer than color prints.

The recent resurgence of scrapbooking has made a wide variety of archival-quality albums and storage systems available, and there are many resources describing how to preserve family photos and heirlooms, so I will not devote a great deal of space to those topics. I will, however, mention one of the cardinal rules a museum professional follows: Don't do anything to a historic object that can't be undone. Don't cut up a photo for which you have no negative. Don't glue or adhere a historic photo into an album so that you can't remove it without damage. Be wary of colorful papers and stickers, even if they are labeled acid-free. Keep the following away from your photos: rubber bands, paper clips, adhesive tapes, food, and drink. Always wash your hands before handling photographs and hold them by the edges to avoid leaving fingerprints. Consider wearing clean white cotton gloves, especially when working with negatives and older photos. In some cases the oil on your skin can react with the chemicals in an image, literally fixing your fingerprints into the photo for posterity.

Whenever possible label your family photos with a pencil (No. 2 or softer) so that you can correct mistakes later. Be careful not to press too hard as you write. If you have nineteenth-century carte-de-visite or cabinet card photos printed on dark cardstock, you might photocopy them and label the copies or write the information on a piece of acid-free paper that you store with the photograph. (This would be the preferred method for daguerreotypes, which you should not attempt to photocopy in any case.)

Modern photographic prints have a plastic coating that requires more specialized marking pencils, available through archival catalogs and photographic and scrapbook supply stores. I know most guides warn you against using ink on your photos, but I personally use the film and print marking pen sold by Light Impressions on photographs for which I have negatives. The ink dries instantly so that it doesn't smear, but it is permanent. If I make a mistake, all I can do is draw a line through the error and start again. I only used ink on our old family photos once, when I had to write inventory numbers on a set of photographs from the early 1900s that a well-meaning relative had unfortunately laminated. Avoid using any sort of adhesive or sticker labels on your old photographs.

The basic information to record for a photograph includes who is pictured and where and when the photograph was taken. If you know more specifically what the photo depicts, who made it and why, all the better! Try to record as much of the story behind the photo as possible, being careful to differentiate between what you can prove and what you can only speculate about. You don't have to write everything on the back of the photo. In many cases, the information might not fit.

As mentioned earlier, writing on photocopies helps associate the stories with the correct photo. In the museum profession, objects and photos in a collection are usually assigned an accession or inventory number, and ideally there is a documentation file for every object in the inventory, with copy photographs, historic records, and other associated paperwork. When I was dealing with accession numbers in house museums for other families' objects, I never thought I would end up using the system to document my own family's history.

In dealing with my grandparents' album and associated loose photos, I have tried to make sense of them as a whole, realizing that the photos represented people and places important enough to my grandparents that they saved them even through the ordeal of the internment camps during World War II when they lost many of their possessions. I needed to remove the photos from the highly acidic album pages, but I wanted to maintain a record of how the photos were arranged in the album. After photographing each page of the album, I started removing the photos and numbering each on the back in pencil: A1-1, A1-2, and so forth. The "A" stood for "Album" (as opposed to the loose photos, which were assigned "L"); the first number was the page in the album; and the second number was the location of the photo on the page. I also wrote this same number on the page where the photo had been, so conceivably the album could be reconstructed, if need be. If another family album comes into my possession, I'll probably number those photos B1-1, B1-2, and so on.

You may develop an inventory system that works best with your particular situation. Some people use surnames and initials as part of their organizational code. Museums often base their inventory numbers on when they receive the object in question. I worked in one house museum where, because everything in the collection came from one family at one time, the type of object determined its number with F-1, F-2, and so forth representing furniture, and P-1, P-2, and so on referring to photographs, prints, and paintings. Perhaps your inventory system will eventually cover all your family heirlooms. Whatever the case, make sure your system is comprehensible to others. Write down what you did so that those who follow you will be able to continue your work.

As I was numbering all the photos, I started a handwritten list, recording a brief description of each photo, including size and format and what I knew about it. As I went through the photos with other family members, it was easier to jot down notes and erase mistakes on my list than on the backs of the photos. I store a copy of the list with the photos and have started a database in which I will eventually enter all the information and perhaps include scans of each photo. Many photos cannot physically be labeled in full because their backs are already filled by my grandparents' descriptions in Japanese or covered with black paper that stuck when the images were removed from an earlier album.

The numbering system also has made a convenient reference tool. When I sent color photocopies to relatives to identify, they could just write back, "Photo A1-2 is your grandmother's mother," and keep the photocopies for themselves. When taking notes while someone looks through the album, I can write the photo number in my interview notes for that person and transfer relevant data to the "master list" later. When I digitized the photos to put online, I could name the file "A1-2.jpg" rather than "tane_matsuda.jpg" (especially useful when you have a lot of similar images).

I have tried to keep track of who identified whom, especially since, in several instances, different relatives assigned different names and dates to the same photo. In my grandparents' collection, I also found group photos taken for school and community organizations, and I circulated these to friends of the family as well. When I went to a community reunion, I brought a binder of color copies of these photos along with outline charts to be filled in (made by taping the photocopies to a window and tracing the silhouettes of each person in the group). Not only did people recognize themselves and their family and friends, they also provided more information about the organizations and the events depicted. I have also posted a number of these community photos on my Web site in hopes that others researching this same

---

RESOURCES FOR ARCHIVAL PHOTOGRAPHIC SUPPLIES

Conservation Resources
5532 Port Royal Rd., Springfield, VA 22151
800-634-6932; www.conservationresources.com

Gaylord Bros.
PO Box 4901, Syracuse, NY 13221-4901
800-448-6160; www.gaylord.com

Light Impressions
PO Box 787, Brea, CA 92822-0787
800-828-6216; www.lightimpressionsdirect.com

University Products
517 Main Street, Holyoke, MA 01040
800-628-1912; www.universityproducts.com

---

community will be able to identify more people.

In dealing with this album I was fortunate that the photos were not pasted to the page, but held in place by "photo corners," many of which had already come loose as the adhesive deteriorated. Also my grandparents wrote their labels on the backs of the photos or on pieces of paper, which they taped to the album page, so that many of these had also fallen out, adding the challenge of matching slips of paper to photos. If you have an album or scrapbook in which the photos cannot be easily removed or the associated text is written on the pages, you may have to consult a conservation expert on how best to proceed.

Finally, after the photos are identified and labeled, spread the wealth. Share copies (all properly labeled, of course) with the rest of your relatives. That way if something happens to your photo of great-grandma, your siblings and cousins will have a backup.

———————————————•———————————————

Selected Bibliography: Frisch-Ripley, Karen. *Unlocking the Secrets in Old Photographs*. Salt Lake City: Ancestry, 1991; "Labeling Your Digital Photographs." *Ancestry Daily News* (January 26, 2001); Morgan, George G. "Along Those Lines." *Ancestry Daily News* (Online at www.ancestry.com/library/view/columns/george/); Taylor, Maureen A. *Preserving Your Family Photographs: How to Organize, Present and Restore Precious Family Images*. Cincinnati: Betterway Books, 2001.

[The author thanks Laura M. Bachelder, Midway Village and Museum Center; Sue Fischer, Cultural Resource Consulting Group; Ramona Duncan-Huse, Indiana Historical Society; and Amy H. Wilson, Chemung Valley History Museum, for reading and commenting on drafts of this chapter.]

Dating Photographs of Women Using Clothing Styles

LAURANN GILBERTSON

———————————— • ————————————

Too often, the photographs in our collections are unidentified. No names or dates are recorded, forcing us to guess who is in a given photograph and when it was taken. There are several ways to estimate the date of a photograph: consider the age of known individuals in the photo, rely on the type of image (for example, photographers made cartes-de-visite from 1859 to the 1890s), and use datable clues such as cars, businesses, and clothing.

Clothing can be a useful tool for determining the date of photographs because women's styles have changed regularly and distinctly over time. By focusing on women's fashions it is often possible to narrow the date down to a decade. Men's and children's clothing changed at a slower pace, so it is more difficult to use men and children to determine the date of a photo. Therefore, this chapter will describe the prevailing women's fashions for each decade from the 1850s through the 1940s after offering general suggestions about the use of clothing to date photographs.

Fashion can be defined as "a prevailing style of dress." Although costume historian Joan Severa cautions that even very poor women were aware of fashion and did what they could to wear stylish clothes, generally, younger and more affluent women fol-

lowed fashion more closely than older or less wealthy women. Photos of Norwegian immigrants show that some women could not or did not follow fashion and were several years behind the prevailing styles for economic or cultural reasons. Many women wore outdated or simplified garments for house and farmwork. In addition, older women sometimes remained in their favorite styles for many years. Figure 1 illustrates this "fashion lag." Therefore, when more than one woman appears in a photograph, look at the fashion exhibited by the youngest adult women.

Readers are encouraged to consult contemporary sources for help in understanding historic clothing. Contemporary materials, those produced at the same time as the photographs, might include women's and needlework magazines, clothing advertisements, and mail-order catalogs. These sources show clothing, accessories, hairstyles, and fashion ideals.

The books in the *Everyday Fashions* series published by Dover are a convenient source of fashion illustrations. They show a nice variety of twentieth-century women's day and evening garments, coats, and accessories. Mid-nineteenth-century fashion plates from the magazine *Godey's Lady's Book* have also been reprinted by Dover.

It is said that photographs don't lie. But fashion illustrations do. Artists subtly exaggerate or deemphasize parts of the body to make them fit the physical ideals of the time. For example, in the 1930s women were drawn with long necks and legs to make the figure look tall, slender, and broad-shouldered. The women in your photographs will not look like the figures in fashion illustrations. Note what is emphasized as "ideal" in fashion illustrations—for example, the broad shoulders of the 1930s—then watch for similar elements in the "real" clothing in photographs, such as the large and capelike collars that gave the fashionable appearance of broad shoulders.

Figure 1. In this multigenerational photograph, the seated woman wears a dress in the 1890s style with large sleeves. The two older women standing are wearing blouses with full fronts and tall collars, the style from the 1900s–1910s. The young woman on the right is wearing what is probably the current fashion, a more tubular dress with a lower collar, from the 1910s. (Courtesy of Laurann Gilbertson)

Whenever possible, use several criteria to narrow down or confirm a date derived by the prevailing style of dress. Notice hairstyles, shape of the neckline, placement of shoulder seams, sleeve and bodice shape, skirt cut and trim, and headwear or outerwear (if any). Even if the entire outfit is not visible, there will be a few fashion clues in almost every photograph with which to work. The sketches in this chapter show the style that

was most common throughout each decade.[1] Consult clothing histories and primary sources, such as fashion magazines, for additional information and examples.

Photographic images from the 1850s may appear in family collections as daguerreotypes, ambrotypes, and ferrotypes. Prints on paper, as cartes-de-visite, were used beginning in the late 1850s. Fashions of this decade, as illustrated in Figure 2, were characterized by a very full, very round skirt shaped by layers of petticoats and later by a hoop. The silhouette was triangular. Bodices, slightly high-waisted, were fitted tightly through the ribs and ended in front with a point or curve. The round neckline was trimmed with ribbons or a white collar. The shoulder seams were set low.

Figure 2. 1850s key features: full round skirt, bodice fitted tightly at ribs, full sleeves

Figure 3. 1860s key features: very low shoulder seams, large round skirt, smooth, center-parted hairstyle

Sleeves were narrow at the top and full below. Flared styles were worn with white undersleeves. The hairstyle was inspired by one worn by Empress Eugénie of France. Hair was parted in the center then shaped smoothly over the ears with a bun in back. Headwear included bonnets that sat toward the back of the head. Shawls, cloaks, and capes were worn as outerwear.

During the 1860s (see Figures 3 and 4), fashions were characterized by a very full round skirt shaped by a hoop, the skirt's fullness slowly moving toward the back as the decade progressed. Dresses had a center front opening with a slightly raised waist. A small white collar at the round neckline closed with a brooch. The shoulder seams were set low, below where the arm naturally bends. Sleeves were fullest at the elbow with cuffs or coat-style openings at the wrist. During the first few years of the decade sleeves were wide and bell-shaped with white undersleeves. Women wore their hair parted in the center, pulled back, and caught with a hair net. Headwear included bonnets that sat at the back of the head. Outerwear was a shawl, hip-length jacket, or long cloak. Military influence was evident in Zouave jackets and Garibaldi blouses.

During the first several years of the 1870s, women wore a combination of bodice, draped-front overskirt, and long full underskirt. Then by 1875 the outfit was reduced to two pieces: skirt and long bodice, as illustrated in Figure 5. The sides of the skirt

Headwear was bonnets and hats. Outerwear consisted of shawls, wraps, and boxy jackets.

Women's clothing styles eased into the 1880s. By 1883 the bustle returned and remained until 1887. The bustle did not cascade from the waist as it had in the 1870s, instead it stuck out straight in back like a shelf. Dresses had less trim but sported asymmetrical swags over a pleated skirt (see Figure 6). The bodice appeared very tightly fitted with narrow shoulder seams. Very tight sleeves ended just above the wrist bones. Bodices became shorter. Buttons were arranged down the front of the bodice first in a single line, then a double line, and finally an asymmetrical placement later in the decade. Collars were low

Figure 5. 1870s key features: long bodice, relaxed smooth sleeves, elaborate hairstyles

Figure 6. 1880s key features: bodice fitted tightly at sleeves and waist, narrow shoulder seams, frizzy bangs

Figure 7. 1890s key features: large sleeves, smooth, gored skirt

Figure 4. The dress worn by this Indiana woman has a large skirt and sleeves that are fullest at the elbow. These were characteristic of 1860s fashions. (Courtesy of the Indiana State Museum)

pulled in and back to accentuate a cascade of back detailing. Until about 1877, extreme back fullness was enhanced by a bustle, which started at the waist and slowly moved down to knee level. Dresses were decorated with self-fabric trim such as pleats, ruffles, and shirring. The shoulder seams were set at the natural bend of the shoulder, and sleeves were looser and evenly shaped. Necklines were ornamented with scarves, cravats, and black velvet ribbons. Hairstyles often had fullness on top or ringlets hanging below.

bands. The hair was pulled straight back into a bun and was often accompanied by frizzed bangs. High, narrow bonnets and a variety of brimmed hats were popular. Coats and jackets were worn for outerwear.

In 1890 sleeves began to loosen at the shoulder, as Figure 7 illustrates, developing from a small puff at the top of the shoulder to mutton-leg-shaped and very large by mid-decade. Sleeves began to deflate after about 1896. The bodice, with slight fullness in front and taller collar, was now very short, ending just at the waist. Outfits had decorated bodices and plain skirts. The bustle left, but a little back fullness remained for the first half of the decade. Skirts were gored (smooth over the hips with a full hem). This

Figure 8. Hoosier Daisy Taylor with her husband, bicycle racer "Major" Marshall W. Taylor, and daughter Sidney. The photograph was taken in Paris on one of Major Taylor's European racing tours. Daisy's large hat, tall collar, and S-shaped posture are the key indicators of a 1900–1909 date. Suit jackets were popular for women during this time period. (Courtesy of the Indiana State Museum)

Figure 9. 1900–1910 key features: very tall collar, full and droopy bodice front, pompadour hairstyle

Figure 10. 1910–1920 key features: shorter collar, hem, and sleeves, gently puffy hair

decade marked the beginning of separates and garments influenced by men's styles. The hair was pulled up, sometimes with a topknot, and short bangs were popular until 1896. Hats had medium brims and vertical decoration. Outerwear included coats with large sleeves and capes, which were especially popular later in the decade. Shoes and boots had pointed toes.

The most distinctive element of a woman's appearance during the years between 1900 and 1910 was the posture, as illustrated in Figure 8. An S-shaped curve was achieved by a straight-front corset; extra rows of ruffles on undergarments gave women a pigeon-breasted look. Blouses showed some fullness in the upper sleeves, but after about 1905 the fullness slid down toward the forearm. Collars were quite high—up to the jawbone. Lightweight and light-colored fabrics were popular including

white, lacy "lingerie" dresses or blouses. Skirts emphasized a curvy lower body and ended fluidly at or near the floor. Hairstyles were characterized by a great deal of fullness. The pompadour, named for hair piled on the top of the head with no part, was popular (see Figure 9). In about 1907, a more tubular silhouette was introduced as a "princess dress." Although there was no distinct waistline, the collar, sleeves, and hair still followed the style of the decade. Footwear included buttoned and laced boots. A variety of suit jackets and coats were worn. Hats were large and horizontal with large trim.

According to costume scholar Geitel Winakor the 1910s are best seen as a transition between the fashions of the nineteenth and twentieth centuries. In the book that she coauthored with Blanche Payne and Jane Farrell-Beck, Winakor states, "Within a given year, there was a bewildering assortment of variations in cut, plus a range of decorative treatments." In the 1910s the prevailing silhouette was tubular, as shown in Figure 10. Long jackets were worn over long narrow skirts. A layered look became popular around mid-decade and hiplines flared with draped hangings. By World War I a squared neckline was in, and the waist became looser and started to sink. Lightweight fabrics and pale colors continued while dark wools became common suit material. New shorter lengths were seen for hems, necklines, and sleeves. Hairstyles deflated but were still somewhat puffy and upswept. Hats were smaller but with strong brims. Lace-up shoes and boots were popular as were small pumps called "slippers."

The style of the early 1920s, dresses with looser and lower waistlines, actually began about 1918. The bustline was flattened so that dresses fell straight from the shoulders to the hem almost without touching the body (see Figure 11). If there was a waistline, it was at hip level, giving ordinary people in photographs a baggy look. Hems were at about mid-calf, but began to creep up to just below the knee in about 1927 (see Figure 12). Shoulder seams were at the natural bend of the shoulder. Dresses were made of lightweight fabrics and decorated, even for daytime, with stitching and trim. Later styles relied more on fabric pleats and tucks for decoration. Many women cut their hair short, at ear or chin level, and wore it straight or in a series of waves. The predominant style of hat in the 1920s was the cloche, which is French for bell. The hats were close fitting, coming down to the eyebrows and over the ears. Popular shoes were high-heeled slippers, often with buckles or ties over the instep.

Figure 11. 1920s key features: extreme tubular silhouette, short hair, cloche hats

Figure 13. 1930s key features: curvy silhouette with flares at the shoulder and hem

Figure 14. 1940s key features: wide padded shoulders, knee-length skirt

Figure 12. Mrs. Carpenter, Elinor Carpenter, and Mrs. Stanfield in Indianapolis. This photo was taken in 1928 when hemlines were at their shortest point of the decade. Close-fitting cloche hats were extremely popular throughout the 1920s. (Louise Carpenter Stanfield Collection, P 0236, IHS)

Outerwear included coats that fastened over the left hip and coats that had to be held closed.

The styles of the 1930s were a dramatic fashion change from the late 1920s. The new styles followed a slim but feminine silhouette. Dresses were belted at about the natural waist and fitted through the hips (see Figure 13). Some of the shaping was achieved by utilizing the diagonal or bias of the fabric and by yokes in the bodice or at the waist. Skirts flared slightly at the hem, which was at the middle of the calf during the mid-1930s. Large and capelike collars emphasized the shoulders. Rayon and acetate (Celanese), the first manufactured fibers to be used for women's clothing, were popular as were knit and all-over lace fabrics. Hair was styled in waves around the face and in a small bun in back. A variety of close-fitting and brimmed hats were worn, but always at an angle. High-heeled slippers continued to be popular. Coats were fitted and had large lapels or collars.

The broad-shouldered look was even more popular in the 1940s and achieved with padding (see Figure 14). The silhouette, until the mid-1940s, was triangular from shoulders to waist and then slightly flared to the skirt hem. Suits and dress/jacket combinations were common. The jackets were shaped with darts and seaming for a defined waist. Government regulations during World War II restricted skirt fullness and length; therefore, hems ended just below the knee. Women relied on bold prints and trim to decorate dresses.

Popular also was a military and menswear style achieved with plain, utilitarian fabrics. It was now acceptable for women to wear pants, but they were usually reserved for casual wear. In 1947, French designer Christian Dior introduced his "New Look," based on 1860s fashions, with a very full skirt, tight waist, and tight torso. As the decade ended, the silhouette became bell shaped. Skirts were fuller and longer while shoulders remained emphasized. Hairstyles in the 1940s ranged from long in a pompadour style that was high in front and on the sides to a short curled style. Headwear, too, ranged from small turbans and pillboxes to larger bonnets and hats. Pumps and high-heeled sandals were the popular shoes for most fashions. Young women preferred saddle shoes. Coats were fitted and had prominent lapels or collars.

1. All sketches in this chapter are by Laurann Gilbertson, 2001, 2002, all rights reserved.

Selected Bibliography: Blum, Stella, ed. *Everyday Fashions of the Thirties as Pictured in Sears Catalogs.* New York: Dover, 1986; Blum, Stella, ed. *Everyday Fashions of the Twenties as Pictured in Sears and Other Catalogs.* New York: Dover, 1981; Blum, Stella, ed. *Fashions and Costumes from Godey's Lady's Book.* New York: Dover, 1985; Dalrymple, Priscilla Harris. *American Victorian Costume in Early Photographs.* New York: Dover, 1991; Danielson, Donna R. "The Changing Figure Ideal in Fashion Illustration." *Costume and Textile Research Journal* 8, no. 1 (1989): 35–48; Gernsheim, Alison. *Victorian and Edwardian Fashion: A Photographic Survey.* New York: Dover, 1981; Olian, JoAnne, ed. *Everyday Fashions of the Forties as Pictured in Sears Catalogs.* New York: Dover, 1992; Payne, Blanche, Geitel Winakor, and Jane Farrell-Beck. *The History of Costume: From Ancient Mesopotamia Through the Twentieth Century,* 2nd ed. New York: HarperCollins, 1992; Severa, Joan. *Dressed for the Photographer: Ordinary Americans and Fashion, 1840–1900.* Kent, OH: Kent State University Press, 1995.

[Thanks to Geitel Winakor, professor emerita of textiles and clothing, Iowa State University, who reviewed the sketches, and Mary Jane Teeters Eichacker, curator of lifestyles, Indiana State Museum, who provided several photographs from the State Museum collections.]

Dramatize Your Family Stories by Placing Them in Historical Contexts

RANDY K. MILLS

———————————————•———————————————

Genealogists spend long hours collecting information about their families. Yet I have observed that, after all this work, many family histories are presented in a list form, void of almost any narrative that might breathe life into them. This chapter suggests ideas to turn your data into meaningful and entertaining packages by writing historical narratives.

Writing historical narratives, as I do, and writing appealing stories about one's family are in many ways the same task. The main difference is that the people I write about are not my relatives. Otherwise, both efforts require an attempt to write accurate and engaging stories. One useful way to create a compelling family narrative is to think of the ancestors you wish to write about as characters in a story. In a story, characters' lives are made more real and significant when the author shows obstacles the characters must strive to overcome. Connected to this idea is that of placing your ancestors' stories in a historical context. This latter effort dramatizes the struggles and highlights the contributions of your ancestors. Following are examples of how these two ideas—presenting family members as characters who must overcome obstacles and placing them in a larger historical context—might be carried out.

A few years ago a friend came to me with some scraps of information about his mother. Let us call her "Alice Jones." My friend showed me a diary his mother had kept as a teenager, some photos, and a recent interview. My friend had a profound respect for his mother and for all the hard work she had carried out to raise a family. Now he wanted to write a narrative about her life—especially the story of how she had decided to become a mother and homemaker—to pass down to future generations.

Teaching has traditionally been a popular career for women. The Indianapolis teacher depicted above is working with students on models of Christopher Columbus's ships, ca. 1895. (Orndorff Family Collection, P 0014, IHS)

Had Alice Jones become a doctor as she originally intended, she would have had few role models, but they did exist. One example is Mollie V. (Lewis) Sarran (1871–1905), a female physician who graduated from the Medical College of Indiana in 1892 and practiced medicine in Madison, Indiana. She was the Jefferson County health officer in 1894. Pictured here are Dr. Lewis's medical degree (left) and her pocket medicine case (right). (Samuel B. Lewis Papers, OM 0079 [left], and Artifact Collection, R 0788 [right], IHS)

Alice's diary offered particular insight, revealing a young woman who hoped to become a doctor or a science teacher. But this did not come to pass. In an interview with her son, Alice tells of receiving a university scholarship to become a teacher. Soon, however, she faced a definitive crisis. Alice grew homesick and discovered that she did not want to further her education after all. Her father held great hopes that she would become a teacher, though, and Alice did not want to disappoint him. Alice experienced a bout of deep depression over this situation. How could she escape her dilemma?

Presenting Alice as a character in a story who must overcome adversity is not difficult. When one places her story in a larger historical context, she also becomes a powerful example of the conflicts many young women endured after the close of World War II. Several historical pieces touch upon these conflicts. I chose Elaine Tyler May's *Pushing the Limits: American Women, 1940–1961* and an article in a 1945 *New York Times Magazine* to help flesh out Alice's tale. Here is a shortened version of the narrative I helped my friend write:

Alice Jones was born on December 3, 1927. Graduating from high school at the top of her class in 1946, she soon faced a painful dilemma—choosing between an outside career or life as a homemaker. In this, she was not alone. In order to win the Second World War, women had been encouraged to work in almost any occupation. Near the end of the war, the New York Times Magazine *noted the new role women in America had carved out for themselves: "Alma goes to work because she wants to go to work . . . now and . . . when the war is over. Alma's had a taste of LIFE. . . . Of course, all the Almas haven't thought through why they want to work after the war or how it's going to be possible. But they have gone far enough to know that they can do whatever is required in a machine shop. They've had the pleasure of feeling money in their pockets—money they've earned themselves."[1]*

It would seem that upon her graduation, Alice had a number of professions from which to choose, and her diary account bears this out. "When I wrote here last June, I wanted to be a doctor. That desire is not less urgent now, but it is not the foremost idea in

my mind. I can accept a scholarship, which amounts to 4 years training at a teacher's college in Illinois if I'll be a teacher. I have decided to accept it. I feel I must have a college education before I can start to do anything. . . . I prefer now to teach sciences in high school. Perhaps I can go to school later beyond the 4 years to become a doctor."[2]

Alice's ambitions were soon challenged by powerful forces. Elaine Tyler May, in her book Pushing the Limits, *notes, "During the war, as women streamed*

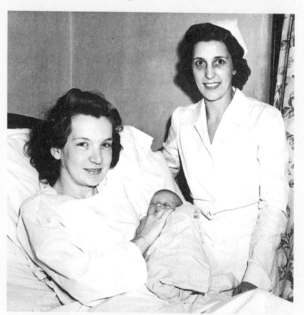

New mother, baby, and nurse at Union Hospital, Terre Haute, Indiana, November 10, 1944 (Martin's Photo Shop Collection, P 0129, IHS)

into the paid labor force, some observers feared that women might not be willing to settle down into family life once the emergency ended. Single women became targets of campaigns that would continue after the war, urging women back into their domestic roles."[3] This pressure to join the homemaking ranks was fierce for women such as Alice who were entering college just after World War II. Alice's diary tells of her struggles. "In about six months after entering the university I became homesick and depressed. For reasons I did not understand, I suddenly found myself wanting to quit school and get a job back home. But my father had great hopes that I would become a teacher. Toward the end of that first semester I found myself wandering around the campus. . . . I even thought about taking my own life. I felt caught between the wish to go to school and the desire to go back home, get a job and eventually marry and start a family. Finally I decided I wanted to return home. Once I made this decision I felt as if a great burden had been lifted off of me. But I still had to deal with my dad. What I decided to do was one of the most difficult things I have ever done in my life. I purposely flunked my chemistry class, then called my dad and told him I was failing school and that he needed to come pick me up. Soon after I returned home, I got a job, met my future husband, married, and raised a family."[4]

May tells us that many women, particularly those who had experienced a taste of college or harbored professional ambitions, did not find much fulfillment in marriage or in raising a family in the early 1950s. One woman of that generation declared, "This problem of the 'educated woman' learning to accept the monotony of housework and child training with cheerfulness and happiness has plagued me. I find much greater happiness now that the children are older." Conversely, many women, according to May, found contentment and significance in raising a family. "Some found that devoting themselves fully to the tasks of homemaking gave them a deep sense of satisfaction. They looked upon marriage and motherhood . . . as a challenging career with numerous rewards."[5]

Alice fit into this latter category. Like many women of her generation, she had difficult choices to make. Reflecting over her life on her seventy-third birthday she observed, "Although I sometimes wonder what my life might have been had I stayed in college, I have never once regretted the choice I made about raising a family. However, I am also thankful that my own granddaughters have greater options than women of my day. As for me, my life has been filled with great challenges, memories of some hard times, but mostly wonderful memories of raising children and running a household. I was married in 1948 and became the mother of four children. Two are teachers, one a sales representative for a large national company, and one is a funeral director. I think God wanted me to be a mother and raise these children, whose lives have reached out and touched so many other lives in such positive ways."[6]

When placed in the context of the dilemma women faced after World War II, Alice's struggles and contributions appear universal, and her story acquires more meaning. Note how her narrative was blended with historical information, how the narrative moved back and forth from her personal experiences to the national scene. Creating such a narrative requires research and writing, but the rewards are well worth the price.

Many readers probably wish to write about pioneer-era ancestors. Suppose that you have the following information on two ancestors named John and Nancy Smith: in 1814 they came from Connecticut to settle in southern Indiana, where they farmed, and Nancy died in 1823 from a fever, leaving John with two young children to raise. This is all the information you can find; there are no written documents or photographs that might enhance the Smiths' story. Fortunately, a vast number of personal accounts are available if you know where to look and how to use them. Following is a narrative I constructed for the fictional couple, using information

This picture of the working pioneer farm at Lincoln State Park in Spencer County, Indiana, shows some of the tools that Hoosier pioneer farmers used. (Courtesy of Allen T. Baer)

G. N. Frankenstein's painting of the Indiana Knobs, near New Albany, Indiana, illustrates the rugged beauty of southern Indiana during the pioneer period. (R. Carlyle Buley, *The Old Northwest Pioneer Period, 1815–1840* [Indianapolis: Indiana Historical Society, 1950])

from regional histories, newspapers, travel accounts, and letters of the day. Again, note how the narrative presents the Smiths as characters who face a number of problems.

John and Nancy Smith came to the southern Indiana frontier from Connecticut in 1814, probably enduring a difficult journey. Virginia and Robert McCormick, in their book New Englanders on the Ohio Frontier, *tell us that travel at this time from Connecticut to the Ohio Valley took six to eight weeks, much of it through a rugged wilderness. They quote a letter from one New Englander who immigrated to the Ohio frontier during this period, "If I were to take the journey again, I would not use one article of crockery. On the road we broke the most of ours."[7] S. A. O'Ferrall, a traveler through southern Indiana, wrote, "We passed through Petersburg to Princeton, but . . . lost the track. After a great deal of danger and difficulty, we succeeded in returning . . . [to] a small village, through which we had passed three hours before. The gloom and pitchy darkness of an American forest at night, cannot be conceived by the inhabitants of an open country, and traversing a narrow path interspersed with stumps and logs is both fatiguing and dangerous."[8]*

Once in Indiana, the Smiths would have staked a claim to their land and begun creating a farm.

The initial process was a daunting one as Morris Birkbeck noted in 1818. "The poor emigrant . . . repairs to the land office, and enters his quarter section, then works his way, without another 'cent' in his pocket, to the solitary spot, which is to be his future abode, in a two horse waggon, containing his family and . . . a few blankets, a skillet, his rifle, and his axe. Suppose him arrived in the spring," Birkbeck wrote, "after putting up a little log cabin, he proceeds to clear, with intense labour, a plot of ground for Indian corn, which is to be next year's support; but, for the present . . . he depends on his gun for subsistence. In pursuit of the game, he is compelled, after his day's work, to wade through the evening dews, up to the waist, in long grass, or bushes, and returning, finds nothing to lie on but a bear's skin on the cold ground, exposed to every blast through the sides, and every shower through the open roof of his wretched dwelling."[9]

Farming on the frontier was an arduous occupation as a farm laborer noted after his first harvest season, "In the beginning . . . I did the easiest work: raking hay. . . . The burning sun was intolerable. . . . After an hour's work I was completely soaked with perspiration. . . . Other kinds of work which I was able to do were turning the swath [cut grain] with a wooden fork, stacking it when it was dry, piling up the hay, loading it on the wagon, then unloading the wagon onto the haystacks. Stacking the hay with an iron fork is . . . almost unbearable. These jobs are nothing compared with mowing, plowing, thinning Indian corn, and grubbing; also stacking oats in stubby fields. It is almost impossible for someone who is not used to this kind of work from his youth to handle the scythe, the plow, and the axe to advantage."[10]

Frontier women like Nancy faced an equally harsh existence. One traveler to southern Indiana observed, "Soap, candles, sugar, cotton, leather, and woolen clothes, of a good quality, are here all made from the land, but not without the most formidable, unremitting industry on the part of the females."[11] Another settler to the region recognized the toilsome situation women faced: "The family meals are to be prepared every day, the washing, the cleaning, the bed-making, the scouring, must be carried on."[12]

Settlers were often beset by illness. In 1821 New England native Samuel Thing wrote from Vincennes, Indiana, to his brother in New Hampshire, "There is so much sickness in this lower country that the northern people suffer very much[.] there was about one hundred and forty or fifty died here last summer and fall and a great many that was sick so long has died thiss winter and some have not got well yet. . . . I see dayly families from the east that is completely broken up by sickness; some taken away and the balance [of] there property all distroyed by sickness."[13]

It is little wonder that sickness prevailed. William Oliver, in his account Eight Months in Illinois, gives a vivid description of insects on the frontier: "The whole earth and air seems teeming with them, mosquitoes, gallinippers, bugs, ticks, sand-flies, sweat-flies, house-flies, ants, cockroaches, etc., join in one continued attack. . . . Sick people in bed, require the constant attention of some assistant to drive them off, otherwise, if the patient were a child, or very weak, I believe they would soon suffo-

cate him."[14] Unhealthy practices added to the danger of disease as a Vincennes, Indiana, newspaper complained in 1808, "It is . . . not uncommon, to see carcass's of horses, dogs, hogs, &c. lying in the streets and on the common near the village."[15]

In 1823 Nancy came down with a fever. It is likely that if a physician treated her, he may have done more harm than good. At this time a doctor would probably have tried bleeding, purges, and plasters to cure Nancy. Regarding bleeding, one Indiana father wrote back East in 1824 that his son "was very nigh falling a prey to an acute . . . fever, which 4 repeated bleedings could hardly check, he is well now but a mere skeleton."[16] If Nancy used a physician, he may have possessed little if any training. In his travelogue, Oliver wrote of one typical doctor, noting, "We happened to apply at the house of a person, who figured as doctor, but whose right to that title was anything but doubtful." According to Oliver, the doctor's wife "praised him to the skies," but "she did not attempt to conceal that he had no diploma."[17]

Nancy died of her fever in 1823. Today, although their remains rest in unmarked graves somewhere in southern Indiana, Nancy and John Smith's legacy continues, for a number of Smith descendants dot Indiana and the Midwest. They can be proud that they possess such courageous ancestors.

During the pioneer era women's chores often included spinning, weaving, and sewing clothes and other textiles. (Chris Aspin, *The Cotton Industry* [Shire Publications Limited, 2000])

These examples demonstrate the main tasks involved in dramatizing family stories and placing them in larger historical contexts. The first step is to note the time and place in which your ancestors lived. Then read sections in local, state, and regional histories about that particular time and place. These histories will enable you to understand and write about the adversities your family members faced and to describe, in general, what your ancestors' world was like. To put a more personal face on the narrative, try to locate firsthand accounts concerning the time and place of your ancestors' stories. Letters, diaries, and other primary documents from the family members in question are the best sources, but you can borrow details from other personal accounts, as in the narratives above, to weave into your story. Interlacing these three elements—the general conditions, first-

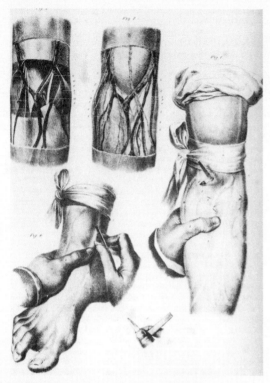

Diagram illustrating the process of bleeding (Joseph Pancoast, *A Treatise on Operative Surgery* [Carey and Hart, 1844])

variety of historical eras. Look at the reference notes at the end of this chapter or browse the Society's History Market or its publications catalogs to get some idea of the wealth of information available to genealogists. Illustrations are another way to enhance family stories. The actual Alice Jones narrative, for example, contained photos of Alice's senior high school class, her wedding, and her family. Even if you are unable to find family illustrations for your stories, you can use general illustrations from the era in question as shown in this chapter.

The stories of common people who have wrestled with daily strife and life-altering decisions are worthy of telling. They are waiting to be discovered and told in memorable ways, to be preserved and at the same time to remind us of what it takes to survive and to live successful lives.

hand accounts, and your ancestor's data—is not easy, but the effort can greatly enhance family stories.

Finding contextual resources may seem like a challenge, but plenty of materials are available. General histories about colonial times, the frontier, the Civil War era, the 1920s, the Great Depression, and so forth abound. And do not forget newspapers and magazines. Newspapers are available on microfilm through interlibrary loan or at the Indiana State Library. Older newspapers can be found in local libraries. Large universities, such as Indiana University, also carry copies of national magazines such as *Time, Newsweek, Ladies Home Journal*, and so forth.

State and local historical societies preserve first-hand accounts such as letters and diaries. For example, a search of the keyword *letters* on the Indiana Historical Society's Web site (www.indianahistory.org) yields a list of hundreds of collections containing correspondence. This Web site provides detailed information regarding the Society's manuscript collections as well. There are also a number of publications called "documentary editions" composed of journals, letters, diaries, and travel accounts from a

1. *New York Times Magazine*, 1945, quoted in Elaine Tyler May, *Pushing the Limits: American Women, 1940–1961* (New York: Oxford University Press, 1994), 47.

2. Alice Jones (pseudonym) Diary, January 1946. The original diary is in possession of the diarist.

3. May, *Pushing the Limits*, 39.

4. Jones diary, n.d.

5. May, *Pushing the Limits*, 67–68.

6. "Alice Jones" interview with her son, December 3, 2000. Copy in author's possession.

7. Virginia McCormick and Robert W. McCormick, *New Englanders on the Ohio Frontier: Migration and Settlement of Worthington, Ohio* (Kent, OH: Kent State University Press, 1998), 44.

8. Shirley McCord, comp., *Travel Accounts of Indiana, 1679–1961*, Indiana Historical Collections, vol. 47 (Indianapolis: Indiana Historical Bureau, 1970), 141.

9. Morris Birkbeck, *Notes on a Journey in America from the Coast of Virginia to the Territory of Illinois* (London: Severn and Company, 1818), 51.

10. Janet R. Walker and Richard W. Burkhardt, *Eliza Julia Flower: Letters of an English Gentlewoman: Life on the Illinois–Indiana Frontier, 1817–1861* (Muncie, IN: Ball State University, 1991), 55.

11. Harlow Lindley, ed., *Indiana As Seen by Early Travelers*, Indiana Historical Collections, vol. 3 (Indianapolis: Indiana Historical Bureau, 1916), 311.

12. George Flower, *The Errors of Immigrants* (London: Cleave, Shoe Lane Fleet Street, 1841; reprint, New York: Arno Press, 1975), 26.

13. Samuel Thing, letter to John Thing, April 22, 1821, Thing Family Papers, 1814–1903, SC 2360, Indiana Historical Society.

14. William Oliver, *Eight Months in Illinois, with Information to Immigrants* (New Castle upon Tyne: William Andrew Mitchell, 1843; reprint, Chicago: Walter M. Hill, 1924), 148, 149.

15. *Vincennes Western Sun*, September 3, 1808.

16. Gayle Thornbrough, ed., *The Correspondence of John Badollet and Albert Gallatin, 1804–1836,* Indiana Historical Society Publications, vol. 22 (Indianapolis: Indiana Historical Society, 1963), 37.

17. Oliver, *Eight Months in Illinois*, 188.

Part 2
Identifying Resources

Indiana State Library building in downtown Indianapolis (Photo by David H. Turk, IHS)

Genealogy Division
Indiana State Library

RANDY BIXBY

———————————————— • ————————————————

The Genealogy Division of the Indiana State Library (ISL) houses one of the Midwest's major collections of family and local history. Emphasis is on Indiana and the states from which Indiana was settled, particularly Virginia, North Carolina, Ohio, Kentucky, Tennessee, and Pennsylvania, but there are also significant holdings on other Mid-Atlantic states, New England, Germany, and Great Britain. Holdings are less extensive for states west of the Mississippi River.

Vital Records

One of the Genealogy Division's great treasures is the set familiarly known as the "red books," or WPA indexes to Indiana births, deaths, and marriages. These indexes were compiled by the Works Progress Administration (WPA) between 1939 and 1941 from records in the various county clerks' offices or county health departments. Sixty-seven of Indiana's ninety-two counties are included in this set.

WPA birth and death indexes span the years 1882 through 1920 for most counties; births and deaths were not officially recorded in Indiana until 1882. WPA marriage indexes usually cover 1850 through 1920. The indexes include the person's name, date of the event, and the record book and page number in which the event is recorded at the county level. Citations for births give parents' names, including mother's maiden name. Indiana marriage records prior to the 1880s do not usually give parents' names or birth dates of the bride or groom. From January 1882 through April 1905 and later for many counties, a supplemental form contained this information. The WPA indexed these supplemental records for many counties. After April 1905, birth dates and parents' names were part of the marriage record itself. For counties not included in the red books, other indexes usually exist for marriage records. Birth and death records are less likely to be indexed.

From printed indexes, microfilmed records, and other sources, the Genealogy Division has compiled a statewide index to pre-1850 Indiana marriage records. This index is available as a searchable database on the ISL's Web site.

The Genealogy Division has a few indexes to Indiana vital records for years more recent than 1920. The Indiana State Board of Health maintains a statewide index of Indiana births that occurred after October 1907 and deaths that occurred after 1900. For a fee, the State Board of Health will search its indexes and can provide copies of the records. Be aware that recent birth records are considered private, and access is restricted by law. The State Board of Health has also created statewide bride and groom marriage indexes for each year beginning with 1958. The Genealogy Division has copies of the indexes from 1958 through 1997. The indexes from 1993 through 2002 are also available as a searchable database on the ISL's Web site. The marriage records can be obtained from the appropriate county clerk's office.

Federal Census Records

When the Founding Fathers mandated a decennial census in the Constitution, they inadvertently created an invaluable tool for family history research. The federal census locates a family in a specific county at the time of the census, and from 1850 on, gives information on each person in the household, such as age, birthplace, and education. The Genealogy Division has all available indexes and microfilmed federal population schedules for Indiana from 1820 through 1930; population schedules and Soundex indexes for all other states 1790 through 1880 and 1930; and population schedules and Soundex/Miracode indexes for many states from 1900 through 1920.

Will and Probate Records

Will and probate records not only give family information by listing spouses and heirs, they also indicate a family's social status or wealth. Because wills are usually filed soon after an individual's death, a close approximation of the death date can be determined by comparing the date the will was written and the date it was filed. The Genealogy Division has printed indexes of many Indiana counties' will records and some microfilm copies of actual wills. The division also holds printed indexes to wills for many counties in states other than Indiana.

Probate records are not as straightforward as wills, in that the probate process can take months or years to complete, so there will likely be more than one probate entry for a person in the county records. Probates can be especially helpful when someone died without a will (probate is required if a person's estate exceeds a certain dollar value or if the decedent

owned real property). There may also be wonderful details about the deceased person's property in the form of inventories. Probate records are more complex than wills, and many probate records are loose papers filed in bundles or drawers in the county clerk's office rather than recorded in books; therefore they are less often indexed than wills. The Genealogy Division has printed indexes to and microfilmed copies of some Indiana counties' probate records. The microfilm often contains an index.

Cemetery Records

Cemeteries have always fascinated genealogists, and many dedicated groups and individuals from the Boy Scouts to the Daughters of the American Revolution have painstakingly recorded tombstone inscriptions for cemeteries across Indiana. The Genealogy Division has extensive listings of tombstone inscriptions for Indiana cemeteries. There are a few countywide indexes to burials; most compilations are for single cemeteries, or sometimes for all the cemeteries in a township. The information in these listings can be extremely helpful, especially if a death occurred before there were official death records. Cemetery records may be the only way of finding a death date for someone who "disappeared" between census years. In addition to the death date, other details can often be found on a tombstone, such as military service, maiden name, birthplace, and so forth.

The Genealogy Division has compiled an Indiana Cemetery Locator File, arranged by county and then by name of cemetery, which gives the call numbers of items in its collections pertaining to specific cemeteries. This file is available as a searchable database on the ISL's Web site. At this time the database does not include the names of the people buried in each cemetery.

Land Records

Land records, in the form of deeds or patents, are another source of family information. They document years during which a family lived in a county, can give family relationships, and also indicate the family's financial status. Deed records are kept at the county level. The Genealogy Division has printed indexes of deeds for many Indiana counties as well as some counties in other states. Many Indiana deed books have been microfilmed, and the microfilms can be found in the Genealogy Division.

If your ancestors were very early Indiana settlers, they may have bought their land directly from the federal government. The Genealogy Division has printed indexes to most original federal land sales in what is now Indiana. Another excellent resource for federal land sales is the Bureau of Land Management's searchable database, which is on the Internet at www.glorecords.blm.gov/default.asp. It can be searched by name of patentee, county, or legal land description (section, town, range).

Genealogy Division of the Indiana State Library (Photo by David H. Turk, IHS)

Passenger Lists

If a researcher has been able to identify an immigrant ancestor, passenger lists can provide further clues about the country of origin. In 1820 the federal government began keeping records of passengers on ships entering American ports. Passenger lists are arranged by port of entry and then by date. The National Archives has indexed and microfilmed many passenger lists. The Genealogy Division has microfilmed indexes for most eastern seaboard, southern, and gulf coast ports for various years, and a few copies of passenger lists themselves. Passenger lists are more difficult to find for pre-1820 voyages, but the Genealogy Division has printed indexes to many lists that are published in books or periodicals.

Naturalization Records

After the American Revolution, immigrants who wanted to become American citizens had to undergo the naturalization process, which involved at least three steps: the Declaration of Intention to become a citizen, the Petition for Naturalization, and the Final [Court] Order of Naturalization. The origi-

nal records for most Indiana counties' declarations and petitions have been transferred to the Indiana State Archives, where volunteers are indexing them for online and print publication. The Indiana Historical Society's book *An Index to Naturalization Records in Pre-1907 Order Books of Indiana County Courts* indexes the Final Orders, which can be found in court order books at Indiana's county courthouses. The Genealogy Division has printed indexes to declarations and petitions from many Indiana counties and microfilm copies of some of these records. It also has a few scattered indexes to naturalization records for counties in other states.

Military Records

Military records can provide a wealth of information on ancestors who served in the armed forces, not only from the time of the American Revolution, but also in the colonial period. Prior to the Revolution, most military service was performed in locally organized militia units. Their records usually reside in the archives of the states formed from the original colonies. The Genealogy Division has many books and printed indexes of colonial military records.

Most records for service in the Revolution, War of 1812, Mexican War, Indian wars, Civil War, and

Spanish-American War are kept by the National Archives in Washington, DC. The Genealogy Division has many printed indexes related to military service from the Revolution through the Civil War and microfilmed pension indexes for Revolutionary War, War of 1812, and Civil War service. The Index to Indiana Enrollment of Soldiers, their Widows and Orphans, 1886, 1890, and 1894, is a card file prepared by the Genealogy Division from a special survey of veterans residing in Indiana in those years. The surveys themselves are held by the Indiana State Archives.

Church Records

Church records can often fill gaps in civil records, especially during the years when births and deaths were not officially recorded. A church record can provide a child's parents' names, give an idea when a family moved into or out of an area, or present a picture of a family's involvement and standing in its community. The Genealogy Division has printed indexes of many Indiana church records, some records for churches in other states, and extensive collections of pre-1850 English church records. The Church of Jesus Christ of Latter-Day Saints has microfilmed many Indiana Catholic Church records; these records are available in the Genealogy Division.

Computer Sources

The ISL has its own Web site, and each division within the library has a Web page with links to in-house databases and other sites of interest. The State Library's Web site can be found at www.statelib.lib.in.us. The library's online catalog is also accessible from the home page. It includes Genealogy Division books cataloged since 1976 and citations for materials in other divisions of the library. At this time some genealogy titles can only be accessed through the manual card catalog in the division's reading room. Several public Internet terminals are available in the reading room.

The library has paid subscriptions to Ancestry Library Edition, HeritageQuest Online, FirstSearch, and New England Ancestors.org (produced by the New England Historic Genealogical Society), accessible through any Internet terminal within the library building. These databases provide information ranging from Civil War pensions to birth indexes, census records, local histories, and more. FirstSearch alone consists of more than one hundred databases, many of them subject-specific—for example, humanities or medicine. One FirstSearch database of particular interest to genealogists is WorldCat, which contains citations from libraries and archives across the country. It is useful for identifying titles of local and family histories not held by the ISL.

A great body of genealogy has also been published on CD-ROM. The Genealogy Division has CDs from several publishers, including Family Search (Latter-day Saints), FamilyTreeMaker, and Generations Archives. Another useful database available on CD-ROM and HeritageQuest Online is PERSI, the genealogy periodical index compiled by the Allen County Public Library in Fort Wayne, Indiana. Periodicals are one of the least-utilized resources for genealogy information. PERSI makes it easy to search for articles by family name, county, or other subject. The Genealogy Division has hundreds of magazines and newsletters indexed in PERSI.

Miscellaneous

Other materials useful to genealogists include maps, pamphlets, family and local histories, heraldry, and manuscript collections. Whether a researcher is a beginner or has years of experience, the Genealogy Division of the Indiana State Library has resources that will advance the work of the family historian.

The Indiana State Library is located at 140 North Senate Avenue in downtown Indianapolis on the corner of Senate Avenue and Ohio Street. The Genealogy Division's printed collections, electronic resources, and reference desk are located on the first floor just inside the Ohio Street entrance; the microform collection and printed census indexes are located on the second floor. The library is open Mondays through Fridays with evening and Saturday hours usually available. It is closed on all state holidays and on the Saturdays of holiday weekends. For the most recent schedule and other information, call 317-232-3689, or visit the Web site at www.statelib.lib.in.us.

Indiana Division
Indiana State Library

ANDREA BEAN HOUGH

⸺⸺⸺⸺⸺ • ⸺⸺⸺⸺⸺

Genealogists and historians regularly use the Indiana Division of the Indiana State Library (ISL) to fill in the gaps of their Hoosier ancestor research. Whether using its extensive collection of Indiana newspapers to locate obituaries; drawing upon its collections of directories, histories, and atlases; or tracking an ancestor through its unique indexes, researchers find hitherto unknown information about their ancestry in the ISL Indiana Division. When the Indiana Division's collections are used in conjunction with the vast holdings of the Genealogy Division, the ISL provides an unparalleled resource for Indiana research.

A Brief History of the Indiana Division

A distinct Indiana collection was part of the ISL as early as 1903, when an *Indianapolis Journal* article noted the two thousand books in the Indiana Section, including novels, histories, and state documents. The Indiana General Assembly formally established "The Division of Indiana History and Archives," which later became known as the Indiana Division, in 1913. Despite the many changes experienced by the Indiana Division over the years, its staff has collected books, periodicals, newspapers, broadsides, oral his-

tories, manuscripts, state documents, and maps to create one of the most comprehensive collections of current and historical materials on all aspects of Indiana in existence today. In addition, Indiana Division librarians have created unique specialized indexes to newspaper holdings and other collections.

The Indiana Division does not replicate the holdings of the ISL Genealogy Division, and, therefore, does not maintain cemetery inscriptions, county records, or family histories. Nor does the Indiana Division duplicate the holdings of the Indiana State Archives, which holds the official records of the state of Indiana. While its collections do not include materials specific to family history research, a wide variety of its materials can be used for that purpose.

The strengths of the Indiana Division collections include periodicals, newspapers, pamphlets, printed histories, directories, clipping files, manuscripts, state documents, and maps. The collection currently holds more than 120,000 printed volumes (books and pamphlets), nearly 80,000 reels of microfilmed newspapers, approximately 3,000,000 manuscript items, and almost 11,000 maps. The card catalog, which provides information on more than 85 percent of the collection, and the online catalog, which shows materials obtained since 1978, provide access to the printed materials in the Indiana Division. Other catalogs provide access to the broadside, manuscript, and picture collections. The print collections are available for use on the ISL's second floor, where librarians are always available to assist patrons in their research.

Locating People in Time and Place

One of the most important aspects of genealogical research is placing an ancestor in a given time and location. This can be done through a variety of methods such as using the Genealogy Division's census records or county records on microfilm. Another way is through using printed resources such as newspapers or city directories, as well as secondary sources such as county histories and atlases. These types of materials are available for use in the Indiana Division.

Newspapers

The Indiana Division contains the largest collection of Indiana newspapers in existence, dating from the first newspaper published in the state in 1804 through the latest editions of more than 220 city and county newspapers from throughout Indiana. These are available for use in the Indiana Division, or they can be borrowed through interlibrary loan from any library in the country.

Several sources identify the newspapers that the Indiana Division holds. Librarians maintain the most comprehensive listings, which are arranged by county and available on the second floor of the ISL and in part through the Newspaper Section on the Indiana Division's Internet Web site (www.statelib. lib.in.us/www/isl/whoweare/indiana.html). Instructions for using the interlibrary loan service to obtain newspapers on microfilm are also available on the Web site.

Although an obituary can provide a wealth of information about an ancestor, newspapers vary in their coverage of the lives of the recently deceased. Small town newspapers have traditionally provided the best articles. However, since many of them are weekly papers, they omit many obituaries of deaths that are "old news" by the time an issue is published.

Large city dailies, such as the *Indianapolis Star*, carried obituaries infrequently until after World War II. Newspapers published obituaries for women less often than for men, and they rarely published obituaries for African Americans until after World War II. When obituaries are not available, death notices or funeral notices may provide some of the information desired.

In addition to obituaries and death notices, community news can provide a wonderful source of information about Hoosier ancestors. Many county-seat newspapers published weekly or semiweekly news columns from outlying towns and villages. These columns provide information on illnesses, engagements, visitors, and various community events. While it is difficult to find genealogical information about an ancestor through the community columns, they may provide unknown details about an ancestor's life.

Directories

The Indiana Division has extensive holdings of Indiana city and county directories that can be used to show that a person lived in a place at a particular time. City directories also show occupation and address of the head of household, and later directories often list the spouse. While the coverage is best for larger communities such as New Albany/Jeffersonville, Indianapolis, Richmond, and Fort Wayne, the collections include directories from almost every county for some time period. Early city directories are available on microfilm or microfiche from the Genealogy Division as well. Many older city directories are currently listed in the card catalog, while newer city directories may be located in the online catalog. Patrons interested in ascertaining whether the ISL holds a directory for a particular city or county in a given year may contact the Indiana Division for assistance.

In addition, the Indiana Division holds a variety of published directories from organizations throughout the state. These include directories by profession such as legal or medical, alumni directories, and political directories. Recently, patrons used banking directories to confirm an ancestor's service on a bank's board of directors. These types of resources are not often considered genealogical; nevertheless, they can be used to fill in gaps of knowledge about an ancestor.

County Histories

County histories can be a good source of information about an ancestor. The Indiana Division has an extensive collection of county histories, which it has supplemented over the years with city, town, church, organizational, business, and other histories covering all aspects of Indiana. When used in conjunction with the Works Progress Administration (WPA) and Indiana Historical Society indexes to county histories and the Indiana Biography Index, they may provide biographical information about an ancestor as well as information about his or her community activities. A word of caution, however: County histories may contain erroneous or conflicting information, so researchers should verify this type of information in other sources when possible.

Atlases and Plat Maps

Nineteenth-century atlases and plat maps can also be used to show that a person was in a given place at a certain time. During the late 1800s, many atlases were published for counties in Indiana. In many cases they provide biographical information about residents who subscribed to the atlas, and they often show the holdings of rural landowners, too. Plat maps, which were published from the 1920s but not collected heavily by the Indiana Division until the 1950s, also show rural landholdings. The Indiana Division has a variety of atlases and plat maps of Indiana counties. While many of the atlases cannot be photocopied because of their condition, the Indiana Division has ordered microfilm of many of them so that patrons may print copies of their pages.

Using Indiana Division Indexes to Trace an Ancestor

Since 1898, ISL librarians have maintained a variety of indexes to make information about Indiana people, places, and events more readily available. Indexes are used to track down information from sources otherwise difficult, if not impossible, to use.

Indiana Biography Index

Decades ago, librarians from the Indiana Division created the Indiana Biography Index. It provides citations to a variety of works with biographical information about people having Indiana connections. The index includes references to books, organizational meeting minutes, magazine articles, and other sources. Approximately two hundred fifty thousand cards are in the index, arranged by name, each with one or more citations. Patrons who are unable to use the on-site card file index may search the index online at http://199.8.200.229/db/bio_cards_search.asp.

The ISL stopped creating entries to the card file index in 1990; however, in 1998 ISL librarians restarted the Indiana Biography Index as an online database, working from sources published since 1990. At present nearly forty thousand entries exist in the online database, accessible at http://199.8.200.229/db/biography_search.asp. Although it is not geared toward genealogists at this time, the online database will be useful to future genealogists.

Newspaper Indexes

From 1898 to 1991, librarians at the ISL indexed the articles in the major Indianapolis newspapers by name, subject, and geographic area. While this particular index does not provide complete coverage of obituaries, it may provide information of use in genealogical research.

A variety of other newspaper indexes are available in the Indiana Division. The WPA created many of these indexes in the late 1930s and early 1940s. Others were created in-house. The Indiana Division has made some of them available over the Internet. Major card file indexes include:

Assorted printed indexes
Indianapolis, 1848–1888, 1898–1978, 1979–1991 (online except 1898–1978)
Logansport, 1848–1855 (online)
Madison, 1849–1899
New Albany, 1849–1889 (online)
Richmond, 1836–1850
Vincennes, 1804–1827 (online)

Periodical Indexes

Citations for periodical articles can be found from the various indexes located in the Indiana Division or through similar periodical indexes created by libraries throughout the state. Whenever a patron has a complete citation for an article (title or content description, name of publication, date, and page of article) from a newspaper, magazine, or other periodical held by the Indiana Division, he or she may contact the division to obtain a copy at a nominal charge. While the majority of the Indiana Division's indexes continue to be available in card format only, some have been converted and placed on the ISL's Web site. Online indexes are available from the Indiana Division's Web page.

A Final Word

The Indiana Division provides valuable information for genealogists. Each week many researchers visit the Indiana Division to fill in gaps in their findings. By combing through newspapers, working with city directories, county histories, and maps, and using the Indiana Biographical Index, family historians learn rare information about their ancestors that may not be available elsewhere.

The Indiana State Library is open Mondays through Fridays with evening and Saturday hours usually available. However, the Manuscript Section of the Indiana Division is open only Monday through Friday 8:00 a.m. until 4:30 p.m.

Patrons may access the collections on the second floor of the library, where the reference desk is located. Patrons may also call, write, or electronically contact the Indiana Division with their questions: 317-232-3670; Indiana Division, Indiana State Library, 140 North Senate Avenue, Indianapolis, Indiana 46204; or visit the Web site, www.statelib.lib.in.us, and use the Ask a Librarian feature. Staff will check the various indexes available in the Indiana Division for entries about specified ancestors. For more information about the ISL Indiana Division or to check its most recent schedule, visit its home page at www.statelib.lib.in.us/www/isl/whoweare/indiana.html.

Indiana Room at the Indiana State Library (Photo by David H. Turk, IHS)

Manuscript Section
Indiana State Library

ELIZABETH WILKINSON

———————— • ————————

The Manuscript Section of the Indiana State Library contains a wealth of historical materials that are often overlooked and underutilized. The Manuscript Reading Room is nestled in a quiet back corner of the second floor where patrons can peruse and research in virtual solitude. The Manuscript Section houses such materials as manuscripts, pictures, broadsides, oral histories, and program collections. A literal summary of the collection would be approximately 3,876 cubic feet of manuscript collections, 144 linear feet of oversized manuscript collection materials, 2,790 bound volumes, approximately 144 cubic feet of program collections, nearly 70 cubic feet of photographs, and 10 cubic feet of oral history tapes.

The collection is used most for research, exhibitions, and publications. As one of the main repositories in the state for Indiana historical documents, our patrons include college students, professors, and family historians. Often cited in dissertations and articles, the Indiana State Library manuscript collection is an invaluable resource for scholars working on projects related to Indiana history.

Of particular interest to genealogy researchers are the manuscript and picture collections. Strengths of the manuscript collection include Civil War-era letters and diaries, papers of Indiana political figures, and family papers. The manuscript items can be located by using a number of methods. The best way to find materials is by looking up specific names of people or organizations and subject headings in the card catalog. Published guides that include access to our materials are *A Guide to Manuscript Collections of the Indiana Historical Society and Indiana State Library* by Eric Pumroy and *Guide to Indiana Civil War Manuscripts* by Ann Turner. While the state library's online catalog contains about 20 percent of the Manuscript Card Catalog, newly processed collections are cataloged directly into the online catalog, and older collections are now being added on a regular basis. Within the next few years the goal is to have all manuscript collections available through the online catalog, eliminating the need for the card catalog.

The picture collection at the Indiana State Library includes thousands of photographs, postcards, and clippings. All of the images have an Indiana connection, and a significant portion is dedicated to portraits of Hoosiers. Access to the picture collection is available through the picture collection card file index, where images can be located by searching

Harvey and Sarah (Waymire) Reser at the time of their marriage, 1857 (*John Rudolph Waymire and the First Three Generations of His Descendants as Known March 1, 1925* [Lafayette, IN: n.p., 1925], 3)

an individual's name, a particular location, or other Library of Congress subject headings. This picture index not only lists images in the manuscript picture collection but also lists images located in historical books and periodicals within the Indiana Division's collections.

A short time ago I processed the William M. Reser Collection (L466), the bulk of which documents Reser's genealogical work and Reser's quest for his roots. William Marven Reser was born in Sheffield Township, Tippecanoe County, Indiana, on June 19, 1863, to Harvey and Sarah (Waymire) Reser. William Reser attended Wabash College and later went to Jefferson Medical College in Pennsylvania, receiving his MD in 1903. He married Mary E. Erisman on November 6, 1907. Dr. Reser practiced medicine in Lafayette for many years, donating his services to the Tippecanoe County orphans' home. He was one of the county's leading historians and a member of the Tippecanoe County Historical Society, serving at different times as its president and vice president. Reser wrote a historical book, *Grist Mills of Tippecanoe County, Indiana* (1945); articles and pamphlets regarding local and state history for the local

newspapers; and "Indiana's Second State Fair" for the *Indiana Magazine of History* (1936). He often gave lectures on local, regional, and state historical topics such as "Wabash and Erie Canal and Its Local Importance." Reser also wrote about his own family history, publishing the pamphlet *John Rudolph Waymire and the First Three Generations of His Descendants as Known March 1, 1925* (1925), and an article "The Jonas Hoover Family" in the *Indiana Magazine of History* (1937).

The Reser Collection consists of papers from 1881–1940, though the bulk of the material covers 1920–1935. The materials within this collection include correspondence, family histories, clippings, DAR ephemerae, sketches of individuals, family tree charts, speeches, and papers related to the Tippecanoe County Historical Society. With the information Reser gleaned from relatives and the documents and information he received from different agencies, he compiled many lengthy family tree charts. Some of the charts he drew up were for Andrew Hoover, Daniel Hoover, David Hoover, Elizabeth Waymire Hoover, and Frederick Waymire.

The majority of this collection deals with Reser's quest to track down and compile as much of his family's history as possible, so much of the correspondence within it is with family members. Some typical exchanges between Reser and his relatives are presented here:

Dr. Reser to Mrs. Maxine Satchel Biggs on September 20, 1936: "Dear Kindred: If you are interested in genealogy—Waymire genealogy—you are the very one I am looking for. I will gladly send one of the old books if you will be kind enough to render some assistance which I badly stand in need of. Among John Rudolph Waymire's 2d set of children was a son Jacob, b. 3/17 or 7/1781, d. 10.7/1857. . . ." What follows is a list of names with blanks for which he is requesting dates of birth, marriage, and death. Mrs. Biggs replied on October 29, 1936, *"Dear Dr. Reser . . . This is such a complicated affair, and so much work, I can appreciate the fact that you get mixed up on the lines and families. . . . Now, don't forget. I'd like ALL the data you have concerning the family (or as much as you see fit to give me) in addition to the printed record. . . . When I start on this, I always get tangled up, and never know when to stop. I'll look forward to hearing from you in the near future, and I thank you again."* Within the letter she also tried as best she could to fill in the blanks for the relatives whom Reser was researching.

It is interesting to see that family research has not changed too much with the digital age. Letters may be sent via e-mail now, but relatives are still trying to contact each other to fill in the blanks on their family charts or to find the next branch to explore. The William M. Reser Collection is not only a record of

genealogical material but also an example of how family research was accomplished in the early twentieth century. By exploring this collection as well as other genealogical resources at the Indiana State Library, researchers can hopefully make new connections while filling in their families' "blanks."

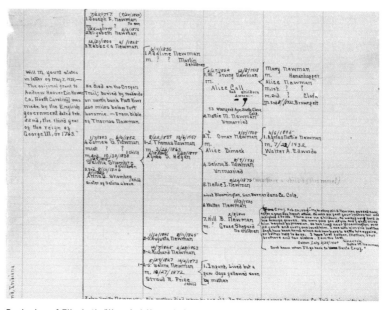

Beginning of Elizabeth (Waymire) Hoover's family tree chart (Reser Collection, L466, Manuscript Section, Indiana State Library)

All the pamphlets, articles, books, and the collection mentioned above are available for perusal at the Indiana State Library. For further information visit the library's Web site at www.statelib.lib.in.us/index.html or call 317-232-3670.

———————————— • ————————————

Selected Bibliography: "Dr. W. M. Reser Dies: Practitioner, County Historian," *Lafayette Journal and Courier,* March 19, 1943; Thompson, Donald E., comp. *Indiana Authors and Their Books, 1917–1966.* Crawfordsville, IN: Lakeside Press, 1974.

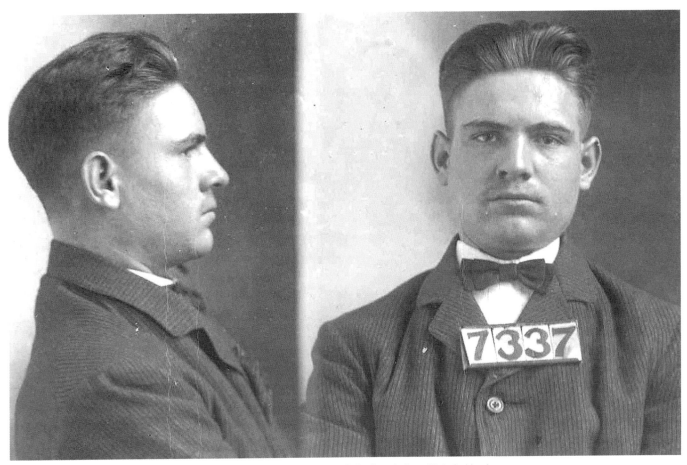

A prisoner at the Indiana State Prison in 1917 (Indiana Department of Correction Collections, Indiana State Archives)

Indiana State Archives

ALAN JANUARY

The Indiana State Archives is the permanent repository for important records of Indiana state and local governments. Its holdings, which include federal, state, and local records and photographs dating from the U.S. territorial period to the present, fill more than 40,000 cubic feet of shelving. The State Archives has important collections of federal records relating to Indiana. Notable among these are the records for the General Land Office, including tract books and the original plats and field notes made by federal land surveyors. The State Archives has the 1820–1880 federal censuses of manufacturers; the 1850–1880 censuses of agriculture; the censuses of social statistics for 1850–1870; and the 1880 census of defective, dependent, and delinquent classes. National Archives' microfilm holdings include the correspondence of four agencies involved in the formative period of Indiana history: the General Land Office, the Surveyor General, the War Department, and the Superintendent of Indian Affairs.

The state government's major collections begin with the records of the executive, legislative, and judicial branches of government from 1784 to the present. These include papers of every governor, bills and reports of the General Assembly, and case files and order books for the territorial General Court and the state Supreme and Appellate Courts.

The State Archives has substantial collections of records from more than five hundred past and present state agencies. Among these are incorporation papers and election returns from the secretary of state's office; muster rolls for state militia and National Guard units from the adjutant general; annual reports filed by railroads and other public utilities; individual patient and inmate records from state institutions dating back to 1822; and important records for the history of health and welfare, education, crime, archaeology, and the environment in Indiana.

Many types of local government records are housed in the State Archives, including naturalization records from circuit courts in more than sixty Indiana counties, physician license books, and enumerations of eligible voters. County records microfilmed by the Works Progress Administration (WPA) and the Genealogical Society of Utah are available for selected counties. Records for Marion County are especially strong.

More than 120,000 aerial photographs are in the State Archives, including some of the earliest ever taken in Indiana. Other significant photographic collections include the Indiana State Fair, the Department of Natural Resources, the Department of Correction, and the Indianapolis Board of Public Safety.

Frequently Accessed Records

Any time an individual's life intersects with federal, state, or local government, there is potential information of value to family history researchers. The possibilities are limitless, for example: a list of jurors in a court order book, quarterly censuses from county asylums, petitions to state or local officials, names of shareholders on incorporation papers, and indexes to inheritance tax schedules. The following list of frequently accessed records is intended only as a starting point for family history research at the Indiana State Archives.

Land Records

The State Archives has the tract books and receipt registers documenting all public land sales at the six Indiana land offices, as well as Indiana sales at the Cincinnati Land Office. A searchable database is available on the State Archives' Web site for sales at the Fort Wayne Land Office, 1823–1852; and the La Porte–Winamac Land Office, 1833–1855. A variety of finding aids is available in-house to sales at the land offices at Jeffersonville, 1808–1855; Crawfordsville, 1820–1853; and Indianapolis, 1820–1876.

Researchers can use these records to find the date a relative actually bought land from the government, which generally antedated by a year or more the date the land was patented in Washington. Many ledgers in the Archives also contain a "residence" column recording where the settler came from or lived at the time of purchase.

Many tracts of public land in Indiana were given to the state to sell for various purposes. The State Archives has certificates of purchase and patents for seven types of land sold by the state: the Wabash and Erie Canal, Michigan Road, Swamp, University, Saline, Seminary, and the Donation Tract (Indianapolis). Additional information on land sales, much of it indexed by the WPA, is available in the journals, letters, and working papers kept by Indiana land officers.

Military Records

The Indiana State Archives' military holdings include records for Indiana veterans of the Battle of Tippecanoe, the War of 1812, the Black Hawk War, the Mexican War, the Civil War, the Spanish–American War, World Wars I and II, the Korean War, and the Vietnam War. Separation papers (DD 214s) from 1941 to the present are confidential. Volunteers at the State Archives are creating a database for the 200,000 soldiers in Indiana Civil War volunteer regiments and batteries. More volunteers are needed so that this database can be brought online.

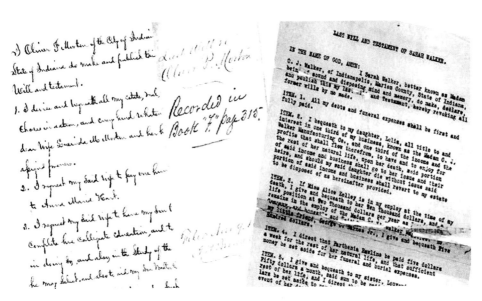

Wills of Gov. Oliver P. Morton and Madam C. J. Walker (Marion County Wills Collection, Indiana State Archives)

Records from the Children's Home Society (Board of State Charities Collection, Indiana State Archives)

The State Archives maintains an index to officers commissioned in the state militia from 1812 to 1861. Muster rolls or service records are available for the Indiana Legion and the Indiana National Guard from 1861 to 1940. Enlistment papers are available for many national guardsmen for the period 1898–1918, including participants in the Mexican Border expedition.

Collections of special interest for the Civil War era include the 1862 Enrollment of Militia and Volunteers, and the 1886, 1890, and 1894 Enrollments of Veterans, Widows, and Orphans. The State Archives also holds the records of the Indiana Department of the Grand Army of the Republic (GAR), including post files and descriptive books. Burial places for veterans in fifty-one Indiana counties who were buried before 1940 can be located in the WPA Veterans' Grave Registration.

Besides the muster rolls for Spanish–American War volunteer regiments and batteries, the State Archives has the files of the Indiana Department of the United Spanish War Veterans. These files include a membership card file, pension applications, death notices, and general correspondence.

Additional World War I resources include draft registration files, the 1913–1922 veteran enrollments, and individual records and photographs of Hoosiers who were decorated for meritorious service or who lost their lives in the war. An alphabetical card index and death notifications are available for Indiana casualties of World War II and the Korean War.

Correctional Records

Indiana's first prison opened at Jeffersonville in 1822. Over the next century the state created additional correctional facilities. The Indiana State Archives has developed searchable databases for inmates confined at specific facilities during the following time periods: the Prison South at Jeffersonville, 1822–1897; the Prison North at Michigan City, 1860–1897; the Indiana Boys' School at Plainfield, 1868–1931; the Indiana Girls' School at Indianapolis, 1873–1945; and the State Prison at Michigan City, 1897–1968. Card indexes are available for inmates confined to two other facilities: the Indiana Women's Prison, 1873–1960; and the Indiana Reformatory, 1897–1950.

Information on most of the inmates in these facilities can be found in a variety of resources at the State Archives, such as descriptive books, commitment papers, and inmate packets. Two collections of special interest for the State Prison at Michigan City are the Life Prisoner Books and a run of prisoner mug shots from 1880 to 1927.

Locating information on persons housed in Indiana correctional facilities between 1889 and 1989 has been simplified in recent years by the transfer from the Indiana Department of Correction to the State Archives of two master card files for inmates confined not only in the institutions discussed above but also in other facilities such as the State Farm. The cards give not only the institutional name and number of the inmate but some personal information as well.

Researchers who discover a prisoner who was pardoned will want to explore the extensive collection of pardon files in the secretary of state's papers. These files typically contain pardon applications, petitions, and newspaper articles concerning the prisoner's case. There are two sets of pardon files. The first covers the period from the 1820s up to 1852. The larger collection begins in the 1850s and continues into the early twentieth century. Additional pardon files can sometimes be found in the governors' official correspondence.

State Hospitals, Schools, and Homes

Indiana's first mental health hospital opened at Indianapolis in 1848. Additional hospitals followed at Logansport (1888), Evansville and Richmond (1890), and Madison (1910). Special facilities were created for persons with a range of disabilities, such as epilepsy, mental retardation, and polio.

In recent years a number of these state institutions have closed. The Indiana State Archives now has all the surviving records for Central State Hospital (the Indiana Hospital for the Insane) at Indianapolis, 1848–1994; the New Castle State Developmental Center (Village for Epileptics), 1907–1998; the Northern Indiana State Developmental Center (Northern Indiana Children's Hospital) at South Bend, 1943–1999; and the Dr. Norman Beatty Memorial Hospital at Westville, 1945–1979. The State Archives has admission registers for all these facilities. Databases have been created for the surviving medical records. Because of privacy concerns, access to information about patients is restricted in accordance with state and federal statutes.

The State Archives preserves many of the older records from state hospitals still in operation at Evansville, Fort Wayne, Indianapolis (Larue Carter), Logansport, Madison, Muscatatuck, and Richmond. Inquiries concerning patient records from these facilities should be made initially to the appropriate institution.

A special resource available to Archives staff is the Index to Patients Discharged from State Hospitals, 1900–1983. This alphabetical card index, created by the Board of State Charities, contains the only surviving information on patients housed at the Southern Indiana Hospital for the Insane at Evansville before 1943, when a fire destroyed the facility.

The State Archives has extensive records for three state schools: the School for the Blind (opened 1844), the School for the Deaf (opened 1847), and the Indiana Soldiers' and Sailors' Children's Home at Knightstown (opened 1867). The State Archives has created searchable databases for children at the Deaf School and the Children's Home. There are applications for admission and other records for these two facilities as well. Volunteers are needed to create a database of pupils at the Blind School. The State Archives stores inactive student files, some of which are still confidential, for the Blind and Deaf Schools.

The Indiana Veterans' Home (State Soldiers' Home) opened at Lafayette in 1896 for Civil War veterans and their dependents. The Home's mission later expanded to serve Hoosier veterans of other wars. Volunteers at the State Archives have created a database for residents at the Home and organized more than twelve thousand resident packets.

The Board of State Charities

The Board of State Charities, established in 1889, was originally given general authority to supervise all state public welfare and penal institutions. The scope of its supervision was later expanded to include county agencies, orphanages, maternity homes and hospitals, day nurseries, and boarding homes for children. An act of 1936 created the Department of Public Welfare in its place.

The Indiana State Archives holds extensive records from the Board of State Charities of value to family history researchers. The quarterly reports from County Poor Asylums, 1890–1942, give information on admissions, discharges, and deaths of residents. The monthly reports of County Orphans' Asylums (ca. 1895–1930) often include the orphans' dates of birth, the names of their parents, and information on their placements or transfers. The reports from state institutions, 1897–1933, include personal information on inmates and patients. For certain institutions, such as the Indiana State Farm at Putnamville and the State Tuberculosis Sanatorium at Rockville, this personal information is not available anywhere else.

The records of the Children's Home Society include files from more than ten thousand orphaned, dependent, or abandoned children placed in foster homes between 1890 and 1920. Volunteers have recently organized these files and created a database searchable by name.

A volunteer at the State Archives has also organized the inspection reports of orphanages, maternity homes, day nurseries, and boarding homes filed by agents of the Board of State Charities. A database for these facilities has been created that is searchable by the name of the institution and by the town in which it was located. The files typically contain applications for licensure, inspection reports, newspaper articles, and correspondence. Occasionally there are lists of children housed in the facilities.

Naturalization Records

Indiana local courts began naturalizing aliens even before statehood. The earliest declarations of intention were on loose sheets of paper. By 1860 most county courts had adopted blank form books for declarations of intention and final oaths. The 1906 Naturalization Act passed by Congress mandated the use of standardized forms and procedures by all naturalizing courts. After 1929 most local courts gradually stopped naturalizing, although courts in some Indiana counties continued to naturalize into the 1950s.

The Indiana State Archives has naturalization records from local courts in more than sixty Indiana counties. In 1997 volunteers from the State Archives began indexing these records. To date records from more than thirty counties have been indexed. A searchable database to many of these documents is available online. Volunteers are still needed to work on this project.

The State Archives also has naturalization records from the Indiana Supreme Court, which are presently being indexed. In addition, researchers should consult the WPA Index to Naturalization Records in Marion County Court Order Books, 1822–1929, which includes not only Marion County local courts but the federal court in Indianapolis as well.

Hours and Services

The Indiana State Archives is currently located at 6440 East 30th Street, Indianapolis, Indiana 46219, between Shadeland and Arlington avenues. Use the Shadeland Avenue exit from I-465 and travel north to 30th Street. From downtown Indianapolis, take I-70 east to the Emerson Avenue exit and go north to 30th Street. Free parking is available in front of the building.

The State Archives is open Monday through Friday, 8:00 a.m. to 4:30 p.m., holidays excepted. Staff members are always available to assist patrons. There are viewing rooms for patrons consulting records on microfilm. Original records may be examined

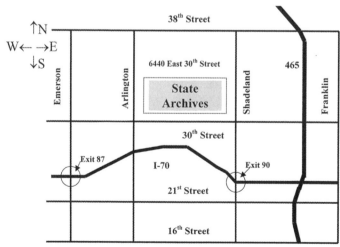

Directions to the Indiana State Archives (Map by Vicki Casteel)

in the Archives' Reading Room under staff supervision. Copying services are available for paper records, micro formats, and photographs, in accordance with the fee schedule approved by the Oversight Committee on Public Records.

The State Archives' staff answers questions by telephone, fax, e-mail, and postal mail. There is a fee for out-of-state residents who request research. The Archives' telephone number is 317-591-5222. The fax number is 317-591-5324. E-mail the Archives at arc@icpr.in.gov.

For more information about the State Archives, please visit its home page at www.in.gov/icpr/archives and the home page of the Friends of the Indiana State Archives at www.fisa-in.org. The Indiana State Archives relies heavily on volunteers to assist in organizing and indexing its collections to make them accessible to the public. For more about volunteer opportunities, please contact volunteers@fisa-in.org or call the Archives.

———————————————•———————————————

[*The author gratefully acknowledges the assistance of Vicki Casteel from the Indiana State Archives staff, who created the illustrations, map, and captions for this chapter, and Casteel and volunteers Sharon Mills and Sandy Ricketts who read and commented on this chapter.*]

Indiana Historical Society Library

SUZANNE HAHN

● ──────────────────

For years the Indiana Historical Society (IHS) has been assisting family history researchers through genealogy programs, Midwestern Roots conferences, and publications, such as *The Hoosier Genealogist*. The Society's William Henry Smith Memorial Library can be of assistance to genealogical as well as historical researchers. Its vast collection of manuscripts, visual materials, and rare published volumes helps create a clearer understanding of the times in which our ancestors lived. The IHS has created more than 20,000 digital images so that researchers can see many of the items in its collection online. Maps, oral accounts, diaries, correspondence, club and organizational records, and personal business papers are among the many treasures that may help illuminate the past. With one of the largest collections of material on Indiana and the Old Northwest, the Smith library has an abundance of resources available to researchers, including:

- 7,350 manuscript collections
- 415 visual collections (1.6 million images)
- 74,000 books and pamphlets
- 1,200 maps
- 400 broadsides
- 3,200 artifacts
- 60+ paintings
- 14,000 pieces of sheet music

IHS Manuscript Collections

Manuscripts such as letters, diaries, journals, notebooks, scrapbooks, ledgers, business accounts, and many other personal items are original sources that cannot be found elsewhere. Primary resources include correspondence and personal accounts of persons living in specific counties—perhaps contemporaries, neighbors, or relatives of individuals being researched. The IHS library specializes in several subject areas, including the following:

African American History
Agriculture
American Civil War
Architecture
Business
Education
Ethnic History
Genealogy
Government
Journalism and Communications

Local History
Medicine
Military History
Notable Hoosiers
Old Northwest Territory
Organized Labor
Politics
Religion
Social Services and Social Organizations
Transportation
Women

Manuscript materials relating to the military history of the state and its citizens, especially the Civil War, are a particular strength of the collection, which includes numerous personal accounts and correspondence of soldiers who served in the war. The collection also includes regimental information such as payrolls, clothing accounts, and unpublished histories. Many veterans of the Civil War were part of the Grand Army of the Republic (GAR). The IHS library has several local membership records from this veterans' organization that can help genealogists track ancestors beyond their military service. In addition to the Civil War, the IHS library also has a growing World War II collection, including written accounts and oral histories of WWII veterans and of those on the home front.

Family history researchers often inquire about records from orphanages and children's homes. Unfor-

tunately, these records can be difficult to find and often no longer exist. The IHS library holds records from a few children's homes in the state, including the Pleasant Run Children's Home and the Indianapolis Asylum for Friendless Colored Children. Church records are another wonderful resource for genealogists. The collection includes several church histories and registers throughout the state. It also includes the meeting records for the Society of Friends, which provide birth, marriage, and transfer information for its members. In addition, the IHS library has an assortment of local history primary sources, such as tax lists, school records, and early election returns for some Indiana counties.

IHS Visual Collections

The 1.6 million items in the visual collections come in a variety of formats, including photographs, postcards, drawings, and moving images. The collection includes scenes from around the state. The images not only capture a specific moment in time but also document how a street or neighborhood has changed over the years. Family history researchers might be able to find a postcard of the town in which their ancestors lived, a portrait of a family member, or a photograph of a Civil War soldier.

The IHS library has recently started a Digital Image Collection available from the IHS Web site, www.indianahistory.org.[1] Thousands of images from some of its most popular manuscript and visual collections have been scanned and are available through the Internet. Just a few of the items that are available to view are pages from the Indiana Woman's Suffrage Association Record Book from 1851 through 1886, Civil War letters from the David Enoch Beem Papers, Indianapolis scenes from the early twentieth century from the W. H. Bass Photo Company, and images from around the state from the Indiana Postcard Collection. The library also recently acquired three nationally significant Abraham Lincoln collections, treasures that can be viewed through its online Digital Image

Genealogy is one of the twenty-one subject areas collected by the IHS library. Images, such as this family portrait of the John Nolcox family, can provide insight not only about the family but also about the time in which the family members lived. (IHS)

At the IHS library researchers can view original diaries, family papers, and other correspondence such as this letter from Indiana Gov. Oliver P. Morton. Morton wrote this letter of introduction for Mrs. Susan Brown, who then met with President Abraham Lincoln to ask for the release of her brother, a Confederate soldier being held as a prisoner of war. Lincoln approved the request, and her brother was released. (McLaughlin-Jordan Family Papers, SC 1030, IHS)

Collection. Researchers can order prints or scans of all of the digital images for display purposes or to be used in a publication.

IHS Books and Pamphlets

One of the most popular and useful sources for genealogists are county histories. The Smith library houses original county histories for nearly every county in the state. For several counties, the library possesses later histories as well. Many of the county histories include a surname index that pinpoints the page where an ancestor is mentioned. County histories can provide a wealth of information, including biographical sketches, lists of county officers, and the history of the communities within the county.

The Smith library is developing its local history collections to include church and religious histories. It also owns unusual publications such as cata-

logs and advertisements of businesses throughout the state. These can provide great insight as to the occupation or livelihood of an ancestor. They can also help identify a family heirloom or antique.

Immigrant guides are another highly useful source for family history research. The early nineteenth-century guides were written to assist overland and waterway travel routes and to give advice on what to expect in Indiana and in the rest of the Old Northwest Territory. Other printed sources about migration show who migrated to Indiana at particular times, where they settled in the state, and what their lives were like.

In addition to its rare books, the Smith library has many other printed reference sources that are useful for genealogical and historical research. Below is a list of some titles that might be of interest to researchers:

CENSUS INDEXES:
- Indiana: 1807, 1820, 1830, 1840, and 1860
- Kentucky: 1810, 1820, and 1830
- Illinois: 1810 and 1820

SOURCE MATERIAL:
- City directories for several Indiana cities, including Evansville, Fort Wayne, Indianapolis, Kokomo, Lafayette, Marion, South Bend, and Terre Haute
- *Indiana Tax Lists*
- County historical society newsletters and quarterly publications

BIOGRAPHICAL SOURCES:
- Biographies of Indiana legislators, including those published in the *Biographical Directory of the Indiana General Assembly* and those found within the William English Papers (M 0098), which laid the groundwork for the biographical publication
- *Indiana Authors and Their Books*
- *Art and Artists of Indiana*

CIVIL WAR MATERIAL:
- Rosters and regimental histories in W. H. H. Terrell's *Report of the Adjutant General of the State of Indiana*

• Select published histories of many Indiana regiments

MEDICAL RESOURCES:
• Numerous nineteenth-century medical guides and directories helpful in studying the maladies afflicting early Indiana settlers and the methods for "curing" or treating them

REFERENCE WORKS:
• The *County Courthouse Book*, featuring addresses and contacts for county courthouses nationwide
• Newspaper bibliography guides for Indiana, Ohio, and Nebraska
• Dictionaries and reference books on slang and colloquial terminology, including regional English and Colonial American English
• A number of self-help books and guides for researchers, including *Bringing Your Family History to Life through Social History, First Steps in Genealogy, Genealogist's Handbook, Organizing Your Family History Search,* and *The Sleuth Book for Genealogists*

IHS PUBLICATIONS:
• A complete run of *The Hoosier Genealogist* (*THG*)
• The *Indiana Source Book* series, a compilation of source material from *THG* complete with every-name indexes
• *Finding Indiana Ancestors*
• *Pioneer Ancestors of Members of the Society of Indiana Pioneers*
• *Abstracts of the Records of the Society of Friends in Indiana*
• *Black History News and Notes*
• *An Index to Naturalization Records in Pre-1907 Order Books of Indiana County Courts*
• *Abstracts of Obituaries in the* Western Christian Advocate, *1834–1850*
• *Centennial Farms of Indiana*
• *Peopling Indiana: The Ethnic Experience*
• The *History of Indiana* series

IHS Map Collection

The IHS library has an impressive holding of maps showing the development of Indiana, first as part of

Maps, such as this 1830 map of Indiana engraved by William Woodruff, can help illustrate settlement patterns and trace the development of counties during early statehood. (Map Collection, DC 0014, IHS)

the Northwest Territory and then as a state. The maps are definitely worth a visit to the Society's library in order to gain a visual sense of where and how people came into Indiana and the uses they made of the state's land. The collection includes numerous county atlases, some of which are originals that are not available elsewhere. The library is fortunate to have a set of the Library of Congress microfiche of land ownership maps for Indiana that are no longer in widespread circulation. This set includes some rare county maps in Indiana, some dating from the 1850s. In addition to the Library of Congress land ownership maps, the library has several plat books for counties throughout the state. Another popular source is the statewide collection of Sanborn Insurance maps that depict the locations of businesses and homes and the physical attributes of buildings, many of which are long gone. In addition, the Society houses maps that show areas of Native American settlement, the National Road, migration routes, stagecoach routes, and boat routes for the Ohio and Wabash Rivers.

Online Databases

The IHS library also provides access to several online databases, such as HeritageQuest Online and the American Civil War Research Database. These databases are free to library users. HeritageQuest Online is one of the premier family history research databases. It assembles extant U.S. federal census records, local histories, tax lists, city directories, land and probate records, birth records, marriage records, death records, and more. HeritageQuest Online also offers the Periodical Source Index (PERSI), a comprehensive, subject-based index covering genealogy and local history periodicals written since 1800.

The American Civil War Research Database is one of the largest, most in-depth, searchable databases of Civil War soldiers and events. It contains information for more than 2.7 million Civil War soldiers, both Union and Confederate. The database also includes regimental rosters, regimental chron-

The Seng family gathers on the front porch of a home to commemorate a wedding anniversary. The image is one of the thousands of items available to view in the Digital Image Collection on the IHS Web site. (Martin's Photo Shop Collection, P 0129, IHS)

icles, soldier photographs, and battle synopses and statistics.

The Smith library also provides access to First-Search, a user-friendly way to search the OCLC, a national online catalog for librarians. FirstSearch gives users access to approximately 62 million items held in libraries throughout the world.

These are just some of the sources in the IHS collection that can be helpful to genealogical and historical researchers. Explore the riches of the IHS collections further by visiting the library, which is open to the public and free to use. Hours are Tuesday through Saturday from 10:00 a.m. to 5:00 p.m. No appointment is necessary. Library staff will be available to assist with your research and answer any questions regarding the collections. Visitors may bring in laptop computers and notes to assist with their research. Photocopies of items can be made depending on the condition of the material and on copyright restrictions. A research service is available for those who are unable to visit the library or who need any noninstructional research requiring substantial time. For more information contact the library or consult "IHS Collections and Library Reference Services, Copies, and Fees" on the IHS Web site. For the most comprehensive listing of the IHS library collections, consult the online catalog, also available from the Society's Web site.

The staff of the Indiana Historical Society's William Henry Smith Memorial Library appreciates your interest and looks forward to assisting you in your genealogical and historical research. If you have any questions about the Smith library, its resources, or its schedule, contact the library reference desk at 317-234-0321, or inquire via the e-mail reference form titled "Ask a Reference Question" at the IHS Web site, www.indianahistory.org.

---

1. For more specific information on the IHS Digital Collections, see Barb Dirks, "Searching the IHS Digital Collections," *The Hoosier Genealogist* 45 (Winter 2005): 4:271.

Historical Genealogy Department
Allen County (Indiana) Public Library

CURT B. WITCHER

⸻ ● ⸻

The Fred J. Reynolds Historical Genealogy Department of the Allen County Public Library was organized in 1961 by the library director for whom it is named. Far from building a national collection of genealogical materials, Reynolds started the department with the vision of providing excellent service and a research sanctuary for family historians during a time when they were not particularly welcome in public libraries. From its humble beginnings, the department's renowned collection has grown to more than 332,000 printed volumes and approximately 362,000 items of microtext. The collection grows daily through generous donations and through department purchases. The department serves approximately 100,000 genealogists each year.

The Genealogy Department seeks to serve anyone interested in family history research. Every hour the department is open, its knowledgeable staff is available to help the beginner get started, the student enjoy a school heritage project, the veteran researcher explore newly acquired records, and those temporarily stymied in their research to find and evaluate new data through a more enhanced understanding of historical research methodology. The department's staff is committed to acquiring appropriate records and

publications and to ensuring access to and understanding of the documents.

The department strives to maintain a comprehensive collection of genealogy and local history material for the North American continent. Materials collected include vital, census, military, passenger and immigration, church, court, obituary and cemetery records, histories, newspaper indexes, yearbooks, journals, daybooks, bibliographies, atlases and plat maps, research methodology guides, genealogies, name dictionaries, gazetteers, and heraldic works. Essentially any work that evidences people in a specific geographic location during a particular time period is a candidate for inclusion in the collection.

There are a limited number of exceptions to the department's comprehensive collection posture. The department, recognizing the role public and state libraries throughout the nation have in collecting and preserving newspapers, and in disseminating newspaper information and understanding the budgetary and space limitations of its parent institution, does not collect actual newspapers unless they are local or one of a select group of large city papers. Indexes, bibliographies, guides, and other finding aids to newspapers and newspaper collections are, however, collected as a part of the department's local history materials.

Other exceptions include family Bibles and personal genealogical software packages. The department's staff gathers the family history data often found in the pages of family Bibles for use by patrons, but the Bibles themselves are sent to the appropriate library, society, or archive for proper storage and preservation. And while the department accepts data on CD-ROM and DVD, personal genealogical software programs such as Family Tree Maker and Origins are not loaded onto the networked computers. Hence, most digital data is output to paper or, when permission by the compiler is granted, queued up for access from the department's Internet home page.

Researchers working in the largest of two Genealogy Center reading rooms at the Allen County Public Library. The largest reading room comfortably accommodates more than one hundred researchers and is located directly adjacent to the nearly six-thousand-volume family history collection. (Photo by Kay Gregg; courtesy of the Allen County Public Library)

A final general note about the department: While the scope of the collection is North America, the department has an extremely rich collection of historical and genealogical research materials from the British Isles as well as some substantial research tomes covering Germany and the old German empire. The online catalog at www.acpl.lib.in.us is the best way to determine specifically what book materials are available to the researchers.

Family Histories

One of the keystone collections of any major genealogical research facility is the collection of compiled family histories. More than 50,000 volumes of compiled genealogies are held in the department, representing work completed on American and European families and ranging from brief typescripts to well-documented multivolume works. Approximately 5,000 genealogies on microfiche and numerous family newsletters complement this collection. The department has also processed numerous manuscript collections into its holdings of family-specific data. Though often not indexed, these unique collections can contain valuable information one would be hard-pressed to find elsewhere.

The collection of family histories continues to grow not only through purchase but also as the result of gifts and the library's long-standing photocopy exchange program. Many individuals realize the benefit of positive exposure their compiled research receives at a national collection while others find the photocopy exchange program quite appealing. With the photocopy exchange program, an author permits the department to make a copy of an original work for its collections in exchange for receiving the original back with an additional complimentary copy. Both preservation and access needs are met with this program.

Censuses and Directories

One of the premier collections of the Genealogy Department is the extensive collection of census records and census-related materials. The department has the complete set of federal population census schedules for all states from 1790 through 1930. In addition to having all these important records on microfilm, the department also provides online access to the entire federal population census schedules and online indexes through Ancestry and Heritage-Quest Online. This access is available for in-house researchers. One can also find all published statewide indexes and soundexes to these federal records, all extant mortality schedules from 1850 to 1880, and all extant schedules of Union army veterans and widows for 1890.

To complement the collection of federal census records, the department also maintains one of the most complete sets of state census records. The state censuses available in the department include enumerations from California, Colorado, Florida, Illinois, Iowa, Kansas, Michigan, Minnesota, Mississippi, Missouri, Nebraska, New Jersey, New Mexico, New York, North Dakota, Oklahoma, Oregon, Rhode Island, Washington, and Wisconsin. State census records tend to mirror their closest federal counterpart in the type and quantity of data they provide. These documents can be invaluable when trying to document ancestors between federal census years, ancestors who moved frequently, and ancestors living in areas and during time periods for which federal census records do not exist. As an example, one can use the 1885 and 1895 state census schedules, where extant, to assist in filling the gap left by the missing 1890 federal census. And while many state census records are not indexed, most contain "extra bits" of information that will entice the researcher. The 1895 Iowa census, for example, not only lists religious affiliation but also the regiment and company in which the individual served if he was a Civil War veteran.

Another outstanding complement to the collection of federal census records is the department's extensive holdings of city directories. Some city directories can be used as substitute census indexes and for those occasions when the census indexes do not pick up the names being researched. The department serves as an R. L. Polk depository library of nearly 50,000 Polk directories dating from 1964 to the present, with significant earlier runs for some cities. The department also holds many directories for smaller cities and rural areas produced by other publishers. The directories in the collection from 1785 to 1935 tend to be in a microtext format while later years are available in book form.

In addition to the obvious information listed in directories relating to the individuals in a particular geographic area, the researcher should keep a keen eye peeled for the unique additional data provided by specialized directories. Some rural and prairie farmers' directories list not only where individuals lived but also where they came from if not native to the area, their political affiliation, the church where they worshipped, and the livestock or grain they raised. The department's large collection of North American local history materials also contains many published school enumerations, special censuses, tax lists, and other unique registers of individuals that are excellent complements to census schedules.

Passenger Lists and Immigration Records

To successfully conduct research on one's immigrant ancestor, it is necessary to understand that immigration is a three-step process: leaving, arriving, and settling down. Each of these steps has the potential to generate records of consequence relating to one's ancestors. Following one of the major tenets of sound historical research methodology, the "settling down" records of the immigrant family are the ones that should be explored at the start of the search as one researches from the most recent information back in time. And it is here that the department's 200,000-volume collection of local history materials becomes consequential for the researcher.

Important immigration information may be found in early deed records, church registers, school records, town and county histories, naturalization records, and other documents that evidence an immigrant family's first years in this country. These "settling down" records often provide invaluable data detailing when the immigrant family came to this country, which port of entry was used, and what Old-World city the family may have originally resided in, as well as the Old-World port from which the family emigrated.

In addition to many important methodology works on passenger and immigration records, such as John Newman's *American Naturalization Records, 1790–1990: What They Are and How to Use Them,* a majority of the National Archives passenger lists and indexes on microfilm are available in the department. Ship manifests and indexes are available in the department for the following major ports: Baltimore, Boston, Detroit, Galveston, New Orleans, New York, Philadelphia, and Atlantic and Gulf Coast ports (Alabama, Florida, Georgia, and South Carolina). Lists and/or indexes are available for sixty-eight minor ports as well. Major print indexes held by the department include such works as Filby's *Passenger and Immigration Lists Index*; *Famine Immigrants: Lists of Irish Immigrants arriving at . . . New York, 1846–1851, German Immigrants . . . from Bremen to New York, 1847–1867*; and *Germans to America*.

Military Records

The holdings of the Genealogy Department include most microfilmed National Archives service and pension record indexes covering every conflict and service period from the Revolutionary War through the Philippine Insurrection. To complement these indexes, a number of microfilmed copies of the actual records are extant in the department, from the Revolutionary War Pension and Bounty Land Warrant Applications to a number of actual Civil War service records and the complete set of World War I draft registration cards.

The department actively collects copies of military records and indexes to those records for all engagements on the North American continent. The types of military records collected include service, pension, claims, regimental/unit histories, letters and diaries, government documents, prisoner lists, and the compiled papers of patriotic and military heritage organizations.

Because the Civil War affected more lives per capita than any other war in this country's history, the department has a particularly robust collection of materials including regimental histories on microfiche and significant microfilmed Confederate records from state archives. The excellent collection of related printed references contains adjutant generals' reports, lineage society publications, soldiers' diaries, and more than several thousand unit, regimental, and divisional histories. The military collection is now expanding into data on twentieth-century conflicts with additions of the World War I draft reg-

istration cards for all states, unit histories for World War I and World War II, and casualty lists for the Korean War, Vietnam War, and Persian Gulf War.

North American Local History Records

The depth and variety of sources found among the local history records make this collection a hallmark of the department. Nearly 200,000 printed volumes make up the core of the department's local history publications. To complement this local history collection, all the standard genealogical reference works are available to the researcher, including *The American Genealogical-Biographical Index* and the *National Union Catalog of Manuscript Collections*.

Significant collections of microfilmed local records, such as the North Carolina Core Collection, are available for the following states: Connecticut, Illinois, Indiana, Kentucky, Massachusetts, New York, North Carolina, Ohio, Pennsylvania, South Carolina, Tennessee, Vermont, and West Virginia. Smaller microfilmed collections are available for most other states. Additional microtext sources that complement the outstanding print collection include the *Genealogy & Local History Series* on microfiche and microfilmed county histories for California, Illinois, Indiana, Michigan, New York, Ohio, Pennsylvania, and Wisconsin.

Several important manuscript collections and reprint series of regional or national scope are contained in the department's local history microtext holdings. These include Library of Congress land-ownership maps, the Draper Manuscript Collection, American Home Missionary Society papers and manuscripts, *Southern Women and Their Families in the 19th Century*, the *Boston Transcript*'s "Notes and Queries" columns, and colonial newspapers from Maryland, Pennsylvania, and Virginia.

The department's collection of local history records contains rich veins of ethnic materials documenting most of the immigrant groups that populated this continent. These substantial collections of materials include records from the British Isles and about those emigrants who settled in North America; extensive collections of research materials for those tracing African American ancestors, including such collections as *Records of Ante-Bellum Southern Plantations from the Revolution through the Civil War, Records of Southern Plantations from Emancipation to the Great Migration,* Freedmen's Bureau records, *Slavery in Ante-Bellum Southern Industries, Papers of the American Slave Trade,* and *State Slavery Statutes*; and a wealth of records evidencing the lives and experiences of the First Nations or Native American peoples.

The department houses a significant collection of Canadiana, especially for the eastern provinces. Print sources include county and town histories, cemetery records, and almost all available published French Canadian parish registers and marriage repertoires, as well as genealogical society publications including the index to the 1871 census of Ontario. Complementary microtext holdings for Canada include all published or microfilmed censuses from 1666 to 1891, passenger lists for Halifax and Quebec, *Quebec Non-Catholic Registers (1760–1941) and Index,* Ontario land and surrogate court records indexes, biographical scrapbooks for Toronto newspapers, 1911–1967, and the *Prince Edward Island Master Name Index.*

Periodicals

A treasure trove of historical and genealogical information is buried in the serials published by insti-

tutions and organizations in the field. Data found in periodicals can include source materials, Bible records, reviews of new publications, ancestor charts and family group sheets, lists of upcoming conferences and seminars, lists of projects and other special activities, holdings of area and regional libraries and archives, unique and forgotten sources of information, and local research tips. Often data found in the periodical literature of this field can be found in precious few other places.

The Genealogy Department holds one of the largest English-language genealogy and local history periodical collections in the world with more than 5,800 current subscriptions and more than 10,200 titles. Individual articles may be accessed through a variety of indexes including the *PERiodical Source Index* (PERSI), compiled by the department's staff in cooperation with HeritageQuest Online.

Pathfinders and Guides

The department has published a series of guides called Pathfinders to assist researchers in using the collection. There are currently fourteen covering the following genealogy topics: Eastern European, English and Welsh, French Canadian and Acadian, German, Irish, Scottish, Swiss, Dutch, newspaper research, census research, adoption and genealogy, sources for twentieth-century research, heraldry and genealogy, and church records. These guides are free and downloadable from the department's Web site (www. acpl.lib.in.us/genealogy/index. html). Two other guides to materials in the department that are available through the respective publishers are *Historical Sources of Fort Wayne, Indiana: An Annotated Bibliography for Doing Historical Research on the Summit City in the Allen County Public Library* and this author's *African American Genealogy: A Bibliography and Guide to Sources.*

The Genealogy Center's more than 362,000 microtext items are complemented with thousands of rolls of newspaper microfilm and biographical microfiche from around the country and world. Microtext remains an outstanding complement to online data. (Photo by Kay Gregg; courtesy of the Allen County Public Library)

Complementary Collections at the Allen County Public Library

The Genealogy Department's holdings are greatly enhanced by the library's other significant collections of biographical sources, government documents, legal references, Native American firsthand accounts, and early American travel and exploration accounts. A number of guides and finding aids are available for these special complementary collections. As examples, the information-rich complete U.S. Federal Government Documents Serial Set with accompanying indexes is available in the library's government document section, while the social sciences and humanities section houses biographical archives collections from K. G. Saur that provide information on many millions of individuals worldwide.

Successful Research in the Genealogy Department

Take full advantage of the library's online catalog when planning a visit. You can find it by going to the library's Web site, www.acpl.lib.in.us, and clicking on the "Search Catalog" link under "Library Catalog." All the Genealogy Department books are listed as well as other valuable information about the department. The microtext catalog is available in a browsable form on the Web at www.friendsofallencounty.org/search_microtext.php. The "Who We Are" link provides a good general description of the department's extensive holdings.

The department's staff handles general postal and e-mail queries, for example, hours of operation, location, holdings, and getting started doing genealogy, without cost. The department's Research Center handles copy requests, consultation, and more in-depth research. "Quick-Search" services are provided by the center for patrons who do not need extensive research but need specific pages from already identified materials. There is a basic fee for this service. Research services are provided for individuals interested in obtaining data from the vast resources of the department's collection but who cannot conduct onsite investigations. The research is performed by individuals experienced in conducting genealogical research surveys and in using the resources of the department. Up to one hour will be spent evaluating the question, exploring primary and secondary sources, obtaining copies of pertinent documents, and composing a research report. The fee for this service is $25, nonrefundable, and paid in advance. Downloadable forms for all Research Center services can be found on the department's Web site (www.acpl.lib.in.us/genealogy/index.html). There is never a fee, though, for using the department in person.

In 2007 the Allen County Public Library completed an extensive expansion and renovation in which the space of the Historical Genealogy Department was more than doubled. The new space accommodates more researchers, more technology, and more traditional print and microtext materials. With its new facility the library continues its commitment to provide the fullest array of services to the nation's genealogists and other historical researchers.

Historical Genealogy Department
Allen County Public Library
900 Library Plaza, PO Box 2270
Fort Wayne, IN 46801-2270
Phone: 260-421-1225
E-mail: genealogy@acpl.info

National Archives
Great Lakes Region, Chicago

MARTIN TUOHY

⚬

Christmas 1868 must have brought hardship and worry to Isaac and Elizabeth Harned of Jacksonburg, Wayne County, Indiana. Looking at the historical documents, one can imagine a scene such as the following: Isaac, a forty-one-year-old shopkeeper, sits at the kitchen table, reading some documents before him. Every so often, he writes two or three words—perhaps his name. Then he turns over the sheet of paper and reads the next one. The room is cold and dimly lit by a single lamp. The heating stove fails to warm the frosty quarters. Elizabeth, his wife, tries to appear occupied at the cook stove. She has sent their nine-year-old son Abner outside to play.[1]

A stranger sits at the small table with Isaac. He, too, has several documents in front of him—ledger sheets topped by some smaller sheets. The stranger writes the following on the first document:

To the Honorable David McDonald, Judge of the District Court of the United States, for the District of Indiana:

The Petition of Isaac F. Harned, of Jacksonburg, in the County of Wayne, and State of Indiana, and District aforesaid, respectfully Represents:

That he has resided for more than six months next immediately preceeding [sic] the filing of this petition, at Wayne County, within said Judicial District; that he owes debts exceeding the amount of three hundred dollars, and is unable to pay all of the same in full; that he is willing to surrender all his estate and effects for the benefit of his Creditors, and desires to obtain the benefits of the Act entitled "An Act to Establish a Uniform System of Bankruptcy throughout the United States," approved March 2, 1867:

That the Schedules hereto annexed, Marked A, and virified [sic] by your Petitioner's oath contains a full and true Statement of all his debts, and (so far as it is possible to ascertain) the names and places of residence of his creditors, and such further statements concerning said debts as are required by the provisions of said Act:

That the Schedules hereto annexed, Marked B, and verified by your Petitioner's oath, contains an accurate inventory of all his estate, both real and personal, assignable under the provisions of said Act:

Wherefore your Petitioner prays, that he may be adjudged by the Court to be a Bankrupt, within the provisions of said Act; and that he may be Decreed to have a Certificate of Discharge from all his Debts provable under the same. . . .

Isaac F. Harned, Petitioner
Subscribed and sworn to, before me, this 24th day of December, A. D. 1868.
E. A. Davis
U.S. Commissioner[2]

Isaac's long list of creditors began with $425 in grocery bills dating back to 1865 and 1866 from Howard and Grubbs, merchants in Richmond, Indiana, followed by $862 in debts to three Richmond and three Cincinnati mercantile houses for goods purchased for Isaac's store between 1864 and 1866. Money borrowed in 1864 and 1865 from two farmers, a "farmiss" (presumably a female farm owner), a widow, and a merchant in Middletown, Henry County, Indiana, as well as an unpaid doctor bill, provide hints of a brief residency there. Isaac also maintained business relations and lines of credit exceeding $2,000 with numerous merchants in Cincinnati in 1865, but surprisingly few in nearby Dayton in 1866. The storekeepers Hoover and Summers of Middletown in Henry County were also owed about $10 by Isaac, and Hoover and Summers were bankrupt, too.[3]

All of Isaac, Elizabeth, and Abner Harned's personal possessions had to be listed and appraised in order to be declared exempt from sale to pay off their debts. The inventory sketches a scene of their household—what historians and anthropologists would call "material culture": two beds and bedding, a cook stove and furniture, a heating stove, a wardrobe, wash stand, bureau, lounge, a dozen chairs, two tables, tableware, woodenware and tin and earthenware, two bowls and a pitcher, a cupboard holding the kitchen items, a lamp, two rocking chairs, clothes, a watch, and twenty-five books. In addition,

Isaac kept two axes, garden tools, a saw plane, chisel, and some other small tools. The family's worldly possessions amounted to $194.50.[4]

The Harned family's story of hardship in the last year of the Civil War and ensuing years conveys the experience of loss more than 135 years after the fact. Like thousands of other Hoosier households caught in the postwar economic recession to the point of declaring bankruptcy, the Harneds' story reveals the nationwide suffering and upheaval that affected ordinary people after the war ended. An estimated one out of every eighty-eight Hoosier households ended up losing their assets to federal bankruptcy sales administered by the U.S. District Courts in Indianapolis and Evansville between 1867 and 1878.[5]

There is a second loss suffered by Isaac and Elizabeth Harned that is implicit in this story. After suffering the indignities of having their possessions handled and appraised by strangers and their massive debts revealed in newspaper announcements of bankruptcy, the Harneds and the other 3,800 Hoosier families who succumbed to federal bankruptcy after the Civil War suffered a posthumous loss: the failure of their descendants to find and tell the stories of their financial tragedies. Genealogists have tradi-

The National Archives and Records Administration–Great Lakes Region, Chicago, holds countless stories about the past that are awaiting discovery by persistent researchers. (Photo courtesy of the NARA–GLR, Chicago)

tionally reconstructed the lives of their ancestors on the basis of records regarding births, marriages, censuses, wars, immigrations, and deaths. It is striking that, at least since the early 1990s, very few, if any, genealogists have visited the National Archives in Chicago to search the Bankruptcy Act of 1867 case records for any midwestern state, let alone Indiana.[6]

This collective failure of genealogists to research past lives in the context of their historical circumstances recalls English historian E. P. Thompson's assertion in his preface to *The Making of the English Working Class*: "I am seeking to rescue the poor stockinger, the Luddite cropper, the 'obsolete' hand-loom weaver, the 'utopian' artisan . . . from the enormous condescension of posterity. . . . They lived through these times of acute social disturbance, and we did not. Their aspirations were valid in terms of their own experience; and, if they were casualties of history, they remain, condemned in their own lives, as casualties."[7] Given the natural historical curiosity of genealogists and historians, many untold stories may be uncovered in National Archives documents that would reveal the roles of ordinary people during historical times—stories such as the suffering of Isaac and Elizabeth Harned in the economic upheaval that followed the Civil War.

Many tens of thousands of stories about ordinary Hoosiers lie recorded but forgotten in folded documents tied with ribbon in the National Archives in Chicago. These stories await rediscovery through the hands-on research labors of avocational historians interested in their ancestors and in their locales. The National Archives and Records Administration (NARA) is the government agency that preserves the historically valuable records of the U.S. government and makes those archival records available for public research use. The historical records of the headquarters offices of federal agencies, the U.S. Supreme Court, and the U.S. Congress are preserved in the National Archives Building in downtown Washington, DC, and in suburban College Park, Maryland. In many ways, the records in the National Archives repositories in the Washington metropolitan area reflect the discussion and formation of federal policy by agency, court, or congressional headquarters.

Federal bankruptcy petitions usually contained detailed inventories of a person's assets, including household furnishings. (Bankruptcy Case, 1865, "In the Matter of William W. Risher and John Risher," Bankruptcy Records, 1867–1878, Records of the U.S. District Court for the Southern District of Indiana at Indianapolis, RG 21, NARA–GLR, Chicago)

During the 1940s and 1950s, however, historical records of federal courts and agencies in cities across the United States remained in their respective regions of origin because of a system of federal record centers. In 1968 the National Archives established a system of regional archives in major cities throughout the continental United States. The NARA–GLR, Chicago, is one of those regional repositories for federal records from the Midwest that possesses enduring historical value.

More than 75,000 cubic feet of archival records—about 188 million pages of paper documents, linen maps, and photographs—are preserved in the National Archives in Chicago. The records, which date from 1800 at the earliest to the 1990s in certain instances, bear witness to the implementation of U.S. government policies and laws in local places throughout Illinois, Indiana, Michigan, Minnesota, Ohio, and Wisconsin. About 60 percent of the archival records in Chicago are federal court records dating from the time of statehood for each Great Lakes state, except for some territorial court records from Michigan and Wisconsin.

Archives are fundamentally different from libraries, so researchers often become confused by trying to impose their library search practices upon archives. Archives are comprised of the older, unpublished records of an organization or institution that retain value for their informational and evidentiary content. Government archivists keep the records of an organization according to their *provenance*—the originator; that is, the agency, bureau, court, legislative body, or other discrete organization that created or received the documents in the course of daily business and from whom the records came to the archives. The term for an organization's records maintained as a unit, apart from those of other organizations, is a *record group* (abbreviated RG). Archivists maintain the *original, intended order* of the records, since that organizational system itself provides some information about the reasons for creating such important documents. A discrete set of files, bound volumes, maps, or other format of records that has some unifying characteristic is called a *series* of records.[8]

All archival records in the National Archives of the United States are organized into record groups according to the U.S. government agency, bureau, court, legislative body, or other unit that created or received the records during regular business. One record group may have several *subgroups*—reflecting the separate bureaucratic divisions of a large agency or busy court. Each subgroup may also have numerous separate series of records, each with its own title, date span, physical characteristics (such as format and size), and informational content (such as written words, graphics, tables or schedules of words and numbers, or photographic images).

Knowing these archival terms and the organizational system for records in the National Archives is crucial for the success of any researcher. They also apply, with some minor modifications, to government records in the Indiana State Archives or in the various county government repositories, most notably the county courthouses. A researcher must relate his or her general research topic to possibly relevant record groups and series. Various published *archival guides* and unpublished *finding aids* are the tools a researcher uses to search the archives. Guides and finding aids describe the records in greater detail and provide the researcher with potential search strategies. However, National Archives guides and finding aids cannot catalogue each document and its content the way a library catalogues each book, magazine, and item, due to the massive volume of historical records. Three essential published descriptions of the records are the overarching *Guide to Federal Records in the National Archives of the United States*, 3rd. ed. (Washington, DC: National Archives and Records Administration, 1995), updated online at www.archives.gov/research/guide-fed-records/index. html; a subject-oriented book, *Guide to Genealogical Research in the National Archives of the United States*, 3rd ed. (Washington, DC: NARA, 2000); and the repository-specific "Guide to Archival Holdings at NARA's Great Lakes Region (Chicago)" updated online at www.archives.gov/great-lakes/ chicago/holdings/index.html.

Researchers should first read the archival guides to identify what records might be intriguing to search and to map out research paths, then discuss any questions or uncertainty about how to proceed with a staff archivist, either by telephone or in writing. (The author personally advocates a letter with full postal address as the most effective way to initiate a research visit, since a letter allows a more thoughtful response than the immediacy of a telephone call.) Published guides provide a solid foundation for informed decision making by a researcher.

Knowledgeable archivists, like reference librarians, are the best added value in any researcher's visit to a repository. Archivists link the guides and unpublished finding aids to the researcher, and the researcher to the records. They do not act as surrogates by conducting research on the behalf of a correspondent or caller, however. Archivists facilitate the interplay between researchers and the historical sources. They foster an intellectual exchange with the researcher that extends far beyond any published guidance and advance the researcher's breadth and depth of knowledge and experience.

When you have first examined the published guides and then corresponded with the archivists to confirm that potentially relevant records are indeed in the National Archives in Chicago, you are ready to arrange a visit. The National Archives is open Monday through Friday, and limited Saturday hours are available as well. Telephone in advance to ask about the Archives' schedule, to notify the staff of your visit, and to confirm that, if necessary, the archivist who has guided you will be available the day you are coming. The National Archives is located at 7358 South Pulaski Road on the far southeast side of Chicago—conveniently accessible to Hoosiers and little more than a three-hour drive from Indianapolis under

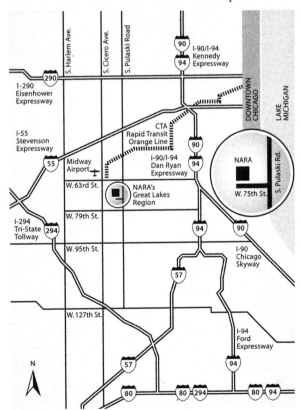

The National Archives in Chicago is conveniently located on the southeast side of the city near public transportation routes and major highways. (Courtesy of the NARA–GLR, Chicago)

ideal conditions. Hours, telephone numbers, a map, and other guidance can be found at www.archives. gov/great-lakes/chicago/. The driveway entrance for the National Archives building is one block west of Pulaski Road on 75th Street. Amtrak riders can also reach the National Archives from downtown using the Chicago Transit Authority's Orange Line rapid transit train and a southbound bus. Currently, Number 53A, the Pulaski Road bus, stops at Richard J. Daley City College at 75th Street and Pulaski Road, one block east of the National Archives.

Affordable and safe hotel accommodations are located along Cicero Avenue near Midway Airport, about one and one-half miles northwest of the archives. The Orange Line train originates at Midway Airport and ends twenty-five minutes later in downtown Chicago's famous elevated Loop, making the National Archives building an ideal and affordable base of operations for additional research work at the Newberry Library, the Chicago Public Library, the Circuit Court of Cook County Archives, the Chicago Historical Society, and the Center for Research Libraries in Hyde Park, all of which are accessible by rapid transit or commuter trains.

This chapter has attempted to dispel some common myths about the logistical aspects of visiting the National Archives in Chicago, establishing instead the relative convenience, safety, and affordability of a research trip from anywhere in Indiana. Federal records in the National Archives–Great Lakes Region reveal rich stories about ordinary Hoosiers who lived from 1819 through the 1950s. Significant archival sources for family history research exist from the territorial and early statehood years of the 1810s through the Civil War and Reconstruction eras. Relatively unknown sources from 1879 through the First World War and the 1920s reveal the stories of industrial workers, immigration and citizenship, military and naval service, and Prohibition. Surprisingly unused records from the Great Depression, the Second World War, and the Korean War include bankruptcies of ordinary Hoosiers, pilot training at Bunker Hill Naval Air Reserve Base, and the ordnance plants of the 1940s. Great stories about your own ancestors' active roles in historical events remain for you to uncover in the

National Archives and Records Administration–Great Lakes Region, Chicago.

———————————— • ————————————

1. Entries for Isaac, Elizabeth, and Abner Harned, p. 103, New Lisbon Post Office, Dudley Township, Henry County, Indiana, Eighth Population Census of the United States, 1860 (National Archives Microfilm Publication M653, roll 266). The description of the room's furnishings is derived from a List of Exempt Property, Schedule B, Bankruptcy Case File 933, "In the Matter of the Petition of Isaac F. Harned," filed 11:30 a.m., December 25, 1868; Bankruptcy Case Files, Act of 1867, 1867–1878; Records of the U.S. District Court, Southern District of Indiana, Indianapolis Division; RG 21, National Archives and Records Administration—Great Lakes Region, Chicago (NARA–GLR, Chicago).

2. Petition by Debtor, Bankruptcy Case File 933.

3. Schedule A, Bankruptcy Case File 933.

4. Schedule B, Bankruptcy Case File 933.

5. The ratio of one bankruptcy for every eighty-eight households is based upon 3,391 cases filed in the U.S. District Court at Indianapolis between 1867 and 1878, another 427 cases filed at the newly created U.S. District Court at Evansville during those same years, a population of 1,680,637 in Indiana in 1870, and a conservative estimate of five persons per household. A small number of the bankruptcy cases involved manufacturing corporations such as breweries, cotton mills, and iron rolling mills. The ratio of 2.2 bankruptcies per 1,000 Indiana residents exceeds an estimate of 2.0 per 1,000 for the entire Midwest. See Beverly Watkins, "'To Surrender All His Estate': The 1867 Bankruptcy Act," *Prologue: Quarterly of the National Archives* 21, no. 3 (Fall 1989): 207–13, especially Table 1 on p. 213; Emma Lou Thornbrough, *Indiana in the Civil War Era, 1850–1880* (Indianapolis: Indiana Historical Bureau and Indiana Historical Society, 1965), 537.

6. This statement is based upon my personal observations working closely with researchers at the NARA-GLR, Chicago since 1992 as well as my familiarity with the reference service slips that document each researcher's use of a particular series or item of archival records.

7. E. P. Thompson, *The Making of the English Working Class* (New York: Vintage Books, 1966), 12–13.

8. Maygene F. Daniels, "Appendix: Introduction to Archival Terminology," in Maygene F. Daniels and Timothy Walch, eds., *A Modern Archives Reader* (Washington, DC: National Archives and Records Service, 1984), 336–42; *Guide to Genealogical Research in the National Archives of the United States*, 3rd ed. (Washington, DC: NARA, 2000), 3–4.

Family History Library System Genealogical Society of Utah

COMPILED BY AMANDA C. JONES

In 1894 in Salt Lake City, Utah, a group of leaders from The Church of Jesus Christ of Latter-day Saints established the Genealogical Society of Utah (GSU). The society's aim was to assist members of the Church in their genealogical searches. To house the growing collection of genealogical material and family history records, the Society began a library in the same year. The undertaking of the GSU resulted in the Family History Library, one of the largest resources for genealogy and family history research in the United States and in the world.[1]

The library, complete with five floors and 142,000 square feet of temperature-controlled space, is home to more than two million rolls of microfilm, 742,000 microfiche, 300,000 books and serials, and 4,500 periodicals recording the lives of individuals from the United States, Canada, Europe, Asia, Africa, and Latin America. The original copies of the documents, microfilms, and records are stored in the Granite Mountain Vault to preserve the collections. The collection continues to grow as genealogists, professional and amateur, contribute their findings. The GSU has microfilmers working in more than forty countries around the globe, gathering useful information. Open to the general public and free of charge, the

library provides a well-trained staff to assist and guide researchers of all experience levels. Library orientation and software classes are also available for patrons to further their skills and ability to access information contained in the library's collections.

The FamilySearch Center, also in Salt Lake City, is an added extension to the main library and is mostly geared toward beginning genealogists. The center allows computer access for the researcher, who can type in a family name and any known dates and receive a list of the records available on the name. Searches made at the center can bring results from the FamilySearch Web site, a collection of eight million paper records of surnames, 70,000 biographies or family histories, the Family History Library Catalog, and the 1920 U.S. census. The FamilySearch Center is also free and open to all, offering, for a small fee, the purchase of photocopies, disks, and computer printouts. Staff and volunteers are on hand to assist with any research or computing questions.

A trip to the Family History Library in Salt Lake City is often not the most convenient way to conduct research for a person living in Indiana. One way from Indianapolis to Salt Lake City is approximately 1,540 miles with a driving time of approximately

The Family History Library in Salt Lake City, Utah (Used by permission, © 1999, 2005, Intellectual Reserve, Inc.)

(Above) Sign for an Indianapolis Family History Center (Photo by Amanda C. Jones)

(Left) View of microfilm reader and resources at an Indianapolis Family History Center (Photo by Amanda C. Jones)

twenty-four hours. One could also spend hundreds of dollars on a coach airline ticket for an entire day of traveling with layovers and connecting flights. With adequate time, a trip to the Family History Library and all of Salt Lake City would be a worthwhile endeavor, but for the weekend genealogist this would be a challenge.

Luckily, the information contained in the Family History Library can be easily obtained at Family History Centers and on the Internet by researchers in any location. Family History Centers are further extensions of the main library and are located in a variety of towns and cities across the world. With more than twenty-five locations in Indiana, the centers give Hoosier researchers great access and convenience to the resources of the Family History Library. Free to anyone wishing to conduct research, many centers are housed in The Church of Jesus Christ of

Latter-day Saints' meetinghouses. To find the closest Family History Center, go to the Family History Library Web site, www.familysearch.org, and click on the "Find the Family History Center" link to search by country, state, county, and city; or to find one by phone, call 866-406-1830. Indiana's Family History Centers are located in all corners of the state. A complete list is provided below:

- Anderson
  200 West 46th Street
  765-644-6417
- Batesville
  Township Line Road
  812-934-3443
- Bedford
  1010 22nd Street
  812-275-6672

- Bloomington
  4235 West 3rd Street
  812-332-0560
- Brownsburg
  10518 East 600 North
  317-852-5688
- Columbus
  3330 30th Street
  812-372-3679
- Crawfordsville
  125 West Road
  765-362-8006
- Decatur
  88 Cardinal Pass
  260-728-9030
- Evansville
  8020 East Covert Avenue
  812-471-0191
- Fishers
  777 Sunblest Boulevard
  317-577-2911
- Fort Wayne
  5401 St. Joe Road
  260-485-9581
- Huntington
  1190 500 North State Road 9
  260-356-7171
- Indianapolis
  900 East Stop 11 Road
  317-888-6002
- Indianapolis
  110 North White River Parkway
  317-917-3210
- Kokomo
  332 West 300 South
  765-453-0092
- Lafayette
  3224 Jasper Street
  (West Lafayette)
  765-463-5079
- Linton
  1000 West (Lone Tree Road)
  812-847-9044
- Marion
  1465 East Bradford Street
  765-662-3311

- Martinsville
  100 Church Street
  765-342-4273
- Muncie
  4800 West Robinwood Lane
  765-288-9139
- New Albany
  1534 Slate Run Road
  812-949-7532
- Peru
  US 31 South
  765-473-4933
- Richmond
  3333 Backmeyer Road
  765-966-2366
- South Bend
  930 Park Place
  (Mishawaka)
  574-243-1633
- Terre Haute
  1845 North Center
  812-234-0269
- Valparaiso
  503 Burlington Beach Road
  219-464-7641
- Vincennes
  1940 North Old Highway 41
  812-882-4022
- Warsaw
  1101 North Circle 175 E
  219-269-2118

The centers have individual operating schedules; and though many show their hours of operation on the library's Web site, you should call ahead to confirm the times or to set up an appointment. Centers will not answer mail inquiries, as staff is limited; therefore, addresses listed are merely for directional purposes. Continue to check the library's Web site for the most up-to-date listings on centers' locations, hours, special arrangements, and holiday closings.

The centers contain a basic collection of the Family History Library's records, including the Family History Library Catalog, the Ancestral File, and the International Genealogical Index (IGI). The Family History Library Catalog search will give a listing of the documents contained in the library. The Ancestral File is a database linking approximately 35.6 million names to families. To search the Ancestral File you need the complete name of a deceased relative. Narrow the search by including an event, such as a marriage, birth or death, year or year range, and/or state or country. The search will also bring up common variations to a surname's spelling, or an exact spelling can be used to narrow the results.

The IGI, which also began with The Church of Jesus Christ of Latter-day Saints, compiled around 250 million names from church members, records, and other donated or collected materials. Year ranges for the IGI are from the early 1500s to the early 1900s. Often included with the results, under "Messages," will be the provenance of the information, relating when the names were added to the list and by what means. Source information given provides the source call number that leads to the actual record of the ancestor, such as a birth, marriage, or death record. With the source call number most records' microfilm can be ordered at the center. The IGI may also refer to the Ancestral File for the submitter. Both the Ancestral File and the IGI can, potentially, pull up the ancestor; his or her birth, marriage, and death dates; as well as parents and children and locales for each. The information may not be complete, but it is useful to initiate searches and guide the next step in family history research. Hence, the resources at the Family History Centers can extrapolate concrete facts on your ancestors from a variety of search engines utilizing the Family History Library materials.

Other benefits of the Family History Centers include the wealth of regional information available, as many centers collect information geared to their areas. Items about the regions do not circulate and are found only at the individual centers. The centers' staffs are volunteer-based, and they will assist in research and can often recommend other points of research in the community. Family History Centers can also circulate most microforms, though not books and periodicals, from the Family History Library, for a small fee to the researcher. Nearly 100,000 rolls of microfilm are circulated monthly between the library and the 3,700 Family History Centers around the world.

The Family History Center south of downtown Indianapolis offers a variety of different resources, especially for state and local genealogists. In addition to the resources listed above typical to a Family History Center, it includes Indiana census records for 1850, 1880, 1900, and 1920. It also has the 1850 census for Kentucky and some 1860, 1870, and 1910 census files for Indiana, Ohio, and Kentucky. This center can also order census film for every state. Included in its Indiana-related materials are Indiana resource books, which list specific Indiana records, and PERSI, the subject index to genealogical and historical periodicals, from the Allen County [Indiana] Public Library. While focusing prominently on Indiana resources, the center also concentrates on Kentucky, as many Indiana ancestors moved from the Bluegrass State to settle in Indiana. Other resources unique to this Family History Center include an A-to-Z Comprehensive Card File that carefully lists most of the holdings in the center under region or surname; the Accelerated Index System, an index of census and tax lists from 1609 to 1860 listed by head of household; and Korean and Vietnam casualty records.

Also available at the center are more general materials, such as how-to genealogy books and films, a variety of state and country atlases, and research outlines with tips on sources and locations. Microforms can be ordered for a small fee and kept for thirty days. In addition, the friendly and knowledgeable staff will gladly answer any questions and help guide research. Many of them have been staff members for a number of years and therefore know the collection and can offer sound advice for both beginning and experienced genealogists. The collection is always expanding as well. The staff is accommodating to special needs; simply call ahead for special arrangements for access or even foreign language skills. The center is regularly open three days a week with morning to afternoon hours, evening hours, and two Saturdays each month.[2]

Another center in Indianapolis is located just west of downtown, offering a more central site. The Family History Center on White River Parkway is only a few years old. It offers the standard resources of the centers and will be steadily adding to its collections as it becomes more established. The creation of a new center demonstrates the continued growth and popularity of genealogy and affirms the status of the Family History Library system as a great resource.

Searching from home is made plausible through the Family History Library Web site, www.family search.org. It contains an abundance of information, searches, and tips for all levels of genealogists. On the initial home page visitors have options to search for ancestors, share information, and learn about the entire Family History system. It has links for Family History news, questions, product support and downloading, and information on The Church of Jesus Christ of Latter-day Saints. It also features a "How-to-Begin Family History Research" section, which contains a helpful step-by-step process of gathering known family history and conducting further searches of a variety of resources.

After determining the ancestor or ancestors to research, use the "Research Guidance" link to further explore the options to search for documents and records. This link provides descriptions, dates, and important information about the United States and other countries. Often the information can help narrow the search through dates and events. Under Indiana, you are given the categories of birth, death, and marriage; click on the year range to receive a list of potential records to search. When you click on the specific record, a step-by-step research process pops up with a "Where to Find It" link available, often including Family History Centers among possible sites. Even for an experienced genealogist, the "Research Guidance" link may provide useful information and new directions for research in the hunt for a family's ancestors.

The "Search" link on the Web site offers the use of FamilySearch via the Internet. Here the ancestor's name can be searched under "All Resources," which includes the Ancestral File, Census, IGI, Pedigree Resource File, the U.S. Social Security Death Index, Vital Records Index, and linked family history Web sites. The searches can also be done under the individual headings. Specifically, the census selection can search, all or individually, the U.S. 1880 census, the 1881 British Isles census, or the 1881 Canadian census. The Vital Records Index is similarly limited, as

it refers specifically to records of Mexico, Denmark, Finland, Norway, and Sweden. The searches will ask for a variety of information, but most important, the ancestor's name, his or her spouse's name, year or year range, and country. The exact spelling restriction is available in some of the searches to further limit the results.

The Family History Library Catalog can also be searched on the Web site and can be found under the "Library" tab on the home page. Using place, surname, title, film/fiche, author, subject, or call number, you can search the entire library catalog. The results of the search will be a full listing of materials in the library. The individual listing will generally provide notes of a biographical nature, subjects, call number, location of the material in the library, physical details such as illustrations or maps, and bibliographical information.

Another resource useful to any genealogist is the "Research Helps" link found on the Search page. In alphabetical order by place, the page provides references for records, research tips on how to read and find various national or state histories, time lines and maps, and examples of census work sheets. The listings for Indiana include multiple census work sheets, a mortality schedule, and vital records. Often the information gives further context to the ancestors' lives and times, while also giving the best direction for tracing the family history. "Research Helps" is linked with the "Research Guidance" tab for further information.

In addition, the FamilySearch Web site provides a sharing capability to anyone willing to publicize his or her family history. The sharing feature allows the researcher to join e-mail lists, leave feedback, share genealogy, or recommend a Web site. Simply create a user name and password and register on the Web site. Membership in The Church of Jesus Christ of Latter-day Saints is not required. The sharing feature allows individual research to be added to the Pedigree Resource File.

The Web site can be used along with a visit to a nearby Family History Center, allowing researchers to be well prepared and ready to look for specific materials with specific questions in mind. Furthermore, searching the library catalog and FamilySearch engine before visiting the center can provide call numbers to more easily find the sources or order the desired microform to make copies of important family documents.

The Church of Jesus Christ of Latter-day Saints has amassed a remarkable amount of information and made it easily accessible to genealogists throughout the United States and the world. Residents in Indiana or any other state can visit one of the many Family History Centers in their areas, receive guidance from staff, and search through a wealth of records. Particularly beneficial for the beginning genealogist, the information available from the Family History Library, at a Family History Center, or on the library's Web site develops a concrete basis for any family history research. Whether planning a research trip to Utah or a nearby Family History Center, the Family History Library provides researchers with the means to begin or to continue assembling their family histories.

———————————•———————————

1. Except where otherwise indicated, the information compiled for this chapter was used by permission, © 1999, 2005 Intellectual Reserve, Inc.

2. The Family History Center of The Church of Jesus Christ of Latter-day Saints, 900 East Stop 11 Road, Indianapolis, Indiana, "Handout," September 23, 2004.

[The compiler thanks The Church of Jesus Christ of Latter-day Saints for allowing this chapter to be compiled from its Web site, www.familysearch.com, and the staff of the Family History Center on Stop 11 Road in Indianapolis for providing additional information and allowing photographs to be taken at the center. The compiler would also like to thank Judith Q. McMullen for her guidance and editing assistance.]

Indiana Historical Society

The Indiana Historical Society (IHS) provides a variety of family history programs and publications each year. The audience for the Society's family history lectures, workshops, conferences, journal, and books traditionally comprises more than half of the IHS membership as well as college students and the general public. To serve this constituency, the Society produces programs and publications at levels from novice to expert.

IHS Family History Programs

The IHS offers a range of family history lectures. Topics vary each year and may feature basic subjects such as migration, military, church, and county commissioner records and more specialized topics such as researching Civil War ancestors, using maps, and researching records of specific ethnic groups, for instance, German, Irish, and African American.

The IHS also hosts a number of research, conservation, and computer workshops. Topics may include working with vital records, using a research library, or organizing family histories. They may cover areas of special interest such as researching historic homes or preserving cemeteries. In addition, the staff of the William Henry Smith Memorial Library presents several workshops each year on conserving original documents and photographs and on collection preservation for professionals and volunteers. The Society's hands-on computer workshops expand access to resources and help beginning and intermediate researchers use the Internet more effectively.

Every two years the IHS hosts the Midwestern Roots Family History and Genealogy Conference in Indiana.[1] National and local speakers present sessions on a diverse array of topics for beginning and experienced researchers. Pre-conference events—including computer labs, special sessions for librarians, tours of local research facilities, and writing workshops—enrich each conference experience.

IHS Family History Publications

The IHS actively promotes family history with its periodicals and books. *The Hoosier Genealogist: CONNECTIONS* (*THG*), a family history journal published since 1961, contains a wealth of information for family historians and other researchers. The journal features articles on research topics; stories of individuals, local communities, and other historic subjects; transcripts of rare Indiana-related source material; family records; and notices of resources and events from the Society and for local, state, and national organizations. In 2006 *THG* received the Award of Merit for its leadership in the field of history from the American Association of State and Local History; and several of its authors have won international writing awards as well. In 2007 *THG* will be published biannually, and related Web publications will be published throughout the year as well. The Society also publishes a popular history magazine, *Traces of Indiana and Midwestern History.*

The IHS has been publishing books since the end of the nineteenth century. The Indiana History series, a five-volume set that covers the state's history from 1800 through 1945, and *Maps of Indiana Counties in 1876* are just two of the many invaluable titles the Society has produced that assist with historical research. A new series, Peopling Indiana, will explore the historical experiences of different ethnic groups in the state. The first volume, *The Irish* by William W. Giffin, was published in 2006. Volumes on German American Hoosiers, Native American Hoosiers, and African American Hoosiers are in the planning stages, and other volumes will be published in the future.

The Indiana History Center building, home of the Indiana Historical Society, in downtown Indianapolis (IHS)

The Society has produced a number of indexes to key resources, for example, indexes for Indiana's Centennial Farms and pioneer ancestors, for the naturalization records in the state's county courts, and for two children's homes in the state. It has published multiple volumes called *Indiana Source Book*s that contain material from *The Hoosier Genealogist* along with every-name indexes for the journal. The Society also regularly produces other books for Hoosier genealogical and historical research. Past subjects have included map books, obituaries from the *Western Christian Advocate*, books on the censuses of 1807, 1820, 1830, 1840, and microfiche for 1860, and guides for research in Indiana libraries and courthouses.

In recent years genealogy has been used in classrooms to help children relate better to history by learning about their family history. In support of these efforts, in 2006 the Society published *Evie Finds Her Family Tree*, a picture book by Ashley B. Ransburg that introduces preschool children to family history. In 2003 the Society published *Casper and Catherine Move to America: An Immigrant Family's Adventures, 1849–1850* by Brian Hasler and Angela M. Gouge. *Casper and Catherine* tells the true story of a typical mid-nineteenth-century family's journey from western Europe to the American frontier. Aimed at primary school children, the book includes an introduction to oral history by Barbara Truesdell and an afterword that introduces young readers to

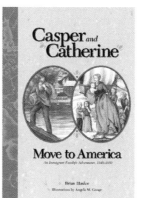

Cover of one of the Indiana Historical Society's family history books for children, published in 2003 (Design by Dean Johnson Design, Indianapolis)

family history research. The Society's Education Department produced a teacher's curriculum guide to accompany this book.

In addition to its programs and publications, the IHS supports genealogical research throughout the state by assisting local historical and genealogical organizations with technical services, traveling exhibits, educational programs, and management expertise; microfilming Indiana newspapers and the papers of pivotal Indiana figures; and providing contact information on its Web site for county historians, historical societies, and local genealogical organizations. To learn more about the Society's family history offerings, to sign up for a program, to purchase a copy of a book, or to become a member, visit the Indiana Historical Society's Web site at www.indianahistory.org.

———————————●———————————

1. In 2003 and 2005, the Midwestern Roots conference was held in conjunction with the Indiana Genealogical Society.

Indiana Genealogical Society

LINDA HERRICK SWISHER

The Indiana Genealogical Society (IGS) was founded on October 29, 1988, during a steering committee meeting in Anderson, Indiana. Curt Witcher, chairman of the steering committee, was also the society's founding president. The society's first convention was held April 21–22, 1989, at the Indianapolis Convention Center.

PURPOSE, BENEFITS, AND STRUCTURE OF THE IGS

Mission Statement

The mission of the Indiana Genealogical Society is to promote genealogical and historical research and education.

Purposes of the Society

The society does not maintain a headquarters or library, instead referring researchers to Indiana repositories. The primary purposes of the Indiana Genealogical Society are:

- Fostering an interest in all peoples who contributed in any way to the establishment and perpetuation of the state of Indiana

- Searching for the reasons and forces behind the migration of early settlers into the state of Indiana
- Preserving and safeguarding manuscripts, books, cemeteries, and memorabilia relating to the early settlers of Indiana
- Securing and holding copyrights, master copies, and plates of books, periodicals, tracts, and pamphlets of genealogical and historical interest to the people of Indiana
- Publishing, printing, buying, selling, and circulating literature regarding the purposes, records, acquisitions, and discoveries of the society
- Aiding others in the publication and dissemination of materials pertaining to Indiana, including biography and family and local history

Member Benefits

The society welcomes new members. Annual membership is $30 for individuals; $35 for joint membership. Individual life membership is $1,000; joint life membership is $1,050. Members receive the *Indiana Genealogical Society Newsletter*, the *Indiana Genealogist* quarterly, and discounts on some IGS publications and conference registration fees.

Educational Opportunities

The Indiana Genealogical Society conducts an annual conference each spring. The location varies so that all Indiana family historians may have the opportunity to attend. The conference features knowledgeable speakers on a variety of topics, as well as exhibits by genealogical vendors and societies.

The IGS holds an annual society management seminar featuring topics of interest to officers of genealogical and historical societies. Officers of IGS chapter societies may attend this seminar at no charge.

The IGS partners with other genealogical and historical organizations to present seminars and conferences. The society also is a frequent exhibitor at national genealogical conferences.

Indiana Genealogical Society Structure

Society officers include a president, vice president, recording secretary, corresponding secretary, and treasurer. The IGS has divided the state into districts, each encompassing several counties and served by a district director. The district director serves as a liaison between the IGS and that district's local historical and genealogical societies, which are autonomous and independent. The IGS offers chapter affiliation to societies, but these societies are under no obligation to become chapters. District directors must reside within the districts they serve. An at-large director serves IGS members who live outside Indiana. Officers may reside anywhere, provided they can attend quarterly board meetings. A chairman of the board presides at board meetings.

The IGS is organized into districts to better serve Indiana family historians. Following are the IGS districts and the counties they encompass:

- West Central: Clay, Fountain, Montgomery, Owen, Parke, Putnam, Vermillion, and Vigo
- Central: Boone, Clinton, Hamilton, Hendricks, Johnson, Marion, Morgan, and Tipton
- East Central: Delaware, Hancock, Henry, Madison, Randolph, Rush, Shelby, and Wayne
- Southwest: Daviess, Dubois, Gibson, Greene, Knox, Martin, Perry, Pike, Posey, Spencer, Sullivan, Vanderburgh, and Warrick

- South Central: Bartholomew, Brown, Clark, Crawford, Floyd, Harrison, Jackson, Lawrence, Monroe, Orange, Scott, and Washington
- Southeast: Dearborn, Decatur, Fayette, Franklin, Jefferson, Jennings, Ohio, Ripley, Switzerland, and Union
- Northwest: Benton, Jasper, Lake, La Porte, Newton, Porter, Pulaski, Starke, Tippecanoe, Warren, and White
- North Central: Carroll, Cass, Elkhart, Fulton, Howard, Kosciusko, Marshall, Miami, St. Joseph, and Wabash
- Northeast: Adams, Allen, Blackford, De Kalb, Grant, Huntington, Jay, La Grange, Noble, Steuben, Wells, and Whitley

Indiana Genealogical Society Chapters

Societies may apply for chapter affiliation. To become a chapter, societies must have ten members who are also members in good standing of the IGS. Benefits of chapter affiliation include:

- Chapters may publish news articles in the IGS newsletter.
- Chapter members may attend an IGS management seminar at no charge.
- Three chapter officers receive complimentary registration for the IGS annual conference.
- Chapters receive complimentary subscriptions to the IGS newsletter and the *Indiana Genealogist.*
- Chapters receive a link on the IGS Web site.
- The IGS will distribute chapter flyers, when available, at all IGS seminars.
- Societies that are chapters of the IGS include Allen County Genealogical Society, Bartholomew County Genealogical Society, Elkhart County Genealogical Society, Genealogical Society of Marion County, Monroe County Historical Society, Northwest Indiana Genealogical Society, Northwest Territory Genealogical Society, Scott County Genealogical Society, Inc., Tri-County Genealogical Society, Tri-State Genealogical Society, and Wabash Valley Genealogy Society.

Society of Civil War Families of Indiana

The Indiana Genealogical Society has established a lineage affiliate, the Society of Civil War Families of Indiana (SCWFI). Any IGS member who is a direct descendant of any person who served in an Indiana Civil War Union military or naval unit or who was a resident of Indiana upon joining a non-Indiana Union unit may apply for membership in the SCWFI. Membership candidates with approved applications will be inducted each year at the annual IGS meeting.

IGS PUBLICATIONS, PROJECTS, AND WEB SITE

IGS Publications

- The *Indiana Genealogist* is a quarterly publication featuring articles from throughout Indiana, including church histories, cemetery records, lists and extractions, rosters and diaries, town and area histories, Bible records, and indexes.
- The *Indiana Genealogical Society Newsletter* is published six times a year. It includes news of the IGS and its chapters. New publications, conferences, and county news are featured along with the "Queries" and "Once a Hoosier" columns. "Once a Hoosier" documents people born before 1900 who lived in Indiana for a while before moving on to another state. In 1997 enough biographies had been published in this column to compile a book for publication, and a second volume will be published on CD-ROM in 2007. Current submissions are being collected for volume 3. A submission form and criteria are included in some newsletters each year or may be downloaded from the IGS Web site, www.indgensoc.org.
- The *Indiana Source Directory* was revised and expanded in 2000. This publication lists sources, societies, and repositories for each county in Indiana, and the information is now available on the IGS Web site under "Counties."
- Indexes to 1890 Soldiers Enrollment Lists are available for more than thirty of Indiana's ninety-two counties. Indexes include the veteran's rank, company, regiment, state served from, and, if deceased, date and place of death, as well as information on a veteran's widow and orphans. These indexes are available on CD-ROM by county.

- *Indiana Cemetery Locations* contains locations and driving directions for cemeteries in fifty-three counties. Two of three volumes of this publication were published on CD-ROM as of 2006.
- The society has published *From A to B: Migration Research—Birds of a Feather* by Richard Enochs. This book features migration examples from North Carolina, but the methodology may be applied to any locale.
- *Once a Hoosier*, volume 1, was published in book format. Volume 2 will be available on CD-ROM early in 2007.

IGS Projects

- The IGS Speakers Bureau: The IGS maintains a free list of speakers and their topics for the benefit of those planning genealogical programs. New speakers may request a speaker's information form. All arrangements are between the requesting organization and the speaker. The IGS assumes no responsibility or liability.
- The IGS Researchers List: The list comprises researchers who will do on-site research in Indiana counties. The IGS does not assume responsibility for the researcher's work. All arrangements must be made between the client and researcher.
- Cemetery Location Project (in progress): The Department of Natural Resources is creating a computerized database of the locations of all Indiana cemeteries. The society has published two of three volumes on CD describing the locations of all known Indiana cemeteries, including driving directions and information about published records for each cemetery, if known.
- Indiana Marriage Index (in progress): On December 6, 2005, the IGS and the Genealogical Society of Utah (GSU) signed an agreement to create a statewide marriage index for Indiana that begins with each county's earliest records and goes through 1950. The records will be digitized by GSU and indexed by IGS volunteers. The completed marriage index will include links to the images of the actual marriage records.
- *Once a Hoosier* (in progress): This is a compilation of submitted entries of family information on peo-

ple who once resided in Indiana before moving on to another state.

IGS Web Site

• The IGS Web site, www.indgensoc.org, offers contact information for members and visitors. The site also offers information on IGS awards and honors, upcoming meetings, and links of interest to genealogists.

IGS AWARDS

The Indiana Genealogical Society bestows several grants, awards, and honors as presented below.

IGS Grants and Scholarships

The society awards the following three $500 annual grants to local Indiana genealogical societies for projects that will advance genealogy in the Hoosier State:

• Cemetery Restoration Grant: For a project to restore and/or renovate an Indiana pioneer cemetery
• Resource Development Grant: For a project to develop a new Indiana electronic and/or printed genealogical resource
• Chapter Resource Grant: For a project to support the operation of an IGS chapter society.

The society awards an annual Librarian's Scholarship. Any librarian serving genealogical patrons within Indiana is eligible. This scholarship is to defray the cost of attending a state or national conference or genealogical institute to help further education in genealogical research and services. The IGS hopes to further the librarian's genealogical knowledge, enabling more effective patron service. In addition, the winner's library shall receive complimentary IGS periodicals for one year. The scholarship must be used within one year of receipt.

IGS Awards

The Honors and Awards Chair accepts nominations for the awards listed below. All awards are presented at the annual IGS conference and meeting. See the IGS Web site for details on submitting a nomination.

Elaine Spires Smith Award

The Society sponsors a creative writing award to honor the late former editor of the *Indiana Genealogical Society Newsletter*. The purpose of the award is to perpetuate the memory of Elaine Spires Smith and her ability to encourage and develop creative writing talent in others who, in her words, "have something to say and a desire to say it." Qualifications for the Elaine Spires Smith Award include the following:

• Only first-time contributors to an IGS periodical are eligible for this award.
• Eligible subjects include research or analytical methodology, public records group, genealogical puzzle solution, and others of Indiana relevance. Transcriptions and abstracts are not eligible.

Service to Local Counties

• Distinguished County Genealogical Service Award: Awarded to an individual for ten or more years of service to the field of genealogy in a local area. The nominee does not have to be a member of the IGS but must be nominated by at least two IGS members.
• Outstanding County Genealogical Contribution Award: Awarded to an individual for recognition of a singular, outstanding contribution to the field of genealogy in a local area. The nominee does not have to be a member of the IGS but must be nominated by one IGS member.

Service to the Indiana Genealogical Society

• Distinguished Service Award: Given to an IGS member for five or more years of distinguished service to the IGS. Nominations must be made by at least three IGS members.
• Outstanding Contribution Award: Given to an IGS member in recognition of a singular service providing exceptional benefit to the society. A person may be nominated for one project. The nominee must be an IGS member, with nomination made by at least three IGS members.

Indiana Genealogical Society Fellow

The honor of Indiana Genealogical Society Fellow may be bestowed for life upon a member of the Society whose contributions meet the following criteria:

- This award is given in recognition of exceptional service to Indiana genealogy and the society over a period of ten or more years.
- A member must be nominated by five members who reside in separate districts of the society or who reside outside Indiana.
- Nominations shall cite qualifying services in the collection, preservation, or dissemination of genealogical or historical information, which pertains to areas beyond the county or adjoining counties of the nominee's residence.

Willard Heiss Award

The Willard Heiss Award may be bestowed upon an individual whose contributions meet the following criteria:

- This award is given in recognition of exceptional lifetime achievement in the field of genealogy throughout Indiana, which emulates the body of Heiss's work.
- The award may be presented once in any given year, but no more than twice in any five consecutive years.
- Individuals must be nominated by three IGS members who reside in separate Indiana counties or who reside outside Indiana.

The Indiana Genealogical Society, a relatively young organization, has contributed greatly to family history efforts in the Hoosier State. The Society will continue to develop its partnerships, publications, and projects with other heritage organizations. The IGS welcomes members from within Indiana, those whose ancestors had ties to Indiana, and any other interested persons. Contact the IGS at Indiana Genealogical Society, PO Box 10507, Fort Wayne, Indiana 46852-0507, or visit the society's Web site at www.indgensoc.org.

Society of Indiana Pioneers

LEIGH E. MORRIS

———————————•———————————

Since its formation in 1915, the Society of Indiana Pioneers has recognized the important role that Indiana's pioneer settlers played in the development of the state, while cultivating the interest of current and future generations in the work and accomplishments of their pioneer ancestors. The society currently has about 1,200 members who are descendants of early settlers of Indiana. Its membership rosters have included Eli Lilly, Robert Todd Lincoln, Gov. Frank O'Bannon and several other Indiana governors, Sen. Richard G. Lugar, and Herman B Wells, who was president and then chancellor of Indiana University for many years. The majority of members have pioneer Indiana ancestors, and the society's membership includes residents of most states and several foreign countries.

The Society of Indiana Pioneers currently sponsors travel outings or pilgrimages, daylong or overnight guided tours of historical sites. The pioneer society's annual meeting is held each fall and features speakers and presentations on historical topics. Members receive a copy of the society's annual yearbook, which includes a list of members and their pioneer ancestors, other information about the society, and some aspect of Indiana history.

Regular members must be at least eighteen years of age and provide proof that one or more of their ancestors lived within the present boundary of an Indiana county on or before December 31, 1840, with the following exceptions: for Howard, Lake, and Tipton counties, the qualifying year is 1845; for Starke County, 1850; and for Newton County, 1855. Junior membership is available for persons under eighteen years of age with a qualifying Indiana pioneer ancestor. Associate membership is available for any person who is interested in early Indiana history and/or the activities of the society but does not have a qualifying ancestor.

Membership applications are available on the society's Web site, www.indianapioneers.com, or by written request to the Society of Indiana Pioneers at 140 North Senate Avenue, Indianapolis, Indiana 46204-2207. Proof of lineage (birth, death, marriage, and the connection between generations) must be provided. The application fee for one ancestor is $25 with each additional line (ancestor) requiring an additional $15. Annual membership dues for Regular and Associate members are $20; $10 for Junior members. Sustaining memberships (which provide additional financial support for the society) are $30.

(Above) The Society of Indiana Pioneers' 2001 Fall Pilgrimage was a day trip to Oldenburg and Batesville, Indiana. Platted in 1837, Oldenburg is often referred to as the "Village of Spires" because of its many old-world steeples. The small town has also retained the German culture wrought by its early settlers. While in Oldenburg, pioneer society members enjoyed German cuisine at the Brau Haus with its distinctive entryway.[1]

(Below) The chapel of the Immaculate Conception Convent and Academy in Oldenburg is the motherhouse of the Sisters of the Third Order of St. Francis, founded by Sister Theresa Hackelmeier in 1851. Sister Theresa came to Indiana from Austria to found an American order that would teach German-speaking children and care for orphans of the 1847 cholera epidemic. During the nineteenth century, the Sisters of St. Francis staffed schools in Indiana, Illinois, Kansas, Kentucky, Missouri, and Ohio; established a school for African Americans in Indianapolis; and operated missions among Native Americans in the western United States. Today the order runs the motherhouse with its attached high school, operates an organic farm—Michaela Farm—and sponsors Marian College in Indianapolis. In addition, the Sisters of St. Francis continue their ministry in sixteen states and in Korea, Mexico, and Papua New Guinea.

Membership pins and charms are available for $25, and membership certificates are available for $10.

————————————•————————————

1. All photos are courtesy of Curt and Christy Morris. Thanks to Kathleen M. Breen for the historical captions for the photos. Sources used for the captions include the following Web sites: "Batesville: A Hillenbrand Industry," www.batesville.com (accessed March 14, 2006); "Franklin County [Indiana] Historical Society," www.franklinchs.com (accessed March 14, 2006); and "Sisters of St. Francis, Oldenburg, Indiana," http://oldenburgfranciscans.org (accessed March 14, 2006).

African American Pioneers and Their Descendants in Harrison County

JUDITH Q. MCMULLEN

T hree separate manuscript collections in the William Henry Smith Memorial Library provide information about early black settlers near Corydon, Indiana. Paul and Susannah Mitchum (also Meacham, Maeachum, Mecham, Mechum, Metchum, Micham, Michum, Mitchem) of Stokes County, North Carolina, wanted to free their slaves before they died. The elderly couple sold their farm and began

a journey that would take almost eight years and bring them to Harrison County in Indiana Territory. The Mitchums knew that if they could get their slaves to Indiana Territory, they could set them free. There are numerous versions of the Mitchums' journey and the number of slaves they brought into Indiana. For example, one version states that Paul and Susannah Mitchum brought 107 slaves from North Carolina; another version states that 75 slaves made the journey; yet another account relates that their trip began in North Carolina with 27 of their own slaves and that they traveled through Virginia, Pennsylvania, and Kentucky, gathering slaves as they went, finally arriving in Harrison County in 1814 with nearly 100 slaves.

Earl Saulman, a Harrison County councilman, has been researching the history of blacks in Harrison County for several years. Saulman has compiled a 158-page manuscript, "Blacks in Harrison County, Indiana: A History," which contains information he has found in deed books, birth and death records, and land transfers. According to Saulman, most of the black families in Harrison County are related to the "48 adults and 50 children who came across the Ohio River to freedom" with Paul and Susannah Mitchum. In an article published in the *Corydon Democrat*, Frederick Porter Griffin, former Harrison County historian, states that the slaves freed by the Mitchums "made up the nucleus of the early Black community in Harrison county." Griffin also states that the Mitchums' story is particularly interesting because "they came here all in one group, before Indiana was even a state." The Frederick P. Griffin Collection in the Corydon Public Library contains a wealth of information about these African American Harrison County pioneers.

According to a 1990 article in *Kentucky Ancestors* by Edwin Burrows Smith, Paul and Susannah Mitchum

Jonathan and Mary Mitchem, on Walnut Street, Corydon, Indiana, ca. 1910. Jonathan was the descendant of slaves who were freed by Paul and Susannah Mitchum in Indiana in 1814. Jonathan and Mary are buried in Cedar Hill Cemetery. (Photo courtesy of Frederick Porter Griffin)

"played an extraordinary role in the emancipation of slaves in the period 1800–1815, long before manumission societies were active (1816–1834) and long before the underground railroad." This same article states that Paul Mitchum was born ca. 1749, probably in Goochland County, Virginia. He was the son of Thomas and Mary Mechum of that county, and he married Susannah Meeks on January 2, 1772. The Mitchums lived in Goochland County, Virginia, until 1798 or 1799, and then in Surry County, North

Carolina, until 1807 when they moved to Kentucky. They settled in Roundstone Creek, Hardin County, Kentucky, and appear on Hardin County tax rolls, 1810–14. Paul died between September 1815 and March 1816 in Harrison County, Indiana.

Smith states that the Mitchums transported and freed an estimated 107 blacks. The tax and census records listed in Smith's article show the number of slaves acquired by

Tombstone of Oswell Wright in Cedar Hill Cemetery. Wright was one of the slaves who came to Harrison County in 1814 with the Mitchum family, who emancipated him. In 1857 Wright was jailed for aiding Charles, a fugitive slave who had escaped from his owner in Meade County, Kentucky. Accused of taking Charles to the train and giving the slave his own free papers, Wright was tried for assisting a slave's escape. Judge William A. Porter defended Wright at his trial but lost the case, and Wright was sent to the Kentucky State Penitentiary for five years. After his prison term, Wright returned to Corydon and died in 1875. (Photo courtesy of Frederick Porter Griffin)

Paul Mitchum: 1780s (Goochland County, Virginia), 10; 1800 (Surry County, North Carolina), 48; 1810 (Hardin County, Kentucky), 27; 1811, 53; 1812, 57; 1814, 91. Some of these slaves were freed in Virginia, but most were freed from 1814 to 1816 in Harrison County, Indiana, where land claims were entered for them and where the Mitchums assisted them in establishing homes and farms. Paul Mitchum did not lead all of his slaves to freedom in Indiana, however. The Harrison County Records Collection, 1807–36, in the Indiana Historical Society library contains a deed, which Paul Mitchum signed on March 2, 1814, giving his property—"my negroes"—to William Vinsett:

Hardin County, Kentucky Deed Book F
Know all men by these presents that I Paul Mitchum of the state of Kentucky and county above Stated do give and proces[?] William Vinsett with my property. To have and to hold as his own bonified <u>right</u> namely, my negroes and the said Vinsett shall dispose of them as he thinks proper. Now the said Vinsett shall be and is possessed this Property from this date namely, Agey and Her five children, Rose

and her child, Oney and her four children, Milly and her five Children, Winney and her two children, Tomas and Paty, and <u>flemen</u>—and dicy—Molly and her three children, and Icem and his Wife, charity and three children, and cary and one Child, Sally and Sukey. Gudy and her boy, John and Rose—Tompson—Jonson,—Nelson & Jesse Mikel and William, all these I do convey and possess to said Vinsett with which I warrant & defend from myself and all others. Given under my hand & Seal in the presence of John Smith & Anderson Page. This 2nd March 1814.

William Vinsett, who according to the *Kentucky Ancestors* article was the Mitchums' adopted son, was designated to oversee the education and improvement of the Harrison County colony after Paul Mitchum's death. However, Vinsett declined the responsibility, which passed to Dr. Littleton Mitchem, one of the freed slaves. Susannah freed the remaining slaves in 1816 after Paul's death. William Vinsett married Aggny Mitchem, a freed slave, on February 25, 1815, in Harrison County, Indiana.

An article in the January 31, 1918, *Corydon Republican*, "Our Colored Pioneers," tells the story of Paul and Susannah Mitchum, who brought 107 slaves into Indiana Territory and freed them. The article states, "After months of travel they reached Charlestown, Ind., where a few of the sojourners were left, then on to Floyd Knobs where some more were left, and ending the journey at Corydon with Bright Mitchem, Littleton Mitchem, Mace [Nace?] Mitchem, Mike Mitchem, Tom Mitchem, Harry Mitchem, George Cousins, James Finley, Lewis Finley, James Powell, Oswald Wright, John Welch, Joe Finley, Solon Carter and their wives, for whom he [Paul Mitchem] entered government land claims."

The largest group from the original slaves brought to Harrison County by the Mitchums took the family name of their former owners: Mitchem.[1] The Mitchem family purchased land in the Corydon area, married, had children, sent their children to the Corydon "Colored" School, died, and were buried near Corydon, many on their own land. In a folder titled "Black Families of Harrison County," the Griffin Collection imparts information from the Harrison County Tract Book. Following is "Land

Ann Mitchem White of Corydon, Indiana, was the sister of Jonathan Mitchem. (Photo courtesy of Frederick Porter Griffin)

Entered from the U.S. Government in Harrison Co. Indiana by Members of the Mitchum Families":

1829—Mitcham, William & Michael, 80 acres, Pt. SW 1/4, Sec 35, T3S, R3E; Southwest of Corydon—Burial place of original Mitchams ("Land located approximately 2 1/2 miles SW of Corydon near Indian Creek.")

1832—Mitcham, Littleton, 40 acres, Pt. SE 1/4, Sect 36, T4S, R3E; South Harrison Township ("Land located in extreme southeast Harrison Township bordering on Heth and Boone Townships.")

1832—Mitchem, Nace, 40 acres, Pt. SE 1/4, Sect 36, T4S, R3E; South Harrison Township ("Land located in extreme southeast Harrison Township near Littleton Mitchem's ground.")

1833—Mitchem, Thomas, 40 acres, Pt. NE 1/4, Sect 1, T5S, R3E, Northeast Heth Township

1833—Mitchem, Thomas, 40 acres, SE 1/4 SW 1/4 Section 34, T3S, R3E

1837—Mitchem, Thomas, 40 acres, Pt. NE 1/4, Sect 1, T5S, R3E, Northeast Heth Township ("Land located in extreme northeast Heth Township bordering on Boone Township on the east and Harrison Township on the north.")

Several Mitchems appear in early Harrison County marriage records, which can be found in the Griffin Collection. The *Corydon Republican* relates that one of the former slaves, Littleton Mitchem, "practiced medicine for many years and was recognized as a man of fine intellect." Littleton was born in 1796 in Virginia. He came to Corydon in 1814 with the original group of slaves. Littleton was parade marshal in June 1870 when the "colored people of Harrison County" celebrated the ratification of the Fifteenth Amendment, giving black males the right to vote. He gave an address to the crowd of two hundred in a grove east of Corydon. The newspaper reports that "everything seemed to pass off quietly and the colored people seemed to enjoy the occasion very much." Littleton died September 24, 1902, at the age of 106.

Many of the original Mitchem settlers were buried in two cemeteries in the Corydon area. One has been lost, but the other one contains the graves of some of the original Mitchems. This cemetery is located on the old James Demoss farm later known as the Michael [Baelz or Baez] farm. According to Griffin, the Mitchem cemetery is located on "a high bluff overlooking Indian Creek and the 'Sinks' on Indian Creek to the south. . . . Sunken graves and native limestone mark some twenty or more graves."

Several branches of the Mitchem family owned land in Cedar Wood, about six miles south of Corydon. Isaiah Mitchem, son of Littleton Mitchem, died March 8, 1920, at the age of eighty-eight. His obituary in the *Corydon Republican* states that he was "an industrious and worthy man" who had "a good farm and a comfortable home." At the time of his death, Isaiah Mitchem owned a ninety-acre farm, where he had lived for most of his life. He was buried in the family burying ground on the Mitchem homestead at Cedar Wood. Mary Ann "Polly Ann" Mitchem, Isaiah's wife, died eight years later at ninety-one and was also buried at Cedar Wood.

In the early 1880s a school was built for black children on East Summit Street in Corydon. School records from the 1884–1885 school term show that the teacher was C. A. Williams and the number of pupils was about seventy-five or eighty. Family names recorded in the records reflect some of the names of descendants of the original Mitchum slaves: Carter, Mitchem, Powell, and Welch.

Fifty-nine names were extracted from a certified copy of the "Register of Negroes and Mulattoes in Harrison County, Indiana, 1857–1863," found in the Griffin Collection. The 1860 census schedule shows the following free blacks in Harrison County: Mary Mitchem, 30F Washer woman; Jonathan Mitchem, 14M Laborer; Julia S. Mitchem, 13F; Marietta Mitchem, 7F; Agnes Mitchem, 3F. Frederick Porter Griffin has also extracted thirteen names of direct descendants of the original black families.

(Left) Annie Belle Lewis worked for forty years as the cook for the Griffin family of Corydon. Her parents were slaves in Meade County, Kentucky. She was born in Corydon shortly after her parents gained their freedom and moved across the Ohio River. Annie Belle was in the first graduating class of the Corydon Colored High School, May 14, 1897. She never married; lived in a log cabin with her parents; died at age sixty-eight on June 2, 1941; and was buried in Cedar Hill Cemetery. Annie Belle is pictured here with William M. Griffin Jr. (left) and cousin Frederick Porter Griffin, ca. 1918. (Photo courtesy of Frederick Porter Griffin)

(Right) Tombstone of Thomas Mitchem, Cedar Hill Cemetery. Many of the Mitchems and their descendants are buried in Cedar Hill, but there were two other Mitchem cemeteries as well. One of the original Mitchem cemeteries was located on the Laconia Pike, but the graves have been lost. Mace/Nace, Littleton, Thomas, and Isaiah Mitchem, who came to Harrison County in 1814, and their family members are buried in another Mitchem cemetery located on forty acres of land that Thomas Mitchem purchased in 1833. The rough limestone used to mark the graves can still be seen today. (Photo courtesy of Judith Q. McMullen)

1. All of the Mitchems in the remainder of this chapter (with the exception of Paul and Susannah Mitchum) are black unless otherwise noted. The name is spelled in various ways; for example, Mitchem, Mitchum, Mitcham, and so forth.

Selected Bibliography: "Black Families of Harrison County." Frederick P. Griffin Collection. Corydon Public Library; Cummings, Holly. "Researching Black History." *Corydon Democrat*, October 6, 1999; Harrison County Court Records Collection, 1806–1817, SC 2508. Indiana Historical Society; Harrison County Records Collection, 1807–1836, SC 2302. Indiana Historical Society; *Kentucky Ancestors* 26 (1990): 14–15; Shannon, Barbara, "Walk Along with Us," unpublished manuscript, folders 21–24, Black Women in the Middle West–Miscellaneous Collection, 1890–1984, M 0499. Indiana Historical Society.

Part 3
Researching Records

		The Name of every Person whose usual place of abode on the first day of June, 1850, was in this family.	Age	Sex	Color	Profession, Occupation, or Trade of each Male Person over 15 years of age.	Value of Real Estate	Place of Birth, Naming the State, Territory, or Country.				
1	2	3	4	5	6	7	8	9	10	11	12	13
		John A. Fuller	6	m				Indiana			1	
19	17	Eli Benham	27	"		Carpenter	100	Vermont				
		Cecillia "	23	f				Ohio				
		Joel Fletcher "	2	m				Indiana				
	18	Silas Benham	25	"		Farmer	400	Vermont				
		Ellen "	18	f				do				
		Lucinda "	1	"				Indiana				
20	19	George Runkle	32	m		Farmer	2000	New Jersey				
		Jane "	29	f				do				
		Sally Hender	15	f				New York				
		William Siguer	22	m				New Jersey				
		Besson Runkle	1	"				Indiana				
21	20	William Baker	32	"		Farmer	600	Kentucky				
		Mary Ann "	25	f				Indiana				
		Orilda "	11	"				do				
		Eliza Jane "	8	"				do				
		Mary C. "	7	"				do				
		Fletcher Daugherty	19	m				do				
		Margaret Ann Baker	11	f				do				
22	21	Thomas Philips	70	m		Farmer	900	do				
		Rachel "	69	f				Pennsylvania				
23	22	Samuel Swartzel	26	m		Farmer	400	do				
		Louisa "	21	f				Ohio				
		Sydia "	1	f				Indiana				
		William Watkins	23	m		Farmer	100	Ohio				
		Jennetta "	2	f				do				
		Louisa "	21	"				Pennsylvania				
25	24	Samuel Frey	53	m		Farmer	1000	Maryland				
		Elizabeth "	57	f				Pennsylvania				
		Edward "	25	m		Farmer	900	do				
		Daniel "	24	"				do				
		William M. "	22	"				do				
		Calet "	20	"				do				
		Rachel "	18	f				do				
		Jerome "	16	m				do				
		Rebecca "	13	"				do				
		Emanuel F.	9	"				do				

Census Records

CURT B. WITCHER

———————————•———————————

Census records are among the most popular records for genealogists and family historians. And it is no wonder—they place individuals in a particular geographic location during a specific time period and provide additional context regarding at least the number of family members and their genders. Census records also provide information on an ancestor's neighbors and list the minor civil jurisdiction where an ancestor lived in addition to the county and state of residence. That censuses were regularly and rather consistently taken is another major research benefit. Their popularity is further evidenced by the fact that among the most frequently visited genealogy sites on the Internet are those that contain census and other enumeration data.

The best known and most frequently consulted census records are the federal population schedules. Indeed, some incorrectly believe that these records are the totality of census records. However, numerous and varied types of enumerations exist. Federal census records alone provide abundant schedules depending on the state and the time period, including population, agricultural, manufacturing/industry, 3-D (or deaf, dependent, and delinquent), slave, social statistics, and mortality. Used as a set of records,

these census materials can provide genealogists with a tremendous amount of consequential data.

National Archives and Records Administration Microcopy Number for Federal Population Schedules

Census Year	NARA Microcopy Number
1820	M33
1830	M19
1840	M704
1850	M432
1860	M653
1870	M593
1880	T9
1890	N/A
1900	T623
1910	T624
1920	T625
1930	T626

Federal Enumerations—Population Schedules

Because Indiana officially became a territory in 1800, no census was taken in 1790. The federal census taken in 1800 for Hamilton County in the Northwest Territory and Knox County in the Indiana Territory was

Census of Indiana Territory for 1807

For genealogists, the first substantial enumeration of individuals in Indiana is the 1807 territorial census. Reprinted with an informative preface and index by the Indiana Historical Society in 1980, the *Census of Indiana Territory for 1807* provides facsimiles of the original Knox, Dearborn, and Randolph County enumerations as well as the 1807 voters list for Clark County as its 1807 territorial enumeration cannot be located. The originals are a part of the William Henry Smith Memorial Library's collections. The enumerations for Knox, Dearborn, and Randolph counties list free males above the age of twenty-one by name. A February 2, 1807, poll list for Kaskaskia, a part of Randolph County, is also included in the work. In most effectively using this work, it is vital to appreciate the boundaries of the Indiana Territory in 1807. For this purpose a map is provided in the work.

lost. The federal census taken in the Indiana Territory in 1810 covering the counties of Clark, Dearborn, Harrison, and Knox was also lost.

The first federal population schedules available for Indiana are for the year 1820—four years after statehood. In this year enumerators were to record for each dwelling or domicile the number of free white males and free white females in the age categories of zero to ten, ten to sixteen, sixteen to twenty-six, twenty-six to forty-five, and forty-five and older. For free white males, the enumerator was also to record the number who fell into the age category of sixteen to eighteen. In addition to the free white categories, the census takers were also to record the number of other free persons (excepting Native Americans), the number of slaves, the number of colored persons, the number of persons not naturalized, and the number of persons engaged in agriculture, commerce, or manufacturing. Consulting the *Map Guide to the U.S. Federal Censuses, 1790–1920* (Baltimore, MD: Genealogical Publishing Company, 1997) will show the actual boundaries of specific counties during particular census years.

While some lament the lack of detailed, specific personal data in these early schedules when compared to the data found on schedules of the mid- to late-nineteenth century, these early schedules are still quite useful. One can identify individuals and families, discover the neighbors of those individuals and families, group individuals and families by minor civil jurisdictions as well as by county, and frequently

Indiana Counties Enumerated on the 1820 Population Schedules According to Microfilm Roll Number

Roll #13	Roll #14	Roll #15
Clark	Crawford	Fayette
Dearborn	Delaware	Ripley
Floyd	Dubois	Spencer
Franklin	Harrison	Sullivan
Gibson	Jennings	Warrick
Jackson	Knox	Wayne
Jefferson	Lawrence	
Pike	Martin	
Posey	Monroe	
Randolph	Orange	
	Owen	
	Perry	
	Scott	
	Switzerland	
	Vanderburgh	
	Vigo	
	Wabash	
	Washington	

glean another fact or two from a careful study of the census pages. Studying how surnames are grouped together within a township and county may also provide leads or clues to migration and settlement patterns.

The 1830 population schedules provide researchers with a more detailed age breakdown for families and dwellings as enumerators were charged to record the names of the heads of households as well as free white males and free white females in the following age categories: zero to five, five to ten, ten to fifteen, fifteen to twenty, twenty to thirty, thirty to forty, forty to fifty, fifty to sixty, sixty to seventy, seventy to eighty, eighty to ninety, ninety to one hundred, and one hundred years of age or more. In addition, the number of male and female slaves and the number of male and female free colored persons were recorded in separate columns and separate sections in the following age categories: zero to ten, ten to twenty-four, twenty-four to thirty-six, thirty-six to fifty-five, fifty-five to one hundred, and one hundred years of age or more.

In 1830 there were also categories for recording the number of white persons who were deaf and dumb and less than fourteen years of age, fourteen to under twenty-five years of age, and twenty-five and older as well as the number of blind individuals. These same categories were provided for slaves and colored persons enumerated in 1830. An additional category was provided for recording the number of aliens—foreigners not naturalized.

All of Indiana's current ninety-two counties were enumerated in 1840 except for Howard, Newton, Ohio, and Tipton. The 1840 population schedules mirror 1830 in many respects including providing the same detailed age breakdowns for free white males and females, and free colored males and females. In addition, there are categories for recording the number of persons in each family employed in mining; agriculture; commerce; manufactures and trades; navigation of the ocean; navigation of canals, lakes, and rivers; and learned professions and engineers. Of particular interest and research benefit is the category asking for the names of pensioners for Revolutionary or military service and their ages.

Additional categories indicate white persons under age fourteen, fourteen to twenty-five, and twenty-five or older who are deaf and dumb, blind, insane and idiots in public charge, and insane and idiots in private charge, as well as colored persons who are deaf and dumb, blind, insane and idiots in public charge, and insane and idiots in private charge. The last section of the 1840 population schedule, titled "Schools, &c," includes universities or colleges, academic and grammar schools and their associated number of scholars, primary and common schools and their associated number of scholars, and the number of scholars in public charge. Careful inspec-

Indiana Counties Enumerated on the 1830 Population Schedules According to Microfilm Roll Number

Roll #26	Roll #27	Roll #28	Roll #29	Roll #30	Roll #31	Roll #32
Allen	Cass	Clark	Hancock	Clinton	Bartholomew	Clay
Boone	Dearborn	Crawford	Jackson	Hendricks	Carroll	Fountain
Decatur	Dubois	Delaware	Owen	Monroe	Daviess	Parke
Elkhart	Franklin	Floyd	Posey	Montgomery	Greene	Ripley
Fayette	Harrison	Jefferson	Randolph	Morgan	Henry	Switzerland
Gibson	Jennings	Marion	Wayne	Putnam	Knox	Union
Hamilton	Johnson	Perry		Scott	Orange	Vanderburgh
Lawrence		Shelby		Vigo	Tippecanoe	Warren
Madison		Spencer			Washington	
Martin		Warrick				
Pike						
Rush						
St. Joseph						
Sullivan						
Vermillion						

tion of these schedules may net considerably more data than one might initially glean with a brief look.

The 1850 population schedules ushered in a new era of more robust census records. This was the first census in which enumerators were to name everyone in the household rather than simply recording the head of household. The other consequential addition to the data collected was the recording of the birthplace of everyone enumerated, typically a state or foreign country. Additional information provided includes age, sex, race, occupation for those over the age of fifteen, value of real estate owned, whether the person was married or attended school within the last

The 1880 federal population schedule for Indiana lists German immigrant Louisa (Wahrenburg) Scheurenbrand along with her husband, John, and their two children, all living in Boswell, Benton County. (Photo courtesy of Fritz Wahrenburg)

year, whether the adults (over twenty years of age) in the household could read or write, and whether anyone in the household was deaf, dumb, blind, insane, or an idiot, pauper, or convict. Newton County was the only one of Indiana's current ninety-two counties not enumerated in 1850.

As a set of records, the 1860 and 1870 censuses are quite significant. With so many participating in and being affected by the War between the States and the massive migration that took place after the war, being able to have a figurative snapshot on either side

of that event is of great historical consequence. Since Indiana was one of the earliest states to contribute soldiers and since, over the course of the war, the state provided more than 208,000 troops, the 1860 and 1870 enumerations help the researcher in evidencing the toll of the war on this state and its residents.

From 1860 through 1930, all of Indiana's current ninety-two counties were enumerated. The 1860 population schedules mirror the 1850 schedules with one additional category of data: the value of personal property. Like the 1850 and 1860 population schedules, the 1870 schedule provides the names of all individuals along with their age, sex, occupation, value of real and personal property, place of birth, whether married in the last year, whether attended school in the last year, whether over the age of twenty-one and able to read and write, and whether anyone in the household was deaf, dumb, blind, insane, or an idiot, pauper, or convict. In addition, 1870 provides the month of birth for those born in the preceding year, whether an individual's father and mother are foreign born, whether a male citizen over twenty-one years of age, and whether a male citizen over twenty-one years of age who has had his voting rights denied or abridged on grounds other than rebellion or other crime. The nine wards of Indianapolis, Marion County, in 1870 were enumerated twice. Both enumerations were microfilmed and are available to researchers (rolls 338 to 341).

The 1880 federal population schedules heralded another significant increase in the data enumerators were supposed to collect. Supplementing the categories that continued to grow in number from the 1850 schedules forward, the 1880 schedules provide not only the place of birth of the individuals being enumerated but also the place of birth of the individuals' fathers and mothers. Complementing the occupational category is a column for number of months unemployed in the last year, and complementing the blind, deaf, and so forth category are the additional elements of maimed, crippled, bedridden, or otherwise permanently disabled. An entirely new category also provides information on whether an individual was sick or temporarily disabled, that is, not able to attend to ordinary business or duties, and the nature of the illness.

The 1890 federal population schedules would have provided genealogists, historians, and demographers with amazing data because they were taken before the depression of that decade but after the Civil War. This schedule asked for information on whether an individual being enumerated was a soldier, sailor, or marine during that war or a widow of such a person. However, a fire in 1921 at the Commerce Department Building destroyed the records for all but slightly more than 6,100 individuals. Only a few fragments from various states survived—regrettably, none from Indiana.

The first population schedules of the twentieth century show that enumerators continued to be charged with gathering more data. The data collected in 1900 included name, sex, race, relationship to the head of household, month and year of birth as well as age at last birthday, station in life (single, married, widowed, or divorced), and if married, number of years married, number of children born to the females listed as well as the number of those children still living, place of birth as well as parents' places of birth, year of immigration to the United States as

the 1910 enumeration included refining the residency and citizenship questions to year of immigration and whether a naturalized citizen or an alien, and recording the language(s) each person spoke. Also modified were the occupation and employment questions so that in addition to occupation or trade, the type of industry was recorded; whether the individual was an employee, employer, or self employed was also indicated; and if the person was an employee, and if unemployed, how long the person was unemployed in 1909. Categories for physical maladies return with this schedule, which records whether an individual was blind, deaf, or

This photo of Friederich Weber was taken in South Erie, Pennsylvania, after he arrived in America but before he came to Lafayette, Indiana. He is listed along with his wife, son, and mother-in-law in the 1880 federal population schedule for Lafayette, Tippecanoe County. (Photo courtesy of Fritz Wahrenburg)

well as number of years residing in this country and whether or not the person is a naturalized citizen, occupation and number of months unemployed in the last year, whether the person attended school in the last year as well as whether the person can read, write, and speak English, and finally whether the family owns or rents, a farm or a house, as well as whether the home is mortgaged.

As happened in the previous century, consecutive enumerations tended to mirror one another. The changes from the 1900 population schedule to

dumb. A new category of high interest on the 1910 federal population schedules was whether the person was a survivor of the Union or Confederate army or navy.

The 1920 population schedules saw the loss of the military question relative to the Civil War and the addition of three columns to capture the native or mother tongue of each person being enumerated as well as those of the person's father and mother—particularly useful for immigrants and first generation Americans.

Native- or mother-tongue categories were dropped with the 1930 census, but a new, similar category was added—language spoken in the home before coming to the United States. In nearly every way this census is at the zenith of data recorded by enumerators, capturing most of all the types of data added for population schedules since 1880. In addition to recording whether the domicile is owned or rented, its value is also recorded. Other new categories include whether the enumerated individual owned a radio set, age at time of first marriage, as well as whether a military veteran—and if so, in what war. The occupation category was expanded to record the kind of work done, the type of industry, and the class of worker. Hence a researcher could find out that in 1930 in Dubois County, Indiana, Alva J. Stutzman was a fireman for the steam railway.

The researcher interested in Hoosier genealogy and history will find the federal population schedules a rich source of information. Before the wide use of personal computers and the advent of an economically accessible Internet, an index was published, in book or microtext form, for every Indiana federal population schedule for the time period 1820 to 1870. It is important to note here that the Indiana Historical Society compiled and published on microfiche a phenomenal every-name index to the 1860 Indiana population schedules. The complete set of microfiche provides both one large alphabetical list-

ing as well as ninety-two county-by-county alphabetical listings. Its accuracy is of particular note.

The 1880 federal population schedules, along with the schedules for 1900, 1920, and parts of the 1910 and 1930 schedules were indexed during the 1930s using the Soundex system patented by Margaret K. Odell and Robert C. Russell in 1918 and 1922. Soundex is a phonetic system, whereby a surname is encoded with numerical values assigned to letters that sound alike. For 1880 only heads of households with children ten years of age or younger were encoded in this manner. While there are challenges to using Soundex as there are with many indexes, there are distinct advantages to having surnames that sound alike grouped together regardless of actual spelling.

The Internet boom of the 1990s ensured that very good access would be available for all of Indiana's population schedules. At Ancestry.com Indiana's federal population schedules for the years 1820 through 1930 have been digitized and placed online along with indexes for each set of schedules. HeritageQuestOnline.com also provides a complete set of federal census records but does not provide indexes for all census years. Whether in print, on CD-ROM, or online, multiple indexes are available for much of Indiana's portion of the federal population schedules. Experienced researchers know that, particularly when they are having a challenging time locating a person of interest, all indexes should be consulted.

Indiana's Statewide Cemetery Registry

JEANNIE REGAN-DINIUS

———————————————— • ————————————————

Cemeteries have been a part of our cultural land-scape as long as people have lived in Indiana. The size, ornamentation, and documentation of these grounds differ with cultural group, wealth of the families, situation surrounding a person's death, and religious affiliation. Native American burial practices varied widely depending on time period, tribal association, and family beliefs. Often graves were unmarked, allowing nature to reclaim the area. Early settlers may have buried their dead on a portion of a farm with marked or unmarked graves. Still others may have lost a loved one while migrating to a new part of the country, and a grave may have been dug along a trail or canal route. As churches developed, so too did religious-specific burial grounds where church members could be laid to rest. Some of Indiana's French Catholic cemeteries date back to preterritorial days. Communities—cities, townships, and counties—also developed ethnic and local cemeteries. All of these resting places, whether marked or unmarked, are important to who we are as a people, and yet many are becoming lost and forgotten.

Both historic cemeteries and prehistoric burial areas can be found in every Indiana county. Many burial sites are visible from the earth's surface. Whether graced by an elaborate marker or a small fieldstone, marked graves are easily identifiable. The Hoosier State boasts dramatic examples of period folk art, especially in and around Bedford, Lawrence County, Indiana, where Indiana limestone is abundant. Many stone carvers lived and worked in this area. Green Hill Cemetery in Bedford contains wonderful examples of folk art—intricate tree stump markers, large monuments, and life-size statues of individuals. One life-size monument features a man with his golf clubs, while another memorializes a World War I soldier.

Most cemeteries offer more than aesthetic beauty; they offer a view to the past and often serve as a valuable resource for historical research. Through inscriptions, monuments, and related records, cemeteries can teach us about our ancestors and what was important to them. On the other hand, the burial sites and accompanying markers of many pioneers are the only records that exist about them. For instance, Jeffersonville, Clark County, Indiana, has some cemeteries that contain the graves of African American slaves. Some of the grave markers list only a first name and the word "slave." No other records exist for some of these folks, so once the markers are lost, all reference to these individuals is gone.

Other cemeteries display no aboveground evidence of their existence. Every Indiana county has cemeteries where markers have been removed. This happens over a number of years and for a variety of reasons. Stones erode away due to environmental influences—from rain to air pollution. They are destroyed by vandalism and purposely removed by private landowners and developers. Although recent legislation protects cemeteries from vandalism and from the intentional removal of stones, many cemeteries are already lost. In some instances, there may be no mention of a gravesite in a land deed, and over time the local community may forget that a cemetery ever existed. Native American burial sites and other unmarked cemeteries are at a greater risk of being lost because there may be no paper documentation of their existence. Those purchasing property today may not know that the land they purchase contains burial plots. People build homes, garages, retail developments, or other structures on the land they own and may unknowingly destroy cemeteries. Because there is little aboveground evidence of some cemeteries, the locations have not been recorded, or the information is not readily available, disturbance and disruption occurs without planning and without community or family involvement.

In recent years the public has become more concerned with the deteriorated condition of historic cemeteries and the number of vanishing cemeteries or cemeteries that are in imminent danger of being lost. For these reasons, in July 2000 the Indiana General Assembly passed IC 14-21-1-13.5, which authorized the Department of Natural Resources (DNR), Division of Historic Preservation and Archaeology (DHPA) to survey and register every cemetery and burial ground in the state.

Many people have asked why the DNR received the responsibility for this project. The National Historic Preservation Act of 1966 mandates that each state appoint one person to serve as the State Historic Preservation Officer. In Indiana this person is the DNR Director. The DHPA Director serves as the Deputy State Historic Preservation Officer and is responsible for the day-to-day administration of preservation and archaeological programs. The DHPA is the logical entity to create and maintain the database since it is the state's lead preservation and archaeological agency.

The statewide Cemetery Registry project started in February 2001 when one staff member was hired to begin the daunting task authorized by the general assembly. Realizing that one person could not survey every site and that many local groups had already been working to document cemeteries and burial grounds in their areas, the DHPA began recruiting allies for the project. The outpouring of support and the number of volunteers have placed the project far ahead of schedule. The local partners comprise

African Americans were buried in the back portion of this early mixed-race cemetery in Jeffersonville, Clark County, Indiana.

One goal of the Cemetery Registry project is to locate and preserve not only cemeteries, but the buildings and structures associated with cemeteries as well.

Many of Indiana's cemeteries contain elaborate collections of funerary sculpture in forms such as grave markers and family memorials.

historical societies and museums, county historians, genealogical organizations, and preservationists. On the state level these contacts include the Indiana Pioneer Cemetery Restoration Committee, the Indiana Genealogical Society, the Indiana Historical Society, the Indiana State Library Genealogy Division, and archaeologists, universities, and other governmental agencies. Nationwide partners are also enlisted: the African American Genealogical Society, the Daughters of the American Revolution (DAR), and the Sons of the American Revolution (SAR).

Each of the historical groups focuses on different aspects of our funerary heritage, for example, pioneer cemeteries, veterans' cemeteries, or county cemeteries. No one group has information on all cemeteries, but, combined, these groups have the wealth of

information necessary to make the DHPA project a success. The information gathered by different organizations varies, but it has extraordinary value for accurate research.

The first step was to gather copies of information from the various repositories found around the state. Once this information was compiled, staff and volunteers began the process of locating, documenting, and mapping every cemetery and burial ground in the state. Divided by township within each county, the information on almost any cemetery can easily be located by staff. While cemetery information is still being collected, the number of new cemeteries decreases each month. Although we will never say we have them all, we do have a relatively complete list of cemeteries in one repository.

From the list, comes the task of filling out a survey form on each cemetery. This task takes longer and will be part of the ongoing project for years to come. Filling out a form requires visiting the site to collect the information needed. The survey form contains a section for general information including a cemetery's name, a description of the site's physical condition, and details of the needed preservation efforts for the cemetery. Other information fields consider a variety of topics such as the religious affiliation of the cemetery, the ethnicity of the people buried at the site, the condition of the stones, an inventory and description of buildings on the property, and bibliographic information regarding the sources researched for each cemetery. The amount of information gathered varies from cemetery to cemetery, depending on available information. For some sites, the only

While Holy Cross Cemetery in Indianapolis, Marion County, Indiana, is currently being used, the older portions of the cemetery are experiencing some of the same deterioration and stone loss as abandoned sites.

completed data field is location; for others, there is a complete record of the site's history.

Because the number of cemeteries is estimated to be around twenty thousand, this project will not record every tombstone to document individual burials, marker inscriptions, or stone types. Various groups have done these types of readings for some cemeteries in the past, and some groups are currently working on such projects. In the 1930s, the DAR and the Works Progress Administration (WPA) surveyed cemeteries throughout Indiana. Current genealogical organizations are rereading the stones to fill in missing information and studying cemeteries missed by earlier groups. The DHPA defers questions about individual burials to local groups.

One of the most difficult but also most important aspects of the project is locating cemeteries where aboveground evidence no longer exists. These include Native American burial grounds, settlers' graves that were never marked, and grave sites where stones have been removed. One tactic the DHPA uses to find these cemeteries is archival research. Volunteers and DHPA staff look through old deeds, newspapers, mortuary records, and other primary sources to find mention of lost cemeteries. Archaeological research and evidence are also used to find these sites.

Even before completed forms come into the office, the information can be placed into the cemetery registry database. By the end of 2008, all cemeteries will be in a searchable database; soon thereafter, the information will be available to all on the Internet.

The scope of the Cemetery Registration project far exceeds that of any other cemetery-recording project conducted in Indiana in the past. The immensity and complexity of the project is a challenge that the DHPA welcomes given both the DHPA's and the public's strong interest in protecting and preserving the state's important historic and prehistoric resources. Developing a statewide registry will help communities identify and protect their ancestors' final resting places while safeguarding the cemetery heritage that belongs to *all* Hoosiers. If you are interested in volunteering to help the DHPA research, document, and/or preserve the cemeteries and burial grounds throughout the state, contact the Cemetery Registry Coordinator, DNR, Division of Historic Preservation and Archaeology, 402 West Washington Street, Room W274, Indianapolis, Indiana 46204; 317-232-1646.

Bibliographic Note: Some of the information for this chapter comes from a DHPA press release about the Cemetery Registry project dated February 15, 2001, *DNR News*. View the cemetery preservation laws via AccessIndiana online at www.state.in.us/legislative/ic/code. All photographs in this chapter are courtesy of Jeannie Regan-Dinius.

County Commissioner Records

CHRIS MCHENRY

A mong the most neglected sources for genealogical information are the minutes and other
records of county commissioners. Historically,
commissioners of Indiana counties have been responsible for verifying and paying the county's bills, and
in times past these have included everything from
medical care and burial of paupers to payment of
Civil War bounty for enlistment to room and board
for prisoners in the county jail.

Over the years, the makeup of the board of commissioners has changed, but its duties have remained,
in essence, the same. In the earliest days of Indiana,
three commissioners were elected in each county. Then
in 1824, the commission for each county was made
up of a justice of the peace, also known as a magis-
trate, from each township. This is probably why commissioners' meetings were also called "commissioners'
court." In 1831 the county commission returned to
its original form of three members, each representing
a specific geographical area of the county.[1]

Until the office of county auditor was created,
minutes of the commissioners were kept by the
county clerk of courts. Today's commissioners are
still responsible for paying the bills, as well as having
the final say on zoning issues and county highways.[2]

From the earliest days of the state, commissioners had special responsibility for care of the impoverished. Commissioners appointed two overseers of
the poor for each township, and each year those who
became "a public charge" were farmed out to people
who were willing to care for them at public expense.
Their destinations were determined by a public sale,
or auction, in which the unfortunate pauper was sent
to live with the person who asked the lowest price for
his or her care. On rare occasions, the commissioners would make a monetary allowance directly for a
person or family who appeared to be in temporary
straits. It is obvious from the records that sometimes
parents or other relatives would be given the funding and the responsibility for people who could not
care for themselves. Occasionally, the relationship is
spelled out in the commissioners' minutes.[3] Finding an ancestor among those appointed as one of the
overseers of the poor can add to your knowledge of
his or her standing in the community because these
people had a real responsibility for their less fortunate neighbors.

Children deemed to be paupers were "bound
out" to families who provided for their care and
taught them some way to make a living.[4] These

children often had no recourse from cruel masters; however, in at least one lawsuit in Dearborn County two children were relieved of their indentured status on charges of cruelty by their guardians.[5]

In the process of making allowances for the care of the poor, commissioners created records about who these people were and, in many cases, when they died. Since these were people who did not own property, made no deeds, and left no estates, the commissioners' records may be the only specific information available about them in the public records. If they lived in the household of someone else prior to 1850, they would not even be listed separately in the census.

Among the bills paid by commissioners were those for coroners' inquests, usually only if someone other than the elected coroner performed that duty. Here you will find the name of the deceased and the date the bill was paid. In these cases the deceased was not necessarily a pauper since the bill was simply to pay the substitute coroner who had investigated an unexplained death.

Even if there was no coroner call, if a pauper died, there were other bills to pay: someone had to make a coffin, cart the body to a graveyard, and dig a grave. Once again the only dates available will be those on which the bills were paid, but that information can considerably narrow down a time frame for the death of an ancestor who is not recorded anywhere else.

County commissioners were not anxious to spend taxpayers' money for the support of paupers who did not actually live in their counties, so on occasion you will find fees paid to individuals for transporting these unfortunates out of the county. Most do not spell out the destination, but in a few cases you may find at least the state to which a pauper was taken.

This example of a pauper's record from the Franklin County Commissioners Records, available at the Indiana State Library on microfilm, states the following: "Ordered that Catherine Lenard be allowed the sum of nine Dollars for Keeping Elizabeth Leonard a pauper from the 6 March to this date —" Written vertically along the left margin is the notation: "Delivered to John Leonard Sen — 4th June 1818." (Courtesy of Chris McHenry)

Commissioners were (and still are) responsible for creating and maintaining roads and bridges. Not unexpectedly, adequate roads to and from all areas of the county were of utmost importance. Under normal circumstances, residents who wanted a new road or bridge would present a petition asking for its establishment. The commissioners would then appoint two or three people to view the proposed route and make recommendations to the commissioners. Both the petitions and the appointments can provide more information about your ancestors.

Many other individuals appear in the commissioners' records. In a time when landowners could satisfy their real estate tax obligations by working on the roads, some were physically unable to do so. They can be found listed in the minutes. Some are identified as blind; others are listed with different physical disabilities. In the early days of Indiana, the county jailer was reimbursed for his expenses in boarding prisoners. Usually these notations include not only the name of the jailer but also the names of his prisoners along with at least an approximate date, leading the researcher to the court records to find out more about the reason for incarceration.

During the Civil War, Indiana counties paid bounty money to men who enlisted in the Union army. Not all of these are noted in the commissioners' minutes. However, in one case a list of names led to an interesting discovery about an entire company from Dearborn County that wound up serving in the 11th Kentucky Regiment. Because of their unusual assignment, the commissioners saw fit to explain why they had paid bounty for them.

The men enlisted in answer to a call from Indiana Gov. Oliver P. Morton, but when they reported for duty, the quota had already been filled. The Indiana governor, acceding to a plea from the Kentucky governor, sent them to Louisville to serve in the Kentucky troops. Had it not been for a note in the commissioners' minutes, their story might not have been known. Their names do not appear on the usual lists of Indiana Civil War soldiers because their service was not in an Indiana unit.[6] In some counties, commissioners reimbursed residents who paid for substitutes to take their places in the Union army.

In most cases, the minutes of the commissioners will be found in the county auditor's office since that person also serves as secretary to the commissioners. You are not likely to find comprehensive indexes to the minutes, but most individual books include an item-by-item index.

Abstracts of commissioners' records for twenty-one Indiana counties were put together by Works Progress Administration (WPA) workers during the Depression, and typescripts of these abstracts are available in the William Henry Smith Memorial Library of the Indiana Historical Society. Those counties are Daviess, Floyd, Jefferson, Johnson, Lake, Marion, Marshall, Monroe, Montgomery, Orange, Pike, Porter, Posey, Rush, St. Joseph, Starke, Tippecanoe, Vanderburgh, Vermillion, Vigo, and Wayne. Most, if not all, cover only the earliest years of the records. The actual records can be found in the auditors' offices of the individual counties. A quick investigation of the abstracts will reveal that the amount of information entered in the different counties varied with the person who was recording the minutes.

The Indiana State Library microfilm department has portions of commissioners' records from the following eleven Indiana counties: Clark (1785–1852); Dearborn (1845–1851); Franklin (1847–1852); Harrison (1844–1853); Miami (1834–1853); Perry (1847–1851); Posey (1817–1855); Scott (1841–1865); Wabash (1835–1868); Warrick (1813–1852); and Washington (1817–1855). Once again some of

these records are full of personal information, and others are frustratingly general.

In Wayne County during the May 1834 term, an associate judge was paid for three days attending to a writ of habeas corpus concerning two women named Evaline and J. Nichols, identified as Negroes from Kentucky. A petition for habeas corpus is used to mandate that prisoners be brought before the court to determine whether they are being held unlawfully. It was often used by opponents of slavery in cases where people were being held as fugitives by slave hunters. This entry begs for additional research in the court records to determine the reason for its issue.[7] Wayne County commissioner records also include reports from various justices of the peace about the fines they had collected and occasionally name the defendants and their crimes.

The researcher will undoubtedly wonder at the difference in charges made for the maintenance of various paupers. In Dearborn County bills for annual care of a pauper named Abraham Peters ranged from $25.00 to $39.99 over a four-year period.[8]

After 1830 the practice of "selling" poor people began to diminish, and provision was made for each county to establish its own asylum for the poor. All Indiana counties at one time had asylums, and many were still in existence until the late twentieth century.[9] The asylums were also under the direction of the county commissioners. Asylum records vary wildly in their content: from simple lists of those in the asylum at any given date to notations of ages, birthplaces, townships of origin, and admission and release dates. If an inmate died at the asylum, that fact may also be noted along with the date, the place of burial, and sometimes the cause of death. The earliest lists of asylum residents may be found in the commissioners' minute books, and beginning in 1850 these residents appear on the census rolls as inmates.

Other facts can sometimes be found in the asylum records, including names of children who were born to pauper mothers at the asylum, names of people to whom the children were sent for care, and transfers to the state insane asylum or the schools for the deaf or the blind. Occasionally the asylum superintendent would be moved to make a more interesting comment, such as the one following, made by a Dearborn County superintendent writing in the margin next to a name: "Too lazy to work, too mean to die."[10]

Circumstances that forced people to seek help at the county asylum could and did happen to families who had been prominent only a short time earlier. In the days before government welfare or social security for the disabled, if a father died or was seriously injured, a normally solvent family could quickly find itself in deep trouble. The rolls of county asylums include many names of former teachers, businessmen, and politicians.

With the advent of social security, welfare, and nursing homes, the county asylums began to close. Most were gone by the end of the twentieth century, although a few are still operating today. It has been estimated that only about 40 percent of their records still exist. County asylum records, where they have been preserved, should be found in the office of the county auditor, who serves as secretary for the commissioners. Records for one county asylum, in Blackford County, were microfilmed and are available at the Indiana State Library microfilm department.

In recent years, some county genealogy and history Web sites have begun including information about their county asylums. For example, abstracts of Henry County asylum records beginning in 1860 can be found on the county's genealogy services Web site, www.hcgs.net/.

An index of microfilms of Allen County asylum records is also online, and the films are available at the Allen County Public Library. Indexes for DeKalb, Kosciusko, and Parke counties are also available online. The abstracts of records for Dearborn County can be found at the Lawrenceburg Public Library, and a list of deaths that occurred at the Dearborn County Asylum from 1867 to 1919 were published in *The Hoosier Genealogist* in the fall and winter 2003 issues. Where graves at county asylums were marked, there is often information in the county cemetery listings.

Although not strictly part of the county commissioners' records, a couple of additional resources can be found in the county auditors' offices, which can be used to help flesh out the lives of ancestors. Annual transfer records, dating from the 1850s, list every parcel of real estate in the county, usually

Postcard of the Fort Wayne Orphans' Home (Jay Small Postcard Collection, P 0391, IHS)

in separate books by township, and note when the property is transferred to a new owner, giving both the name of the seller and that of the buyer. This record also gives the assessed value of the property and improvements each year, information that does not appear in deeds. A large increase in the value of improvements can provide a clue about the time that someone built a new house or a barn. The second record also deals with real estate. Each county keeps land ownership plat maps. These have often been preserved back into the 1850s. In counties where commercially published land ownership atlases may be few and far between, these records can give you a clear picture of your ancestor's holdings.

With the surge in popularity of genealogical research in recent years, most county clerks and recorders have become accustomed to researchers poring over their little-used, old books, but the same is not true of county auditors. Most of them have not had any reason to look at their outdated records, and many do not even know exactly what they have. As a result, you may find yourself being told that it will be necessary to make an appointment with someone on the courthouse staff to accompany you to the attic or the basement storage room and help move boxes of neglected records out of the way before you can even determine if the records you need still exist. Nevertheless, if your ancestor is one of those elusive people who simply do not appear in the more common records, a search of commissioner and other records may provide the information you thought you would never find.

1. *Western Statesman* (Lawrenceburgh, IN), February 18, 1831; *History of Dearborn, Ohio and Switzerland Counties, Indiana* (Chicago: F. E. Weakley and Co., 1885), 230, 283, 1,021, 1,022.

2. *Indiana Code: Comprising All Statutes of a General and Permanent Nature, Including Statutes Enacted Through the 1998 Regular Session of the Indiana General Assembly* (Indianapolis: The Council, 1998), 12:36-2-2-2.

3. *Western Statesman*; Thomas B. Helm, *History of Hamilton County, Indiana, with Illustrations and Biographical Sketches of Some of Its Prominent Men and Pioneers, to Which Are Appended Maps of Its Several Townships* (Chicago: Kingman Brothers, 1880), 43.

4. Gayle Thornborough and Dorothy Riker, comps., *Readings in Indiana History* (Indianapolis: Indiana Historical Bureau, 1956), 492.

5. Dearborn County, Indiana, Circuit Court Complete Record Book No. 3. April term 1831, Sylvanus Crowell and Elmira Crowell v. Davis Woodward, 199.

6. Dearborn County Commissioners' Record Book No. 7 (December 20, 1862), 36.

7. *Commissioners Record for Wayne County, 1830–1835*, vol. 3 (Indianapolis: Indiana Historical Society, n.d.), 162.

8. Dearborn County Commissioners' Record Book No. 1 (n.d.), 33, 48, 73, 109, 143.

9. Thornborough and Riker, *Readings in Indiana History*, 491–92.

10. Records of the Dearborn County Asylum for the Poor, June 9, 1897. (Note: These records were kept in nondescript notebooks of varying sizes, with no volume numbers and no page numbers.)

Church Records

TIMOTHY MOHON

One of the more underused and misunderstood documentary sources for the genealogist is church records. Many do not understand that these are private, not public, documents and were never meant to substitute for vital records.

When family historians are willing to enter the world of church records—and accept their unique nature and limitations—they will more than likely discover that these sources can be of great value to their research. To read and interpret this record group correctly one must be willing to set aside biases and misconceptions and seek to comprehend the religious world of his or her ancestor.

Gaining a Basic Understanding

With missing census years and sparse birth records, many researchers turn to church documents to fill the vacuum. The hope is that church records will be a perfect substitute for vital records. This inappropriate assumption is dashed when one grasps a basic understanding of this type of record.

A common fallacy among many is that "everybody went to church back then." In reality church attendance has increased over the nineteenth and twentieth centuries. According to Roger Finke and

Rodney Stark, professors of sociology and religious studies, the rate of religious adherence in 1776 was only 17 percent; the other 83 percent of the population did not attend worship services regularly or identify with a church. In what Finke and Stark call "the churching of America," the adherence rate had increased to 62 percent by 1980.[1]

According to the U.S. Census Bureau, Indiana's estimated population in 1906 was 2.7 million. In that year's census of religious bodies the bureau reported that 938,405 Hoosiers were connected with a religious denomination—less than 35 percent of the state's population. Since 65 percent were not identified with any religion in that year, the names of these individuals will not likely appear in church documents or membership records.[2]

With this basic understanding in mind, the researcher must have a rationale to look for an ancestor among church records. Reasons might be clues found in family records or traditions that suggest a religious orientation for a particular ancestor or household. Without a solid reason a search will be like looking for the proverbial "needle in the haystack."

Once a foundation to look among church records is established, the genealogist must narrow his or her focus upon a definite faith or denominational family. In 1906 the Census Bureau identified 101 denominational groups or bodies within Indiana's boundaries, while listing 189 in the entire nation.[3] Of these 101 groups, the five largest denominational families in Indiana were the following:

1. Methodist 228,091
2. Roman Catholic 174,849
3. Christian 118,447
   (Disciples of Christ and Churches of Christ)
4. Baptist 88,532
5. Presbyterian 55,417

These five groups represented nearly 80 percent of all religious adherents in Indiana in 1906. Approximately one of four Indiana residents was associated with one of these five denominations.[4]

Four Crucial Aspects about Churches

Once the researcher decides on a likely denomination, he or she needs to become familiar with four aspects of that group to focus and understand the research process. These four aspects are theology, polity, history, and terminology.[5] The most basic piece of theology that needs to be understood is baptism. An awareness of a faith's teaching on baptism will help to decrease frustration in the use of church records.

Most genealogists long for a baptismal record for their ancestor since it might substitute as a birth certificate and supply a birth date or at least a good estimate of one. But not all denominations baptize infants. Using the "top five" denominations as examples, only three—Methodist, Catholic, and Presbyterian—practice this mode of baptism.

Both Baptist and Christian bodies administer believer's baptism by immersion. It is believed by each group that the only proper baptismal candidate is one who has made a conscious decision for Christ. Baptisms in each of these bodies will occur many years after an individual's birth, normally in adulthood. One must also understand that, even with groups that practice infant baptism, adult converts also receive baptism. The date of birth is infrequently noted in these instances.

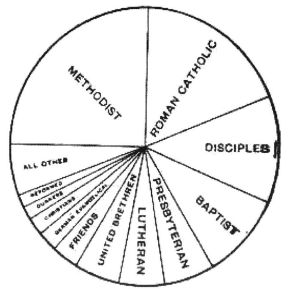

Visual representation of the percentage distribution of denominations in turn-of-the-century Indiana (*1906 Religious Census* [Washington, DC: Government Printing Office, 1910], 50)

It is important to be familiar with the polity, or government, of a denomination. Is there a bishop outside the congregation who mandates record keeping (Catholic)? Is there a conference or presbytery that requires the archiving of documents (Methodist and Presbyterian)? Or is the local congregation self-governing—not accountable to an outside authority (Christian and Baptist)? In other words, the more hierarchical the structure, the more likely that records will be available. Of course, this is not a given.[6]

Being aware of a denomination's history will help to clear up confusion and will assist in locating records. The disagreements over episcopal control versus local determination, as well as the slavery issue, partially explain the listing of eight different Methodist bodies in the 1906 census. A familiarity with the "anti-mission movement" in Baptist history helps in understanding the presence of eight distinct Baptist groups in nineteenth-century Indiana.[7]

In addition to the divisions, it is wise to be familiar with the occasional merger. In 1939 three of the Methodist bodies listed in 1906—Methodist Episcopal, Methodist Protestant, and Methodist Episcopal, South—merged as the Methodist Church. The Evangelical United Brethrens (which was a 1946 union of the Evangelical Church and the United

Brethrens) joined with the Methodists to form the United Methodist Church. Though not as complete a union, the Presbyterian Church and the Cumberland Presbyterians reunited in 1905.[8]

Terminology of the various denominations can also confuse the researcher. The sessions, presbyteries, synods, and general assemblies of the Presbyterian bodies, while not identical, are very similar to the charges, districts, annuals, and general conferences of the Methodist bodies, respectively.

Misleading to many is identical or comparable terminology used in different ways. The classic example is when the family historian learns that an ancestor was a deacon. A frequent assumption is that this individual was a clergyman. This is correct in both the Methodist and Catholic settings, since diaconal orders are part of the process to full ordination. But in Christian, Baptist, and Presbyterian circles a deacon is a layman who assists clergy in congregational life. The person might have become an ordained minister later, but this cannot be assumed.[9]

What Can Be Learned from Church Records?

Keeping the four aspects of churches in mind, the researcher's question becomes: "What will this particular set of records tell me?" Presuming that your ancestor was a member of or associated with one of the one hundred plus denominations of Christianity in Indiana, these records may be helpful in several areas of research:

1. If the particular faith practices infant baptism, then not only a birth date but also the parents' names can usually be ascertained.
2. If the individual transferred his or her membership from one congregation to another, the minutes of the receiving church will frequently give the name and community of the previous congregation.
3. In many denominations marriage records can be obtained (Baptist and Christian congregational sources seldom include matrimonial records). However, it is not unusual to find that the most faithful church member's wedding was officiated by a justice of the peace

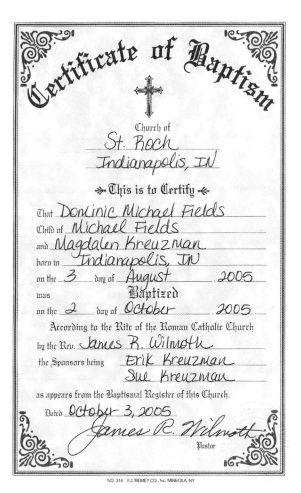

Example of a recent Catholic baptismal record for Dominic Michael Fields. The reverse side is used to record dates of future religious ceremonies. (Courtesy of Michael and Maggie [Kreuzman] Fields)

(these marriages will rarely be found in church records).

4. If your ancestor was active in church life, this can usually be inferred from the person's leadership positions and memberships. This is especially true in Protestant congregations with their multiplicity of auxiliaries, such as Sunday schools, mission organizations, education societies, and women's groups.
5. Especially in congregationally governed churches, the records will give accounts of disciplinary procedures against members. Was your ancestor challenged on theological principles? Was he or she tried for various moral charges? Did proceedings lead to the dismissal of the member?

6. Was your forebear well-regarded by the church? Did this individual fill positions of responsibility (class leader, trustee, elder, deacon, moderator, and so on)? Did he or she represent the congregation in higher jurisdictions (associations, conventions, conferences, presbyteries, synods, for example)?

7. If your ancestor was a member at the time of death, this will normally be noted in church records. This does not mean that the date will always appear. This author has seen numerous examples of names being crossed off membership registers with only "dead" being attached to the name.

Where Can I Find Church Records?

The records that offer the best chance of providing helpful information are those produced by local congregations. The seven items listed above are primarily of local concern and will not normally appear in larger denominational documents.

In the case of the congregation being defunct, the researcher will want to consult the appropriate denominational archive for assistance. The aspiration of the archivists at these repositories is that local churches will place their records in these holdings (though, for a multitude of reasons, this does not always occur). If not found in these archives, the records might be held by another local congregation, or they could have been placed in the care of a state or local public library, archive, or historical society. Fortunately, as researchers discover the importance of church records, more of these documents are being transcribed and published.

The major exception to this "local" rule is when one's ancestor was a minister or a layperson who was active in larger denominational life. The presence of congregational leadership listings in jurisdictional proceedings (which were normally published annually) are a godsend in discovering the whereabouts of pastors. Ministers and prominent leaders usually warranted obituaries or at least notices of their death in these annuals. In the postbellum years, Baptist associational minutes began to list all church members (not just church leaders) who died in the previous year (never universal, but a practice still popular with many Baptist associations today).[10]

Many repositories of Indiana's church documents are readily available. The best first step for the researcher is the extensive bibliographic work by L. C. Rudolph and Judith E. Endelman in preparation for Rudolph's *Hoosier Faiths: A History of Indiana Churches and Religious Groups*. This work is divided into three sections: a listing of published works (books and articles) dealing with religious topics in Indiana, a catalog of published Hoosier congregational histories, and a nationwide register of relevant repositories.[11]

Indiana Conference, 1847.   185

New-Philadelphia, *Ezra L. Kemp.*
Salem, *Elijah Whitten.*
Greenville, *Silas Rawson*, J. B. Lathrop.
Fredericksburg, *George Havens.*
Corydon, Giles C. Smith.
Elizabeth, *E. W. Cadwell*, W. Coldren.

EVANSVILLE DISTRICT.
John Kiger, P. E.
Evansville, *William V. Daniels.*
Mt. Vernon station, R. S. Robinson.
Mt. Vernon circuit, to be supplied.
New-Harmony, *John W. Julien.*
Cynthiana, William C. Hensly, Henry O. Chapman.
Princeton, F. A. Hester, C. C. Holliday.
Boonville, *Thomas J. Ryan*, Peirce B. Pennel.
Lynnville mission, James H. Noble.
Rockport, *Wm. M. Fraley.*
Rome mission, Thomas Wallace.
Jasper mission, *George W. Walker.*
Petersburg, *Asbury Wilkinson.*

VINCENNES DISTRICT.
Joseph Tarkington, P. E.
Vincennes, *Thomas C. Crawford.*
White River mission, James B. Hamilton.
Washington, *Samuel Hicks.*
Carlisle, Elijah W. Burruss.
New-Lebanon, *James R. Williams*, David Williamson.
Prairieton, Elijah D. Long.
Scotland mission, *Alfred B. Nisbet.*
Point Commerce, Jacob Miller.
Bowling Green, *Stephen Ravenscroft.*
Spencer, H. S. Talbott, Nathan Shumate.
Putnamville, *John Talbott.*

INDIANAPOLIS DISTRICT.
Edward R. Ames, P. E.
Indianapolis—
Central Charge, F. C. Holliday.

West & South charge, *James Corwine*, Thomas Beharrel.
Burlington, Erastus Lathrop.
Edinburg, *Philip I. Beswick.*
Shelbyville, *James Crawford.*
Franklin, *James Mitchell.*
Sugar Creek, Ami H. Shafer.
Palestine mission, *Lealdes Forbes.*
Mooresville, *Zelotes S. Clifford.*
Belleville, *William Morrow.*
Greenlee H. M'Laughlin, Agent for the current expenses of the Indiana Asbury University.
Matthew Simpson, President of the Indiana Asbury University.

BLOOMINGTON DISTRICT.
Anthony Robinson, P. E.
Bloomington, *Isaac M'Elroy*, William Stevenson.
Bedford, *Eli C. Jones*, Basil R. Prather.
Orleans, John W. Powell.
Paoli, *Daniel M'Intire.*
Livonia, *Thomas Ray.*
White Creek mission, Jacob R. Odell.
Leesville, S. Tincher, C. Carran.
Morgantown, *Landy Havens.*
Martinsville, *Henry S. Dane.*
Brownstown, B. F. Crary.
Leavenworth mission, John W. Dole.
Isaac Owen, Agent for the Indiana Asbury University.

Augustus Eddy, transferred to the Ohio Conference.
John L. Kelly, transferred to the Iowa Conference, and appointed to Colony mission.

Quest. 18. *Where and when shall our next Conference be held?*
At New-Albany, Indiana.

Quest. 12. *Who have died this year?*

1. ALLEN SEARS was born in the state of New-York, in the year 1806. When a young man he removed to the western part of Pennsylvania; and in a few years afterward he visited Cincinnati, where he remained but a short time, and then removed to Kentucky. There was considerable wildness and irregularity in his early career, yet the counsels, tears, and prayers of a pious mother ever pursued him; and he was restrained, by their influence, from many acts of wickedness. Brother Sears professed religion and joined the M. E. Church, some time previous to the year 1838, but the precise period is not known. The church was soon convinced that his conversion was genuine, and that the Lord had called him to labor in his vineyard. He was persuaded himself that a dispensation of the gospel was committed to him; but he was so distrustful of his qualifications for the work, that it was with considerable difficulty that he could be prevailed upon to ask for license to preach. In the year 1838, however, by the advice of his more experienced brethren, he was induced to submit his case to the church, and was properly recommended to the quarterly meeting conference, when he was licensed to preach, and recommended to the Kentucky Conference as a suita—

The volume *Minutes of the Annual Conferences of the Methodist Episcopal Church* gives a synopsis of each annual session's proceedings, including this portion from the 1847 Indiana Conference, on page 185. (Indiana United Methodist Archives, Depauw University, Greencastle, Indiana)

Most nationwide denominational archives have Internet listings that are easily accessible to the researcher. An excellent register of these sites can be accessed on the Web site of the Archives of the Episcopal Church.[12]

Indiana residents are blessed with the presence of several state denominational repositories. Though this list is not exhaustive, among Indiana's repositories are the following:

- Baptist Historical Collection
  Franklin College, Franklin
- Catholic Archdiocesan Archives
  Archdiocese of Indianapolis, Indianapolis
- Christian Manuscript Collection, CTS Library
  Christian Theological Seminary, Indianapolis
- Methodist Indiana United Methodist Archives
  DePauw University, Greencastle
- Presbyterian Archives and Special Collections
  Hanover College, Hanover
- Friends (Quakers) Indiana Quaker Archives
  Earlham College, Richmond
- United Brethren Archives
  Church of the United Brethren in Christ
  Huntington, Indiana

Besides the many denominational sources, the genealogist must not forget the various private and public institutions with strong religious record holdings. In downtown Indianapolis both the Indiana Historical Society's William Henry Smith Memorial Library and the Indiana State Library have selections of congregational histories and denominational proceedings as well as excellent samplings of local church records.

Also never underestimate the local library. In addition to locally produced congregational histories that can be found in many collections (often found in the 200 call numbers), great untapped potential exists in the vertical files that are mainly associated with local genealogy departments. Many items that are not easily cataloged are placed in these cabinets and, needless to say, do not appear in traditional or online library catalogs.

It is important to remember that church records—just like census records, deeds, and wills—

INDIANA SYNOD.   5.

WEDNESDAY, DEC. 4, 1907, 9 A. M.

The Synod met and was opened with song and prayer. The roll was called and the following Ministers answered present:

MORGAN PRESBYTERY.
J. B. Hadlock,   G. B. Harbison,
J. M. Stafford,   S. E. Wilson.

WABASH PRESBYTERY.
G. W. May,   Joseph Wood.

INDIANA PRESBYTERY.
J. L. Stocking

The call of roll of all churches in each Presbytery, as per list in 1907 General Assembly Minutes, was made and the following Ruling Elders answered present:

James Allen Smith, Bethel.
B. F. Musgrave, Chandler.
H. J. Graf, Jefferson Avenue of Evansville.
O. H. Miller, Oatsville.
Warren Horrell, Petersburg.
P. H. McNabb, Algiers.
D. W. Summit, Herman.
J. A. Myers, Herman (alternate)
Q. A. Harper, Algiers.

Synod and presbytery meetings list both clergy (ministers) and lay members (ruling elders), as shown in the *Minutes of the Cumberland Presbyterian Church, Held at Petersburg, Indiana, December 3–4, 1907* (Otwell, IN: Star Printing House, 1907), 5.

were not developed to be genealogical sources. Family historians are allowed to use these records for their own purposes, and they are always guests. While enjoying the treasures discovered in church records, researchers must accept the limitations of this, as well as any, record type.

———————————•———————————

1. Roger Finke and Rodney Stark, *The Churching of America, 1776–1990: Winners and Losers in Our Religious Economy* (New Brunswick, NJ: Rutgers University Press,

1992), 15–16. In their study, Finke and Stark use the term "adherents" instead of "church members" since they were required to balance congregations that counted children in membership against those that did not in their statistical analysis.

2. Department of Commerce and Labor, U.S. Census Bureau, *Religious Bodies: 1906, Part 1: Summary and General Tables* (Washington, DC: Government Printing Office, 1910), 42, 46, 58; hereafter cited as *1906 Religious Census*; 1906 will be used throughout as an example year, and it must not be assumed that membership statistics or numbers of denominations have remained static throughout the state's history.

3. *1906 Religious Census*, 16–191.

4. *1906 Religious Census*, 308–11.

5. A basic reference in the study of Indiana religious history is L. C. Rudolph's *Hoosier Faiths: A History of Indiana Churches and Religious Groups* (Bloomington: Indiana University Press, 1995); another handy source is Frank S. Mead's *Handbook of Denominations in the United States*, 10th ed., revised by Samuel S. Hill (Nashville: Abingdon Press, 1995).

6. The family historian must remember that, even where required, records can disappear, for example, through fires, floods, or neglect.

7. Mead, *Handbook of Denominations in the United States*, 197–98; Timothy Mohon, "The Joys and Frustrations of Researching Indiana Baptist Records," *The Hoosier Genealogist* 42 (Fall 2002): 3:138–45.

8. Chester E. Custer, *The United Methodist Primer, 2001 revised ed.* (Nashville: Discipleship Resources, 2001), 49–51; Rudolph, *Hoosier Faiths*, 122.

9. A listing of Methodist terminology can be found on the Web site of the United Methodist General Commission on Archives and History, www.gcah.org/glossary.html (accessed March 15, 2006); various Baptist terms can be deciphered by consulting Mohon, "The Joys and Frustrations of Researching Indiana Baptist Records," 144.

10. An example of this "every member listing" can be seen in Timothy Mohon, "Death Notices in the Annual Minutes of the Friendship Baptist Association in Central Indiana, 1855–1900," which appeared in three installments in *The Hoosier Genealogist* 42 (Fall 2002): 3:164–67; 42 (Winter 2002): 4:238–41; 43 (Summer 2003): 2:96–101. In the Fall 2002 issue the obituary of Elder William S. Cole (p. 166) is an excellent example of the detailed notice that can appear for pastors, while the note for Elder Brenton (p. 165) is the opposite.

11. L. C. Rudolph and Judith E. Endelman, *Religion in Indiana: A Guide to Historical Resources* (Bloomington: Indiana University Press, 1986).

12. Web site of The Archives of the Episcopal Church, www.episcopalarchives.org/religious_archives.html (accessed March 15, 2006).

[The author and the editors of Finding Indiana Ancestors *thank genealogical researcher, author, and lecturer Lloyd Hosman, chair of the Indiana Historical Society's Family History Publications Advisory Board, 1999–2006, for reviewing and commenting on an initial draft of this chapter.]*

Courthouse Records

PATRICIA K. JOHNSON

•

When researching your family lines, you must document your information. Documentation can be from either one or more primary sources or at least two secondary sources, but primary sources should be used if at all possible. A primary source is one that was recorded at the time an event took place. This information would be given by an individual with firsthand knowledge of the event, in other words, a person who witnessed the event. Courthouses are one of the best places to find primary sources. In most cases, these records contain information recorded at the time of the event by a person directly involved in that event. For this reason, researching courthouses is a very important part of compiling your family history.

In conducting courthouse research, it is important to know what county your ancestor was in at the time of the event you are researching. As Indiana became more populous, new counties were formed from the old counties. Your ancestor may have lived in the same location but may have lived in different counties as new ones were formed from existing counties and county lines shifted. Before you start your search, determine if the current county was in existence at the time your ancestor was in

that area. If the county did not exist, then determine what county or counties it was formed from. Several books will give you this information, including *The Handybook for Genealogists*, edited by George B. Everton, and *Ancestry's Red Book*, edited by Alice Eichholz.[1]

Indiana became a state on December 11, 1816, with a population of approximately 147,000.[2] At this time there were thirteen counties: Wayne, Franklin, Dearborn, Switzerland, Jefferson, Clark, Washington, Harrison, Knox, Gibson, Posey, Warrick, and Perry.[3] By 1830 there were sixty-three counties, and by 1845 all ninety-two counties of Indiana were formed. One county, Richardville, was renamed Howard in 1846.[4] As new counties were formed, new courthouses were built, and, of course, the collections of records from the new counties were begun (in most cases, previous records were kept at the old courthouses). You can now see how an ancestor's records might be found in several county courthouses even though your ancestor never moved.

Before going to the courthouse for research, do your homework. You will accomplish more in a shorter time, and your time at the courthouse will be better spent. You should check for hours and days the

Marion County Courthouse, 1920 (W. H. Bass Company Collections, P 0130, 69902-F, IHS)

courthouse is open. This information can be found by calling the courthouse before you visit. Telephone numbers for the courthouses can be found in *The Handybook for Genealogists.*[5]

A visit to the library in the town where the courthouse is located would also be beneficial before beginning your courthouse research. Many genealogical and historical societies as well as other groups have copied and/or indexed the records from the local courthouses. You may also want to go to the genealogical Web site for the county in which the courthouse is located.[6] Many counties have indexes of various courthouse records on their Web pages. Use this information for guidance in where to search for primary records. A couple of examples are Jefferson County marriages, 1850 to 1873, which gives the names of the grooms and brides and the dates of marriage, and Kosciusko County divorces, 1908 to 1933, which lists plaintiffs, defendants, dates, and box and case numbers. However, please remember that what you find in a compiled book or on the Internet is not considered a primary source. Additionally, a date, place, or name spelling may have been transcribed incorrectly. Use this information as a *guide* only for locating your ancestor's original records more quickly.

Your search will go faster if you know the location of your ancestor's information in the courthouse before you visit it. Be aware that the location of court records may differ in the state's ninety-two counties. Also, courthouses are becoming overcrowded, and many counties now store their records off-site or at inaccessible locations. You may have to give some courthouses several days notice before you arrive so these records can be retrieved. In any case, if you are not sure of the location of the records you are searching, do not hesitate to ask any of the courthouse employees.

Most records found in the courthouse are considered public records. However, some are not. The researcher must respect those records that are not public and accept the fact that the records cannot be searched. Some of the records considered confidential are for adoptions, cases involving juveniles, grand jury proceedings, paternity records, most records that pertain to medical or mental health, and wardships.[7] You may want to call ahead and confirm that the records you are looking for are available. Always show respect for the courthouse employees. Be aware that they have their regular jobs to perform and may be extremely busy at the time you arrive. If so, see if they would prefer you to come back later in the day or the next day. Obey any rules that they may have (use pencils only; look at one box of records at a time; and so forth). Before using a camera, always ask for permission. Do not remove any records from the courthouse. Ask if you can make copies or if copies can be made for you.

If you are told that the records do not exist or that the courthouse burned, check with others in the courthouse, library, or local historical and genealogical societies. Sometimes courthouses did have fires; however, many times only a few records were involved. Some employees may say the records do not exist because they do not have time to retrieve them or they are not aware they are available elsewhere. The county courthouses known to have lost records due to a natural catastrophe are listed in Willard Heiss's essay "Courthouse Catastrophes in Indiana."[8]

Health Department—Births and Deaths

Some county health departments are located in the county courthouses; however, many are located in annexes, separate buildings, or even in a town other than the county seat (for example, the Elkhart County Courthouse is located in Goshen, while the health department is located in Elkhart). Both birth and death certificates are located in the health department. Registration of birth and death certificates was made mandatory beginning in 1882. However, many counties did not record all births and deaths until 1885 or later. Therefore, it is possible that you may not be able to locate a birth or death certificate

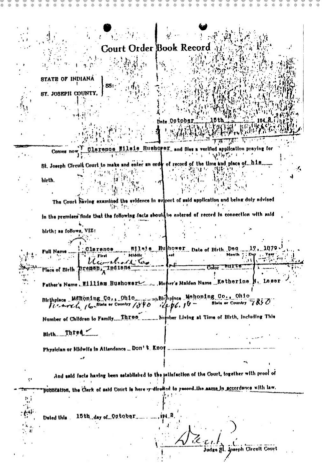

Delayed birth certificate for Clarence Wilsie Hushower, born December 17, 1879, in Bremen, Marshall County, Indiana, who applied for the certificate on October 15, 1942, in St. Joseph County, Indiana

during the early years of mandatory recording. Prior to October 1907 all birth certificates were filed at the local level. After October 1907 birth certificates were also filed at the Indiana State Department of Health. Death certificates were filed locally only before 1900 and filed at the state level also after 1900.[9]

In order to provide access to a birth certificate, most health departments will ask for proof of relationship due to the federal Privacy Act. If you cannot show a relationship, you may not be able to obtain the certificate. The certificates issued are certified copies. However, some health departments will give you an uncertified copy at a lower rate if you specify that it is for genealogical purposes. Several county health departments, such as Elkhart County, actually have genealogists volunteering to search for birth certificates.

When requesting a birth certificate, ask for a *copy of the original certificate for genealogical purposes.* The original birth certificate will often give parents' names, how many children the mother had and how many were still living, addresses, and occupations. If you do not request a full copy of the birth certificate for genealogical purposes, you most likely will get a newly typed certificate with only the individual's name and birth date. Information on the original birth certificate can be considered primary for the parents' names and the child's information.

When requesting a death certificate, the same holds true. Ask for a copy of the original certificate for genealogical purposes. Not all the information on a death certificate can be considered primary. The name of the deceased, the death date, and the name of the nearest kin are primary. The deceased's birth date and location may be incorrect and therefore not considered primary proof (the person reporting the information was not present at the deceased's birth). Also, the names of the deceased's parents may not be correct for the same reason.

If you had an ancestor who was born at the end of the nineteenth century or early in the twentieth century, and you are unable to locate the ancestor's birth record, the ancestor may have filed for a delayed birth certificate. Many older individuals who did not have birth certificates, but who retired under the 1936 Social Security Act, applied for what was called a "delayed birth certificate."[10] These individuals brought to the courts documented papers attesting to their birth dates. When an individual's birth date was proven satisfactorily, he or she was given the certificate. Keep in mind that records regarding delayed birth certificates will be found in the county and state the individual was living in at the time of application, not necessarily in the county or state in which he or she was born. Most of these applications were filed in the late 1940s and 1950s. Delayed birth records can be found in court order books in the year the individual filed the application. Many individuals needed a birth certificate to apply for Social Security, so look in the time frame when they would have turned sixty-five. Several Indiana counties have indexed these records in published format or on their Web site.

Marriage Records

Marriage records are normally found in the clerk's office. An index is usually found in each marriage record book. The Works Progress Administration (WPA) indexed marriages up to 1920 in sixty-eight of the ninety-two counties in Indiana. Most courthouses have copies of these books located with the marriage records. However, researchers must remember spellings and dates were transcribed and, therefore, may have errors. Use these books as guides only. A law making marriage licenses mandatory occurred in 1800.[11] Therefore, marriages in all Indiana counties were recorded from the time of the formation of the county. In 1905 a new Indiana law provided for a book in the clerk's office called "application for marriage license."[12] These applications give more information, including names of the parents with mother's maiden name, age, and the number of previous marriages. When looking at the marriage records, it must be noted that three different dates are listed. Usually

One-half of the application for a marriage license for Frank J. Finch and Lena Keene, dated June 26, 1905, in Elkhart County, Indiana the first date is the date for the marriage license application. The other two dates are the date the couple was "united in marriage" and the date the marriage license was filed at the courthouse. Make sure you copy the "united in marriage date." These last two dates may be in different orders.

Probate Records and Wills

Probate records and wills are usually found in the circuit court records. These records were begun at the formation of the county. Most counties have a general index (by name of the deceased) to the probate records (wills and estates). This index will give the book and page number for the various records involved in the probate procedure. Wills may name children and grandchildren. A husband's will may give his wife's name, but many times just states "my wife." A will normally specifies the distribution of the real and personal property. A will is considered a primary source for proving the ancestry of a child. If a person dies without a will and has property (died intestate), he or she will be listed in the probate record book, which may or may not be indexed.

It is important to look at all the records in a probate packet. Many of the small items can provide clues to an individual's lifestyle. An inventory of the estate may include numbers of cups and bowls, coverlets, beds, jars of canned vegetables, family bibles, tobacco, alcohol, cows, and so on. If the estate went to auction, there is usually a list that will include who bought each item and the price each buyer paid. You may also find a record of the purchase of a gravestone and the location of the stone's placement. If burial is in a different location from where the person died, you may find money allocated to ship the corpse to that location.

Guardianship Records

Guardianship records are found in the probate court, most likely in the guardian's docket. The records will show who was appointed guardian for minor children and incompetent or aged individuals. Minor children may have had a guardian appointed when they received an inheritance from a parent or relative. Be aware that the term "orphan" does not necessarily

mean that both of a child's parents were deceased; in some cases the term was used when only one parent was deceased (usually the father).[13]

Divorce Records

Divorce records are found in the court clerk's office. Divorces can be found by looking in the general index books (which also include civil cases, petitions for name changes, back taxes, and other miscellaneous items) for parties (plaintiffs and defendants) who have the same last name. The index will give the order book number and page number. In turn, the order book will give the jacket number and location of the actual papers. The papers most likely will include the date and location of the marriage, date separated, and reason for divorce. The date the divorce was granted and the terms of the divorce will also be listed.

Naturalization Records

Naturalization records can be found in a number of locations. Many are found in various nonindexed court order books (circuit, common pleas, probate, and superior). In more recent times, the court may have a book strictly for naturalization papers. Traditionally, several steps were taken for naturalization. First, an individual declared his or her intention to become a citizen. Then after an allotted period (which varied depending on the naturalization rules at the time), an individual filed his or her petition to become a citizen, and finally, he or she received citizenship. Keep in mind that each of the steps could have taken place in a different state or county. Consider this example from the Stark County, Ohio, Court of Common Pleas: Peter Fisher was born in Bavaria and immigrated to the United States in May 1837, arriving in New York in June 1837. In 1840 he was forty-eight years old and a farmer in Stark County, Ohio. On April 20, 1840, Fisher filed his intention to become a citizen of the United States of America. He later moved to Indiana, and on August 14, 1848, brought his declaration of intent to Marshall County, Indiana, Probate Court and filed a petition to become a citizen. Fisher became a U.S. citizen on September 7, 1848.[14]

In the early 1940s the WPA set out to compile a list of all naturalization records (that is, *notations* regarding naturalization proceedings) found in court order books in Indiana prior to 1906. In 1981 the Family History Section of the Indiana Historical Society (IHS) published a book of these records titled *An Index to Indiana Naturalization Records Found in Various Order Books of the Ninety-Two Local Courts Prior to 1907.* However, each county in Indiana filed these records differently, and few counties were consistent in their filings. Therefore, many of these records were not listed in the 1940s and, thus, cannot be found in the IHS book.[15]

In the 1980s the Indiana Supreme Court ruled that the Indiana State Archives was to be the official repository for all naturalization records prior to 1951. The exceptions to this rule were the notations involving the naturalization process documented in the court order books previously mentioned. The Friends of the Indiana State Archives, a volunteer group, is indexing the naturalization *documents* sent to the Archives by the majority of Indiana's counties (forms, certificates, and bound naturalization books). These indexes are published on the Archives' Web site at www.in.gov/icpr/archives/. Copies of the documents indexed here may be obtained by contacting the Archives.[16]

Land Records

Land records may be one of the least used records found in the courthouse. However, they are very important in determining where your ancestors lived and, in some cases, when they moved to and from an area or when they died.

Deed records were some of the first items recorded by the courts. According to author Wade Hone, "More than 85% of our ancestors who lived before 1900 owned land at one time or other."[17] In Indiana these records are found in the recorder's office. To find a deed, you must first use the deed index. The index is by grantor (seller) and grantee (buyer). The two indexes are located in the same book. The grantor index is on one side of the page, and the grantee index is on the other side. These indexes give the names of the grantor and the grantee, a descrip-

NAMES OF ARTICLES	AMOUNT SOLD FOR	TO WHOM SOLD
3 bu. potatoes @40¢	$ 1.20	Harrison Horner
	.40	Jonas Yoder
Hoe	.25	Everett Corl
Shovel	.60	Jonas Yoder
Mattock	.85	Frank Smith
Buck Saw	1.00	Jesse Keyser
Wheelbarrow	.10	Charles Jeandervin
Wash basin	.10	Lowell Fredericks
Potatoes	.75	L. Wolfe
Cabinet	6.00	Eli Berkholder
Cupboard	1.30	Mr. Farmwald
Cook stove	4.00	Eli Berkholder
Cupboard	.75	Oliver Ringle
Sink	.10	Eli Berkholder
Slaw Cutter	.20	H. H. Feldman
Coal	10.50	Eli Berkholder
Carpet	2.50	Jonas Yoder
Carpet	.80	Harry Kling
Can of pop-corn	.10	
Comfort	3.50	Troxel
German Bible	10.00	Carpenter
Comfort	2.50	O. Warburger
"	2.50	Elwood
"	2.75	Heltzel
Picture	$ .75	William Petcher
Chair	5.00	Walter Schlosser
Couch	3.50	Wood
Melodian	20.00	William Petcher
Music Box	13.00	Troxel
Piano	55.00	Welcome Cuppp
Organ	1.00	F. E. Powlby
Clock	2.85	Hatfield
Box of Mdse;	2.00	Anna Ditty
Stove	1.00	Florence Kline
Rags & Paper	6.82	Silberman Bros.

Total amount of Sales — — $910.37

This bill of sale for the estate of Catherine Hushower of Marshall County, Indiana, lists articles sold, the amount each item sold for, and the name of the person who bought each item.

tion of the property and its cost, and the location of the record in the deed books. Indexes are alphabetical (by first letter of the surname only) but recorded by the date the transaction was registered. Therefore, you need to search all the pages in the section of the index with the first letter of the name being searched.

Deed records can be instrumental in determining when your ancestors came to the area and, in some cases, where they came from. Many times when a person was going to move, he or she would buy the new property before actually moving into the area. Therefore, the deed may very well list the location where the individual currently lived (Example: Grantee, John Jones of Mahoning County, Ohio). By finding the original land records for all the land an ancestor ever owned and mapping the land descriptions (section, township, range, and acreage) across space and time, you may get a more complete picture of your ancestor's life.

Land deeds vary in their content. Some give very little information while others give much more than one would ever expect. A deed recorded March 5, 1915, in Elkhart County for John B. Miller and heirs (grantors) and Ira E. Miller (grantee) is a good example. The indenture mentions that John B. Miller is the surviving husband of Barbara Miller. It also names all their children and where they were living: James Albert Miller and wife Daisy Miller; Harvey A. Miller and wife Eva Miller; Idella Myers and husband W. H. Myers; Maude Fribley and husband Harry Fribley, all of Elkhart County; Ethel Miller, guardian for Gerald Miller, a widow and only heirs of Chris Miller, deceased; John B. Miller by power of attorney for Louis F. Miller and wife Jessie Miller of Los Angeles, California.[18]

With diligent searching in land records, a person may be able to locate the formation of a cemetery (private, church, or township). You will need to know the approximate time of the cemetery's formation and the name of the person who donated or sold the property, or the group who purchased the land (township, city, or church).

Also to be found in the recorder's office are the Miscellaneous Records books. These books began as early as 1850 but are different for each county. They contain numerous varied items such as incorporation papers, affidavits, bills of sale, leases, mortgage assignments, powers of attorney, and more.[19]

Tax Records

Tax records can be very useful. Nevertheless, many counties disposed of them to conserve space. If your county has a county archives, the tax records may have been moved to that location.

Pre-1900 tax records show the taxes paid for various items such as schools, roads, county, state, and polls. The records also give the description and acreage of property owned. Polls can be quite interesting as they indicate those men who were considered eligible to vote. When he reached the age of twenty-one, a man was eligible to vote and to pay a poll tax, but a man was exempt from paying poll tax when he obtained a certain age (usually about fifty). This age varied as new state laws were enacted, so, you will need to check the laws for the time you are researching. In 1826 a law was passed in Indiana that exempted anyone who served in the Revolutionary War from paying poll tax and tax on personal property. However, keep in mind that some of these veterans may have been overlooked.[20]

If the Indiana county you are researching has any of the 1889, 1890, or 1891 tax lists, they can be used to fill in gaps in your ancestors' family history caused by the destruction of the 1890 census. Tax lists may also help to distinguish individual men with common names who were living in the same area.

Military Records

If your ancestor served in any capacity in the military, he or she would have filed for a discharge in the county where he or she lived at the time of the discharge. These papers are found in the county recorder's office.

In 1886 and 1894 enrollments were taken of deceased Civil War soldiers and their widows and orphans.[21] These records show the name of the deceased soldier, his rank, company, regiment, number of children under sixteen years of age, and a description of injuries received in the service, among other items. The enrollments may or may not be located in the recorder's office. For example, in Elkhart County these records are found in the County Microfilm Department located in a separate building from the courthouse.

Summary

Courthouses are excellent places to find primary sources to document your ancestors. When researching in a courthouse, do not stop when you find an answer to your immediate question. Continue to look at all the information regarding that event. You may find something you do not think is important at the time, but when you "flesh out" the family later, you may find it is very important.

If at all possible, photocopy the original record (be sure to get permission). Always document information about the source and its location on the copy of the source. If you cannot photocopy the record, abstract it on a preprinted form, available from a number of sources, or make your own form before you arrive at the courthouse.

Courthouses have a wealth of information on your ancestors. However, it will require time to locate the information you are looking for. Come prepared and enjoy researching your ancestors in the Indiana courthouses.[22]

———————•———————

1. George B. Everton, ed., *The Handybook for Genealogists: United States of America,* 8th ed. (Logan, UT: Everton Publishers, 1991), 70–78; Alice Eichholz, ed., *Ancestry's Red Book: American State, County and Town Sources* (Salt Lake City: Ancestry Publishing, 1989), 177–83.

2. Eichholz, *Ancestry's Red Book,* 171.

3. *History of Elkhart County, Indiana* (Chicago: Chas. C. Chapman and Co., 1881), 118.

4. Eichholz, *Ancestry's Red Book,* 179, 182.

5. Everton, *The Handybook for Genealogists,* 74–78.

6. You can find genealogical information on Indiana counties on the INGenWeb Project Web site at http://ingenweb.net/ (accessed March 29, 2006). Click on the county you will be searching. Click on the local genealogical society, historical society, or the topic you are interested in.

7. For more information about court documents that are considered confidential and those available to the public, visit the Web site for the Indiana Supreme Court Division of State Court Administration at www.in.gov/judiciary/admin/ (accessed March 29, 2006) and click on "Public Access to Court Records Handbook."

8. Willard Heiss, "Courthouse Catastrophes in Indiana," in *Working in the Vineyards of Genealogy* (Indianapolis: Indiana Historical Society, 1993), 107.

9. Eichholz, *Ancestry's Red Book,* 172.

10. Christine Rose, *Courthouse Research for Family Historians: Your Guide to Genealogical Treasures* (San Jose: CR Publications, 2004), 149.

11. Eichholz, *Ancestry's Red Book,* 172.

12. Heiss, "Courthouse Catastrophes in Indiana," 112.

13. Rose, *Courthouse Research for Family Historians,* 96–97.

14. Marshall County, Indiana, Probate Book A, p. 396.

15. In 2001 the Indiana Historical Society reprinted the index with a modified title, *An Index to Naturalization Records in Pre-1907 Order Books of Indiana County Courts.*

16. To search the Indiana State Archives database for naturalization records, go to the Archives' Web site; click on "Databases" and then click on "Naturalization Records Databases." The counties that are covered can be seen by clicking on the pull-down menu. Enter the first name and last name (required) and submit.

17. E. Wade Hone, *Land and Property Research in the United States* (Salt Lake City: Ancestry, 1997), 192.

18. Elkhart County, Indiana, Deed Book 126, p. 430.

19. Heiss, "Courthouse Catastrophes in Indiana," 116.

20. Arlene Eakle and Johni Cerny, eds., *The Source: A Guidebook of American Genealogy* (Salt Lake City: Ancestry Publishing, 1984), 235.

21. There was a Civil War enrollment of deceased soldiers taken in 1890, but half of these records were destroyed by fire, including those for Indiana.

22. See also John J. Newman, *Research in Indiana Courthouses: Judicial and Other Records* (Indianapolis: Indiana Historical Society, 1990).

Inventories of County Archives

PATRICIA SHIRES ORR

•

During the Great Depression the Historical Records Survey, a program of the Works Progress Administration (WPA), undertook the task of inventorying every public record—federal, state, county, and municipal—found in offices outside the agencies of the federal government in Washington, DC.[1] The centerpiece of this project was the inventories of county archives. Before World War II brought an end to the WPA and its programs, inventories were published for twenty-one Indiana counties. These inventories and draft inventories for sixty-nine other Indiana counties are a valuable resource for genealogical and historical research.

BACKGROUND OF THE HISTORICAL RECORDS SURVEY

The Beginning

Early histories of America focused on major military and political events and the lives of prominent people involved in those events. At the end of the 1800s historians began to look at ordinary men and women and their roles in shaping the country. Local government records were fundamental to this research. The increasing use of these records heightened awareness of their importance to American culture and raised

concerns about their condition, accessibility, and preservation. During the early years of the Depression a few states, with grants from federal relief agencies, employed professional and clerical workers to sort, index, and transcribe records. These efforts received a positive response from state and local officials and historians and fostered the belief that such programs should be extended to all states. One suggestion put forth by a committee of university and government historians was to conduct a nationwide survey of all local, public archives. This suggestion caught the attention of Harry Hopkins, the first administrator of the WPA, who was looking for opportunities to create jobs for unemployed, white-collar workers. In the summer of 1935, he hired Luther Evans, a former Princeton University political science professor, to draft plans for the survey.[2]

Evans proved to be an excellent choice for the position. Young and energetic, he drew upon the expertise of interested archivists, historians, and educators to supplement his skills in developing the program and submitted his proposal by late summer. The proposal was to create two projects—one to inventory records in federal offices located in the states and a second to inventory state, county, and other local records. The National Archives became the cosponsor with the WPA of the first project, known as the Survey of Federal Archives.[3] Evans continued to plan the implementation of the second project with financial support from the National Park Service. In November 1935 President Franklin D. Roosevelt approved funds for the inventory of state and local records, titled the Historical Records Survey (HRS), with the WPA as its sole sponsor. The WPA appointed Evans national supervisor of the HRS and placed it under the Federal Writers' Project (FWP). States began to set up HRS offices in January 1936; by May all states and the District of Columbia had initiated projects. Almost from the beginning the relationship between the HRS and the FWP proved incompatible at both the national and state levels, in part because of the inherent differences in the programs—the HRS was to a large extent clerical; the FWP was creative—and in part because of poorly defined lines of authority. Evans asked that the HRS be separated from the FWP; and in October 1936, it became an independent, WPA-sponsored program.[4]

Implementation and Expansion

The HRS concentrated first on producing inventories of county archives (town archives in New England states) with state and municipal records to be addressed afterward. Each inventory was to contain the following:

- The history of the county
- An essay on the county's governmental organization and records system
- An essay on the storage and care of the county's records
- A bibliography of the county's records, organized by the department responsible for the record[5]

Evans's objective was to ensure that the inventories were comprehensive, that the information in them was correct, and that they conformed to a nationwide standard in both quality and content. His challenge was to produce the inventories while adhering to the WPA's employment quotas and

requirements: his workforce was made up primarily of unemployed workers with no training in archival work. To overcome this challenge, he devised a hierarchical organization structure with well-defined processes and strict controls at each level and wrote a manual that was used to train workers at all levels. The manual consisted of instructions and master forms. When Evans made changes in procedures, format, or style, he issued supplements to update the manual.[6]

At the top of the organization were Evans and his staff of editors, field supervisors, and assistants in the national office in Washington, DC. The state offices were composed of a director, district supervisors, researchers, writers, and clerical personnel. Field workers were hired in each county to go into the courthouse to collect data about the records on forms and to advise clerks on maintaining their records.[7] More often than not, the workers had to locate, clean, and organize the records before they could fill out their forms. The completed forms were submitted to the state office where the staff wrote drafts of the inventories. These drafts were checked against the records by supervisors, amended as necessary, and forwarded to the national office. There the editors corrected the drafts and returned them for revisions before giving permission to publish the inventories. As a final control, regional and field supervisors performed spot checks of both the fieldwork and the state office operations.[8]

The HRS met the WPA's employment quotas by hiring professionals with relevant backgrounds for upper management positions and unemployed, white-collar workers who could be trained for other positions. State directors and regional and field supervisors were professionals; some were historians, university professors and deans, librarians, and archivists. The district supervisors, writers, editors, and field-workers had more varied backgrounds. In some cases, teachers, business executives, magazine and newspaper editors, ministers, attorneys, and similarly skilled individuals filled these positions.[9]

Although the inventories of local archives remained the priority at both the national and state HRS offices, Evans added several projects at the suggestion of some of his advisers. These included surveying private manuscript collections, church archives, early American imprints, and portraits in public buildings; compiling a union list of newspapers and newspaper indexes; microfilming public records and newspapers; and writing bibliographies of American history and literature. The choice of whether or not to undertake most of these additional projects was left to the states. The HRS also assumed responsibility for the Survey of Federal Archives in 1937.[10]

The End of the WPA

The boost to the economy that resulted from the country's growing involvement in World War II obviated the need for the Depression's relief programs. The Emergency Relief Appropriation (ERA) Act of 1939 prohibited the WPA from sponsoring such

programs and turned the programs over to the states. For a short time thereafter the Library of Congress provided office space and funding for the national HRS staff so it could continue to give editorial support. The HRS was eventually placed under the WPA's Research and Records Section, a part of the Professional and Services Division. Evans resigned in November 1939 to become director of the Division of Legislative Reference at the Library of Congress.[11] Sargent Child, the assistant director, assumed the directorship of the HRS and carried on Evans's work to the extent that reductions in personnel and funding allowed. With the end of the program in sight, Child instructed each state to inventory its unpublished material—the completed forms and drafts in various stages of editing—and to place it in a repository within the state for completion after the war.

On the back of this photograph, found at the NARA, College Park, Maryland, is the following information, "Office staff of HRS." The photo was in an envelope marked, "Indiana."

In January 1942 a presidential order terminated the WPA; by 1943 all state HRS projects had been phased out.[12]

Most HRS projects were unfinished when the program ended. With respect to its central project, inventories were published for only 664 of the 3,066 counties in the country. In 1942 Child and Dorothy P. Holmes prepared *The Check List of Historical Records Survey Publications*, revised in 1943, as a guide to the published material of all HRS projects.[13]

Drafts and other unpublished material "remained in storage where they were frequently neglected, occasionally forgotten, and in some cases even discarded by the agencies that had taken them in." A revival of interest in the HRS during the 1970s prompted the Society of American Archivists to undertake an inquiry into the fate of this material and to publish a state-by-state listing of the repositories and their contents, *The WPA Historical Records Survey: A Guide to the Unpublished Inventories, Indexes, and Transcripts.*[14]

THE HRS IN INDIANA

The State Organization

The Indiana HRS office opened February 19, 1936, at 217 North Senate Avenue, Indianapolis, with Samuel J. Kagan as director. Prior to accepting this position, Kagan was superintendent of Public Archives at the Indiana State Library. Because Evans had found his national advisory committee so helpful, he recommended that each state form such a committee. Christopher B. Coleman, director of the Indiana Historical Bureau, served as chairman of Indiana's Committee for the Survey of State and Local Historical Records. In that capacity he provided technical advice and support and acted as a liaison with state agencies. Other committee members were Frank Bates, professor at Indiana University, Bloomington; Lemuel A. Pettenger, president of Ball State Teachers College; R. N. Tirey, president of Indiana State Teachers College; Esther U. McNitt, head of the Indiana Division, Indiana State Library; and Judge Harold C. Phelps, Peru, Indiana. As was the case in many states, Indiana's committee rarely, if ever, met; however, individual members contributed to HRS projects.[15]

While the state HRS followed Evans's organizational structure, Kagan had some discretion in implementing procedures in his office. Edythe Weiner, editor of county archives in the national office, visited the Indiana office on April 27, 1937, and reported, "[T]he editorial set-up . . . appears to be the best I have ever seen."[16] The thirty-two people on Kagan's staff worked in rooms devoted to different functions. As the field-workers' material arrived in the state office, staff in the "checking room" screened the forms for errors and omissions, returning them to the field-workers for corrections and additions as needed. Kagan observed, "Forms have to be returned two, three, and even four times for information which has been omitted."[17] Once a county's forms were complete, they were sent to the "classifying room," where the record forms were separated from the history and building notes and arranged in a prescribed order. This group also supplied the table of contents and index. From the history and building notes, the "research division" produced a county history, essays on housing and governmental organization, and an organizational chart. The forms went to the writers in "condensing," who turned the comments into "a complete, concise picture of the records in bibliographical form." The finished manuscript was proofread, typed, and proofread again. These steps resulted in the first draft that was sent to the editors in Washington for review.[18]

After the national office had approved an inventory for publication, the state office solicited funds to pay for the printing. HRS budgets allowed only for mimeographing or multigraphing the inventories. Kagan and Governor Clifford Townsend wrote the commissioners in each county asking that they contribute a portion of the costs so that their county's inventory could be professionally printed. As an increasing number of inventories reached the publication stage and funds were not forthcoming from most counties, Kagan acquired a multigraph machine and established an in-house operation to reduce costs.[19]

Kagan feared from the start of the program that time and funding would run out before work was completed. He requested that his staff write preliminary drafts of all county inventories soon after the initial fieldwork was concluded. By January 1938 the drafts had been written and typed in triplicate with one copy deposited in the Indiana State Library for safekeeping and the other two used as working drafts in the state office and the field.[20]

With the passage of the ERA Act in 1939 and its mandated transferal of responsibility for WPA programs to the states, the Indiana Historical Bureau became the sponsor for the state's HRS and provided financial, as well as technical, support. Kagan resigned as state director the following year. Roger A. Hurst assumed the position and managed the HRS for the program's waning years.[21]

Indiana's County Inventories

When the HRS ended in Indiana, it had published twenty-one county inventories—five were professionally printed, and sixteen were multigraphed.[22] The inventories were assigned numbers corresponding to the county's position in an alphabetical listing. Their standardized title is *Inventory of the County Archives of Indiana*, followed by the county number, county name, and the county seat in parentheses. The table below lists the published inventories with some descriptive information.

Draft inventories, completed for all counties except Hancock and Wayne, were deposited in the State Archives at the Indiana State Library. The Archives, now a part of the Indiana Commission on Public Records, continues to be the repository for all of Indiana's unpublished HRS material.

Availability of the Inventories

Copies of Indiana's published inventories were distributed within the state and sent to several organizations outside the state. Each public office in a county received a copy of its inventory to aid personnel in identifying and locating records; each county's libraries, schools, and historical societies received copies for use by the public. Eighty libraries across

No.	County (County Seat)	Pub. Date	Length[23]	Pub. Method	No. Published
2	Allen (Fort Wayne)	1939	379 pages	Multigraph	500
6	Boone (Lebanon)	1937	143 pages	Print	300
11	Clay (Brazil)	1939	404 pages	Multigraph	500
18	Delaware (Muncie)	1940	386 pages	Multigraph	500
25	Fulton (Rochester)	1942	391 pages	Multigraph	400
28	Greene (Bloomfield)	1939	500 pages	Multigraph	500
34	Howard (Kokomo)	1939	152 pages	Print	200
38	Jay (Portland)	1940	399 pages	Multigraph	500
46	La Porte (La Porte)	1939	189 pages	Print	500
49	Marion (Indianapolis)	1938	219 pages	Print	500
50	Marshall (Plymouth)	1941	465 pages	Multigraph	450
53	Monroe (Bloomington)	1940	433 pages	Multigraph	500
55	Morgan (Martinsville)	1941	436 pages	Multigraph	500
65	Posey (Mount Vernon)	1940	378 pages	Multigraph	500
71	St. Joseph (South Bend)	1939	248 pages	Print	300
73	Shelby (Shelbyville)	1940	415 pages	Multigraph	500
79	Tippecanoe (Lafayette)	1941	516 pages	Multigraph	500
80	Tipton (Tipton)	1941	404 pages	Multigraph	450
82	Vanderburgh (Evansville)	1939	268 pages	Multigraph	500
87	Warrick (Boonville)	1940	378 pages	Multigraph	500
90	Wells (Bluffton)	1941	431 pages	Multigraph	450

County archive inventories were published for the Indiana counties listed here. (Table by Patricia Shires Orr)

the country, at least one in each state, participated in an exchange program and received a copy of all the states' published inventories. The national HRS office requested copies to place in the Library of Congress, the National Archives, and a few other federal agencies. In addition, copies of some inventories were available for sale.[24]

Because of this wide dissemination, finding copies of the published inventories today is relatively easy. In Indiana most county libraries and historical societies have a copy of their county's inventory and may have copies of those of other counties. In Indianapolis the Indiana State Archives, the Indiana State Library, and the William Henry Smith Memorial Library at the Indiana Historical Society have copies of all published inventories, as does the Fred J. Reynolds Historical Genealogy Department of the Allen County Public Library in Fort Wayne, Indiana. Colleges and universities around the state may have copies in their collections as well. The Family History Library, Salt Lake City, Utah, has microfilmed Indiana's published inventories and loans the microfilm through its local Family History Centers. Finally, a researcher may be able to obtain a specific inventory via interlibrary loan at his or her public library.

Only two organizations have copies of all of Indiana's draft inventories. The originals are at the Indiana State Archives, as discussed above. Several years

NEW COURT HOUSE.
Built in 1893-94. Size 84x120 ft. Height of Tower 170 ft. Cost $143.665.

The Tipton County Courthouse, 1893. Drawing from the *Tipton Advocate*, Sept. 8, 1893. The newspaper was found in the Tipton County Commissioners' Records, Book 2, page 442.

ago that organization microfilmed the collection and encourages the use of the microfilms rather than the originals.[25] The Historical Genealogy Department of the Allen County Public Library has bound photocopies of the draft inventories. While the draft inventories can provide useful information, they did not undergo the rigorous rechecking and editing process to which the published inventories were subjected and are more likely to contain errors and omissions. The remainder of this chapter examines the inventories' contents in greater detail and explores their value to genealogists.

Research Examples from Tipton County's Inventory

The inventories of county archives, published for twenty-one Indiana counties by the HRS, are guides to identifying and locating the county records that are essential to genealogical research. These inventories enable a researcher to determine what records— marriage books, tax lists, deed books, school records, court minutes, and such—were kept in a county

In an envelope marked, "Indiana," found at the NARA, College Park, Maryland, is this photograph. The back side of it states, "La Porte County Courthouse Storage Room No. 1."

during an ancestor's residency and which were extant when the inventories were written. Because Indiana's county records are retained in the county of origin and only a small portion have been microfilmed or transcribed, most genealogists will visit a county courthouse at some point. The inventories can help in determining when such a trip might be fruitful and can help in preparing for it.

The contents and format of Indiana's inventories reflect a nationwide standard established by Luther Evans, national director of the HRS, which is designed to facilitate collecting data for the inventories and writing and editing them. Some variations occur, but each should include the following sections:

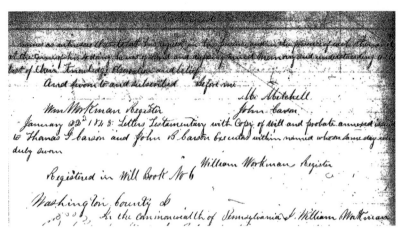

Part of a page from Tipton County Deed Book A, pages 426 to 427, shows that letters testamentary and copies of a will and a probate that were issued to Thomas G. and John B. Carson were registered in Tipton County Will Book 6 on January 22, 1848.

- Foreword
- Preface
- List of County Officials
- Table of Contents with List of Illustrations
- Historical Sketch of the County
- Essay on the Governmental Organization and Records System of the County
- Essay on the Housing, Care, and Accessibility of the Records
- Bibliography
- Abbreviations, Symbols, and Explanatory Notes
- County Offices and Their Records
- Index

The prefatory material is an overview of the national and state HRS organizations. The foreword gives a brief history of the national program while the preface goes into some detail on Indiana's program. Most inventories name the staff in the state office responsible for that inventory; some name county field-workers and specify the date of the original fieldwork (the process of going into the courthouse to collect data on the records) and the date of the final check of that work. According to Tipton County's preface, the fieldwork began in

June 1936 with a final check made in August 1941 prior to the inventory's publication the same year. Mitchell S. Kelly performed the final fieldwork; Charles A. Ferry, an assistant state supervisor, conducted the final check. A photograph of the courthouse serves as the frontispiece.

The county history provides background for a researcher unfamiliar with the county. It was intended as a "sketch," not a definitive history, and drew from published county histories and commissioners' records in an effort "to combine historical accuracy, human interest, and local color, into a vivid narrative."[26] The history may suggest additional avenues of research that do not appear elsewhere in the inventory. For instance, the Tipton County history lists seventeen active and defunct newspapers for the county.

The essay on the county's governmental organization and records system is a history of county government in Indiana and describes changes that occurred as the counties grew. Although Indiana state laws regulate county organization and mandate the records to be kept, differences exist among counties because of size and other factors. This section points out those differences and cites the legal basis for the county's organization and records.

The essay on the housing, care, and accessibility of the records with a floor plan of the courthouse is the least useful portion of the inventory for current research. In most cases the construction of new courthouses and the remodeling of old ones have rendered this information obsolete.

An extensive bibliography concludes the introductory section. It lists the primary and secondary sources used to compile the history and essays.

The listing of the county offices and their records is the essence of the inventories. This section follows a prescribed arrangement with the legislative, executive, and administrative agencies first, followed by the courts and judicial officers, then the taxation and finance functions, and finally the service agencies such as the school, health, and highway departments. The functions of each agency or office are described, followed by the records for which it was responsible. This section comprises almost two-thirds of the Tipton County inventory.

Just as the content and format of the inventories were standardized, so were the compositional elements of the record entries. Explanatory notes and a list of abbreviations and symbols help in deciphering the entries. The following excerpt from the entry for Tipton County's deed records found in the Recorder's office is an example of the content and style of the entries:

72. Deed Record, 1838–. 109 vols. (A–I, K–Z/ 1–84).

Transcripts of deeds for conveyance of titles to real property, showing dates of deed and recording, names of grantor and grantee, entry number, kind of deed, amount of consideration, and location and description of property. Also contains: Sheriff's deed record, 1847–69, entry 75; cemetery deed record, 1849–1924, entry 76; tax title deed record, 1846–64, entry 77 . . . miscellaneous record, 1838–54, entry 95; and apprenticeship record, 1849–52, entry 98. Arr. chron. by date of recording. Indexed alph. by names of grantor and grantee. Also separate index, entry 70. Hdw. 1838–June 15, 1915; typed June 16, 1915–. 586 pp. 18 x 12 x 3.

This excerpt reveals that:

- The deed record is the seventy-second entry in the records section. (The entries are numbered

consecutively throughout the section and are indexed by those numbers rather than by page numbers.)
- Deed records existed from 1838 (some of the deeds predate the county's founding in 1844) to the date of the last field check, 1941, with no loss of records.
- In 1941 Tipton County had 109 deed books.
- The deed books were designated, or titled, by letter originally, later by number.
- There is no volume J. (The comma between the letters "I" and "K" would ordinarily mean that the volume is missing; however, because there is no corresponding skip in the years, the omission simply means that the letter "J" was not used as a volume designation.)
- Sheriff's deeds were kept with these records from 1847 to 1869 and separately after 1869. (A description for those later deed records can be found in entry 75; a similar separation occurred for cemetery deeds, tax title deeds, and others.)
- Recorded deeds appear in the books in chronological order by date of recording.
- Each deed book has an alphabetical index of grantors and grantees.
- There is a master index for all deed books, described in entry 70.
- The deed records were handwritten until June 15, 1915, and typed after that date.
- Each deed book has 586 pages and is 18 in. x 12 in. x 3 in. (The size was recorded in anticipation of later microfilming the books.)

The information in this entry and that in the adjacent deed entries are all that would be necessary to locate the record of most deeds and similar instruments recorded in Tipton County before 1941. Moreover, knowing in advance how the deed books are indexed enables a researcher to estimate the amount of time required for the research.

The inventories are indexed by page and entry number. This can be confusing to the person who does not notice the following on the first page of the index: "Figures in roman type refer to entry numbers;

figures in italics to pages." Indexes are missing from the Fulton, Tipton, and Wells inventories. The absence of the index is an obvious handicap to the user.

In spite of the measures taken to ensure the quality of the inventories, they have defects. In addition to the missing indexes, noted above, anyone who uses the inventories frequently will find other errors, omissions, and weaknesses. The name of the probation officer was left out of the La Porte County inventory.[27] The history section in the Boone County inventory contains a factual error that was corrected in the Marion County inventory.[28] Notwithstanding these problems, the value the inventories add to research far outweighs their defects.

There is one final caveat: The inventories describe records that existed when the inventories were written. In the ensuing years some of these records have been lost or discarded. In most cases their locations have changed. A phone call to the courthouse can verify a record's current status and location. The Indiana State Archives' Web site lists the addresses and telephone and fax numbers of the state's county courthouses at www.in.gov/icpr/archives/family/maillist.html. County Web sites may also provide this information as do several genealogy guides.

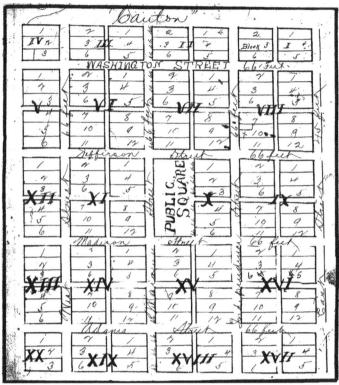

This town layout for Canton was found in Tipton County Deed Book A2, page 533, with a notation, stating, among other things, that Samuel King donated the land for the town.

●

---

1. The name was changed to Work Projects Administration on July 1, 1939. See *United States Government Manual* (Washington, DC: Office of War Information, 1943), 451.

2. Luther H. Evans, "Archives as Materials for the Teaching of History," *Indiana History Bulletin* 15 (1938): 1:139–46; Luther H. Evans, "The Historical Records Survey," in *Public Documents*, ed. A. F. Kuhlman (Chicago: American Library Association, 1936), 209; William F. McDonald, *Federal Relief Administration and the Arts* (Columbus: Ohio State University Press, 1969), 751–59.

3. *United States Government Manual* (Washington, DC: Government Printing Office, 1937), 341.

4. Evans, "The Historical Records Survey," 209–10; S. J. Kagan, "A Statement Concerning the Historical

Records Survey in Indiana" [Dec. 22, 1936], 1–3, Indiana folders, General Project Correspondence (1936–42), Records of the HRS, Records of the WPA, RG 69, NARA, College Park, MD. This typescript gives the year of presidential approval for the HRS as 1932, apparently in error; McDonald, *Federal Relief Administration and the Arts*, 759–65. The Indiana HRS separated amicably from the FWP in August 1936. See S. J. Kagan to Luther H. Evans, Aug. 18, 1836, Indiana folders, General Project Correspondence (1936–42), Records of the HRS, Records of the WPA, RG 69, NARA, College Park, MD.

5. Christopher B. Coleman to Luther H. Evans, Feb. 26, 1936, Indiana folders, General Project Correspondence (1936–42), Records of the HRS, Records of the WPA, RG 69, NARA, College Park, MD; Sargent B. Child, "Status and Plans for Completion of the Inventories of the Historical Records Survey," in *Archives and Libraries*, ed. A. F. Kuhlman (Chicago: American Library Association, 1940), 14; Luther H. Evans, "The Local Archives Program of the WPA Historical Records Survey," in *Public Documents*

with *Archives and Libraries*, ed. A. F. Kuhlman (Chicago: American Library Association, 1938), 289–93.

6. A finalized version of Evans's manual was published in 1941 as *Instructions for the Preparation of Inventories of Public Records by Historical Records Survey Projects* and has been used in archival courses by both the National Archives and Records Administration and universities. Evans, "The Historical Records Survey," 212; Luther H. Evans, "The Historical Records Survey: A Statement on Its Program and Accomplishments Presented to the Sub-Committee of the Senate Committee on Education and Labor, in Connection with the Bill to Create a Permanent Bureau of Fine Arts, March 1, 1938, by Luther H. Evans, National Director" (Washington, DC: WPA, 1938), 5, 13–14, Indiana State Archives; Kagan to Evans, Aug. 18, 1936; McDonald, *Federal Relief Administration and the Arts*, 793–96.

7. For forms and instructions used by field-workers in Indiana, see Form 12–13, rev., and "Instructions for Preparing Form 12–13, rev.," box 1, L1713, HRS, Indiana State Archives; "Instructions to Field Workers for Briefing Historical and Legal Material in County Archives" and "Instructions for Collecting and Preparing Material for the Housing Essay of the Inventory to the County Archives of Indiana" (Indianapolis: The HRS of Indiana, 1938). The last two documents are in the collection of the Indiana State Library, Indianapolis, Indiana.

8. Evans, "The Historical Records Survey: A Statement . . . by . . . Evans, National Director," 4–5, 9–10; McDonald, *Federal Relief Administration and the Arts*, 770–81, 795–96. For examples of the Washington office's editorial work, see corrected drafts in Indiana folders, Editorial Correspondence (1936–42), Records of the HRS, Records of the WPA, RG 69, NARA, College Park, MD; Kagan, "A Statement Concerning the Historical Records Survey in Indiana."

9. Evans, "The Historical Records Survey: A Statement . . . by . . . Evans, National Director," 13; William R. Hogan, "The Historical Records Survey: An Outside View" (Paper presented at the annual meeting of the Society of American Archivists, Annapolis, MD, Oct. 13, 1939), 13–14; McDonald, *Federal Relief Administration and the Arts*, 768–70, 774–82.

10. Luther H. Evans, "Next Steps in the Improvement of Local Archives," in *Public Documents with Archives and Libraries*, ed. A. F. Kuhlman (Chicago: American Library Association, 1937), 276–79; Evans, "The Historical Records Survey: A Statement . . . by . . . Evans, National Director," 10–13; Herbert A. Kellar, "An Appraisal of the Historical Records Survey," in *Archives and Libraries*, ed. A. F. Kuhlman (Chicago: American Library Association, 1940), 44–45; McDonald, *Federal Relief Administration and the Arts*, 792–93, 802–27; [S. J. Kagan], "Summary Report of the Procedure and Operation of the Historical Records Survey in Indiana," Oct. 1938, [1], Indiana folders, General Project Correspondence (1936–42), Records of the HRS, Records of the WPA, RG 69, NARA, College Park, MD.

11. Evans served as Librarian of Congress from 1945 to 1953 and as Director General of the United Nations Educational, Scientific and Cultural Organization (UNESCO) from 1953 to 1958 (Verner W. Clapp, "Luther H. Evans," *Library Journal* 90 [1965]: 15:3,388, 3,390–91).

12. A. F. Kuhlman, "Introduction," in *Archives and Libraries*, ed. A. F. Kuhlman (Chicago: American Library Association, 1940), 7–8; Child, "Status and Plans for Completion of the Inventories of the Historical Records Survey," 13–16; Kellar, "An Appraisal of the Historical Records Survey," 49; McDonald, *Federal Relief Administration and the Arts*, 765, 786–89.

13. McDonald, *Federal Relief Administration and the Arts*, 800; Sargent B. Child and Dorothy P. Holmes, comp., *Check List of Historical Records Survey Publications: Bibliography of Research Projects Reports*, WPA Technical Series, Research and Records Bibliography No. 7, rev. Apr. 1943 (Baltimore: Genealogical Publishing, 1969).

14. Loretta L. Hefner, ed., "Introduction," *The WPA Historical Records Survey: A Guide to the Unpublished Inventories, Indexes, and Transcripts* (Chicago: The Society of American Archivists, 1980), 1.

15. S. J. Kagan to Joseph Gaer, Mar. 10, 1936, Indiana folders, General Project Correspondence (1936–42), Records of the HRS, Records of the WPA, RG 69, NARA, College Park, MD; Christopher B. Coleman, "Indiana Archives," *The American Archivist* 1 (1938): 4:205–06; McDonald, *Federal Relief Administration and the Arts*, 766–68; Kagan, "A Statement Concerning the Historical Records Survey in Indiana," 2–3; [Kagan], "Summary Report of the Procedure and Operation of the Histori-

cal Records Survey in Indiana," [1–2]; Coleman to Evans, Feb. 26, 1936; Kagan to Evans, Aug. 18, 1936.

16. Weiner later became assistant to the national director of the HRS and "next to Evans, was most influential in shaping the policies and practices of the Washington Office" (McDonald, *Federal Relief Administration and the Arts*, 770); Weiner to Evans, May 2, 1937, 1, Indiana folders, General Project Correspondence (1936–42), Records of the HRS, Records of the WPA, RG 69, NARA, College Park, MD.

17. Kagan, "A Statement Concerning the Historical Records Survey in Indiana," 10.

18. This description of the state office is based on Weiner to Evans, May 2, 1937; and Kagan, "A Statement Concerning the Historical Records Survey in Indiana," 5, 9–16. By October 1938 Kagan had made some minor organizational changes. See [Kagan], "Summary Report of the Procedure and Operation of the Historical Records Survey in Indiana," [3–20].

19. [Kagan], "Summary Report of the Procedure and Operation of the Historical Records Survey in Indiana," [20–23]; S. J. Kagan to Luther H. Evans, Aug. 9, 1937, and M. Clifford Townsend to Board of Commissioners, Allen County, Indiana, Apr. 16, 1938, Indiana folders, General Project Correspondence (1936–42), Records of the HRS, Records of the WPA, RG 69, NARA, College Park, MD.

20. [Kagan], "Summary Report of the Procedure and Operation of the Historical Records Survey in Indiana," [1].

21. *Year Book of the State of Indiana for the Year 1940* (Indianapolis: C. E. Pauley, 1940), 99; Mildred Schmitt to Florence Kerr, Feb. 10, 1940, Indiana folders, General Project Correspondence (1936–42), Records of the HRS, Records of the WPA, RG 69, NARA, College Park, MD.

22. Blackford County's inventory, labeled a preliminary edition, can be found in several library collections. It was the only draft inventory to be distributed, but the reason for its distribution is unknown.

23. Excludes prefatory material.

24. Kagan, "A Statement Concerning the Historical Records Survey in Indiana," 2; Evans, "The Historical Records Survey: A Statement . . . by . . . Evans, National Director," 13; Coleman to Evans, Jan. 15, 1938, Indiana folders, General Project Correspondence (1936–42), Records of the HRS, Records of the WPA, RG 69, NARA, College Park, MD.

25. The original draft inventory for Madison County is missing at the Indiana State Archives, but the microfilm copy is available.

26. [Kagan], "Summary Report of the Procedure and Operation of the Historical Records Survey in Indiana," October 1938, [8], Indiana folders, General Project Correspondence (1936–42), Records of the HRS, Records of the WPA, RG 69, NARA, College Park, MD.

27. Elmer H. Wilhelm to John K. Jennings, Aug. 8, 1939, General Project Correspondence (1936–42), Records of the HRS, Records of the WPA, RG 69, NARA, College Park, MD.

28. The history in the Boone County inventory contains a statement about the Treaty of Paris (p. 11) that is incorrect. See Frank E. Ross to Luther H. Evans, June 24, 1938, General Project Correspondence (1936–42), Records of the HRS, Records of the WPA, RG 69, NARA, College Park, MD.

[The author is grateful to Betty Warren, Indiana Genealogical Society; Ruth Dorrel, Indiana Historical Society and Society of Indiana Pioneers (retired); Diane Sharp, Indiana State Library; and Rick Applegate, Indiana State Archives, for sharing their experiences with the inventories; and to Alan January, Indiana State Archives, and Rick Applegate for reading and commenting on this chapter prior to publication.]

Naturalization Records

M. TERESA BAER

———————————•———————————

Becoming a naturalized citizen has traditionally been a multistep process, and before the 1950s candidates could file the necessary paperwork at any court from the federal level down to the local level. Therefore, researchers looking for naturalization records must be aware of the categories of naturalization records and where they are located. Currently in Indiana, naturalization records fall into two categories: "naturalization documents," which are manuscript items such as forms, certificates, and bound naturalization books; and "naturalization proceeding notes in court order books," which are notes about court proceedings jotted down by court clerks.

Naturalization Documents at the Indiana State Archives

Naturalization documents encompass paperwork for four steps of the naturalization process: 1) alien report and registry (few, if any of these documents appear in Indiana records), 2) declarations of intention to become a citizen, 3) petitions for naturalization, and 4) stubs for certificates of naturalization. Clerks of the circuit court in each Indiana county retained these documents until the 1980s when the Indiana Supreme Court mandated that the counties give the paperwork to the Indiana State Archives. To

date nearly two-thirds of Indiana's ninety-two counties have turned these four types of naturalization documents over to the Archives. Therefore, although most of these documents are located at the Archives, some are still held by clerks of various circuit courts.

In an ongoing project since 1997, Archives staff members and volunteers have been indexing the naturalization documents and publishing the indexes on the Archives' Web site: www.in.gov/icpr/archives/. Indexes for the following counties have been available since 2006: Blackford, Dubois, Elkhart, Floyd, Hamilton, Hancock, Henry, Howard, Jefferson, Marshall, Monroe, Morgan, Noble, Owen, Parke, Putnam, Randolph, Switzerland, Union, Wayne, and Whitley counties. The indexes are cross-listed for spelling variations such as for people who Americanized their names or for women who arrived in the United States under one name but subsequently married and were naturalized under the second name.

Information online consists of names of persons being naturalized; their nationalities, ages, and dates of arrival in the United States; and the volumes and page numbers of the naturalization records in which their names are located. If a researcher finds an ancestor here, he or she should contact the Archives online:

TRIPLICATE
(To be given to declarant)

No. 2031

UNITED STATES OF AMERICA

DECLARATION OF INTENTION
(Invalid for all purposes seven years after the date hereof)

United States of America | *In the* District Court

Southern District of Indiana | *of the* United States *at* Indianapolis, Ind.

I, Joe Zuppardo
now residing at 1133 E. Markland Ave., Kokomo, Howard Indiana
occupation Fruit & Veg. dealer, aged 45 years, do declare on oath that my personal description is:
Sex male, color white, complexion dark, color of eyes brown
color of hair dark brown, height 5 feet 2 inches; weight 135 pounds; visible distinctive marks
none
race Italian (South); nationality Italian
I was born in Siculiana, Italy, on May 1, 1895
I am married. The name of my wife or husband is Mary
we were married on Oct. 25, 1935, at Louisville, Ky.; she or he was
born at Siculiana, Italy, on Oct. 14, 1912, entered the United States
at New York, N.Y., on about 1920, for permanent residence therein, and now
resides at Kokomo, Indiana. I have one children, and the name, date and place of birth,
and place of residence of each of said children are as follows:
John Zuppardo, born June 1920 in Siculiana, Italy (child by first wife
now resides in Siculiana, Italy

I have heretofore made a declaration of intention: Number on year 1923
at Kokomo, Indiana Howard County Circuit Court
my last foreign residence was Siculiana, Italy
I emigrated to the United States of America from Naples, Italy
my lawful entry for permanent residence in the United States was at New York, N.Y.
under the name of Giuseppe Zuppardo now Joe Zuppardo, on April 1, 1922
on the vessel SS Tristicka

I will, before being admitted to citizenship, renounce absolutely and forever all allegiance and fidelity to any foreign prince, potentate, state, or sovereignty, of whom or of which I may be at the time of admission a citizen or subject; I am not an anarchist; I am not a polygamist nor a believer in the practice of polygamy; and it is my intention in good faith to become a citizen of the United States of America and to reside permanently therein; and I certify that the photograph affixed to the duplicate and triplicate hereof is a likeness of me.

I swear (affirm) that the statements I have made and the intentions I have expressed in this declaration of intention subscribed by me are true to the best of my knowledge and belief: So help me God.

Joe Zuppardo

Subscribed and sworn to before me in the form of oath shown above in the office of the Clerk of said Court, at Indianapolis, Ind.
this 2nd day of January, anno Domini, 19 41. Certification No. 9 R 26677 the Commissioner of Immigration and Naturalization showing the lawful entry of the declarant for permanent residence on the date stated above, has been received by me. The photograph affixed to the duplicate and triplicate hereof is a likeness of the declarant.

[SEAL]

Joe Zuppardo

U. S. District Court.
Clerk of the
By Deputy Clerk.

Form 2202-L-A
U. S. DEPARTMENT OF LABOR
IMMIGRATION AND NATURALIZATION SERVICE
[See instructions on reverse hereof]

Declaration of Intention for Joe Zuppardo filed in U.S. District Court, Southern District of Indiana, Indianapolis, January 2, 1941. The original is in the Indiana State Archives.

arc@icpr.state.in.us; by phone: 317-591-5222; or by letter: Indiana State Archives, 6440 East 30th Street, Indianapolis, IN 46219. *Ask the Archives staff to pull the Naturalization Records for the given county, stating the volume(s) and page number(s).* The naturalization documents that the Archives possesses may identify wives and children, list dates and ports for departure to and arrival in the United States, and sometimes include photographs. Archives staff will photocopy the material for a nominal fee depending on the number of pages in the record. Photograph reproductions may also be purchased for an extra charge.

Naturalization Proceeding Notes in Order Books at the County Courts

The second category of naturalization records in Indiana encompasses notes regarding naturalization proceedings in order books at the county courts. Each time an immigrant took a step in the naturalization process, a court clerk noted that the proceeding occurred in an order book of the court for which he or she served. The note is called a "filing" or a "pleading" if it states that an immigrant filed a declaration of intention to become a citizen or a petition for naturalization. The note is called a "final order" if it states that a judge ordered that an individual is officially a citizen. Clerks of the circuit courts in Indiana's counties retain the order books that contain these filings/pleadings or final orders. To obtain a copy of one of the notes, a researcher must know which county clerk to contact. The best way to begin this research is to consult the Indiana Historical Society publication *An Index to Naturalization Records in Pre-1907 Order Books of Indiana County Courts* (2001).[1] This book is an index to filings/pleadings and final orders in Indiana from 1906 and before for four types of courts found in both the civil and probate court systems: superior, common pleas, probate, and circuit. It contains an alphabetized list of immigrants. Next to each immigrant's name is the county where the immigrant completed a step of the naturalization process, the type of court order book (superior, common pleas, probate, or circuit) that contains

the filing/pleading or final order, and the volume, page(s), and year(s) where the note is located in the order book. If a researcher finds an ancestor listed in this index, he or she should call or visit the circuit court for the county indicated and *ask the circuit court clerk to pull the civil AND probate order books for the type of court listed (superior, common pleas, probate, or circuit) and state the volume, page(s), and year(s) of the filing/pleading or final order. (To avoid confusion, do not ask for "naturalization records.")*

───────── ● ─────────

1. This book was published in 1981 under the title *An Index to Indiana Naturalization Records Found in Various Order Books of the Ninety-Two Local Courts Prior to 1907*. For further research, see John J. Newman, *American Naturalization Processes and Procedures, 1790–1985* (Indianapolis: Indiana Historical Society, 1985), updated version, *American Naturalization Records, 1790–1990: What They Are and How to Use Them* (Bountiful, UT: Heritage Quest, 1998).

[The author thanks the following people for their generous assistance with this chapter: John Newman, Supreme Court of Indiana; Alan January, Indiana State Archives; Stephen Towne, IUPUI University Library; Kathy Breen and Eric Mundell, Indiana Historical Society; and Ruth Dorrel, George Hanlin, and Judy McMullen, formerly of the Indiana Historical Society.]

Name	County	Court	Vol.	Page	Years
Grear, John	Vigo	Sup[erior]	27	97	
Green, Michael	Faye[tte]	Com. [Pleas]	1	228	[19]00
Greenwood, Josiah	Dear[born]	Pro[bate]	6	436	[18]47–[18]49

Excerpts from *An Index to Naturalization Records in Pre-1907 Order Books of Indiana County Courts*. The entries in this book will lead researchers to notes in court order books in Indiana's county courts.

Land Records

TANYA D. MARSH

‒‒‒‒‒‒‒‒‒‒‒ • ‒‒‒‒‒‒‒‒‒‒‒

The ownership of land is a major part of what America is all about. Many of our immigrant ancestors left crowded industrial cities or picturesque but tiny farms, crossing oceans to seek a new life that promised, in part, the ability to own land. Land records can tell us a great deal about our ancestors, fleshing out migration patterns and locating collateral relatives. They can give us leads for future research by helping us locate abandoned family cemeteries and identify local parishes and schools. Perhaps more important, knowledge of where our ancestors lived can create a sense of place and can help us understand the texture and rhythm of their lives. The documentation of the ownership of land is a matter of state law, and, therefore, research methods vary greatly from state to state. This chapter is designed to provide genealogists researching Hoosier predecessors with the background sufficient to research, obtain, and use land records to learn more about rural and urban ancestors.

Interests in Land

Ownership of land is often compared to a bundle of sticks. Sometimes people own the entire bundle, called "fee simple absolute," and sometimes they own

less. Ownership of land can be broken up into shares, such as when several people own land as "tenants in common" or as "joint tenants" or when spouses own as "tenants by the entirety." Alternatively, land ownership can be broken up temporally, such as when a person has a "life estate" in a farm (ownership until death) subject to another's "future estate" (the right to inherit the farm upon the first person's death). Ownership of land can also be divided into uses, such as when one person holds an "easement" to cross the land of another. Normally, people buy and sell land in "fee simple absolute," the whole bundle of sticks, but when confronting an unusual land record, it may be useful to remember that the only limit to the variety of land ownership arrangements is the human imagination.

Ownership of land can be transferred in one of several ways. Initially, for the vast majority of land in Indiana, the federal government either sold or granted land to various groups of people.[1] Since that initial transfer, privately owned land has been either sold or gifted during the lifetime of the owner or after death. If land was sold or gifted while the owner lived, a document called a "deed" was created that, at a minimum, contains the names of the seller(s) (the "grantor") and the buyer(s) (the "grantee"), and a legal description of the land. The deed may also reflect the grantee's former or the grantor's future address. A deed indicating that land was sold "for love and affection" (referred to in deeds as "consideration"), rather than money, usually indicates a familial relationship between grantor and grantee.

Land may also have been transferred at death either via a written will, which was hopefully probated and filed with the county judge, or via "intestate succession," which means that if a person did not indicate who should own the property after his or her death, the state transferred it to family members in a particular order determined by law. If land was passed after death, either via will or intestate succession, it is likely that no land record may have been generated.

Often, as is the case today, a grantee borrowed funds to pay part or all of the purchase price of the new land, and the lender of those funds required a mortgage on the property as security for the repayment of the loan. From time to time, a landowner may have generated a variety of documents granting different interests in the land. Depending on the nature of the interest granted and the timing, these documents can be helpful in informing us about our ancestors' lives, as well as giving us clues about familial and other relationships.

The Recording System in Indiana

The foundation of the Indiana land records system is the county recorder, an elected official in each county who is charged with maintaining government records, the majority of which pertain to the ownership of real estate.[2] Indiana law requires each recorder to maintain at least three separate sets of books for (1) deeds, (2) mortgages, and (3) miscellaneous records. Each book is required to be indexed separately by the last name of the grantor and grantee, or mortgagor (owner of land) and mortgagee (bank or other lender).[3] Recorders are also required to maintain a single set of books, called the "Entry Book," in which all recorded instruments are indexed in the order of recording.[4] However, the usual caveats apply: Recorders are only human and sometimes

make mistakes; and courthouses occasionally burn down. Although Indiana counties began recording and indexing documents with the assistance of computers in the mid-1980s, recorders in many small and rural counties still exclusively use books to record and index land records. Even recorders who use computers to document and index current records maintain their old books and are generally quite helpful to researchers who wish to use them.

Because land records in Indiana are organized by county, the first step in researching them is figuring out the county where an ancestor lived. It is also very helpful, especially if the county is populous, to narrow the search to a particular time period. For example, suppose that you have an ancestor named Hiram Calvert who was identified in the 1860 census as a resident of Saline County, Missouri, and in the 1850 census as a resident of rural Bartholomew County, Indiana. Beginning with the Bartholomew County Deed Book index for 1860, scan the grantor index for the name "Calvert." Then work backwards through time until you come to the deed by which Hiram Calvert sold his farm in Indiana. Let's say your research reveals that Calvert sold this farm in 1857. Starting with that date, you can scan backwards through the grantee index to the Deed Book for the name "Calvert," searching for the deed by which Hiram Calvert purchased his farm. Imagine that you find a deed in 1843 naming Hiram Calvert as the purchaser of a farm that matches the legal description of the farm sold in 1857. You now know the period of time in which Calvert owned this Indiana farm. Armed with these dates, you can explore the other index books in the recorder's office, searching for mortgages and other records that may give additional information about Calvert's ownership of the farm. If you have no further information about Calvert's origins, you could repeat the process by searching the Deed Book indexes from 1843 backwards to see if he previously owned another farm in the same county.

As discussed above, it may be that no deed can be located because (1) Calvert inherited the land; (2) a deed was executed but never recorded; or (3) Calvert did not own another farm in Indiana. If the search for a deed is unsuccessful, undertake similar searches of the Mortgage Book index and the Miscellaneous Records index. If Calvert inherited the farm or failed to record the deed, he may have still mortgaged it. If he farmed the land under a lease, then perhaps the lease or a memorandum of it was recorded in Miscellaneous Records. If nothing turns up in these searches, it is also a good idea to see if a will was probated or an intestate estate was administered for a "Calvert" before 1870.

Because of the manner in which land records in Indiana are indexed—that is, by the name of the parties to the document—it is easy to scan for surnames and to look for likely collateral relatives. Establishing the geographical relationship between land or homes owned by potential collateral relatives may help in teasing out familial relationships.

Legal Descriptions

Indiana is a federal land state, which means that, for the most part, the initial private ownership of the land that became the state of Indiana was controlled by the federal government. Researchers working in federal land states have a definite advantage—unlike researchers of older states along the eastern seaboard where land was initially handed out by European governments through varying systems. The federal system is predictable and consistent, and the method of describing land makes it easier for laypersons to locate. The legal description of the land conveyed is one of the most important pieces of information on a land record. The way to translate legal land descriptions is discussed below.

Rural Land Records

After the American Revolution, Congress turned to expanding the new nation westward. Surveyors were dispatched to draw imaginary lines in the wilderness to help create an orderly system for distributing land that few had ever seen. The surveyors began with lines called "meridians." Meridians run directly north and south around the Earth, more or less equally spaced, linking the North Pole to the South Pole. Next, they drew a horizontal line called the "base line" around the Earth east to west, intersecting the meridians at right angles. Two meridians run through Indiana—

6	5	4	3	2	1
7	8	9	10	11	12
18	17	16	15	14	13
19	20	21	22	23	24
30	29	28	27	26	25
31	32	33	34	35	36

Figure 1: Guide to the section numbering in a congressional township (Leigh Darbee, "Basic Township Divisions" map in the article "The Township and Range Survey System," *The Hoosier Genealogist* 40 [December 2000]: 4:inside back cover)

the First Principal Meridian and the Second Principal Meridian. They are the starting points for any legal descriptions of land.

Each meridian region is divided into tracts, which are approximately twenty-four miles square. Imaginary lines running north and south, called "ranges," are set six miles apart and help subdivide the tracts into sixteen congressional townships—squares approximately six miles across. Each congressional township is then subdivided into thirty-six sections, each a one-mile square consisting of approximately 640 acres.

Sections are numbered in a uniform but not particularly intuitive manner. It is useful to keep a section numbering guide handy, such as that in figure 1, when looking at land records because farms that appear to be far apart by their legal descriptions may actually adjoin one another. Sections can be subdivided in any number of creative ways, but they are normally divided into squares and rectangles. A sectional breakdown graph can also be very useful when trying to work out legal descriptions.

Note that the word "township" is used to describe two different kinds of land groupings. "Congressional townships" are those described above as part of the meridian grid system. This type of township will be referenced in legal descriptions in the context of the section, township, and range of a particular piece of land. The more commonly understood townships are "civil townships," which are normally made up of one or more congressional townships and are known by a name such as "Washington Township." When census records and other nonland records refer to named townships, they inevitably mean civil townships.

Plat Maps

A "plat map" is a snapshot in time and normally indicates the names of then-current property owners as reflected in the county recorder's records. Plat maps are essential tools for translating legal descriptions and for allowing genealogists to figure out geographical relationships. Plat maps divide each county into civil townships and then into congressional townships and sections. Modern plat maps for fifty-nine of Indiana's ninety-two counties are currently produced by a company called Great Mid-Western Publishing. Ordering information for those plat maps may be found at www.platmaps.com. For other counties, contact the local chambers of commerce, title companies, or county recorder offices for information.

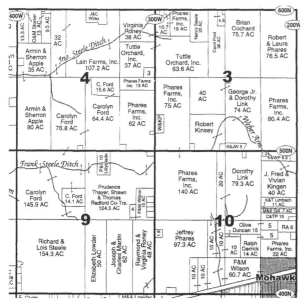

Figure 2: Portion of a plat map showing Sections 3, 4, 9, and 10 in Township 16 North, Range 6 East, Buck Creek Township, Hancock County, Indiana (*Hancock County, Indiana, Plat Directory*, Great Mid-Western Publishing, 2003)

Historic plat maps for most counties may generally be found at the county seat's public library, the Indiana Historical Society, or the Indiana State Library.

A sample legal description reads as follows: "The East half of the Southeast quarter of Section 3, Township 16 North (congressional township), Range 6 East, Buck Creek Township (civil township), Hancock County, Indiana." Each piece of information in this legal description is vital to locating the land. We begin with the name of the county, which tells us which plat map to consult. We then turn to the appropriate page(s) for the named civil township and locate the appropriate congressional township, section, and portion of section. Applying the legal description to the plat map in figure 2, we find that the current owner of the parcel is Phares Farms, and that the farms are located in the northwest corner of County Road 200 West and County Road 500 North in Hancock County.

You may find it useful to doctor modern plat maps for counties where your ancestors lived, erasing the names of the current owners and adding the names of your ancestors and their neighbors for specific periods of time. This may help you to visualize the relationships between people and lead you to discover collateral ancestors and family cemeteries.

Urban Land Records

Locating urban ancestors, depending upon the towns or cities in which they lived, can be much easier than locating rural ancestors. However, it may be less than satisfying to discover that great-great-grandma's house was demolished to make way for an industrial park, and that no local cemeteries, schools, or churches remain to convey a sense of the old neighborhood or to provide further leads for research.

The process for researching land records in the recorder's office is the same regardless of whether the land in question is rural or urban. The main difference is that towns and cities mainly consist of land that has been platted into subdivisions. The modern understanding of a subdivision is a uniform residential development in the suburbs, but the word simply means that a large piece of land was divided into smaller chunks. At the time of subdivision, a docu-

Figure 3: Plat of Milledgeville, Boone County, Indiana. This figure is a plat, as opposed to a plat map, because it does not identify any owners of the lots but simply splits the town into lots. (Boone County, Indiana, recorder's office)

ment called a "plat" (not to be confused with a plat map) should have been filed with the county recorder to identify the name of the new subdivision as well as to assign lot numbers to the new smaller parcels of land as shown in figure 3. Plats also normally document new roads and possibly parks or other common areas. Plats are recorded in a Plat Book (which may or may not be an actual book) in the county recorder's office and are searchable by the names of the subdivisions.

For example, assume that a deed has been located showing that Katherine Sherman sold lot 4 in Newman Oaks Park, a subdivision of the city of Indianapolis, in 1910. Unfortunately, the deed does not indicate the street address of the home. The next step is to ask the recorder for the subdivision plat of Newman Oaks Park, take note of the names of the surrounding streets, and then try to match up the location on a map of Indianapolis from around 1910, if possible, or on a modern map of Indianapolis. Matching our legal description to the subdivision plat reveals an address of 1905 Halloway Street. Figure 4 shows a portion of a 1935 map of Indianapolis that includes Halloway Street.

Many urban areas have undergone tremendous change in the past hundred years. It is not uncommon to see a subdivision replatted into a large parcel for industrial or commercial development. Even if this is

the case, the recorder should have the original plat with a cross-reference to the new plat of the same land.

Another resource available for larger cities in Indiana is the city directory.[5] Depending upon the year, these directories allow researchers to find people both by last name and by street address. In this manner, surnames can be browsed and neighborhoods can be reconstructed. As an added benefit, city directories generally indicate whether a person owns or rents a home and may indicate the name of the person's employer.

Genealogical discovery often reaps intangible rewards—we rejoice when we find new collateral relatives, but most will never mean more to us than names on paper. Land records, plat maps, and city directories can lead us to far more tangible and satisfactory results—we can locate ancestral homes, gaze across the horizons where those homes stood, and briefly walk in our ancestors' shoes.

———————————•———————————

1. Although a description of this process is outside the scope of this chapter, the documents generated by this initial transfer are stored at the National Archives, the Bureau of Land Management, or the Indiana State Library.

2. Indiana Constitution, art. 6, sec. 2 (amended Nov. 4, 1952 and Nov. 6, 1984).

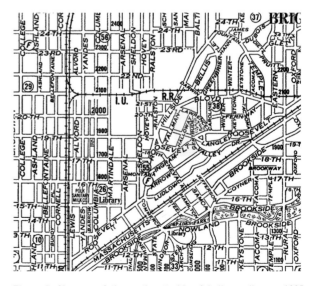

Figure 4: Close-up of the northeast side of Indianapolis, ca. 1935 (George F. Cram and Co., 1935)

3. Indiana Code, tit. 36, art. 2, chap. 11, sec. 12 (1980, 2001).

4. Ibid., sec. 9 (1980).

5. The downtown branch of the Indianapolis–Marion County Public Library maintains a collection of city directories dating back to the mid-1800s for Indianapolis and several other large Indiana cities. The Indiana State Library has a large collection of city and county directories, both current and historical, as does the IHS library.

Other libraries across Indiana may have city directories for smaller communities.

[The editors of Finding Indiana Ancestors *thank Lloyd Hosman who served as an outside reviewer for this chapter. A professional genealogical researcher, author, and lecturer, Hosman served as chair of the Family History Publications Advisory Board from 1999 to 2006.]*

Military Records in Federal and State Repositories

DOUGLAS E. CLANIN

———————————— • ————————————

Genealogists and other researchers who wish to examine military records in an effort to uncover the services of Hoosier residents in peace and war face a bewildering array of sources that may or may not yield positive results. In this brief chapter I will attempt to steer researchers to some key sources and Web sites that will help them get started.

The best single source on how to obtain military records is the book *How to Locate Anyone Who Is or Has Been in the Military: Armed Forces Locator Guide*, written by the late Richard S. Johnson and Debra Johnson Knox and available in the Genealogy Division of the Indiana State Library and in other major libraries. In 1999 MIE Publishing, Spartanburg, South Carolina, published the eighth edition of this book. In addition to chapters on how to locate active duty and retired military personnel, the book also contains chapters on family histories for veterans, military records, and Internet searches. The eighth edition of the Johnson and Knox book also has ten appendixes, which include a list of useful publications, a directory of military and patriotic organizations, lists of state-held military records, and a directory of state resources.

Principal Federal Repositories Containing Military Records

Major military personnel records created after 1912 are located in the National Personnel Records Center (NPRC) in St. Louis, Missouri. The Internet address for this repository is www.archives.gov/st-louis/military-personnel. The NPRC is a significant repository that contains millions of personnel, health, and medical records of discharged and deceased veterans of all military services in the twentieth century following 1912. Researchers need to be aware, however, that most of these records are covered by privacy restrictions. Interested persons need to consult with the staff of the NPRC before they attempt to gain access to the military records stored there.

It is also worth noting that a 1973 fire led to the loss of between sixteen and eighteen million military records and may affect a researcher's inquiry for information. The NPRC has estimated a loss of 80 percent of all U.S. Army records for persons discharged between November 1, 1912, and January 1, 1960. The NPRC has also estimated a 75 percent loss of U.S. Air Force records for individuals discharged between September 25, 1947, and January 1, 1964, whose names follow Hubbard, James E., alphabeti-

Easier Access to Military Records Provided for Veterans and Their Families

"The National Personnel Records Center (NPRC) has provided the following website for veterans to gain access to their DD-214s online: http://vetrecs.archives.gov/. This may be particularly helpful when a veteran needs a copy of his/her DD-214 for employment purposes. NPRC is working to make it easier for veterans with computers and Internet access to obtain copies of documents from their military files. Military veterans and the next of kin [surviving spouse that has not remarried, father, mother, son, daughter, sister, or brother {NPRC Web site}] of deceased former military members may now use a new online military personnel records system to request documents. Other individuals with a need for documents must still complete the Standard Form 180, which can be downloaded from the online website. Because the requester will be asked to supply all information essential for NPRC to process the request, delays that normally occur when NPRC has to ask veterans for additional information will be minimized. The new web-based application was designed to provide better service on these requests by eliminating the records center's mailroom processing time." (The GRENADE, newsletter of the Service Club of Indianapolis, 80 (May 1, 2006): 17:[2])

cally. The NPRC utilizes alternate sources to recover a limited amount of this information; see this repository's Web site for more information.

For military records dating before 1912, including personnel records, researchers can find an enormous number of documents in the buildings of the U.S. National Archives and Records Administration (NARA) in Washington, DC; College Park, Maryland; and in other NARA research centers located across the United States. A good place to begin a search of this institution is the principal NARA Web site, www.archives.gov. It links the researcher to dozens of finding aids and research guides and gives useful background information. Researchers of Hoosier veterans will find NARA's regional archives in Chicago particularly useful.

Principal Indiana Repositories Containing Military Records

The Indiana State Archives, Indianapolis, holds a valuable collection of military records. Initially, the researcher should access the State Archives' Web site, www.in.gov/icpr/archives, to obtain an overview of the scope of the collection.

The Indiana State Archives offers several handouts detailing the contents of the repository, including military records. Researchers may examine records that cover the participation of Hoosiers in the Battle of Tippecanoe on November 7, 1811, the War of 1812, the Black Hawk War, and the Mexican War. In addition, the Archives houses card files for Indiana Civil War volunteers, Indiana Legion (Civil War state militia), and Civil War substitutes, as well as a veterans' graves registration file for veterans buried prior to 1940 for fifty-one of Indiana's ninety-two counties. The State Archives also possesses an index for members of the Indiana militia, 1877–1896, and the Indiana adjutant general's registration cards for Spanish-American War volunteers, 1898–1899.

Numerous documents detail the military service of Hoosiers in the wars of the twentieth century. Among these are the names, addresses, and serial numbers of Indiana residents who served in World War I, 1917–1918; a World War I draft registration index, 1917–1918; World War I service records; World War II discharge certificates, 1941–1945; Indiana's U.S. Army and U.S. Navy casualties in World War II, 1941–1945; Korean War discharge certificates, 1950–1955; and a list of Indiana's Korean War veterans, 1950–1953. Use of service records from World War II, the Korean War, and the Vietnam War housed at the Archives is restricted under federal government confidentiality requirements.

This photograph, taken by the W. H. Bass Photo Company, shows men and women of the Motor Corps, 1918, World War I. (W. H. Bass Company Collections, P 0130, 63465-F, IHS)

Other military records in the Indiana State Archives include the Indiana Legion and Indiana National Guard service records, 1880–1917, and Indiana National Guard service records, 1917–1940. Indiana National Guard applications from 1898 to 1921 are currently being processed by volunteers. The "Veterans' Enrollments of 1886, 1890, and 1894" is a statewide listing of veterans and their widows and orphans. Arranged by county and township, the list provides a veteran's name, the war in which the veteran participated, the state from which the veteran served, and the veteran's regiment and company information. The State Archives is also the repository for the records of the Indiana Soldiers' and Sailors' Children's Home, which opened in 1867. This collection contains information on the military service of the children's fathers. An index to these records was published by the Indiana Historical Society in 1999 titled *An Index to Records of the Indiana Soldiers' and Sailors' Children's Home in the Indiana State Archives.* The Indiana State Archives also holds records on the Indiana State Soldiers' Home of Lafayette, which opened in 1896, including information on veterans and spouses who resided at the home.

The Indiana Historical Society (IHS) holds a relatively small collection of Hoosier military records; researchers can gain an understanding of the nature of those records by accessing the IHS Web site,

This discharge form for David L. Weatherford gives Weatherford's date of birth, describes him physically, itemizes his military service, tells his level of education and what occupation he practiced in civilian life, and lists his immunizations. (Douglas E. Clanin World War II Oral History Collection, 1944–2002, IHS)

```
                    INDIANA HISTORICAL SOCIETY
                    MILITARY HISTORY SECTION
                    ORAL HISTORY DATA SHEET
I.  Interviewee/Narrator
    1.  Name  Helen (Clanin) Ellis
    2.  Birthplace Indianapolis, Ind.    3.  Date of birth March 7, 1918
    4.  Address 8427 175th St., W.Illinois 5.  Phone   309-798-2294
                               City, Ill
    6.  Ethnic origin Pa. Dutch and German 7.  Religion   Presbyterian
    8.  Current occupation  Home Economics Teacher
    9.  Occupational history   1940-1944:  teacher Metz High School
                               1944-1946:  U.S. Navy gunnery instructor
                               1949-1952:  Franklin Jr. High School, Rock Island, Il
    10. Education 1936--Swayzee High School graduate
                  1940--Ball State Teachers College graduate

    11. Military service
        Branch WAVES--U.S. Navy          Date of entry  July 13, 1944
        XXXXXXXX/enlisted Ft. Wayne, Ind.  Discharged   July 13, 1946
        Units Naval T.S., Newport, R.I.   Theatres  United States
    12. Marital status  Widow            Wedding date & place Sept. 7, 1946
    13. No. of children Male  2          Female    1
    14. Father's name  (George) Arthur Clanin
        Birthplace  Swayzee, Ind.        Date  Aug. 12, 1882
    15. Mother's maiden name  Clara (Matilda) Rissiek
        Birthplace  Sweetser, Ind.       Date   Oct. 15, 1883
    17. Special  interests, hobbies, etc.
            handicrafts of all types; travel
    18. Interviewing sessions with interviewee
        date        time           location        interviewer
    June 18, 1983   6 P.M.         4314 Columbus Ave.  Doug Clanin
    June 19, 1983   Noon           Anderson, Ind.
```

Top portion of an Oral History Data Sheet, completed by the author to accompany an interview with Helen (Clanin) Ellis, who was in the U.S. Navy during World War II (Douglas E. Clanin World War II Oral History Collection, 1944–2002, IHS)

---

www.indianahistory.org. Genealogical information can be gleaned from the hundreds of oral military history interviews and written recollections housed in the IHS library. Volunteers conducted many interviews from the late 1970s to the present, and many of these interviewee files contain biographical data sheets that list basic information about the veterans and their parents.[1] Also, to mark the fiftieth anniversary of the beginning of World War II, the IHS library staff solicited veterans and family members to submit written recollections and copies of original documents and photographs. These sources also contain some biographical information about Hoosier World War II veterans.

Finally, in addition to the federal and state repositories mentioned here, researchers should check the holdings of Indiana public libraries and college and university libraries. Many of these institutions possess index card files and computer files for local newspapers, which are often excellent sources of information about active duty military personnel and veterans.

1. The author donated to the Indiana Historical Society the Douglas E. Clanin World War II Oral History Collection, 1944–2002 (Collection M 0783; CT 0974–1487; 1529–1567; 1569–1631). An Air Force veteran from the Vietnam era, Clanin began interviewing World War II veterans in 1983 and had amassed interviews with more than three hundred veterans by 2003. The collection, which includes correspondence, newspaper clippings, photographs, copies of service records and discharges, and other information related to either the individual being interviewed or his or her unit, comprises a significant source for World War II scholars and family historians with Hoosier veterans from this era.

[The author and the editors of Finding Indiana Ancestors *would like to thank Alan January, program director, Indiana State Archives, for reviewing and commenting on an initial draft of this chapter.]*

Civil War Records

AMY JOHNSON CROW

Indiana provided nearly 200,000 soldiers to the Union forces during the Civil War. These men (and a few women) left behind a legacy rich in resources and records. Family historians who have such a veteran as a direct ancestor or collateral relative should avail themselves of the voluminous amount of records created as a result of that service.

The exact sources a researcher should examine are far too numerous to detail in a single chapter. Instead, this chapter will describe major resources and provide a template of record groups and repositories that researchers should consult.

The Search for Service

Which men in the family tree were likely to have served in the Civil War? A good guideline is to consider all men born between 1820 and 1845 as candidates for Civil War service. It is important to remember, however, that not all men in this age group served. Members of pacifist denominations such as Mennonites and Quakers and the infirm are not going to be found as members of the fighting forces. In 1863 and 1864 a man who was drafted could hire a substitute or pay a $300 commutation fee.

The search for possible Civil War service can start at home. Family photographs, letters, and journals may give clues about service if not specific information about the unit in which an ancestor served.

Those who have delved into researching their ancestry may have collected sources that are valuable in beginning Civil War research. It is not uncommon to find Civil War service mentioned in obituaries and county histories (especially those published in the late 1800s). The 1910 federal census asked if the enumerated was "a survivor of the Union or Confederate Army or Navy."

Tombstones are another possible source of Civil War service information. Figure 1 shows Eli H. Heaton's tombstone in Union Chapel Cemetery in Indianapolis. On it are listed the two units in which he served—the 8th Cavalry and the 39th Indiana Volunteers [infantry]. Other tombstones are not so specific but still give good clues. For example, the Grand Army of the Republic (GAR) was a fraternal organization of honorably discharged Union veterans. A GAR symbol on a tombstone or flag holder is indicative of Civil War service.

Specific Service: The Key to Research

It is not enough to know that an ancestor served in the Civil War; his unit (or units) must be identified. Much as counties are the key to finding relevant genealogical records such as vital records and wills, the unit or regiment is key to finding the Civil War records created by and about that particular ancestor. The Civil War Soldiers and Sailors System Web site (discussed in more detail later in this chapter) has 203 entries for men named John Miller serving in Indiana units. Although some entries undoubtedly refer to the same man, it is obvious more than one John Miller served in an Indiana regiment. Finding the ancestor in the correct unit is paramount.

If tombstones, obituaries, or biographies in county histories do not list the exact regiment, there are several sources to consult. One such source is the *Report of the Adjutant General of the State of Indiana* by William Terrell (Indianapolis: A. H. Connor, 1865–1869), an eight-volume roster of Indiana Civil War regiments. It is available in many libraries across the state and on microfilm through Family History Centers of the Genealogical Society of Utah. It is arranged by regiment and contains a separate name index. Information in this roster includes the soldier's name, rank, date of enlistment, residence, and remarks (such as transfer, date mustered out, and so on). The residence can be a huge help in differentiating between men of the same name.

For those who do not have access to the Adjutant General's roster, the Civil War Soldiers and Sailors System Web site (CWSS) might be of help. The CWSS is a cooperative project of the National Park Service, the Federation of Genealogical Societies, the Genealogical Society of Utah, and several other national and regional partners. This Web site, found at www.civilwar.nps.gov/cwss/, is free and contains rosters, unit histories, battle summaries, and information about selected cemeteries and prisoners of war.

Searches can be done by soldier's name or by regiment. To use the CWSS site to help narrow the field of possible regiments for a particular person, search by name. The results screen will list all of the entries with that name, along with a regiment for each entry. Clicking on the regiment will yield a brief unit his-

tory, which usually includes where the regiment was raised. While not foolproof, it does help to prioritize further research, as a man was more likely to join a unit raised near his home than one raised on the other side of the state.

Another source for determining the correct service is the set of Indiana Civil War cards, available at the Indiana State Archives and on microfilm as "Indiana Civil War records" through Family History Centers. The information on these cards was taken from the unit muster rolls. Facts on the cards include name, age, eye color, hair color, height, complexion, and (most important for genealogical research) birthplace.

Researchers who know where their Civil War ancestors are buried can check another source—the grave registration card. Graves registration started as a Works Progress Administration (WPA) project in many states, including Indiana. The goal was to record the location of the graves of each veteran in a particular county. The criterion for being on the card in a specific county is being buried there, regardless of the place of death. The Indiana State Archives has cards for the fifty-one counties listed below and for Jefferson Township in Wayne County:

Adams	Huntington	Morgan
Blackford	Jasper	Orange
Brown	Jay	Owen
Cass	Johnson	Parke
Clark	Knox	Pike
Clay	Kosciusko	Posey
Crawford	La Grange	Pulaski
Daviess	Lake	St. Joseph
DeKalb	La Porte	Spencer
Delaware	Lawrence	Starke
Elkhart	Madison	Steuben
Floyd	Marion	Sullivan
Gibson	Marshall	Tipton
Grant	Martin	Vanderburgh
Greene	Miami	Vermillion
Harrison	Monroe	Vigo
Howard	Montgomery	Washington

Research Strategies

Once the correct unit has been determined, the real research begins. There are three ways of approaching any record group. All three approaches should be used to discover the most pertinent information.

Figure 1. Eli H. and Nancy Ann Heaton tombstone, Union Chapel Cemetery, Indianapolis (Photo by Amy Johnson Crow, March 31, 2005)

The first way is by name. This may seem obvious, but searching by name is not limited to the name of the ancestor. Other names in the regiment should be researched including the commanding officer. Many family historians are not fortunate to find letters or journals written by their Civil War ancestor; however, such items may still exist for other members of that regiment. Examining them may reveal details about the ancestor. At the very least, they offer context in which to place the ancestor.

The second approach is by unit. Searching by unit will assist in finding records such as unit histories and regimental reunion booklets. Finally, it is important to search by battle. Reading about battles in which the ancestor participated may not help in determining who his parents were, but it will greatly add to his context. Many battles were known by two (or more) names. Union forces tended to name battles for geographic features (for example, Bull Run), while Confederates tended to name them for the nearest town (for example, Manassas). Searching by both names will help ensure that the most records have been discovered.

Pensions

The ancestor's pension file is the most basic record to search for. Drawing a pension after the war did not carry the stigma it did for Revolutionary War or War of 1812 veterans. In addition, there were fewer criterions for receiving a pension than there were for earlier wars. Information in the pension file usually includes information about the veteran's marriages, children, and residences. It is not uncommon to find references to parents and siblings as well. If a researcher had to choose one record to find for a Civil War ancestor, the pension file would be the one to choose.

Pensions are held at the National Archives and can be ordered online at www.archives.gov/research/order/. (This site is also the place to order military service records.) At a minimum, a successful request will have the veteran's name and regiment. Including the pension number will expedite matters.

The National Archives has issued Microfilm Publication T288, "General Index to Pension Files, 1861–1934," which is available in many formats. On microfilm, it can be found at the Allen County Public Library in Fort Wayne, Indiana, and through Family History Centers. Digitized images of the index cards can be found online at Ancestry.com, a subscription service available to individuals and also available at some public libraries. The cards list the veteran's name, the widow's name, service (regiment), and pension application and certificate numbers for the veteran and widow (if applicable).

Enrollment of Soldiers

Along with the 1890 federal census, the government compiled a special schedule of Union veterans and their widows. Unfortunately, the schedules for Indiana no longer exist. However, there are three censuses, taken in 1886, 1890, and 1894, that family historians should be certain to look for: Indiana's Enrollment of Soldiers, Widows, and Orphans. These statewide enumerations are arranged by county and then by town or township. An index is available at the Indiana State Library, and the records may be searched at the Indiana State Archives. The records, but not the index, are also available on microfilm through Family History Centers. Not all enumerations for all counties exist, but with the exception of Dearborn and Marion counties, each county has at least one enumeration.

As the example in Figure 2 shows, these enrollments include the veteran's name, his widow (if applicable), regiment, number of children under age sixteen, and post office. If a widow was listed, the record often includes information about the veteran's death as well as any subsequent marriage of the widow.

GAR Records

The Grand Army of the Republic (GAR) was founded in 1866 as a fraternal organization for honorably discharged Union veterans. It quickly became a major force in the political landscape as it pertained to pensions and medical benefits for those veterans.

The local GAR posts kept many types of records of interest to genealogists. The most detailed are the books of "personal sketches," which are, in essence, biographies of the camp members. The questionnaire asked for the member's name, date and place of birth, date and place of enlistment, list of battles, and details of hospitalizations or imprisonments. The last question was to name his "most intimate comrades" in the service. When searching for other records by name, these are names that should definitely be researched.

In addition to the personal sketches books, other records include post rosters (membership lists), which often include death dates and information about members transferring to other posts. Even the minutes of the business meetings can contain biographical information. For example, the minutes of GAR Post 227 in Hartford City, Indiana, mention that Comrade William Smelwarte died in the Marion Home since the last meeting and that Comrade Crabtree "was quite sick."

The difficulty in using GAR records is locating them. As posts disbanded, many of the records were simply discarded. Others are hiding in attics, closets, and barns. The Indiana Historical Society has some GAR post records in its collection. Local historical societies and libraries sometimes have records for the posts in their areas.

Unit Histories

Many regiments published a unit history in the years following the war. Some researchers are lucky and find detailed accounts of their ancestors' exploits in these histories. More common, however, the worth of these histories lies in the "rolls of honor" (lists of deceased unit members) and in the accounts of the regiment's activities.

Unit histories were usually published in small quantities. The public library in the area where the unit was raised is an excellent place to start looking for these books. The Allen County Public Library has an extensive collection of unit histories.

The Civil War Soldiers and Sailors (CWSS) Web site is a free, online source for unit histories. Each regiment in the database has at least a

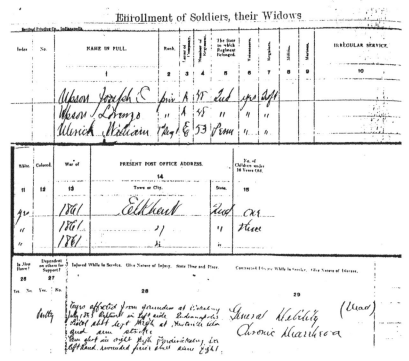

Figure 2. Sample page from the Enrollment Book of Soldiers, Widows, and Orphans for Concord Township, Elkhart County, Indiana, in 1894 (Courtesy of Patricia K. Johnson)

short history; some go on for several screens. The site takes advantage of its Internet format by adding links from the unit histories to battle summaries. A visitor to the site can read the unit history for the 31st Indiana Infantry, for example, and find links to summaries of seventeen battles in which the regiment participated.

Just as careful researchers expand their searches beyond the ancestor's name and include names of others in the regiment, a search for unit histories should be expanded beyond the ancestor's unit. When reading accounts of battles, take note of the other regiments involved in the action and search for histories of those units. For example, *Four Years with the Iron Brigade: The Civil War Journals of William R.*

ters of unit members with their residences. Reunion booklets usually contain a list of veterans who died since the last reunion; some booklets give biographies of these veterans rather than a simple list.

Because of their ephemeral nature, reunion booklets can be hard to find. Local public libraries and historical societies are excellent places to look, as are the Indiana Historical Society library and the Allen County Public Library.

Major Web Sites

The National Park Service recently launched a sister Web site to the CWSS site. The American Civil War Web site (http://cwar.nps.gov/civilwar/) has time lines, battlefield information, and other articles of

Photo of a Civil War veterans group taken in 1931 by Martin's Photo Shop, Terre Haute, Indiana (Martin's Photo Shop Collection, P 0129, IHS)

Ray, Company F, Seventh Wisconsin Volunteers, edited by Lance Herdegen and Sherry Murphy (Cambridge, MA: Da Capo Press, 2002) is probably not the first book one would think of if researching an Indiana regiment. However, the book is filled with references to Indiana units that fought alongside the 7th Wisconsin.

Reunion Booklets

When the war was over, some veterans felt the need to stay in touch with their comrades. Some regiments held organized reunions annually or biennially, often beginning in the late 1870s. Most produced some amount of ephemera—programs, ribbons, and the like. Some regiments produced booklets with ros-

general interest. The site will grow and change as the nation approaches the sesquicentennial of the beginning of the Civil War (2011).

Other Web sites with Civil War information are the county USGenWeb sites. From the INGenWeb state page (www.ingenweb.org) researchers can find links to all ninety-two county INGenWeb sites. Each site is independent, so content will vary from county to county. It is not uncommon, however, to find rosters of local units, veterans' burials, and abstracts of pension files.

Two Civil War "portal" sites that are national in scope are the American Civil War Homepage (http://sunsite.utk.edu/civil-war/warweb.html) and the United States Civil War Center at Louisiana State

University (www.cwc.lsu.edu). Each site features categorized links to other Civil War Web sites.

The Civil War Indiana Web site (www.civilwar indiana.com) is a portal site specifically linking Indiana sites. Unlike the two mentioned national portals, Civil War Indiana has data on the site, including unit histories, photographs, and an extensive Indiana Civil War bibliography.

Finding the Records

The Indiana Historical Society has an extensive collection of Civil War letters, diaries, and journals, as well as some local GAR post records. The Indiana State Library and the Indiana State Archives have original records, as well as published materials (unit histories, for example). The Allen County Public Library has an outstanding Civil War collection for Indiana and beyond.

Researchers should always check with local public libraries, genealogical societies, and historical societies. Many of the records mentioned in this chapter are rare or one-of-a-kind. These types of records often find their way to local repositories.

Many libraries have copies of C. E. Dornbusch's classic work, *Regimental Publications and Personal Narratives of the Civil War: A Checklist* (New York: New York Public Library, 1961). This extensive bibliography is arranged by unit and is a must for finding out-of-the-way resources. One such record is listed

under the 35th Indiana: "The War Letters of Father Peter Paul Cooney" in a 1933 issue of the *Records of the American Catholic Historical Society.*

The Library of Congress's National Union Catalog of Manuscript Collections (NUCMC) lists more than 1,400 manuscript collections across the United States. The online version (www.loc.gov/coll/nucmc/) has more than 500,000 entries and is an excellent resource for finding manuscript items such as letters and journals.

Conclusion

The Civil War shaped this nation and affected in some way, great or small, every person who lived here during those four tumultuous years. The records created by, for, and about those who served are invaluable to family historians—from biographically rich records such as pension files to more contextual records such as unit histories. Those who have Indiana Civil War ancestors are fortunate for they have innumerable sources to seek out and examine.

———————————————— • ————————————————

1. Account Book, 1904–1917, GAR Jacob Stahl Post, No. 227, Allen County Public Library, Fort Wayne, Indiana, 47. For other GAR records, see Mary Blair Immel, "Grand Army of the Republic, Post Number 4, Covington, Indiana, parts 1–21," *The Hoosier Genealogist* vol. 41, no. 1–vol. 46, no. 1.

Civil War Records in Indiana

STEPHEN E. TOWNE

Genealogists searching for information on an ancestor who served in the American Civil War (1861–1865) are more fortunate than those whose ancestors served in the country's earlier wars and military conflicts. The large scale of the war, involving millions of combatants, and the serious stakes involved—nothing less than the survival of the United States of America—ensured that the full efforts of the federal government and the state governments that supported it were mobilized. With government effort comes bureaucracy. From bureaucracy comes paperwork. From paperwork comes information.

Researchers with Civil War ancestors can also be thankful that the conflict was significant in the minds of those who fought it and understood its consequences. Civil War veterans, their families, and the families of the many thousands of combatants who were killed in battle or who died of disease chose to remember the costs and to memorialize the efforts of those who fought—whether they lived or died. These people insisted that memorials be erected and that records be preserved as a means to ensure a lasting memory of the great national struggle. Compare this effort to that of the previous major war the United States had embarked upon—the Mexican

War of 1846–1848. A significant conflict against a neighboring country reflecting the growing ambitions of the nation, the Mexican War, nonetheless, did not evoke a national remembrance. Indeed, so little did Indiana's government care about its role in the Mexican War that Indiana government records relating to the raising and organizing of its five Mexican War volunteer regiments were already lost from neglect by the time of the Civil War, less than fifteen years later.

So genealogists with ancestors who served in Indiana units in the Civil War should take heart that such an abundance of records survives. The question then becomes how to sort through it all to find the needed information on great-great-grandpappy Enoch. This chapter is an effort to help guide the researcher through the thicket of Indiana Civil War records. But be warned that documentation is often uneven: some soldiers' service generated more documentation than others. This chapter will focus on documentation relating to the roughly 200,000 soldiers who served in approximately 175 volunteer infantry, cavalry, and artillery regiments and batteries formed for national service with the assistance of Indiana's state government. It does not address the relatively small number of Indiana soldiers who served in the United States (regular) Army or the relatively small number who served in the United States Navy. Regular army and navy service records can be found exclusively at the National Archives in Washington, DC. This chapter will provide no assistance for the small number of Indiana men who fought for the Confederate cause. Records for them will be found in the state archives of the southern states that rebelled against the United States.

Where to begin? The search for information on a Civil War soldier depends on what information the researcher already possesses. Perhaps an ancestor left a trunk full of letters recounting his Civil War experiences; only a tidbit of extra data would be needed to fill in a few gray areas. Or perhaps the researcher knows only the vague family story that old Enoch might have been a soldier in an Indiana Civil War unit but nothing more. In either case, and for all cases in between these two extremes, the first place to check is the Civil War Volunteer Card File in the Indiana State Archives. The card file, alphabetically arranged, contains information on every soldier listed on the muster rolls of all the volunteer units raised in Indiana. The card file, created at the time of World War I at the behest of the Indiana General Assembly, contains the information listed on the regimental and battery muster rolls and descriptive rolls then in the state's custody. It includes name, rank, company, regiment, and date and place of enlistment and muster in and muster out. It may include the date of discharge if the soldier became sick or was wounded in service and could not continue to serve. It also will note if a soldier died of disease or wounds, deserted, or was taken prisoner. In many (but not all) instances, the card will give physical description information that appeared on the muster roll or descriptive roll, including age; height; color of eyes, hair, and complexion; nativity (that is, where he said he was born); and occupation. The one

Civil War Volunteer Card for Sgt. Ambrose G. Bierce, Company C, 9th Indiana Regiment (Indiana State Archives)

item of information that the card does not provide that might have been on the muster roll or descriptive roll was the yes/no answer to the question asking if the soldier was married. These cards have been microfilmed. The staff of the Indiana State Archives with assistance from volunteers from the Friends of the Indiana State Archives are entering information from these cards into a database that, when completed, will be available online.

The Civil War Volunteer Card File may yield multiple cards for soldiers with common names. For example, say that you are looking for information on a soldier named—you guessed it—John Smith. After lamenting that your ancestors had not the imagination to give their son a slightly more distinct name (Enoch, for instance), you discover that dozens and scores of John Smiths served in Indiana volunteer units. So you should next search by whatever other bits of information exist on old John. Did he have a middle name or initial? Where was he from? Do you know when he was born? Answers to these questions will allow you to narrow the search. Okay, you know that John Q. A. ["Quincy Adams"] Smith was born in Huntington County in 1828. Equipped with this information, you should be able to narrow the field significantly to find the right John Smith.

An important thing to remember is that nearly all of the Indiana volunteer units were raised in specific geographical regions of the state. Most of the regiments and batteries were raised from an assigned congressional district in the state. So if your ancestor was from Posey County down on the Ohio River in the extreme southwest corner of the state, you can be fairly sure that he would not have enlisted in a regiment in Steuben County in the extreme northeast. You can be fairly sure but not absolutely sure. People in nineteenth-century America were much more mobile than we typically credit them. Young men ranged far and wide for work. Consequently, many Indiana men found themselves in other states when the war began and enlisted there thinking to get in on the action before the war ended. Likewise, thousands of men from other states mustered into Indiana units. This mobility also led men to shop around later in the war when counties and townships offered large

bounties to volunteers if they would enlist from their county or township jurisdiction, thus reducing their draft quotas. Indiana boys traveled to eastern cities to cash in on the lucrative bonuses offered there. So, while most Hoosiers enlisted in units raised in their home locales with their neighbors and friends, this was not always the case.

The quickest way to learn where a unit was raised is to look at the rosters of the regiments published in the *Report of the Adjutant General of the State of Indiana.* Published in eight volumes shortly after the end of the rebellion, the rosters list the names of all the soldiers in all the volunteer units raised in Indiana, along with their home counties. Thus, you will see that the 47th Indiana Volunteer Infantry Regiment came from the counties around Fort Wayne;

Civil War soldiers from the 80th Indiana Volunteer Infantry Regiment: Col. Lewis Brooks, Loogootee; Lt. Col. James L. Culbertson, Edwardsport; Maj. John W. Tucker, Orleans; and Adj. Alfred Dale Owen of New Harmony (Indiana Carte-de-Visite Collection, ca. 1862–ca. 1893, P 0415, IHS)

the 1st Indiana Cavalry Regiment was from southwestern Indiana around Evansville; and the 71st Indiana Volunteer Infantry (later reorganized as the 6th Cavalry) came from the 7th Congressional District around Terre Haute. Knowing where the units came from will help the researcher identify the Civil War soldier ancestor.

Perhaps a researcher is trying to confirm the family story that Henry Clay Johnson served in the Civil War but has nothing to go on except that he lived throughout his life in Indiana and died

```
NAME    Ebrecht, Henry          SERIAL NO._____

HOME ADDRESS  Haubstadt, Indiana _____

BORN 1-27-1838 AT    Germany       DIED 9-8-1923

CEMETERY      Nobels Chapel    COUNTY   Gibson

                                        AR.
GRAVE NO. 25 AR LOT_____  BLK.___ ROW 1  SEC_____

WAR    Civil   RANK_____   OUTFIT Co.K,11th.Vol.

ENLISTED  8-31-1861    DISCHARGED  2-21-1865

REMARKS _____


_____

GRAVES REGISTRATION FORM NO. 1 - THE AMERICAN LEGION
```

Veterans' Graves Registration Card for Henry Ebrecht, Company K, 11th Indiana Volunteer Regiment (Indiana State Archives)

there in 1904. The researcher should use that bit of information—his year of death—to work backwards. The Grand Army of the Republic (GAR) was the organization of Union veterans. It wielded tremendous political clout in its heyday (1880s–1890s). The GAR had thousands of local "posts" throughout the country where Union veterans could meet and swap stories. Indiana had hundreds of GAR posts in its cities and towns. Few veterans did not join their local GAR post. Each year the Indiana GAR headquarters published a list of GAR members who had died in the previous year. Listed by post number and by date, a researcher can often find quickly the name of a GAR member who died in that year. The Indiana State Library has a collection of each GAR annual report, including the annual death rolls.[1] The roll list provides the Civil War unit in which the soldier served. The researcher can then go to the card file with the name and unit. Some surviving GAR post records and correspondence of the state headquarters also can be found in the Indiana State Archives.

Another information entry point is a cemetery. A researcher may find that an ancestor, Martin Van Buren Jones, was buried in a family cemetery but has little or no information beyond the grave marker, which might be a government-supplied veteran's marker. In the late 1930s the Works Progress Administration (WPA), a federal government entity created

to give work to the unemployed during the Great Depression, cooperated with the American Legion to produce a card file of veterans' graves in Indiana cemeteries. Fifty-one of Indiana's ninety-two counties were surveyed, and a Veterans' Graves Registration card file was produced listing alphabetically the veterans buried in cemeteries in a given county. These card files are available at the Indiana State Archives. WPA researchers compiled information from the grave markers and any cemetery records that they could find. Thus, Civil War veterans have their units listed. As well, WPA workers drew plats of these cemeteries, helping to locate sometimes obscure and hard-to-find cemeteries. These plats are in the Indiana State Archives.

Perhaps a researcher knows that Andrew Jackson Murphy lived in a given Indiana county after the war but is not sure that he served in the Civil War. One source to check would be the Enrollments of Soldiers, Widows, and Orphans of 1886, 1890, and 1894. In the 1880s, under political pressure from the GAR, Congress passed laws greatly expanding eligibility for Civil War veterans' pensions. Instead of just wounded men and the families of dead and badly injured soldiers receiving pensions, all Union veterans became eligible for pension payments from the U.S. government. However, the federal government needed to ascertain how many people might be involved, so it requested local government assessors to collect information on veterans in their neighborhoods. The result was the Enrollments, which compile information on unit, wounds received in action or illnesses contracted while in service, and the number of children under sixteen years old. The Enrollments are available at the Indiana State Archives and may be searched by county and township. An alphabetical index to the 1886 Enrollment is available in the Genealogy Section of the Indiana State Library.

Federal pension records can be found in the National Archives, Washington, DC.

Sometimes a researcher may search high and low to find a record that ancestor Daniel Webster Anderson served in an Indiana Civil War unit but to no avail. The researcher might check the Draft Enrollment Lists for the state-administered draft of 1862, the country's first draft, resorted to when enlistments slipped as the war bogged down and casualties mounted. State officials were charged with appointing local officials to compile lists of eligible men. Thus, for each township in each Indiana county there are two lists. The first lists all men from a township who had already enlisted in the armed services, showing the men's names, ages, occupations, and units. The second lists the white males only who were between the ages of eighteen and forty-five years and were eligible to be drafted. The list contains their names, ages, and occupations. It also notes any physical disabilities that a man might have had (for example, blindness, deafness, syphilitic, tubercular, missing fingers, and so on), or if the man was a member of a religious group that opposed military service ("conscientious exempts"), such as the Quakers or the Brethren. In this way, the researcher might check the lists for the township where

Application for admission into the Indiana Soldiers' Orphans' Home at Knightstown, Indiana, for Mary Hofmeister of Evansville, Indiana. According to the application, her father, Henry Hofmeister, served in Company E, 14th Indiana Volunteer Regiment. (Indiana State Archives)

Daniel resided to see if he had enlisted or if he was physically disabled. These records are housed in the Indiana State Archives. In 1863 Congress passed a law placing the administration of the federal draft in the hands of federal officials. Consequently, draft records for 1863 and later are in the Provost Marshal Bureau Records in the National Archives, Washington, DC.

The State of Indiana provided special services to veterans and the orphans of veterans after the war. The Soldiers' and Sailors' Children's Home applications provide information on children of veterans, showing the units in which the veterans served. A searchable database is available at www.in.gov/icpr/archives/databases/issch. Likewise, the Indiana State Soldiers' Home applications provide information on Civil War veterans who applied for residence and care at the state home in Lafayette. Both sets of records are found in the Indiana State Archives. The federal government established a series of veterans' homes across the country, including one in Marion, Indiana (now the Veterans Administration hospital). Records for these federally run facilities can be found in the National Archives, Washington, DC, and in the National Archives' regional repositories.

The above records apply to all soldiers in all ranks, but officers generated more documentation. Governors had the power to appoint all the commissioned officers of all the volunteer units raised in the war. It was a huge responsibility, involving more than ten thousand appointments in Indiana. Indiana Gov. Oliver P. Morton used the opportunity to appoint men to his liking. Information relating to the appointment and promotion of officers exists in the copious correspondence of the governor, the adjutant general of Indiana, and each of the volunteer units, all to be found in the Indiana State Archives. A searchable database of the telegraph books of Gov. Oliver P. Morton is available online at www.in.gov/icpr/archives/databases/civilwar/s_morton.html. Thus, if Thomas Jefferson Thompson was appointed to be an officer in one or more of the Indiana units, there is likely to be correspondence of or about him in the regimental files.

The above examples are just a few of the many entry points into the documentation of Civil War military service in Indiana volunteer regiments and batteries. Many more exist. It is always advisable to consult the archivists and librarians of the Indiana State Archives and the Indiana State Library for assistance in using these and other Civil War sources. They can help you find the information you need.

---•---

1. See also Dennis Northcott, comp., *Indiana Civil War Veterans: Transcriptions of the Death Rolls of the Department of Indiana, 1882–1948* (St. Louis: D. Northcott, 2005).

For the Record: Was William Park Herron Wounded at Chickamauga?

ERNIE MOORE

O ne fascinating thing about genealogy research is that it sometimes proves that generally accepted family legends are untrue. Secondary sources of information, such as history books, can mislead or contain factual errors. A little inquisitiveness and in-depth research of original documents may show that a family legend is incorrect, initiated innocently by one source and, over time, repeated by

other storytellers until the legend becomes accepted as fact. I believe this is the case with the story below about William Park Herron.

Being a novice Civil War buff, I was reading Glenn Tucker's *Chickamauga: Bloody Battle in the West* (1961), when I came across the account of an incident the morning after the battle, which was fought September 19–21, 1863: "Youthful Captain W. P. Herron of Wilder's brigade—'I never saw a man fight so hard'—wounded severely in the battle on the Federal right, bled during the night and had to be chopped loose from the ground in the morning. His side wound had stuck to the frosty ground. It was freed carefully by comrades. But the bullet that

hit his head so blinded him that he had to stay in a darkened room for five years."

My maternal grandmother was a Herron. I wondered, "Is this Civil War hero a relative?" Upon reviewing my copy of "The Family of Thomas Herron, 1755–1936" by Harriett Harding Millis and William A. Millis, I found that William Park Herron is my fourth cousin. I was thrilled that one of my relatives was mentioned in a historical account of a major Civil War battle and wanted to learn more about Herron.

From information in the Millis's family history and an article about Herron family history, by Gen. Charles D. Herron, William's son, I learned that William Park Herron was born on June 17, 1843, in

Montgomery County, Indiana, on a Ripley Township farm.[1] Herron was the ninth of eleven children born to James Douglas and Rebecca Herron. When he was nine years old, his parents sold the farm and bought another just south of Crawfordsville, Indiana.

Charles's history indicates that when the Civil War began in 1861, Herron was a Wabash College junior, not yet eighteen. He promptly enrolled in President Lincoln's "Hundred Day Volunteers." After the release of these volunteers, William joined the Seventy-second Indiana Volunteer Infantry on July 12, 1862, as a private and was made first sergeant of Company B that day. By February 24, 1863, Herron was promoted through the ranks to captain, becoming the commanding officer of Company B.

To learn more about Herron's Civil War record, I requested copies of his pension papers from the National Archives, Department of Veterans Affairs, and received eighty-three pages regarding Herron's disability pension. Although eleven documents address his physical condition and the basis for his disability, none of these pages mentions Chickamauga. Herron's disability pension application, dated November 16, 1867, and signed, "W. P. Herron, Late Capt of Co. B. 72nd Regt. Ind.," states:

Capt. William Park Herron (Courtesy of John Sickles, Civil War collector)

On the 20th day of March, 1865, he [Herron] contracted a disease of the Lungs or hemerage [sic] of the Lungs. Said disease was produced or brought on by a Severe cold which he had contracted during his March from: Waterloo, Miss, to Selma, Alabama. . . . the result of Exposure to all kinds of weather and constant marching. . . . And was affected more or less with said disease until the date of his discharge and that said disease still affects him and at times he is utterly & wholly prostrated and is at no time able to procure his subsistinc[e] by manual labor.

The document is signed by two witnesses and certified by the clerk of the Circuit Court of Montgomery County, Indiana. Six more documents, dated November 27, 1867, to May 16, 1868, state essentially the same thing—attributing Herron's physical condition to his march across Mississippi and Alabama in March 1865. A March 19, 1868, document adds, "For the past eight or nine months the patient has been unable to leave his room."

However, a surgeon's certificate dated September 6, 1873, states the "alleged disability result[ed] from Gunshot wound of right Lung . . . received in . . . the military service of the United States." The physician further states that inflammation of Herron's "Larynx, Trachea and right Bronchial tube" was "assuming a Tuberculous Type." A similar surgeon's certificate of September 8, 1875, attributed Herron's disability to a "shell wound of the right side":

The pensioner states that he suffers a great deal of pain in the right side in the region of the wound when he takes colds and . . . that he has hemorages [sic] from the lungs and that he looses so much blood at times that he becomes . . . prostrated so as to confine him to his room for a week at a time. I find this to be a concussion wound . . . and find dullness on percussion . . . and absence of the respiratory murmur over lower lobe of right lung with a very fe[e]ble respiratory murmur in the middle and interior lobes of right lung[.]

Two other surgeons' certificates, dated June 25, 1877, and September 25, 1877, cite "disability resulting from injury [?] shell" and "disability resulting from concussion shell wound in right side," respectively. Note that it was six years after the submission of Herron's pension application before the terms "gunshot wound" or "shell wound" appear in government disability pension documents. Interestingly, none of the last four documents provides a place where Herron contracted his lung problems. Five of the earlier documents cite Selma or Alabama.

None of the documents mentions a head wound from the Battle of Chickamauga, and, although the claim of May 16, 1868, mentions that Herron was unable to leave his room for "eight or nine months," none of the documents states that Herron had to stay in a dark room for five years due to blindness. Thus, the pension documents contradict Tucker's account.

The obvious question is: Was William Park Herron wounded at Chickamauga? I think not, but let's look further.

The Montgomery County Historical Society published a documentary edition in 1997 titled *Battles, Skirmishes, Events and Scenes: The Letters and Memorandum of Ambrose Remley.* A friend of Herron's, Ambrose Remley was from Crawfordsville and was a member of the Seventy-second, Company E. During the war, Remley wrote numerous letters to his family and friends in Crawfordsville that provide significant details about the day-to-day activities and battles of his unit. In nearly every letter Remley comments on his health and that of the "boys" from the Crawfordsville area, at times giving names. Remley specifically mentions Herron nine times. On September 26, 1863, six days after the Battle of Chickamauga, Remley reports, "There was

only one wounded in Co B. His name I believe was Martin. I havent seen Will Herron for a day or two but I guess he is well." In letters dated October 6 and October 30, 1863, Remley writes, "I am well. All the boys are well." Remley's letters do not state or imply that Herron was wounded at Chickamauga. Had Herron sustained a wound, I believe his friend would have mentioned it in a letter home. However, let's continue our search.

The book *Blue Lightning: Wilder's Mounted Infantry Brigade in the Battle of Chickamauga,* written by Richard A. Baumgartner, was also published in 1997. The Seventy-second was a part of Wilder's Brigade. In the book Baumgartner includes Herron's picture and mentions him three times, twice regarding his military duties and once relating his participation after the war in the erection of a monument to the Wilder Brigade at the Chickamauga & Chattanooga National Military Park in Fort Oglethorpe, Georgia. The most significant reference to Herron follows: "Private David Martin of Company B, after being shot, was hoisted onto a horse by Captain William Herron and told to ride to the regimental field hospital at Crawfish Springs." This statement coincides with Remley's letter stating that a person in Company B named Martin was wounded. *Blue Lightning* provides no hint that anyone other than Martin in Company B was wounded at Chickamauga.

Charles Herron's family history relates

The front side of Capt. Herron's disability pension certificate, dated November 27, 1867 the following about William Herron and the Battle of Chickamauga:

The main Confederate effort was against the Union left and on that flank was Company "B." In the next day's fighting William was severely wounded and, according to a letter now on file at battlefield headquarters, the writer on the following morning chopped Captain Herron loose from the ground to which he was frozen in his own blood and got him to a field hospital! The unseasonable cold of that night and the wound are of official record, but . . . in so far as I know, the Captain never even once related that very remarkable episode to any of his family!

The question remains: Was William Park Herron wounded at Chickamauga?

Copies of records for the Seventy-second kept at the Chickamauga & Chattanooga National Military Park and two additional publications, *History of the 72d Indiana Volunteer Infantry of the Mounted Lightning Brigade* by Benjamin F. Magee and William R. Jewell (1882), and *War of the Rebellion: Official Records of the Union and Confederate Armies*, published by the federal government (1899), provide evidence that Herron was *not* wounded at Chickamauga.[2] On July 18, 2001, a staff member of the military park advised me that he had searched the Seventy-second's file but failed to find a letter containing the story told by Charles about his father's alleged wound. Nor was there anything in the file to support Tucker's statement.

In their regimental history Magee and Jewell state the following respecting the Battle of Chickamauga: "In the case of David Martin, of B [Company], as soon as he was shot Capt. Herron put him on Sergt.-Major Tompson's horse and told him to go to the hospital. Neither he nor the horse was ever heard of afterwards." They also relate that on October 4, 1863, while Company B was chasing rebels through McMinnville, "Capt. Herron in command . . . says that . . . he was, for the first time, sure that he saw one man shoot at and kill another."

In his official report from Selma, Alabama, on April 5, 1865, which was published in *War of the*

William Herron and his wife, Ada (Courtesy of Louise Herron Ripple)

Rebellion, Lt. Col. Chester G. Thomson of the Seventy-second states, "My regiment having had the advance on the 1st was by the general order of march assigned to the rear on the 2d, and four companies, under command of Captain Herron, were detailed to guard the division train. . . . Herron brought the train in safely."

I have been unable to find any original documents stating that Herron received a head wound or that he was temporarily blinded in the Battle of Chickamauga so that he had to stay in a darkened room for five years. If he had suffered a head injury, Herron would not have been chasing rebels less than two weeks after the battle as his regimental history states, nor marching to Selma in March 1865 as his pension paperwork states, nor commanding a detail guarding the division train in April 1865 as the government's official records state.

Herron's pension documents through 1868 make no mention of a wound. Rather, his condition is attributed to a disease or hemorrhage of the lungs caused by a severe cold. Remley and Baumgartner speak of only one person from Company B being wounded at Chickamauga, and it was not Herron. The official government record agrees with these accounts. Finally, Charles states that his father never mentioned being wounded. I believe the reason he never mentioned it is because it did not happen.

Nevertheless, the legend continues to be passed along as fact. An essay by Ruth Blakeslee, "The Successful Herron Family—150 Years in Montgomery County," published in *Montgomery County Remem-*

bers in 1997 by the Montgomery County Historical Society is a good example. Blakeslee writes of Herron, "Returning home . . . [he] had typhoid fever and was severely wounded at the battle of Chickamauga. When the war ended in 1865, he was discharged in

William Herron built this house, locally known as "The Gingerbread House," in Crawfordsville, Indiana, in 1890. Note the front gate, featuring two herons. (Courtesy of Ernie Moore)

poor condition, suspect of tuberculosis." No doubt Blakeslee read sources or interviewed individuals who gave her this version of Herron's story and accepted in good faith that the story was true.

According to Herron's pension papers, he was honorably discharged July 6, 1865. Blakeslee and Charles relate similar accounts of Herron's postwar career. Although too sick to work, he enrolled again in Wabash College. In 1868 Herron went to work for the First National Bank of Crawfordsville, remaining with them for sixty years except while serving two terms as county treasurer. He eventually became pres-

ident of the bank, the Crawfordsville Wire and Nail Mill, the city's first gas company, the local theater, and the central heating company and a director of other local enterprises. Herron also served as president of a large Indianapolis bank and as board president of the Indiana School for the Deaf. Herron was a member of the commission that placed the Indiana monuments on the Chickamauga Battlefield and a member of the committee that erected the Soldiers and Sailors Monument on the Circle at Indianapolis. He and his wife, Ada, were married for fifty-two years and were the parents of seven children. Herron died at the age of eighty-four on June 19, 1927.

Was William Park Herron wounded at Chickamauga? At the time of this writing, Herron's eighty-three-year-old granddaughter, Louise Herron Ripple, told me she did not know; but her father, Charles, had told the story many times, and she had always assumed it was true. What is your opinion?

———————•———————

1. Gen. Charles [Douglas] Herron, "Capt. William P. Herron Served in the Civil War," *Montgomery Magazine* (April 1978): 7–9. This article is excerpted from an undated family history manuscript of fifteen pages titled "Herron" with the initials "C. D. H." at the end. The last four pages are devoted to William Herron's life, two pages providing an overview of William's military service.

2. U.S. War Department, *War of the Rebellion: Official Records of the Union and Confederate Armies* (Washington, DC: Government Printing Office, 1899), for Battle of Chickamauga: ser. 1, vol. 30, pts. 1 and 2 (reports), 3 and 4 (correspondence); for Lt. Col. Chester G. Thomson, "Official Report. Seventy-second Indiana (Mounted) Infantry, April 1–2, 1865": ser. 1, vol. 49, pt. 1; for supplemental reports, Union correspondence, etc., January 1, 1861–June 30, 1865: ser. 1, vol. 52, pt. 1.

Selected Bibliography: National Park Service. "Chickamauga & Chattanooga National Military Park." www. nps. gov/chch/index.htm (accessed March 23, 2006); National Park Service, et al. "Soldiers & Sailors System." www. itd.nps.gov/cwss/ (accessed March 23, 2006); National Archives and Records Administration. "Military Resources: Civil War." www.archives.gov/research/alic/reference/ military/civil-war-resources.html (accessed March 23, 2006).

Part 4
Researching with Maps

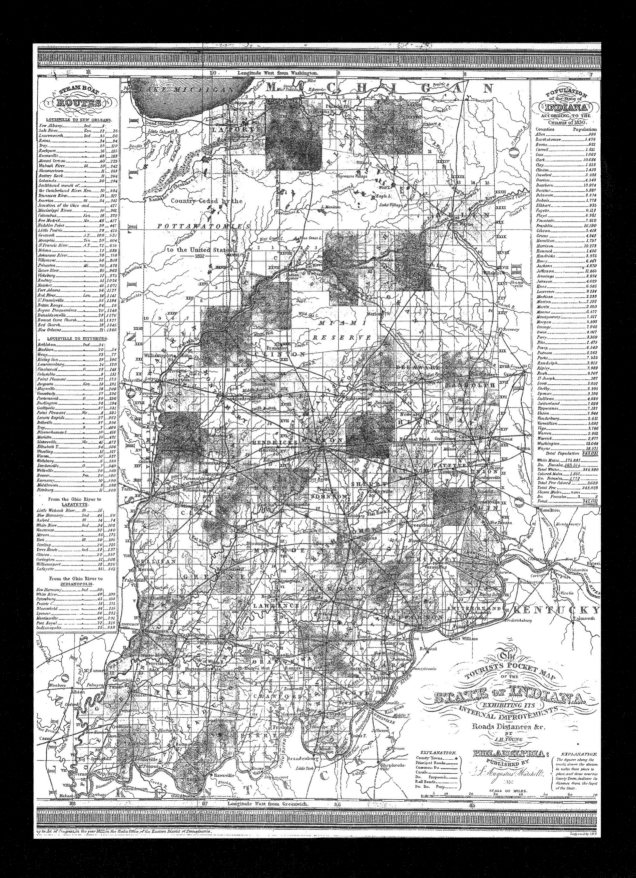

STEAMBOAT ROUTES

LOUISVILLE TO NEW ORLEANS.

New Albany	Ind.	2
Salt River	Ken.	23	25
Leavenworth	Ind.	35	60
Rome		34	94
Troy		25	119
Rockport		16	135
Evansville		48	183
Mount Vernon		40	123
Wabash River	Ill.	10	242
Shawneetown		11	243
Battery Rock		11	264
Golconda		30	294
Southland mouth of			
the Cumberland River.	Ken.	10	304
Tennessee River		13	317
America	Ill.	34	361
Junction of the Ohio and			
Mississippi Rivers		6	367
Columbus	Ken.	18	372
New Madrid	Mo.	48	427
Riddles Point		20	447
Little Prairie		28	475
Greenock	A.T.	100	574
Memphis	Ten.	30	604
St Francis River	A.T.	15	639
Helena		12	639
Arkansas River		70	758
Villemont		50	808
Princeton	Mi.	70	878
Yazoo River		85	963
Vicksburg		12	975
Rodney		51	1026
Natchez		45	1071
Fort Adams	Lou.	56	1127
Red River		14	1141
St Francisville		53	1194
Baton Rouge		24	28
Bayou Plaquemines		20	1248
Donaldsonville		28	1276
Bonnet Carre Church		51	1327
Red Church		18	1345
New Orleans		21	1366

LOUISVILLE TO PITTSBURG.

Bethlehem	Ind.	34
Madison		20	54
Vevay		23	77
Rising Sun		29	106
Lawrenceburg		24	130
Cincinnati	O.	23	148
Columbia		3	151
Point Pleasant		28	151
Augusta	Ken.	18	201
Maysville		18	209
Vanceburg		27	236
Portsmouth	O.	20	256
Burlington		38	294
Gallipolis		37	331
Point Pleasant	Vir.	2	333
Letarts Rapids		27	362
Belleville		37	390
Troy	O.	9	409
Blennerhassets I.		6	416
Marietta		15	431
Steubenville	Vir.	41	472
Elizabeth T.		34	506
Wheeling		11	517
Warren		10	527
Wellsburg		6	533
Steubenville	O.	7	540
Wellville		20	560
Beaver	Pen.	30	590
Economy		10	590
Middletown		8	598
Pittsburg		11	609

From the Ohio River to LAFAYETTE.

Little Wabash River	Ind.	16
New Harmony	Ind.	44	60
Oxford	Ill.	14	74
White River	Ind.	34	103
Vincennes		32	140
Merom		35	175
York	Ill.	30	105
Sterling		20	225
Terre Haute	Ind.	22	237
Clinton		20	257
Covington		32	289
Williamsport		12	320
Lafayette		35	361

From the Ohio River to INDIANOPOLIS.

New Harmony	Ind.	60
White River		45	105
Petersburg		45	153
Prairie C.		18	171
Bloomfield		34	205
Spencer		36	251
Martinsville		40	291
Port Royal		22	313
Indianapolis		25	338

POPULATION of the State of INDIANA ACCORDING TO THE Census of 1830.

Counties	Population
Allen	996
Bartholomew	5.476
Boone	622
Carroll	1.611
Cass	1.162
Clark	10.686
Clay	1.616
Clinton	1.423
Crawford	3.238
Daviess	4.543
Dearborn	13.974
Decatur	5.887
Delaware	2.374
Dubois	1.778
Elkhart	935
Fayette	9.112
Floyd	6.361
Fountain	7.619
Franklin	10.190
Gibson	5.418
Greene	4.242
Hamilton	1.757
Harrison	10.273
Hancock	1.436
Hendricks	3.975
Henry	6.497
Jackson	4.870
Jefferson	11.465
Jennings	3.974
Johnson	4.019
Knox	6.525
Lawrence	9.234
Madison	2.238
Marion	7.192
Martin	2.010
Monroe	6.577
Montgomery	7.317
Morgan	5.593
Orange	7.901
Owen	4.017
Perry	3.369
Pike	2.475
Posey	6.549
Putnam	8.262
Parke	7.535
Randolph	3.912
Ripley	3.988
Rush	9.707
St Joseph	287
Scott	3.092
Shelby	3.295
Spencer	3.196
Sullivan	4.680
Switzerland	7.028
Tippecanoe	7.187
Union	7.944
Vanderburg	2.611
Vermillion	5.692
Vigo	5.766
Warren	2.861
Warrick	2.877
Washington	13.064
Wayne	18.571
Total Population	343.031
White Males	175.885
Do. Females	163.514
Total White	352.390
Colored Males	1.857
Do. Females	1.772
Total Free Colored	3.629
Total Do.	343.028
Slaves Males	none
Do. Females	3
Total	343.031

The TOURIST'S POCKET MAP OF THE STATE OF INDIANA EXHIBITING ITS INTERNAL IMPROVEMENTS Roads Distances &c. BY J. H. YOUNG

PHILADELPHIA: PUBLISHED BY S. Augustus Mitchell. 1833.

EXPLANATION.

County Towns	—
Principal Roads	—
Common Do.	—
Canals	—
Do. Proposed	—
Rail Roads	—
Do. Do. Proy.	—

EXPLANATION.
The figures along the roads shew the distances in miles from place to place, and those nearest County Town, indicate its distance from the Capital of the State.

SCALE OF MILES.

Tourist Pocket Maps

JUDITH Q. MCMULLEN

————————————•————————————

One of the maps in the Indiana Historical Society's map collection is *The Tourist Pocket Map of the State of Indiana, Exhibiting Its Internal Improvements, Road Distances, &c.* This map, shown opposite, was created in 1833 by the engraver James Hamilton Young and published by Samuel Augustus Mitchell. Pocket maps, maps that are intended to be folded so they can be easily carried in a pocket or purse and referred to in the field, were common in the 1830s. The maps were printed on vellum paper (which was thought to resist folding) and fit into a small leather case. The maps often included indexes and historical information about the area.

According to Brian J. McFarland, "Pocket maps showed the growth of the transportation network, reflected ideas about the capitalist economy, and were central information resources about western lands." They were visual representations, "both realistically and metaphorically, of the progress and growth of the United States." Mitchell, who published many of the early pocket maps, founded a map-publishing house in Philadelphia in 1831, which, "during its most prosperous years employed 250 people and sold more than 4000 publications annually."[1]

Although Mitchell was not an engraver or cartographer, his pocket maps were created by a large team of engravers, compilers, printers, and binders. Mitchell began his business by purchasing the 1826 engravings from Anthony Finley's *New American Atlas.* He hired Finley's chief engraver, James H. Young, "to improve and update the plates, keeping them current with America's rapid growth in the early years of the nineteenth century."[2] Young became the Mitchell Company's principal compiler and draftsman, as well as chief engraver from 1830 on.

The Mitchell tourist pocket maps were widely available and produced in large numbers. A "tourist" was defined as "someone who completed a circuit or made a round trip."[3] Maps were of individual states only and focused on the developing transportation networks—roads, canals, steamboat routes, and railroads—in Ohio, Indiana, Illinois, and Michigan, the main destinations of many westward immigrants, travelers, and tourists.

The covers of the tourist pocket maps were 4¾ inches by 3 inches, made of pasteboard covered with plain leather (usually brown or deep maroon), with a simple gold-stamped title. The maps opened out to 18¾ inches by 13½ inches.

The 1833 Indiana tourist pocket map featured here focuses on internal improvements: existing roads, proposed roads and canals, and existing and proposed railroads. Population figures, reportedly from the 1830 census, are also given along with steamboat routes and distances in miles "from place to place" and from the state capital. The emphasis is on the state's growth. McFarland explains that the orderly design of this early Indiana map points to "future hopes of progress" and reveals the state as "a place of order and growth."[4] Tourist pocket maps helped travelers, tourists, and immigrants understand both the natural geography and the man-made internal improvements of the western expansion states.

1. Brian J. McFarland, "From Publisher to Pocket: Interpreting Early Nineteenth Century American History through the Pocket Maps of Samuel Augustus Mitchell" (PhD diss., University of Texas at Arlington, 2002), 5, 14.

2. Pierre Joppen, "Mitchell, Samuel Augustus," entry made January 20, 2003, in "Dictionary of Mapmakers" on Paulus Swaen's Web site, www.maphist.com (accessed June 6, 2006).

3. McFarland, "From Publisher to Pocket," 58.

4. Ibid., 70.

Gazetteers

LEIGH DARBEE

●

Gazetteers are valuable geographic sources that can be used in conjunction with maps. The word "gazetteer" was originally used to describe a person who wrote for a gazetteer—a newspaper— that is, a journalist. Gradually the word became identified with a thing rather than a person, and the meaning of the word changed. According to the *Oxford English Dictionary*, the transition between the old and new meanings of the word occurred during the last quarter of the seventeenth century.

The first gazetteer for the state of Indiana was compiled and published by John Scott and William M. Doughty in Centerville in 1826. The complete title of the work is *The Indiana Gazetteer, or Topographical Dictionary, Containing a Description of the Several Counties, Towns, Villages, Settlements, Roads, Lakes, Rivers, Creeks, Springs, &c. in the State of Indiana, Alphabetically Arranged.* Around July of 1826, Scott had published a map of the state. The gazetteer probably appeared in September and was intended as a companion piece to the map. While the work was not perfect—for example, it omitted Clarksville, an important Ohio River town—it was the first systematic attempt to provide information about Hoosier locales. Besides descriptions of location and, for larger

towns, brief histories, the gazetteer includes estimates of population for each city and town. According to the preface, these figures were calculated "from the official returns of the voters in 1825, by multiplying those numbers by five; which, however, is deemed, by some, too small a ratio."

An Indianapolis publishing firm, Douglass and Maguire, purchased the copyright from Scott and Doughty and published a second edition of the gazetteer in 1833, "carefully revised, corrected, and enlarged." James Scott was given credit for assisting with the revisions. The third edition, which appeared in 1849 with a similar title, was compiled by E. Chamberlain, who also produced an edition in 1850. Chamberlain's editions contain more extensive information, including, for larger towns, number and denomination of churches, number of doctors, and kinds of businesses operating in each place. Later gazetteers appeared at irregular intervals and under many titles. The Indiana Historical Society holds a representative sampling of gazetteers from the mid–nineteenth century to the early twentieth century:

G. W. Hawes' Indiana State Gazetteer and Business Directory, 1858/59 and 1860/61.

Indiana State Gazetteer and Shippers' Directory,
    1866/67.

Higgins and Ryan, *New Topographical Atlas and*
    Gazetteer of Indiana, 1870.

Indiana State Gazetteer and Business Directory,
    1880/81–1895/96.

Polk's Indiana State Gazetteer and Business Directory,
    1916/17.

Several of the volumes include reference maps and miscellaneous illustrations.

The early gazetteers were particularly chatty productions, offering qualitative assessments of the places described. These books included a fair amount of promotion for the state. For example, on pages 38 and 69, respectively, the 1826 volume describes Blue River as "a very handsome stream" and states that Indianapolis and its surroundings are "in an eminent degree beautiful and fertile." The early gazetteers could also be fairly political. Chamberlain was particularly pointed about what he was trying to accomplish and managed to find fault with a number of groups of fellow citizens in the process:

There are some circumstances that render it more difficult to prepare a good Gazetteer of this State than of almost any other. There have been few books written about the State to refer to, rapid improvements have been constantly going on, of which little is known, even in the vicinity; other improvements are loudly talked *of and supposed to be done almost before they are commenced, and the real business men meet at no common point where they could be consulted and the truth ascertained. . . . They . . . know little of the State, except where their immediate business lies. The politicians, the speculators in companies and in town lots, and others without pressing business, who assemble at Indianapolis, have time to talk, when they meet there, but the information they give is not always the* most *certain. These matters render it the more important that a book like this should be published. It will correct some errors, it will lead to inquiries as to others, and the tendency will be to aid in forming a State character of which the citizens may be proud.[1]*

TOPOGRAPHY AND STATISTICS.   293

LITTLE WHITE LICK rises in the west part of Marion, runs south through a corner of Hendricks into Morgan, where it unites with the main stream, two miles below Mooresville.

LITTLE WILD CAT, a branch of the main stream of that name, in Howard county.

LIVONIA, a small town in Washington county, twelve miles west of Salem, and nine east of Paoli.

LOCKPORT, a small town on the canal, in Carroll county, ten miles north-east of Delphi.

LOCKPORT, a small town in Vigo county, nine miles south-east of Terre Haute.

LOGAN, a township in Dearborn county, population 660.

LOGAN, a township in the north of Fountain, population 1,515.

LOGAN, a southern township in Pike county, population 650.

LOG LICK, a small stream in Switzerland county, running south-west into the Ohio six miles above Vevay.

LOGANSPORT, the Seat of Justice of Cass county, is situated in the forks of the Wabash and Eel river, in latitude 40 deg. 45 min. and in longitude 9 deg. 16 min. west. It was first settled in 1829, by G. McBean, J. H. Kintner, D. Patrick, James Smith, C. Carter, H. Todd, J. and C. Vigus, Gen. J. Tipton, who was the principal proprietor, J. B. Duret, and others. The whole number of buildings at this time in Logansport is 373, of which twenty-nine are of stone, forty-eight of brick, and 296 of timber. The population is about 2,700. The Court House, built of cut stone, is one of the finest buildings in the west. Three of the Churches, the Old School Presbyterian, the Episcopalian and the Catholic, are fine stone buildings, and the Methodists and New School Presbyterians also have good Churches there.

The favorable situation of Logansport for trade and business, the immense amount of water power there, and the fertile country in the vicinity, must make it among the best towns in the State. While the Miami Reserve, lying immediately south of the Wabash, was held by the

A page from Chamberlain's 1850 gazetteer

While the later gazetteers gradually lose the sense of their compilers' personalities, they nonetheless trace the growth of the state over time. The most recent and thorough gazetteer in the IHS collection is the Indiana volume of *The National Gazetteer of the United States of America,* published in 1988. According to its foreword, "'The National Gazetteer of the United States of America' is the result of a long-term effort to provide a standard reference to the Nation's named places, features, and areas." Thus, what the book lacks in idiosyncrasy, it redeems by standardizing descriptions of places across the country. It also includes references to many kinds of features that were generally not covered in the older gazetteers. Each entry includes the name, the feature class (such as stream, cemetery, dam, canal, locale), status of the name (for example, established by the Board of Geographic Names, unofficial, variant), county, geographic coordinates, source (of valleys, streams, and arroyos), elevation, and map reference in the U.S. Geological Survey 7.5 minute topographical maps.

Gazetteers can be helpful to family historians in providing information about the size and character of places in which their ancestors lived. They are particularly helpful for information about towns that have vanished from current maps.

1. *The Indiana Gazetteer, or, Topographical Dictionary of the State of Indiana* (Indianapolis: E. Chamberlain, 1849), [vii]–viii.

County Boundary Changes

LEIGH DARBEE

———————————— • ————————————

Family historians are aware of the importance of county history to genealogical research, but some may not realize that the history of a county's formation can affect one's success in locating information. County boundaries are not static. Although they do not change significantly any more, during much of Indiana's history one boundary or another was changing almost all of the time. An extremely useful resource on the changes in Indiana county boundaries is *Indiana Boundaries: Territory, State, and County*. The compilers outline why such a book is needed for Indiana: "Unlike some commonwealths, Indiana did not, upon admission to statehood, lay out a framework for the future county organization of her entire territory. Nor did county organization in Indiana follow any other carefully prepared plan. . . . [County] organization actually followed irregularly behind the lines of Indian cessions and pioneer settlements."[1]

Scott County can be used to demonstrate how boundary changes might affect research. Following is a summary, taken from volume 2 of the *Historical Atlas and Chronology of County Boundaries, 1788–1980*, of how the shape of Scott County has changed since its founding:

February 1, 1820: Scott County created from Clark, Jackson, Jefferson, Jennings, and Washington Counties
December 26, 1820: Lost land to Washington County
January 22, 1830: Gained land from Jefferson County
February 16, 1839: Gained land from Clark and Washington Counties
December 5, 1842: Lost land to Clark County
February 13, 1851: Gained land from Jefferson County

The compiler of this volume lays out why changes like those Scott County experienced may be of concern to researchers:

Counties or their equivalents cover nearly all the territory of the coterminous forty-eight states and operate as the highest level of local government and administration. They are the primary units for the administration of justice, the assessment and collection of taxes, the recording of births, deaths, marriages, and wills, the organization of census data and other kinds of statistics, and they have long

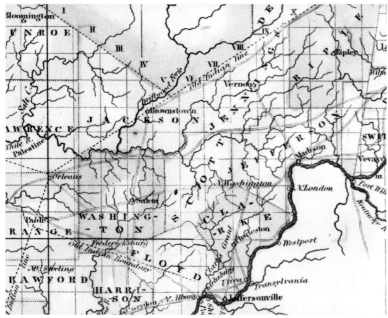

1821 map of Scott and surrounding counties, excerpted from map titled *Indiana* by Lucas Fielding Jr. (Baltimore, 1821)

1838 map of Scott and surrounding counties, excerpted from map titled *Indiana* by T[homas]. G. Bradford (Boston, 1838)

served as the basis for national and state legislative apportionment. Any change in county boundary lines can effectively "move" people and resources in the affected area from one county to another.[2]

As one can see, although families may have lived in a particular county at a given time, they may not have stayed there—even if they never moved!

———————————— ● ————————————

1. George Pence and Nellie C. Armstrong, *Indiana Boundaries: Territory, State, and County*, vol. 19, Indiana Historical Collections (Indianapolis: Indiana Historical Bureau, 1967), 28.

2. Stephen L. Hansen, comp., *Historical Atlas and Chronology of County Boundaries, 1788–1980*, vol. 2, *Illinois, Indiana, Ohio* (Boston: G. K. Hall, 1984), 1, 250.

Selected Bibliography: *Atlas of Historical County Boundaries: Indiana.* Edited by John H. Long. Compiled by Peggy Sinko. New York: Charles Scribner's Sons, 1996.

County Atlases

LEIGH DARBEE

County atlases can be a valuable source for family history information. Michael P. Conzen, an historian of the county atlas, summarized its function as follows: It "was built on the principle of showing the ownership of all land parcels within the rural parts of a given county, set in the context of the area's main natural and cultural features such as rivers, hills, roads, railroads, towns, and administrative boundaries."[1]

More than seven hundred county atlases were published between 1862 and 1886. Most of the seven hundred were published in the 1870s, with 1875 being the peak production year. Two-thirds of the atlases covered the areas north of the Ohio River and in the upper Mississippi River valley. Indiana counties garnered more than fifty atlases of this total.[2]

Atlases were sold by subscription. Therefore, salesmen persuaded many county residents to pay for the atlases in order to have their biographies, portraits, and pictures of their farms and/or prize livestock included. These atlases were published before photographically illustrated books were common, so the largely lithographed illustrations were originally hand drawn. Because the cartographic entrepreneurs needed a certain critical mass of population to turn a profit, many areas of the United States were never documented in atlases, while other areas—such as the booming Midwest—had an abundance of volumes.

The content of atlases gradually became standardized. A majority of volumes produced during the heyday of county atlases included most of the following features: a state map; a county map; page-sized maps of individual townships; town and city plats done on a large scale to show detail; natural and man-made features such as rivers and roads; names of landowners and number of acres owned; locations of churches, schools, stores, businesses, factories, rail lines and facilities, and so on.

While searching for mentions of ancestors and their landholdings in county atlases, pay attention to other features that may tell something about these people's lives: Who were their neighbors? Where did they establish their farms, not only in relation to towns, but also to schools, churches, and woodlots? How close did they live to rail lines, major roads, or other transportation routes? Imagine how their location in relation to these other features might have affected their daily lives.

1. Michael P. Conzen, "North American County Maps and Atlases," in *From Sea Charts to Satellite Images: Interpreting North American History through Maps,* edited by David Buisseret (Chicago: University of Chicago Press, 1990), 186.

2. Walter W. Ristow, *American Maps and Mapmakers: Commercial Cartography in the Nineteenth Century* (Detroit: Wayne State University Press, 1985), 420.

Map of Center Township, from *Combination Atlas Map of Grant County, Indiana* ([Chicago]: Kingman Bros., 1877)

Thematic Maps

LEIGH DARBEE

———————————————— • ————————————————

Once geographic knowledge about a given area has become well established, mapmakers compile other kinds of maps offering information that can be layered over basic geography. Such cartographic works fall into the broad category of thematic maps. Thematic maps provide a way to convey a great deal of knowledge in graphic shorthand, assuming that the viewer has some familiarity with basic geography and cartographic conventions. Thematic maps often impart social or economic information and can be qualitative, recording the presence of features, or quantitative, attaching some sort of value to those features. As map historian Alan Hodgkiss comments, "Mapmakers began to consider not just 'where is it?' but 'what is there?' and eventually 'how much is there and what is its value?'" Both types of thematic maps are invaluable in historical research since they often record features that have either changed radically over time or no longer exist. This chapter describes two qualitative thematic maps.

One example of a qualitative thematic map is reprinted in William Ingraham Kip's *The Early Jesuit Missions in North America* (Figure 1). Jesuit missionaries were responsible for much of the early mapping of the Great Lakes region, basing their work on both their own observations and on maps and verbal descriptions supplied by Native Americans. For about fifty years after the death of Samuel de Champlain in 1635, the Jesuits were the primary explorers and mappers of what became the upper Midwest. The French government barred other explorers and fur traders from the Great Lakes region between 1632 and 1681 to provide the Jesuits the opportunity to establish religious missions free of secular influence. Jesuit efforts to lay spiritual claim to the region and its inhabitants had as a byproduct dramatically improved geographical knowledge of the area, which was incorporated into the first printed European maps of Lake Superior and the Mississippi River.

The geographical features in the Jesuits' map (Figure 1) are limited to lakes and rivers, the vital transportation routes used by both the Jesuit missionaries and the Native Americans they hoped to convert. Portages are shown because they were links between those waterways; familiarity with their locations enhanced the Jesuits' mobility.

Along these bodies of water are shown forts, native villages, and missions. A few of these are depicted using shorthand symbols, but most are miniature delinea-

(Left) Figure 1: Portion of the map captioned "Copy of a Map, Published by the Jesuits, in 1664" by William Ingraham Kip in his book *The Early Jesuit Missions in North America* (New York: Wiley and Putnam, 1846)

(Below) Figure 2: *Owen County, Indiana* in A. T. DeGroot, *The Churches of Christ in Owen County, Indiana* (Spencer, IN: Samuel R. Guard and Co., [1935])

tions of structures, with a European twist: Forts are shown turreted and castlelike, while both missions and Indian villages are represented by western-style buildings. These representations bore scant relationship to how the sites actually looked, but the architectural depictions would have been meaningful to the Jesuits' audiences back in Europe. At the same time, they symbolized the increasing European presence in North America, of which the Jesuits were the vanguard.

Another thematic map with a religious subject shows a different way to impart qualitative information. It locates Churches of Christ in Owen County as of 1935 (Figure 2). As in the Jesuit map, the cartographer included only enough geographical features to allow the viewer to place the area shown; in this case, the only "standard" geographical details are the outline of the county, township boundaries and names, and the course of the White River. The rest of the information pertains specifically to the subject at hand. Abstract symbols represent individual church buildings, with meanings as follows:

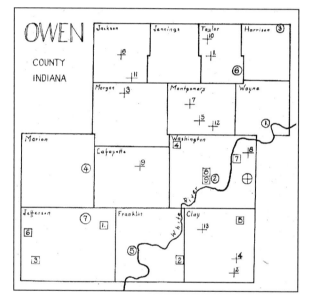

« Closed churches
⊕ Chambersville (New Light) Christian Church
£ Churches of Christ
○ Christian Churches

The numbers associated with each symbol refer to an accompanying list that identifies specific churches by name. While the manner of depicting individual sites differs radically from the method used by the Jesuits,

the information is conveyed in a manner that is appropriate to the compiler's intent. The remainder of the book contains narrative descriptions of each church, along with transcriptions of membership rolls.

Family historians can use information from thematic maps as one way to understand the social and economic contexts in which their ancestors lived. While the availability of these specialized maps is unpredictable, when they are found they can provide information not available in any other source.

Selected Bibliography: Hodgkiss, A. G. *Understanding Maps: A Systematic History of Their Use and Development.* Folkestone, UK: Dawson, 1981.

Indiana's Pioneer Periods

COMPILED BY JUDITH Q. MCMULLEN

———————————————————— • ————————————————————

When the Society of Indiana Pioneers began in 1916, a member had to have at least one ancestor who had lived in Indiana during the year 1830 or earlier. It was soon recognized, however, that few people could qualify on the basis of an ancestor who had lived north of Indianapolis since much of the northern part of the state was in the hands of the Native Americans in 1830. Charles N. Thompson, president of the society in 1925, appointed a committee to study this problem. The committee recommended allowing membership to those applicants whose ancestors had come to an Indiana county within five years of the earliest land entry in the county as well as to those whose ancestors had been in the state by 1830. After the constitution was amended to reflect this change in 1927, it was found that the determination of land entries created other problems. Upon more study, the date of the organization of the county was seen as a significant factor also.

In 1932 Thompson compiled a map grouping the counties of Indiana into three sections, "divided approximately according to the progress of settlement," showing for each county the dates of the first white settlement, the organization of the county, the

convening of the first court, and the first land entry. The sections reveal three pioneer periods of settlement in Indiana: 1) that of the southern part, including thirty-six counties, from 1800–1818; 2) that of the central part, including twenty-two counties, from 1818–1830; and 3) that of the northern part, including thirty-four counties, from 1830–1850. From this data, a schedule for membership eligibility was adopted in 1933.

Thompson found that the three main determining factors in the settlement of southern Indiana were transportation, closeness of earlier settlements, and the release of lands occupied by the Native Americans. Settlers before 1816 came primarily from Virginia, Kentucky, Tennessee, and North Carolina. In the Whitewater region, many came from Ohio and Pennsylvania, along with large numbers of Quakers from the South, immigrating because of their opposition to slavery.

Thompson cited two additional factors that made the settlement of central and northern Indiana difficult—disease and the physical condition of the land. Old-growth forests had to be cleared, and virgin sod had to be broken. Central and northern Indiana were settled by native Hoosiers; immigrants from Ohio, the eastern states, and Europe; and central Indiana by people from the southern states as well. The National Road, Michigan Road, and smaller roads aided access to the northern Indiana counties during the 1830s. As the map shows, there was slow development from the earliest pioneer settlements in southern Indiana to the final pioneer settlements in northern Indiana.

Selected Bibliography: Holliday, Murray. "Qualification—Membership." *A History of the Society of Indiana Pioneers, 1916–1980.* Greenfield, IN: Mitchell-Fleming Printing, 1980–1983.

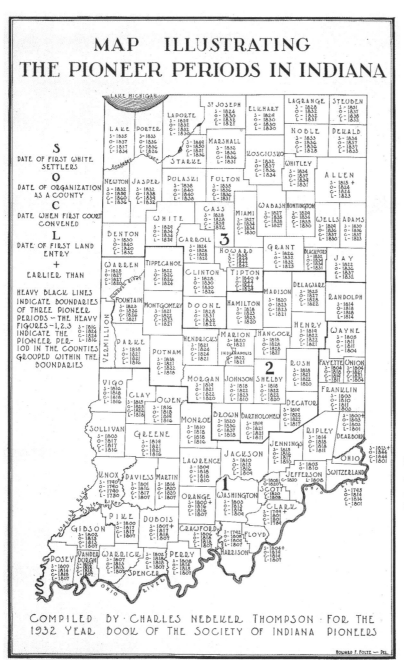

Charles Nebeker Thompson, *The Pioneer Periods in Indiana*, map in *Year Book of the Society of Indiana Pioneers, 1932* (Original map in IHS collections)

1879 Political Map of Indiana

JUDITH Q. MCMULLEN

Maps showing political divisions are one example of thematic maps that depict a particular subject rather than natural geographic details. Political maps show the boundaries and names of districts, which are determined by census data. The holding of regular censuses in the United States after 1790 provided a large potential source of mappable data.

The *New Political Map of Indiana* divides the state into thirteen districts, showing the counties in each district and the number of male inhabitants over twenty-one in each county in 1877. It depicts in marginal tables the breakdown by districts and counties of the gubernatorial election of 1876 between James Douglas Williams and Benjamin Harrison. Harrison was unsuccessful in his bid for governor, losing to Williams by 5,139 votes; however, he became the twenty-third president of the United States in 1889. The breakdown of votes by counties for the secretary of state election of 1878 is also given in the margins of the map. For this election, there is also a listing of the number of "colored voters" in the state "as enumerated by the Township Trustees in 1877." According to this enumeration, there were 442,972 white voters in the state in 1877 and 8,056 colored voters. The

breakdown of colored voters by district shows that the largest numbers were in the First District (1,553) and the Seventh District (1,967), while the smallest number was in the Twelfth District (71). The following counties had the largest numbers of colored voters: Marion County, 1,907; Vanderburgh County, 693; Clarke County, 486; and Wayne County, 380.

Other marginal information on the map includes the "Total Vote in 1876" for governor and for president of the United States. The 1876 presidential election had many similarities to the 2000 election—with similar controversy over the outcome. Samuel Jones Tilden (1814–1886), the Democratic candidate, received about 250,000 more votes than Rutherford B. Hayes (1822–1893), the Republican candidate. Tilden had 184 uncontested electoral votes versus 163 for Hayes. After the election, however, the Republicans challenged votes from South Carolina, Florida, Louisiana, and Oregon. The Electoral Commission, set up to decide the outcome of the contested votes, decided all the states in favor of Hayes, who was elected president by one electoral vote.[1] According to historian James H. Madison, "Nearly all of the Indiana electorate voted in late nineteenth century presidential contests," and

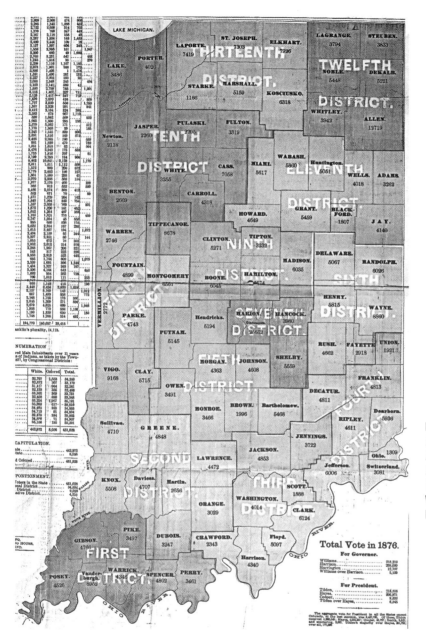

Portion of *A New Political Map of Indiana which Shows the Total Number of Male Inhabitants in the State over Twenty-One Years of Age* (Fort Wayne, IN: Wm. Fleming, Sentinel Printing House, [1879])

the largest turnouts in 1876 and 1896 were close to 95 percent.[2] Tilden, who carried Indiana by about 6,000 votes, always maintained that he was "wrongfully deprived of the election."[3]

1. *Merriam-Webster's Biographical Dictionary* (Springfield, MA: Merriam-Webster, 1995), 1,026.

2. James H. Madison, *The Indiana Way: A State History* (Bloomington: Indiana University Press; Indianapolis: Indiana Historical Society, 1986), 211.

3. *Merriam-Webster's Biographical Dictionary*, 1,026.

Mapping the Ohio River

LEIGH DARBEE

F ighting a war on a frontier is always a tricky business, and the struggles among the French, British, and Americans on North American soil in the eighteenth century were no exception to this rule. Among the many needs of frontier armies were engineers to perform tasks such as building forts and other defensible structures and analyzing for commanding officers the navigability of rivers and streams, the quickest travel routes at the time. The engineers who played a vital role in American victories during the French and Indian War and the American Revolution were the skeletal beginnings of what became the U.S. Army Corps of Engineers. A 1992 history of the Ohio River Division of the corps by Leland R. Johnson summarizes the achievements of these engineers in the Ohio River basin: "The first missions of Army Engineers in the basin had . . . a military character, in support of troop units operating on the trans-Appalachian frontier and as a contribution to the security of the basin's first settlements. This dual military-civil mission has continued in the basin under direction of the U.S. Army Corps of Engineers."

The Corps of Engineers was permanently established by Congress in 1802. In order to train engi-

neers on American soil, Congress established the U.S. Military Academy at West Point, New York, the same year. Since its inception, the corps has pursued innumerable projects throughout the country. Those have included building roads (for example, the corps worked on constructing the National Road), railroads, bridges, lighthouses, and water control features such as dams and levees.

The Ohio River basin was, and has remained, a major focus of the corps' work. Much of that work has centered on improving Ohio River navigability for the purposes of both national defense and the promotion of commercial interests. The corps has worked on the river in a succession of fifty-year projects, beginning in 1824 with one to open and maintain a safe and sufficiently deep navigation channel. In 1875 the corps undertook its second Ohio River program, the "canalization" of the river including constructing fifty-three locks and dams to control the river's level and flow to prevent flooding. The first dam was started near Pittsburgh in 1879, and the last was completed in 1929.

From 1911 to 1914, the corps compiled a series of 280 charts, plus an index sheet, covering the Ohio River from Pittsburgh to its mouth near Cairo, Illi-

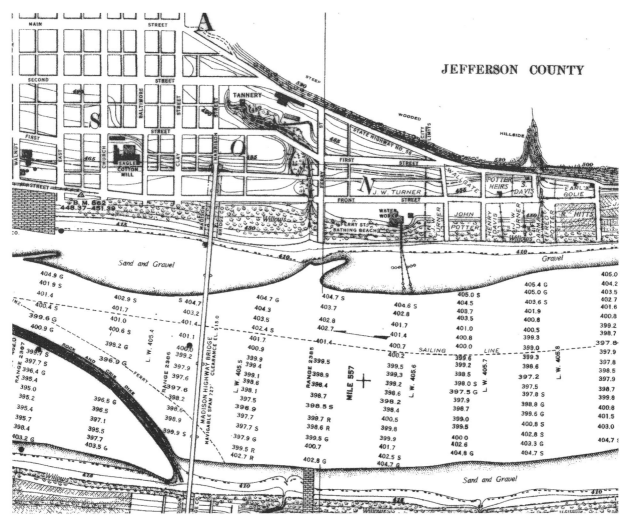

Detail from Chart No. 155 (Mile 557–60), United States Army Corps of Engineers, *Atlas of the Ohio River, Consisting of 280 Charts and Index Sheet: Survey of 1911–14, Ohio River, Pittsburgh, Pa., to Mouth* (Detroit: Photolithed and printed at U.S. Lake Survey Office, ca. 1914)

nois, which is available at the IHS library. These charts, published under the title *Atlas of the Ohio River*, were likely done in response to a 1910 act by Congress that authorized the construction of the locks and dams on the lower part of the river. The charts were executed by the corps' district engineer officer in Louisville, Kentucky.

Similar to many maps that were originally drawn for a very specific purpose, these river charts contain many features of interest to general researchers today. Drawn at a scale of 1 inch = 600 feet, they show a great amount of detail. The charts depict between 2,000 and 3,000 feet of land on either side of the river and about 300 feet on either side of tributary rivers and streams, which are charted approximately 1,200

to 1,500 feet upstream from where they enter the Ohio. With this much land shown on the riverbanks, researchers can get a fairly detailed picture of what the riverfront looked like anywhere along the Ohio during the first dozen years of the twentieth century.

As one would expect, many of the features shown are ones that would be of particular interest to the corps. These include such things as river depths; the length and elevation of bridges; which bridges are navigable; the main navigation channel and channel markers; retaining walls and dikes; sewers; features of the riverbed such as sand, gravel, mud, boulders, and rock; locations of locks and dams; and historical information on low water, high water, and "normal pool" along the river.

Railroads are shown and labeled by name, and supporting structures such as roundhouses and stations appear clearly. Factories are named, and the charts show "footprints" of all buildings in factory complexes. In addition, the charts locate a wide variety of other features, including parks, streets, schools, penitentiaries, quarries, streetcar tracks, and racetracks. There are useful notations such as "residences on hillside" and "pasture" versus "cultivation."

In the middle of the corps' second fifty-year project, in late March 1913, a flood ravaged the Ohio River basin, making abundantly clear the need for a flood protection and control plan. This flood and others led Congress to pass the Flood Control Act of 1917, which authorized federal flood control of the Mississippi and its tributaries, including the Ohio. The charts in the series *Atlas of the Ohio River* that were completed before the catastrophic flood must have proven invaluable to the corps in placing the flood in historical context and in documenting what the flood destroyed.

The *Atlas*'s charts were superseded by a new set of charts created by the corps in 1930, the year following the completion of the original system of locks and dams. This new set was also done in anticipation of the corps' third fifty-year plan for the Ohio River basin, which concentrated on flood control. All but two of the original locks and dams have been replaced under the corps' fourth plan, the Ohio River Modernization Project, which since the 1950s has concentrated on building locks and dams that are larger and higher.

———————————— • ————————————

Selected Bibliography: Johnson, Leland R. "Engineering the Ohio." In *Always a River: The Ohio River and the American Experience*. Robert L. Reid, ed. Bloomington: Indiana University Press, 1991; Johnson, Leland R. *The Falls City Engineers: A History of the Louisville District, Corps of Engineers, United States Army*. Louisville, KY: U.S. Army Corps of Engineers, 1974; Johnson, Leland R. *The Ohio River Division, U.S. Army Corps of Engineers: The History of a Central Command*. Cincinnati: U.S. Army Corps of Engineers, Ohio River Division, 1992.

Railroad Maps

LEIGH DARBEE

T he romantic image of westward migration usually involves a Conestoga wagon laboriously making its way across the prairie. Means of migration evolved as time passed, however, and modes of travel generally became easier and faster. Migrants coming to Indiana certainly came by wagon in the early days, but they also used water transportation, when possible, to ease their way. These modes were supplemented by canals, which took routes that diverged from natural watercourses and allowed settlers to penetrate farther inland. After the first quarter of the nineteenth century, however, rail travel quickly eclipsed other forms of transportation in speed and in the variety and extent of travel routes.

The earliest rail passenger line in the United States was the Baltimore and Ohio, which had fourteen miles of track in operation by the end of 1830. Indiana was not too far behind: The Madison and Indianapolis (M&I) Railroad, which connected the Ohio River to the fast-growing state capital, was chartered in 1836, had fifteen miles of track completed out of Madison by 1838, and reached the capital by 1847. Indianapolis quickly became a rail hub, a windfall after early discovery that the White River was not, after all, navigable for boats of any

size and after the city's section of the Wabash and Erie Canal was left as a fragment by the boondoggle of the internal improvement schemes of the 1830s. One nickname for Indianapolis from the late nineteenth century was, indeed, "Railroad City."

Maps have always been a vital accompaniment to railroad construction and operation. Maps have been used in prospectuses for new rail lines, to attract investors to support one line or another and to promote passenger travel on particular railroads. Compilers of such maps were not above distorting them to their own ends: emphasizing the track route by the thickness or color of the line to make it appear as the most vital component of the map or altering routes to make them look as straight—and therefore as quick—as possible. In fact, many of the mapped routes were never built.

The map illustrating this chapter displays some of those features. It was issued with an 1850 report to M&I Railroad stockholders. The text, compiled by M&I president John Brough, begins:

Aware of the deep interest you [as stockholders] take, not only in your own road, but the various other roads now in process of construction in the State of

Indiana, which connect with, or are by some supposed as promising, in the future, to compete with the Madison Road . . . I have caused to be prepared an accurate map of the State, with all the railroads projected, and in process of execution, laid down upon it.

Col. Thomas A. Morris, former chief engineer of the M&I, created the map. It emphasized the route of the M&I, and several other lines shown on the map were never built. Though the report was represented by Brough as informational, he also wanted to make M&I stockholders aware of possible *competition* from other lines, competition that might affect the return on their investments in the M&I.

Thomas A. Morris, *Railroad Map of Indiana*, created for the Madison and Indianapolis Railroad, 1850. Morris's map depicts projections for rail lines from fourteen possible competitors with the M&I Railroad (listed on the right side of the map). However, several of these lines were never built.

Genealogists trying to flesh out their family histories with details about their ancestors' experiences, including the mode of transportation they might have used in migrating to Indiana or elsewhere, might want to consider using railroad maps for supplemental information. As has been pointed out, however, these maps—like all primary sources—must be viewed with a certain amount of skepticism; the information in them cannot necessarily be taken at face value. If you find a rail route on a map that makes sense in terms of what you know about your ancestors' travels, you will want to determine whether that line was built and, if so, whether it existed at the time your forebear would have been traveling in a given area. If you are fortunate, you may locate timetables for a particular route and be able to add a little extra detail to your story. You should also be aware that rail lines are notoriously subject to mergers and reorganizations, so the name of a line may have changed substantially over time. Many books on railroads are available that may help you figure out the details; a small selection of them is mentioned below. You can also find references for many more titles by searching the Indiana Historical Society's online catalog through its Web site, www.indianahistory.org.

Selected Bibliography: Modelski, Andrew M. *Railroad Maps of North America: The First Hundred Years.* Washington, DC: Library of Congress, 1984; Modelski, Andrew M. *Railroad Maps of the United States.* Washington, DC: Library of Congress, 1975; *Railroad Map of the State of Indiana, with a Statement of the Condition of the Roads Now in Process of Construction.* N.p.: Madison and Indianapolis Railroad, 1850; Simons, Richard S., and Francis H. Parker. *Railroads of Indiana.* Bloomington: Indiana University Press, 1997; Sulzer, Elmer G. *Ghost Railroads of Indiana.* Indianapolis: Vane A. Jones, 1970. Reprint, Bloomington: Indiana University Press, 1998 (volumes for Kentucky and Tennessee are also available).

Urban Transit Maps

LEIGH DARBEE

A popular souvenir item in recent years has been a T-shirt displaying the London Underground transit system, primarily because of its pleasingly bold and colorful graphic design. Most U.S. cities would be hard-pressed to offer a similar item to their out-of-town visitors because of the rapid decline of America's urban transit systems since the mid-twentieth century. However, many American cities, including several in Indiana, once did boast extensive systems and substantial ridership.

Urban transit systems generally developed as the growth of cities grew beyond the point where people were within walking distance from home to work. This radius is commonly estimated to be between one and two miles. Early systems used animal-powered omnibuses, which—as their Latin-derived name indicates—were vehicles "for all." These gave way first to horse- or mule-drawn streetcars and later to electric trolleys and streetcars.

The need for urban transit grew in part out of the increasing diversification of the working class and as the middle class became sufficiently affluent to move out of the city center. In his seminal study of the Boston area, *Streetcar Suburbs*, Sam Bass Warner Jr. states the following about the "central middle class":

They "had stricter transportation needs. Their hours of work were long, but unlike the lower middle class their places of work tended to be stable so that they had a predictable route of travel. Nor was multiple employment a necessity for these families. As a result good linear streetcar service, or even railroad service if the stations were handy, was all they required."[1]

The history of transit systems in Indiana followed patterns similar to those found in Boston and other major cities. A few examples: The transit system in Anderson developed in the 1890s but was nonexistent by the 1960s. In Columbus the street railway started about 1890; streetcars were discontinued in 1932 in favor of buses. Evansville's system started with a metropolitan rail line in about 1865; streetcar service was discontinued in 1939. Kokomo had a street railway beginning about 1892; its streetcars ran until 1932. Terre Haute's system was started about 1866; streetcar service ended in 1939.

Streetcar service in Indianapolis began about 1864, provided by the Citizens' Street Railway Company. This company was succeeded by the Citizens' Street Railroad Company in 1890, the Indianapolis Street Railway Company in 1899, and Indianapolis Railways, Incorporated, in 1932. The People's Motor

Coach Company offered competing service by bus in 1923, but it was bought out by the Indianapolis Street Railway Company in 1927; the latter company had started offering bus service in 1924 as an extension of its streetcar service. By the 1940s, Indianapolis Railways offered trolleybus service on most of the streetcar routes. The last streetcar operated on the Broad Ripple line in 1953.

The map shown here dates from about 1937 and shows the transition in progress from streetcars to buses. It was issued by Indianapolis Railways and likely was meant to be displayed in a public area for passengers to find their routes. The map shows streetcar lines, trackless trolley lines, feeder bus lines, "connecting with [street]cars," and motor coach lines "direct to Circle." An inset map shows "downtown car and bus routings." Other information includes frequency of service during rush hours and the rest of the day, at night, and on Sundays.

After World War II, the development of city bus service, the dramatic increase in individual automobile ownership, and explosive suburban growth brought about rapid changes in the transit picture. The Indianapolis area is one of many textbook examples of these changes, with its ever-expanding suburbs and roadways to serve them. The transit picture in 1937, while it too shows society in transition, seems refreshingly simple in comparison.

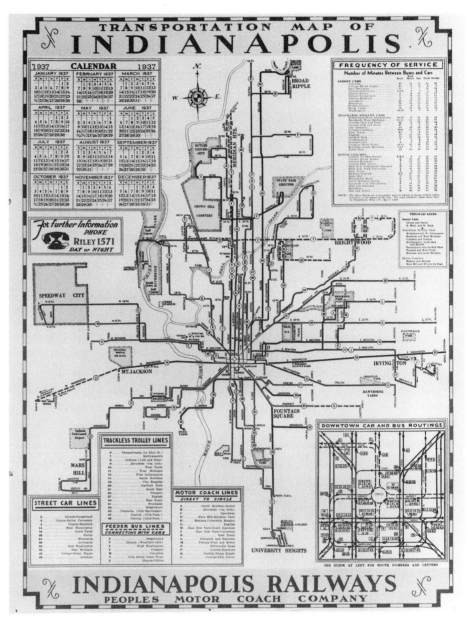

Indianapolis Railways, *Transportation Map of Indianapolis* (Indianapolis, 1937)

1. Sam Bass Warner, *Streetcar Suburbs: The Process of Growth in Boston, 1870–1900* (Cambridge, MA: Harvard University Press, 1962), 55.

[The author thanks Bill Vandervoort and his Chicago Transit and Railfan Web site, http://hometown.aol.com/chirailfan/, for permission to use information he compiled about the history of transit systems in Indiana.]

Automobile Maps

LEIGH DARBEE

———————————•———————————

Railroad maps as a category of transportation maps were produced for a variety of reasons, from information to propaganda. Train travel was over routes and by schedules set by the railroads, so maps were not needed for directions. Other travel was generally fairly circumscribed; one historian estimates that people rarely traveled farther than about twenty-five miles from home, so they likely had little need for directional signs or maps. The late nineteenth century, however, saw the beginnings of more extensive, self-directed travel for pleasure and recreation. This began with the growth in popularity of cycling, which in turn led to calls for improvements in road mapping. The first organized national cyclists' group, the League of American Wheelmen (LAW), founded in 1880, spearheaded the development of maps and guides.

Automobile drivers gradually eclipsed cyclists as the largest group of individual travelers starting with the introduction of the Model T in 1908. Thus, as map historian Walter W. Ristow has pointed out in a quote from an early motorist, development had to continue to make road maps truly useful for automobilists: "Road maps are not very helpful, as they are usually made for wheelmen. A road may be good for bicycles, as they need only a narrow strip, but an automobile must have wide wagon roads." Early motorists had a number of concerns, since early-twentieth-century highway technology lagged behind developments in automobile technology. As with cycling, a pervasive problem was the lack of hard-surfaced roads and the resulting problems of driving through mud and snow. In addition to the lack of road maps, there was no extensive system of road signage, though cyclists had begun to remedy that through the LAW's "Good Roads" movement.

Automobile guides and maps compensated for the lack of route markings in different ways. An early solution was the production in book form of verbal descriptions accompanied by photographs of routes, so a driver—or his navigator—could literally see the route to be followed. The IHS has an example of one of these guidebooks, *Chicago to South Bend and Michigan City*, published in Chicago in 1905. It is a cumbersome and expensive means to an end, however, so guides and maps gradually became more standardized and used increasingly stylized methods to convey precise information. Guides of this kind in the IHS collection include *Automobile Blue Book* (1909), *Bowen's Automobile and Sportsmen's Guide for*

Indiana (1917), *The Complete Official Road Guide of the Lincoln Highway* (1924), *Goodrich Route Book: Ohio and Indiana* (1913), *King's Official Route Guide* (1910 and 1915), and the one illustrated here, *Scarborough's Official Tour Book: Indiana, Ohio, Michigan, Illinois, Wisconsin and Trunk Lines* (1917).

The page shown is a segment of Trip No. 724, Indianapolis to Fort Wayne. There are advertisements at the top of the page for two businesses whose services would interest motorists. These are followed by part of the narrative description of the route, with mileage from the center of Indianapolis on the left and, on the right, directions about landmarks to note and turns to make. Potentially hazardous points in the journey—in this segment a railroad grade crossing—are marked with a boldfaced star and the word "Danger." Under the city of Anderson, three businesses are listed; there are display ads for all of these on the page before the one shown here. The final element is a city map—in this case, Marion—showing the route through town for Trip No. 724 and also showing where four other trip routes intersect it.

Even though signage, route marking, and highway construction continued to change and improve, there has continued to be a need for road maps, and those maps have become more detailed and inclusive. More and more, however, electronics are being applied to highway travel. Paper road maps and guidebooks may soon become strictly collectors' items, as cars increasingly come equipped with global positioning systems and other high-tech driving aids.

Scarborough's Official Tour Book: Indiana, Ohio, Michigan, Illinois, Wisconsin and Trunk Lines (Indianapolis: Scarborough Motor Guide, 1917), 14

Selected Bibliography: Belasco, Warren James. *Americans on the Road: From Autocamp to Motel, 1910–1945.* Baltimore: Johns Hopkins University Press, 1997; Hokanson, Drake. *The Lincoln Highway: Main Street Across America.* Iowa City: University of Iowa Press, 1999; Jakle, John A. *The Motel in America.* Baltimore: Johns Hopkins University Press, 1996; Ristow, Walter W. "American Road Maps and Guides." *The Scientific Monthly* 62 (1946): 397–406;

"Road Maps: The American Way," an online exhibit by the Osher Map Library, University of Southern Maine, Portland, at www.usm.maine.edu/maps/exhibit9 (accessed March 14, 2006); Schlereth, Thomas J. *U.S. 40: A Roadscape of the American Experience.* Indianapolis: Indiana Historical Society, 1985; Yorke, Douglas A., et al. *Hitting the Road: The Art of the American Road Map.* San Francisco: Chronicle Books, 1996.

Highway Maps

LEIGH DARBEE

●

The early guidebooks for the use of automobilists tended to be highly pictorial, wordy, or both. As the number of automobiles and drivers increased and the building and marking of roads improved, people were able to drive longer distances. Bulky guidebooks became impractical and were gradually replaced with highway maps.

Road improvement allowed people to travel in an increasingly larger radius from their homes. Consequently, the idea of automobile travel for pleasure quickly became a major growth industry in the United States. The prestige of being an auto-touring pioneer, with the attendant hardships of that status, quickly gave way to a clamor for ease of travel. While during much of the nineteenth and early twentieth centuries road building and maintenance were seen primarily as state and county issues, this view changed as auto touring became increasingly popular. Federal funds for highway improvement and construction were made available to the states for the first time with the Federal Aid Road Act of 1916. The American Automobile Association (AAA), founded in 1902, was a strong advocate of the act and joined with the American Association of State Highway Officials (AASHO) to witness the law's signing by President Woodrow

Wilson. Funds were allocated based on a number of factors, including miles of existing post roads in a state, that is, routes over which mail was carried. In addition, the states had to have established highway departments to administer the funds.

Prior to the 1916 act, and soon after its founding, AAA (according to information on its Internet Web site) "established a bureau of touring information to supply members with all available data on roads, hotels, service facilities and motor vehicle laws." Road maps were one of the many services AAA provided. Maps are still available from the organization today, but they are offered as a membership benefit only and are not available to the general public.

Even more ubiquitous than the AAA guides and maps were the free highway maps available at gas stations. While there was no membership requirement for receiving these, the oil companies anticipated that people would pick them up at the same time as purchasing a tank of gas from their pumps. These road maps were an unparalleled marketing tool for the oil companies, which lavished much attention on offering attractive designs to the consumer. The example pictured here, from 1936, was produced by Cities Service (now CITGO). The illustration shows a well-dressed couple in a late-model convertible, getting directions from the attendant in his spotless white uniform. The attendant is handing the motorists a road map, thereby encouraging map users to identify with the stylish couple—or to aspire to be like them—by using the same map in their own travels.

The map showed basic features that motorists came to expect, most of which are present on today's maps. Roads were divided into four grades: paved—asphalt, brick, concrete, or surface treated; improved—gravel, stone, shell, or topsoil-sandclay; graded—drained and maintained; and dirt—unimproved. Both town-to-town and accumulated mileages were listed, as well as locations of airports, state parks and monuments, and other points of interest. Other features included mileage charts and individual city maps. Advertising by Cities Service was also a prominent feature on the map: the company logo appeared in all four corners and in the title block. In addition, the green corporate trefoil symbol indicated towns where Cities Service products were available.

The oil companies' free maps gradually became more functional, less decorative, and increasingly hard to find, particularly after the oil crisis of the 1970s. They have largely been replaced by state highway maps, issued as official state government publications. Highway maps from the first half of the twentieth century, however, remain valuable documentation for both transportation and social history.

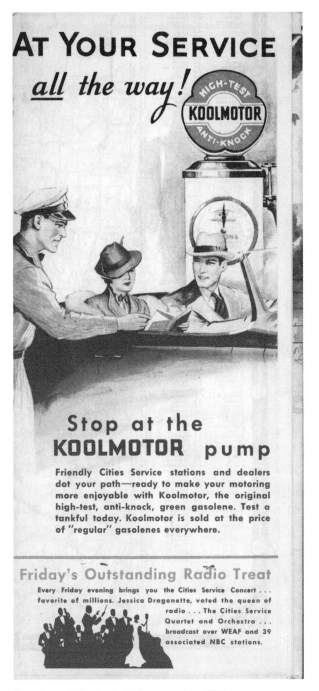

Cover from a Cities Service highway map from 1936

Bird's-Eye Views

LEIGH DARBEE

It is now a commonplace that during the Victorian era Americans loved to cram their homes with heavy furniture and draperies, busily patterned carpets and upholstery, and knick-knacks of every description. It is thus not surprising that they were also mad for all kinds of decorations to hang on their walls; one has only to think of the popularity and nostalgic appeal of things such as compositions of dried flowers or human hair, or prints by Currier and Ives. Much of this popular artwork was inspired by patriotic feelings generated by both the Civil War and the national centennial in 1876. According to map historian John Reps, in his *Bird's-Eye Views: Historic Lithographs of North American Cities,* panoramic maps of cities and towns "may have been the single most popular category in this mass of printed images."

"Bird's-eye view" is the evocative name of a form of panoramic map that was particularly popular in the United States from just after the Civil War to the beginning of the twentieth century. As its name implies, this kind of map showed a city or town from the perspective of a bird flying over it, at the equivalent of as much as 3,000 feet in the air, and thus allowed for depiction of street patterns, individual

buildings, and surrounding countryside. The viewpoints from which truly elevated views were drawn were fictional, and thus an artist had to possess some skill to execute a convincing image. As Reps describes the process:

> *By combining some imagination with a hilltop location as an initial viewpoint for the scene before him, the artist could create an urban portrait giving the appearance of being drawn from a much higher elevation. He could enhance this impression by introducing foreground figures or objects drawn as if seen from a point well above their true position.*

The maps were generally drawn by itinerant artists who specialized in the genre and were usually sold by subscription and/or through newspaper advertisements. They were primarily commercial, mass-produced items, so their artistic merit was a secondary consideration. They did, however, have a certain mesmerizing quality that derived from the artist's ability to freeze a moment of a town's history and decide what elements that moment would contain. By their nature these images were selective in the degree of realistic detail they included. Because

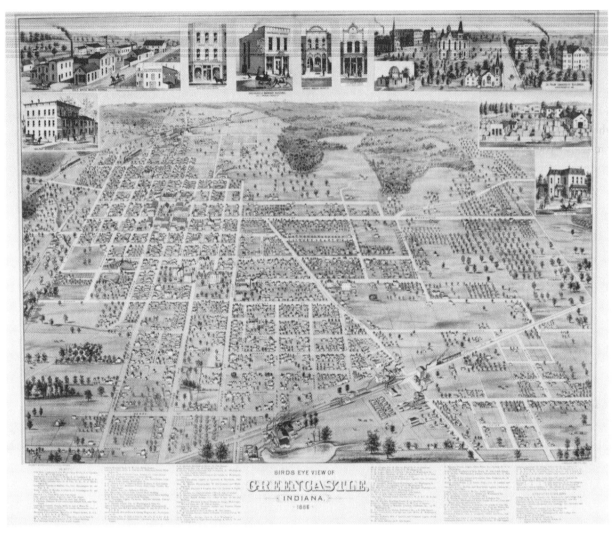

A portion of J. Wallis Smith's *Birds Eye View of Greencastle, Indiana* (Chicago: Shober and Carqueville Lith. [1886]), 62 x 72 cm. The map includes detailed illustrations and a list of businesses and churches.

of their physically distant points of view, they filtered out the less picturesque aspects that all towns and cities had, such as garbage in the streets, roaming stray animals, slums, and so on. Factories benignly puffed smoke, symbolizing prosperity but not pollution. The surrounding countryside appeared not so much as a pastoral alternative to the crowded streets, but rather as fallow ground awaiting further growth and development.

Despite their distant, fictional perspectives, bird's-eye views are among the most accurate records of what cities and towns looked like. They are also, like old photographs, arresting reminders of what has been lost. A case in point is James T. Palmatary's 1854

"View of Indianapolis" (technically a panoramic map done at a slightly oblique angle), which, like many bird's-eye views, features ground-level depictions of individual buildings as vignettes around the edges of the print. Of all the buildings included in both the main view and the vignettes, only one survives today.

Bird's-eye views were unabashed tools of civic boosterism. They were sold to residents, who framed and hung them for visitors to admire. They were also used by town fathers to attract new businesses and residents. Many of the maps were produced by lithography, which was cheap and simple compared to earlier engraving and etching methods and also easily accommodated the use of color. Reps estimates that approximately five thousand city views were produced, documenting some twenty-four hundred places (many larger cities are represented by several views from different times), and that many of these views had runs of several hundred copies. Given the relatively small scale of production, originals are scarce today. Reps's union catalog of views indicates that there are forty-eight such maps relating to Indiana. Approximately one-quarter of these are currently represented in the Indiana Historical Society's collection.

Bird's-eye views are useful to family historians on at least a couple of levels. Specifically, they can be used to find an image—albeit likely on a minute scale—of a family dwelling in a city or town, where photographic documentation might be difficult to find. On a larger scale, they can give historical scholars an almost three-dimensional view of a town an individual once called home.

Selected Bibliography: Danzer, Gerald. "Bird's-Eye Views of Towns and Cities." In *From Sea Charts to Satellite Images: Interpreting North American History through Maps*, edited by David Buisseret. Chicago: University of Chicago Press, 1990; Reps, John W. *Bird's-Eye Views: Historic Lithographs of North American Cities*. New York: Princeton Architectural Press, 1998; Reps, John W. *Views and Viewmakers of Urban America: Lithographs of Towns and Cities in the United States and Canada, Notes on the Artists and Publishers, and a Union Catalog of Their Work, 1825–1925*. Columbia: University of Missouri Press, 1984; "Panoramic Maps, 1847–1925," in "American Memory," a Web page of the Library of Congress at http://lcweb2.loc.gov/ammem/pmhtml (accessed on February 28, 2006). This Web site allows searching and viewing of the Library of Congress's collection of bird's-eye views, with the further ability to zoom in on details of these maps.

Fire Insurance Maps

LEIGH DARBEE

●

Determining an ancestor's locale at various times during his or her life is an interesting aspect of family history research. County maps and atlases that show land ownership are particularly useful sources for rural locations. The job is a bit more challenging in urban areas. One useful tool is the fire insurance map.

As one can deduce from the name, fire insurance maps and atlases were originally developed to serve the insurance industry. "With uniformity and clarity, these maps relay architectural details of residential, commercial and industrial buildings. They provide at a glance, through the use of symbols, colors and labels, a snapshot of the built environment. For countless underwriters, who were unable to personally inspect properties, fire insurance maps were a vital part of their fiscal survival."[1] The first fire insurance map was for Charleston, South Carolina, and was published in 1788. Fire insurance maps started appearing regularly in the mid-nineteenth century and were produced in large numbers for the next hundred years. Although several companies produced the maps, the Sanborn Map Company (incorporated in 1876) came to dominate the market and absorbed many of the smaller companies. Sanborn monopolized the field by 1920.

Because of the complexity and expense in producing fire insurance maps, there was an elaborate system for distributing and updating them. "They were not sold to individual customers, but rather issued on a subscription basis, with the Sanborn Map Company recalling outdated volumes when new editions were prepared, or replacing corrected pages, or applying paste-on revisions as construction changes were noted."[2]

The maps record a large amount of data concerning individual properties, showing a "footprint" of each building, including outbuildings of all kinds. Through the use of color, they depict various construction materials. They impart other information that is helpful in historical research, too, such as building use type and house numbers, both old and new as numbering systems in given locales changed. In a broader context, the maps reveal the character of given sections of a city by providing an overview of the relationship of industry to residential areas, the locations of churches and schools, what kinds of parks and other open spaces were easily accessible, and so on. They also show change over time in neighborhoods through new editions and updates.

1. Diane L. Oswald, *Fire Insurance Maps: Their History and Applications* ([College Station, TX]: Lacewing Press, [1997]), 7.

2. Robert Karrow and Ronald E. Grim, "Two Examples of Thematic Maps: Civil War and Fire Insurance Maps," in *From Sea Charts to Satellite Images: Interpreting North American History through Maps*, ed. David Buisseret (Chicago: University of Chicago Press, 1990), 215.

Selected Bibliography: *Fire Insurance Maps in the Library of Congress: Plans of North American Cities and Towns Produced by the Sanborn Map Company: A Checklist.* Washington, DC: Library of Congress, 1981; Hoehn, R. Philip. *Union List of Sanborn Fire Insurance Maps Held by Institutions in the United States and Canada.* Santa Cruz, CA: Western Association of Map Libraries, 1976–1977.

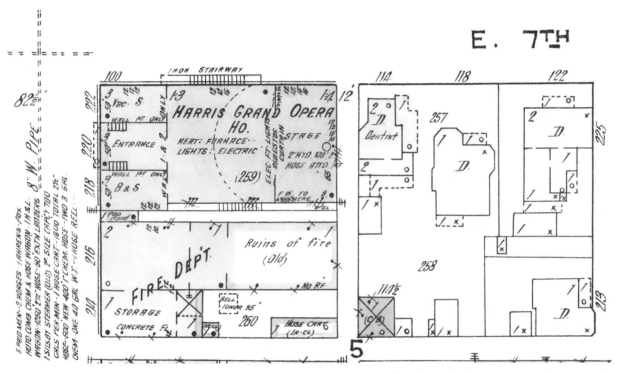

This Sanborn insurance map of the north half of plan 5, Bloomington, 1913, shows the Harris Grand Opera, the fire department, and a square to the east, which includes a dentist's office and several residences. (New York: Sanborn Map Company)

Traugott Bromme's
Travel Account of Indiana in 1848

TRANSLATED AND INTRODUCED BY RICHARD L. BLAND

During the early part of the 1800s Europeans were coming to the United States in large numbers. One such person was Traugott Bromme. Born near the German city of Leipzig, Saxony, in 1802, Bromme came to the United States in 1821, studied medicine, and subsequently became a doctor in the "Columbian service." Before returning home, he served aboard a Columbian

vessel in the West Indies and spent time in Haiti.[1] During his travels he undoubtedly faced the types of problems encountered by immigrants in a new land.

Many nineteenth-century immigrants to America arrived with no prospect of a job and unable to speak English, the dominant language. A sizable portion of these people looking for a new start in life were German.[2] To fill the need for information that would help them know what to expect, Bromme wrote a travel guide for German immigrants. This book was relatively popular, going through at least five editions by the year 1848. It was titled *Traugott Bromme's Hand- und Reisebuch für Auswanderer nach den Vereinigten Staaten von Nord-Amerika, Texas, Ober- und*

Unter-Canada, Neu-Braunschweig, Neu-Schottland, Santo Thomas in Guatemala und den Mosquitoküsten, which translates as *Hand- and Travel-Book for Emigrants to the United States of North America, Texas, Upper and Lower Canada, New Brunswick, Nova Scotia, Saint Thomas in Guatemala, and the Mosquito Coast.* The fifth edition, which was used for this chapter, was published in 1848 in Bayreuth, Bavaria, by Verlag der Buchner'schen Buchhandlung.

On page v of his book, Bromme touts it "as the most crucial and accurate purveyor of information on the conditions of the western world, in so far as emigrants might be interested." In fact, his travel guide indicates that he did substantial research on the various states within the United States, using the maps of Henry Schenck Tanner.[3] The book has more than 550 pages divided into two main parts. In the first part Bromme gives a general overview of the United States, including a thumbnail sketch of most of the states, territories, or countries an immigrant was likely to enter in North America. He devotes more attention to those places most likely to benefit an immigrant; for example, about one and a half pages concern Indiana (pages 209–11), and less attention to those places he felt were of less benefit; for example, less than half a page is written on the territories of Missouri and Oregon (pages 225–26). About the briefness of the latter section, Bromme explains that for "settlement, this recommendation comes still too early" because these are "Indian territories with the wild inhabitants of the same." In the second part of the book Bromme deals with the problem of who should and who should not emigrate, discussing about one hundred professions.

According to bibliographer Joseph Sabin, Bromme produced at least twenty-three titles, some multiple volumes, and some as supplements to the works of others, such as Alexander von Humboldt.[4] All his works were geographic in nature. However, Bromme did not intend for all his books to be used solely as guides. For example, in 1842 he published the second volume of his two-volume set *Gemälde von Nord-Amerika in allen Beziehungen von der Entdeckung an bis auf die neueste Zeit—Eine pittoreske Geographie für Alle, welche unterhaltende Belehrung suchen und ein Umfassendes Reise-Handbuch für Jene, welche in diesem Lande wander wollen* (*Portrait of North America in All Connections from the Discovery to the Most*

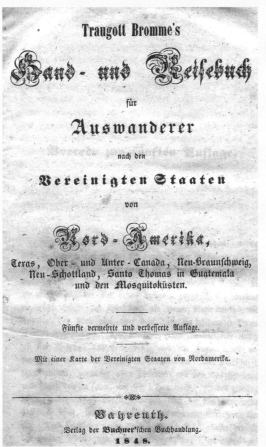

Title page for Traugott Bromme's *Hand- and Travel-Book* (Courtesy of Richard L. Bland)

Recent Time—A Picturesque Geography for Everyone Who Seeks Entertaining Instruction and a Comprehensive Traveler's Handbook for Anyone Who Wants to Travel in This Land). As is apparent in the title, these volumes were intended not only as travel guides but as entertaining instruction as well.

The 1848 edition of Bromme's *Hand- and Travel-Book* was given to me by an uncle who was somewhat of a book collector. Having an interest in the early contact period of the Northwest Coast, I looked to see if Bromme mentioned that coast. Although he did not, I nevertheless took his book to Alaska where I was working on a project. There I translated a number of the descriptions of the states, amounting to about half the book. I did the work for personal satisfaction and because I felt that people might be interested in Bromme's views of the individual states.

I have been publishing sections of Bromme's *Hand- and Travel-Book*; the articles include "Traugott Bromme's Handbook," *Vermont History News* 46 (Montpelier, 1995), 4:41–44; "'A noble-minded, honest people, full of high patriotism': Observations on Kentucky and Kentuckians," *Register of the Kentucky Historical Society* 94 (Frankfort, 1996), 1:59–66; "Translation of the Arkansas Section of Traugott Bromme's Handbook," *The Arkansas Historical Quarterly* 55 (Fayetteville, 1996), 2:194–98; "The State of Rhode Island," *Rhode Island History* 56 (Providence, 1998), 1:28–32; "The Handbook of Traugott Bromme: A Nineteenth-Century German Immigrant's Guide to Maryland," *Maryland Historical Magazine* 98 (Baltimore, 2003), 1:73–77; and "The State of Ohio in 1848 as Seen by

Traugott Bromme," *Ohio History* 112 (Columbus, 2003), 2:87–92. I have also published translations of Bromme's book sections on Pennsylvania, Tennessee, and New Brunswick, Canada.

I have left Bromme's spellings, errors, and omissions as they are in the original, trying not to intrude upon the author. However, I have changed his punctuation and word organization in order to bring the text somewhat more in line with modern idiomatic English, and I have broken the text into paragraphs (there was only one in the original).

The State of Indiana

Traugott Bromme
Indiana lies between 37° 45' and 41° 50' north latitude and between 7° 40' and 10° 47' west longitude.[5] It is bordered in the north by Michigan and Lake Michigan, in the east by Ohio, in the southeast and south by Kentucky, and in the west by Illinois. It has a north-south extent of 240 miles, an east-west extent of 138 miles, and embraces an area of 35,093¼ square miles or precisely 22,459,669 acres. The entire land forms a high plain that offers a softly rolling surface, which finally transforms into a chain of hills that are called knobs and whose highest point lies elevated 800 feet above Lake Michigan. The bottomland of all the rivers of the state, except that of the Ohio, contain rich alluvial soils. Fertile plains, bounded by tall forest, mixed with moist, damp areas and inferior meadows cover the entire land.

The climate of the high-lying middle and northern parts of the state is healthy, although in the rich lowlands the evaporation from the damp prairies annually produce intermittent fever. This part of the land, which is found primarily in the south, is more and more acquired, and annually the number of settlers increases. Winter begins here rarely before the end of December, is milder than in the eastern states, and does not last long. Spring begins in the last days of February. In the beginning of March peaches and cherries are already in bloom, and by the middle of April all the woods are the most beautiful green.

Cereals of all kinds, hemp, and tobacco are the chief products of the state. Game is still present in large quantity, and trade with the Indians, which

is briskly carried on here, is concerned chiefly with hides of bears, beavers, otters, foxes, etc.

The most considerable rivers of the state are: the Ohio, Wabash, White, Tippecanoe, Vermillion, De Page, Kankakee, Big Blue, and St. Josephs. The products of nature are like those of Ohio.

Art and industry are still of little significance here.

The inhabitants, 765,464 in number, are originally French Canadian and Americans from the southern and eastern states, and, since 1810, a multitude of European immigrants: Scots, Irish, and 309,000 Swiss and Germans. In the north 20,000 Indians still live. The majority of the first settlers were poor and had no means when they entered Indiana, but, sober and industrious, they have courageously labored forward by their own power and are always engaged in moving ahead. Luxury has not yet taken the upper hand here, as in other states of the Union. Drunkenness is rare. The old respectability, the hospitality of the woodsman living alone has remained with the resident of Indiana.

The church circumstances are always as usual: the Baptists have 334 churches and 218 clergymen, Methodists 70 preachers, and Presbyterians 109 churches and 73 clergymen in the land. Catholic clergymen wander through the wilderness like the Apostles, and rarely does a settler of the sparsely inhabited north miss the comfort of religion from the mouth of one such clergyman wandering about without prospect of pecuniary gain.

School instruction is up to now still poorly appointed. However, 54 academies have already been built in various cities, and 1,521 elementary schools can be counted, with 48,189 pupils, and the institutions of higher learning are: Indiana College at Bloomington, South Hanover College in South Hanover, Wabash College at Crawfordsville, and the Indiana Asbury University, altogether with 322 students.

Significant public works in the state that have been completed are: the Wabash and Erie Canal, which goes from Lafayette on the Wabash 187 miles to Toledo on Maumee Bay in Lake Erie, with 87¼ miles built in Ohio and 99¾ miles in Indiana; the Whitewater Canal, which stretches from Lawrence-

burg 30 miles to Brookville; the Central Canal, which is to connect the Wabash and Erie Canal at Peru with the Ohio at Evansville and to run through Indianopolis [sic]. It is only partially completed, and its entire length amounts to 290 miles. The Terre Haute and Eel River Canal will connect the southern end of the Wabash and Erie with the Central Canal in Greene County and have a length of 40½ miles. It is not yet completed. The Madison and Indianopolis Railroad, the only railroad up to now completed in the state, is 95 miles long.[6]

The government consists of a governor and lieutenant governor, a senate, and a house of representatives, of which the members of the former are renewed every three years and of the latter, every year.

The state is divided into 87 counties and still contains several Indian reservations in the north.

Indiana does not yet have large cities. Indianopolis, on the eastern bank of the White, somewhat below the mouth of Fall Creek, is an indeed still small but quickly flourishing place, with 4,561 inhabitants, 331 houses, 11 churches, and 2 banks, and the capital of the state. New Albany, the larg-

est city up to now, counts 560 houses and 5,520 inhabitants. Madison has 4,208, Vincennes 3,400, Richmond 2,840, and Salem 1,826 residents. All other cities are small and only a few have 800–1,000 inhabitants.

———————— • ————————

1. It is stated in *Appleton's Cyclopaedia of American Biography*, James Grant Wilson and John Fiske, eds., 7 vols. (New York: D. Appleton, 1888), 1:384, that Bromme "settled in the United States in 1820, and afterward travelled extensively in Texas and Mexico, became surgeon on a Columbian war-schooner cruising in the West Indies, and was detained for a year as a prisoner in Hayti." In contrast, Klaus Dieter Hein-Mooren in "Gediegene Schriften für Auswanderer," *Buchhandelsgeschichte* (2001), 2:B42–B46, states that Bromme came to the United States in 1821 and studied medicine, though he does not say where, only that later Bromme became a doctor in the Columbian service and spent some time in Haiti, returning to Saxony in 1824.

2. Hein-Mooren, 2:B42, states that "from 1816 to 1845 about 300,000 people left the German states to seek a new homeland. Many of them traveled to the United States. The famine of 1816–1817, the Karlsbad decrees of 1819, as well as the social, economic, and political unrest of the 1830s form the background for these emigration movements" (author's translation).

3. Tanner created numerous maps in the early 1800s. As a result, it is difficult to say with certainty which ones Bromme used. Tanner's maps for Indiana can be found on the Internet by typing "tanner maps indiana" in the search line. [The IHS library has several Tanner maps.]

> MODERN FRAME BUILDING PUT
> OVER IT TO PRESERVE IT 1907.

> FIRST M.E. CHURCH BUILT IN INDIANA BUILT IN 1808.
> 3 MILES NORTH OF CHARLESTON.

(Above) The images of this early First Methodist Episcopal Church near Charleston, Indiana, appear on a postcard in the Jay Small Postcard Collection, P 0391, Indiana Historical Society.

(Right) This depiction of the Wabash and Erie Canal Aqueduct over the St. Marys River at Fort Wayne, Indiana, was drawn by Ellis Kaiser and is part of the W. H. Bass Company Collections, P 0130, Indiana Historical Society.

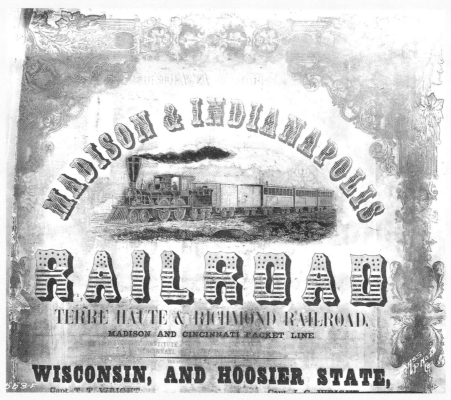

The image above is part of a broadside for the Madison and Indianapolis Railroad from 1852 and is part of the W. H. Bass Company Collections, P 0130, Indiana Historical Society.

4. Joseph Sabin, *Bibliotheca Americana: A Dictionary of Books Relating to America, from Its Discovery to the Present Time,* 29 vols. (New York: Bibliographical Society of America, 1868–1936), 2:516–18. Alexander Freiherr von Humboldt (1769–1859) was a German explorer, scientist, and cartographer who conducted expeditions to Cuba and Central and South America. His greatest work was *Kosmos,* in five volumes. Bromme, who edited the volumes, is credited with working on the illustrations in *Kosmos* (Hein-Mooren, 2:B45). For von Humboldt, see Wilson and Fiske, eds., *Appleton's Cyclopaedia of American Biography,* online at "Virtual American Biographies," http://famousamericans. net/ (accessed March 29, 2006).

5. Bromme separates east and west longitude, that is, forms a prime meridian, at the present longitude of 77° west. This is apparently because 77° west longitude runs through the nation's capital, Washington, DC.

6. The population figure given by Bromme (765,464) and the statement that the Madison and Indianapolis Railroad was complete at 95 miles indicates that Bromme either wrote or revised this essay during the mid-1840s. See James H. Madison, "Appendix A. Indiana Population, 1800–1980" in *The Indiana Way: A State History* (Bloomington: Indiana University Press; Indianapolis: Indiana Historical Society, 1986), 326, for population figures by decade, and Phil Anderson, "Pioneer Railroad of the Northwest: History of the Jeffersonville, Madison, and Indianapolis Railroad" on the Internet at http:// hometown.aol.com/ma393/railroad (accessed March 29, 2006), for information about the Madison and Indianapolis Railroad.

Part 5
Researching Ethnic Groups

Deutsche Haus-Athenaeum in Indianapolis, ca. 1910 (W. H. Bass Company Collections, P 0130, 313035F, IHS)

German American Heritage Organizations in Indiana

JAMES R. FEIT, GILES R. HOYT, GREGORY HUNTER MOBLEY, AND RUTH REICHMANN

ince the first Germans arrived at Jamestown, Virginia, in 1608 more than seven million people have immigrated to America from Europe's German-speaking areas. The 1990 U.S. census reports 2,084,667 Hoosiers (37.6 percent of the state's population) as having roots in German-speaking lands. The impact of German Americans on Indiana's development is a history that needs to be told. Several organizations in Indiana are working to preserve and to help researchers tell that history. Three of them, the Indiana German Heritage Society, the Max Kade German-American Center, and the Indiana Chapter of Palatines to America, are discussed in this chapter, along with a description of the German American holdings in the University Library Special Collections and Archives at Indiana University–Purdue University at Indianapolis (IUPUI).

The Indiana German Heritage Society

On March 16, 1984, the Indiana German Heritage Society was founded as a statewide historical and educational membership organization. Headed by a volunteer board of directors, it is a nonprofit organization, qualifying for tax-deductible donations. The society has its seat in Indianapolis in the Deutsche Haus-Athenaeum, a famous historic landmark. Offices and meeting rooms are shared with the Max Kade German-American Center of IUPUI.

The Indiana German Heritage Society is nonpolitical. It looks at "German" in terms of ethnic traditions of culture and language. Indiana's German heritage thus includes contributions from Austria, the Federal Republic of Germany, Liechtenstein, Luxembourg, German-speaking Switzerland, Alsace-Lorraine, Southern Tirol, and other German-speaking regions of Europe. The society cherishes the cultural diversity of the Hoosier State and is proud of the German American contributions to its way of life.

The Indiana German Heritage Society seeks the participation and support of individuals and organizations in fulfilling its mission. Thus, it works closely with organizations such as the Athenaeum Foundation, the Indiana Historical Society, the Society for German-American Studies, the Indiana Religious History Association, Palatines to America, and others, as well as social organizations such as the Federation of German Societies of Indianapolis and the American Turners. The society's principal academic partner for research activities and publications is the Max Kade German-American Center.

The Max Kade German-American Center

The Max Kade German-American Center is operated by IUPUI's School of Liberal Arts as a research center for German and German American studies, which the center coordinates with faculty in other university departments. It provides Indianapolis and Indiana, the eastern Midwest, and areas south of Indiana with a center for conducting research into its German American history and heritage. German immigration was heavy in these areas, but relatively little research has been done. The center's purpose is to support such research and to disseminate the results.

In step with IUPUI's tradition of joint public-private endeavors, the center receives most of its support from the Max Kade Foundation, named after a prominent German American pharmaceutical industry leader. It also receives help from the Indiana German Heritage Society.

Anchoring the center's research and teaching mission is an endowed professorship, the Hoyt-Reichmann Chair of German and German American Studies. The center also offers student scholarships and faculty stipends for research in German American studies. The IUPUI University Library Special Collections and Archives holds an impressive collection of German American research materials and is the national repository for materials on the American Turners. Part of the endowment for the professorship goes toward library materials support.

Indianapolis is an ideal location for the Max Kade German-American Center, being located near the middle of the U.S. "German quadrangle." It is also equidistant from Max Kade organizations in Madison, Wisconsin, and Lawrence, Kansas.

The center coordinates lectures, exhibitions, performances, conferences, seminars, and workshops, with both historical and contemporary dimensions, and runs an extensive publishing program. The center is proud of its involvement with the IUPUI German program, which offers a Saturday language school for children and, in cooperation with the IUPUI International Affairs Office, a bilingual preschool in the university's child-care center that serves as a laboratory for research in German-language pedagogy. The Max Kade German-American Center also conducts orientation sessions for the German program, which administers exchange programs for business and engineering students.

The center contributes to Deutsche Haus-Athenaeum intellectual and cultural activities and networks and cooperates with organizations such as the Society for German American Studies, the German Historical Institute (Washington, DC), the Indiana German Heritage Society, the Indiana Historical Society, the Indiana Religious History Society, the Indiana Humanities Council, and Indiana Sister Cities. The center conducts summer institutes for teachers, works with the Indiana Department of Education and German Studies programs throughout the state, and develops primarily Web-based teaching materials for social studies and language classrooms. The Max Kade German-American Center gives presentations (slide and video) and has information tables at schools, other organizations, and such events as the Indianapolis International Festival. The center works closely with the Research Center for Emigration from Lower Saxony to North America at Oldenburg University. It also partners with the University of Bremen for emigration studies.

Palatines to America

Several national societies help people research German-speaking ancestry. Palatines to America has an Indiana chapter, which meets twice a year and publishes a newsletter. Meeting lectures provide German American immigration history and research advice. The meetings also encourage researchers to ask questions of others doing similar genealogical work. Therefore, joining a genealogical society such as Palatines to America is greatly beneficial for solving difficult German research problems.

But, what is a Palatine? In the eighteenth century, thousands of German-speaking farmers came to North America. Two large groups settled in the colonies of New York and Pennsylvania. In 1709 thousands of farmers along the Rhine River migrated to England. Queen Anne agreed to settle many of them in her colony of New York, intending for them to supply pitch and tar for the Royal Navy. However, the settlers wanted to farm. When the pine trees along the

The top half of a page from the member account book of the Damenverein (Women's Society) of the Indianapolis Socialer Turnverein (now Athenaeum Turners). The writing here in Fraktur, a German style of black letter, shows one research challenge of nineteenth-century German American records. (Courtesy of IUPUI University Library Special Collections and Archives)

Hudson River proved unsuitable to supply pitch and tar, the Germans were allowed to farm. Many stayed along the Hudson River, but others moved into the Mohawk River Valley.

William Penn recruited settlers for his colony of Pennsylvania from the Rhine River Valley. Because the English translation for the Rhine River region was "the Palatinate," the settlers in New York and Pennsylvania were called Palatines. Thus, as eighteenth-century German farmers arrived in Philadelphia, the port authorities reported that a shipload of Palatines had arrived.

In the mid-1970s a group of genealogists formed Palatines to America to help people research their German-speaking ancestry. They chose the name to honor the thousands of German farmers who had braved the rigors of early travel to settle in America, although all German-speaking ancestors are considered for research. The organization's national office in Columbus, Ohio, has a research library that can be accessed by anyone needing help. Members receive written answers to specific questions. The holdings of the library are listed on its Web site. Once each year a national conference is held. This conference rotates between the member chapters.

German-American Resources in IUPUI's University Library

IUPUI delved into German American collecting because of its School of Physical Education, which

the American Turners started in New York in 1866 to train gymnastics instructors for Turner societies. The school moved to the Athenaeum in Indianapolis in 1907 and remained there until 1970, becoming part of Indiana University's (IU) system in 1941. The IUPUI University Library first acquired the records of the Athenaeum Turners and then records from the national Turner organization and other local German American groups. The collections described below, the core of IUPUI's German American holdings, have drawn the most genealogical interest. Many of the early records are in German, but translations are available for some of the material. Items in these collections include membership lists or directories, minutes of board meetings, committee records, and publications, such as the national newsletter and anniversary publications. For more information, consult the online catalog.

- Athenaeum Turners Records, 1876–1999: These records document the activities of Indianapolis's oldest surviving German organization. Much of the pre–World War I material is handwritten in Fraktur.
- Athenaeum Damenverein (Women's Society) Records, 1876–1999: Much of the Damenverein's early efforts focused on supporting the activities of the Athenaeum and on philanthropic activities. In more recent years social and cultural activities have been predominant.

- Indianapolis Maennerchor Records, 1866–1992: These records document one of the nation's oldest and continuously active men's singing societies.
- Indianapolis South Side Turners Records, 1893–1956: Includes minutes and cash book of the Southside Turnverein Hall Association (organization that built and owned the South Side Turners' building on Prospect Street). Many of these records are in Fraktur.
- American Turners Records, 1853–2002: Information about Turner society members can be found in the newsletter, *American Turner Topics*. The collection contains information on national leaders and is especially valuable

for studying the impact of acculturation and changing attitudes about ethnicity on a German American immigrant organization. The library has completed a project converting *American Turner Topics* into searchable, digital images, which will be available at http://indiamond6.ulib.iupui.edu/TurnerTopic/.

- American Turners Local Societies Collection, 1866–1997: Constitutions and bylaws and other materials for Turner societies across the United States. The files for the Louisville, St. Louis Concordia, and Detroit Turners include long runs of their newsletters.

Indiana German Heritage Society, Inc.
and/or Max Kade German-American Center
401 East Michigan Street
Indianapolis, Indiana 46204
mkgac@iupui.edu (email)
http://www.ulib.iupui.edu/kade/

Palatines to America Headquarters
611 East Weber Road
Columbus, Ohio 43211-1097
Pal-Am@juno.com (email)
http://www.palam.org

IUPUI University Library
Ruth Lilly Special Collections and Archives
755 West Michigan Street
Indianapolis, Indiana 46202-5195
speccoll@iupui.edu (email)
http://www.ulib.iupui.edu/special/

First page of the first issue of *Der Deutsche Pionier*, March 1869, a publication that provided articles about early German immigrants to the United States, helping to keep a sense of German culture and heritage alive in the German American community (Courtesy of IUPUI University Library Special Collections and Archives)

Selected Bibliography: Hoyt, Giles R. "Germans." In *Peopling Indiana: The Ethnic Experience*. Edited by Robert M. Taylor Jr. and Connie A. McBirney. Indianapolis: Indiana Historical Society, 1996; Jones, Henry Z, Jr. *The Palatine Families of New York: A Study of the German Immigrants Who Arrived in Colonial New York in 1710*. 2 vols. Universal City, CA: H. Z. Jones, 1985 (and this book's two sequels); Knittle, Walter A. *Early Eighteenth Century Palatine Emigration: A British Government Redemptioner Project to Manufacture Naval Stores*. Baltimore: Genealogical Pub-

German Roots of Indiana's Heritage

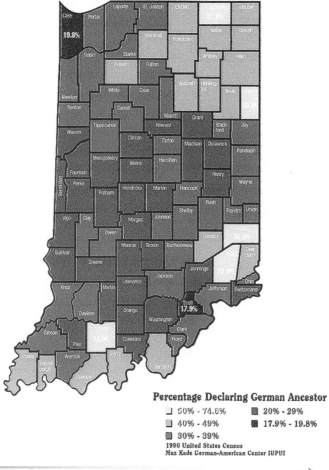

Percentage Declaring German Ancestor

- ☐ 50% - 74.8%
- ■ 20% - 29%
- ☐ 40% - 49%
- ■ 17.9% - 19.8%
- ☐ 30% - 39%

1990 United States Census
Max Kade German-American Center IUPUI

GERMANY IN US

Indiana Humanities Council
Strengthening the ties between us.

This map illustrates Indiana's German heritage. The 1990 census shows the state's northeast corner as having from 40 to 49 percent German ancestry. Only two counties declared less than 20 percent German heritage, and five declared more than 50 percent German ancestry. For a color image of the map, consult the Germany in US Web site, hosted by the Indiana Humanities Council at http://liberalarts.iupui.edu/giu/. (Developed by Eb Reichmann for the Max Kade German-American Center at IUPUI)

lishing, 1965. Reprint, 1970; Pumroy, Eric L., and Katja Rampelmann, comps. *Research Guide to the Turner Movement in the United States.* Westport, CT: Greenwood Press, 1996.

[The editors of Finding Indiana Ancestors *thank Dr. Ann Whitlock Swedeen, formerly of the Indiana Humanities Council, for her help in procuring a copy of the German heritage map for use in this article.]*

African American Research
A Bibliography

WILMA L. MOORE

•

African American family history has become increasingly popular over the past two decades. Author Alex Haley first serialized the family chronicle *Roots* in the *Reader's Digest*. He wrote the novel and the subsequent screenplay that became the most watched television miniseries to that point (1977). Haley romanticized the family history search of a young, attentive boy in Henning, Tennessee, who grew up and traced his ancestors back to a village in West Africa. Roughly based on his life search, Haley captured the imagination of genealogists and crossed the formidable and brutal barrier of slavery. In April 1999, in its cover heading for an article series, "How to Search for Your Roots," *Time* magazine declared, "Genealogy is America's latest obsession. And thanks to the computer, it is as easy as one, two, tree."[1] Although computer programs and the Internet have simplified access to some tools, developing family trees can be an arduous task. The following bibliography, with a focus on African American family history, provides numerous useful sources for anyone doing genealogical research.

Guides to Repositories

Cerny, John, and Wendy Elliot, eds. *The Library, a Guide to the LDS Family History Library*. Salt Lake City: Ancestry Publishing, 1988.

Genealogy Division of the Indiana State Library. *Genealogy Subject Catalog*. Indianapolis: The Library, 1976–1999.

Genealogy Division of the Indiana State Library. Indianapolis: Indiana State Library Video Service Center, 1991. Video recording.

Neagles, James C. *The Library of Congress, a Guide to Genealogical and Historical Research*. Salt Lake City: Ancestry Publishing, 1990.

Newman, Debra L. *Black History: A Guide to Civilian Records in the National Archives*. Washington, DC: National Archives Trust Fund Board, General Services Administration, 1984.

Parker, J. Carlyle. *Going to Salt Lake City to Do Family History Research*. Turlock, CA: Marietta Publishing, 1989.

Szucs, Loretto Dennis, and Sandra H. Luebking. *The Archives: A Guide to the National Archives Field Branches*. Salt Lake City: Ancestry Publishing, 1988.

Thackery, David T. *Afro-American Family History at the Newberry Library: A Research Guide and Bibliography*. Chicago: The Newberry Library, 1988.

U.S. National Archives and Records Service. *Guide to Genealogical Research in the National Archives*. Washington, DC: National Archives and Records Service, 1982.

Washington, Reginald. *Black Family Research: Records of Post-Civil War Federal Agencies at the National Archives*. Washington, DC: National Archives and Records Administration, 2001.

Genealogical Guides

Barksdale-Hall, Roland C. *The African American Family's Guide to Tracing Our Roots: Healing, Understanding and Restoring Our Families*. Phoenix: Amber Books, 2005.

Baxter, Angus. *In Search of Your Canadian Roots*. Baltimore: Genealogical Publishing, 1994.

Beasley, Donna. *Family Pride: The Complete Guide to Tracing African-American Genealogy*. New York: Macmillan, 1997.

Blockson, Charles L. *Black Genealogy*. Baltimore: Black Classic Press, 1991.

Braxton-Secret, Jeanette. *Guide to Tracing Your African Ameripean Civil War Ancestor*. Bowie, MD: Heritage Books, 1997.

Burroughs, Tony. *Black Roots: A Beginner's Guide to Tracing the African American Family Tree*. New York: Simon and Schuster, 2001.

Byers, Paula K., ed. *African American Genealogical Sourcebook*. New York: Gale Research, 1995.

Casper, Gordon, and Carolyn Casper. *The Genealogists Video Research Guide*. Spanish Fork, UT: Video Knowledge, 1994–1995. Video recording.

Cooper, Kay. *Where Did You Get Those Eyes? A Guide to Discovering Your Family History*. New York: Walker, 1988.

Crandell, Ralph J. *Shaking Your Family Tree: A Basic Guide to Tracing Your Family's Genealogy*. Dublin, NH: Yankee Publishing, 1986.

Croom, Emily Anne. *Unpuzzling Your Past: A Basic Guide to Genealogy*. Cincinnati: Betterway Books, 1995.

Day, Johnnie M. *A Quick Step in Genealogy Research: A Primer for Blacks, Other Minorities, and the Novice in This Area*. Minneapolis: North Star and Day Publishing, 1983.

Do Your Family Tree: Advanced Research. Provo, UT: Horizon Home Video, 1992. Video recording.

Drake, Paul E. *In Search of Family History—A Starting Place*. Bowie, MD: Heritage Books, 1992.

Ferraro, Eugene. *How to Obtain Birth, Death, Marriage, Divorce, and Adoption Records*. Santa Ana, CA: Marathon Press International, 1989.

Heinegg, Paul. *Free African Americans of North Carolina and Virginia: Including the Family Histories of More Than 80% of Those Counted as "All Other Free Persons" in the 1790 and 1800 Census*[es]. Baltimore: Genealogy Publishing, 1994.

How to Trace Your Native American Heritage. Dallas: Rich-Heape Films, 1998. Video recording.

Krause, Carol. *How Healthy Is Your Family Tree? A Complete Guide to Tracing Your Family's Medical and Behavioral Tree*. New York: Simon and Schuster, 1995.

Linder, Billy Royce. *Black Genealogy: Basic Steps to Research*. Nashville, TN: American Association for State and Local History, 1981.

Out of Your Tree! Crazy about Genealogy. Austin: Rondo Films, 1993. Video recording.

Pengra, Nancy. *Family Histories: An Easy, Step-by-Step Guide to Capturing Your Family's Precious Memories Now, before They're Lost*. St. Paul, MN: Family Histories, 1995.

Redford, Dorothy Spruill. *Somerset Homecoming: Recovering a Lost Heritage*. New York: Doubleday, 1988.

Reed, Robert D. *How and Where to Research Your Ethnic-American Cultural Heritage: Black Americans*. Saratoga, CA: Reed, 1979.

Rose, James M. *Black Genesis: A Resource Book for African-American Genealogy*. Baltimore, MD: Genealogical Publishing Company, 2003.

Schafer, Louis S. *Tombstones of Your Ancestors*. Bowie, MD: Heritage Books, 1991.

Smith, Franklin Carter. *A Genealogist's Guide to Discovering Your African-American Ancestors: How to*

Find and Record Your Unique Heritage. Cincinnati, OH: Betterway Books, 2003.

Smith, Jessie Carney, ed. *Ethnic Genealogy, a Research Guide.* Westport, CT: Greenwood Press, 1983.

Smith, Lorna Duane. *Genealogy Is More Than Charts.* Elliot City, MD: Life Times, 1991.

Stryker-Rodda, Harriet. *How to Climb Your Family Tree: Genealogy for Beginners.* Boston: G. K. Hall, 1990.

Szucs, Loretto D., and Sandra H. Luebking, eds. *The Source: A Guidebook of American Genealogy.* Salt Lake City: Ancestry Publishing, 1997.

Thackery, David, and Dee Woodtor. *Case Studies in Afro-American Genealogy.* Chicago: The Newberry Library, 1989.

Thackery, David T. *Finding Your African American Ancestors: A Beginner's Guide.* Orem, UT: Ancestry, 2000.

Walton-Raji, Angela Y. *Black Indian Genealogy Research.* Bowie, MD: Heritage Books, 1993.

Woodtor, Dee Parmer. *Finding a Place Called Home: A Guide to African-American Genealogy and Historical Identity.* New York: Random House, 1999.

Young, Tommie M. *Afro-American Genealogy Sourcebook.* New York: Garland Publishing, 1987.

Putting Genealogy in a Historical Context

Ball, Edward. *Slaves in the Family.* New York: Ballantine Books, 1999.

Black History News and Notes. Indianapolis: Indiana Historical Society, 1979–2006.

Bremer, Ronald A. *Compendium of Historical Sources: The How and Where of American Genealogy.* Bountiful, UT: American Genealogical Lending Library, 1997.

Danky, James P., and Maureen Hady, eds. *African-American Newspapers and Periodicals: A National Bibliography.* Cambridge, MA: Harvard University Press, 1999.

Davis, Thulani. *My Confederate Kinfolk: A Twenty-First Century Freedwoman Confronts Her Roots.* New York: Basic Civitas Books, 2006.

Gibbs, Wilma L., ed. *Indiana's African-American Heritage: Essays from* Black History News and Notes. Indianapolis: Indiana Historical Society, 1993.

Greene, Robert Ewell. *Black Courage, 1775–1783: Documentation of Black Participation in the American Revolution.* Washington, DC: National Society of the Daughters of the American Revolution, 1984.

Ham, Debra Newman, comp. *List of Free Black Heads of Families in the First Census of the United States, 1790.* Washington, DC: National Archives and Records Service, General Services Administration, 1974.

Indiana Magazine of History. Bloomington, IN: Indiana University, 1905–.

Streets, David H. *Slave Genealogy: A Research Guide with Case Studies.* Bowie, MD: Heritage Books, 1986.

Thornbrough, Emma Lou. *The Negro in Indiana before 1900: A Study of a Minority.* Bloomington: Indiana University Press, 1993.

Traces of Indiana and Midwestern History. Indianapolis: Indiana Historical Society, 1989–.

Woodson, Carter G. *Free Negro Heads of Families in the United States in 1830.* Washington, DC: The Association for the Study of Negro Life and History, 1925.

Genealogical Sources

African American Lives. Alexandria, VA: PBS Home Video, 2006. Video recording.

Frisch-Ripley, Karen. *Unlocking the Secrets in Old Photographs.* Salt Lake City: Ancestry Publishing, 1991.

Hyman, Rick. *My Texas Family: An Uncommon Journey to Prosperity: Featuring Photographs from 1912 to 1927.* Charleston, SC: Tempus, 2000.

Lawson, Sandra M. *Generations Past: A Selected List of Sources for Afro-American Genealogical Research.* Washington, DC: Library of Congress, 1988.

Steuart, Bradley W., ed. *The Soundex Reference Guide.* Bountiful, UT: Precision Indexing, 1990.

U.S. Department of Commerce, Economics and Statistics Administration, Bureau of the Census. *1990 Census of Population. Ancestry of the Population in the United States.* Washington, DC: U.S. Government Printing Office, 1993.

Witcher, Curt B. *African American Genealogy: A Bibliography and Guide to Sources.* Fort Wayne, IN: Round Tower Books, 2000.

Indiana Genealogical Sources

Beatty, John D. *Research in Indiana.* Arlington, VA: National Genealogical Society, 1992.

Carty, Mickey Dimon. *Searching in Indiana: A Reference Guide to Public and Private Records.* Costa Mesa, CA: ISC Publications, 1985.

Darlington, Jane E. *Marion County, Indiana, Records Miscellanea.* Indianapolis: Indiana Historical Society, 1986.

Ebony Lines. Bloomington: Indiana African-American Historical and Genealogical Society, 1989–1992.

Gibbs, Wilma L. *Guide to African American Printed Sources at the Indiana Historical Society.* Indianapolis: Indiana Historical Society, 1997.

_____. *Selected African-American History Collections.* Indianapolis: Indiana Historical Society, 1996.

Heiss, Willard C. *Working in the Vineyards of Genealogy.* Indianapolis: Indiana Historical Society, 1993.

The Hoosier Genealogist. Indianapolis: Indiana Historical Society, 1961–.

Howard County Genealogical Society. *Howard County, Indiana, Family History, 1844–1994.* Paducah, KY: Turner Publishing, 1995.

Miller, Carolynne L. *Indiana Sources for Genealogical Research in the Indiana State Library.* Indianapolis: Indiana Historical Society, 1984.

Peterson, Roger A. *African Americans Found in Owen County, Indiana, Records, 1819–1880.* Spencer, IN: Roger Peterson, 1996.

Robbins, Coy D. *Forgotten Hoosiers: African Heritage in Orange County, Indiana.* Bowie, MD: Heritage Books, 1994.

_____. *Indiana Negro Registers, 1852–1865.* Bowie, MD: Heritage Books, 1994.

_____. *Reclaiming African Heritage at Salem, Indiana.* Bowie, MD: Heritage Books, 1995.

_____. *Source Book: African-American Genealogy in Indiana.* Bloomington: Indiana African-American Historical and Genealogical Society, 1989.

Schweitzer, George K. *Indiana Genealogical Research.* N.p. 1996.

Witcher, Curt B. *Bibliography of Sources for Black Family History in the Allen County Public Library Genealogy Department.* Fort Wayne, IN: The Library, 1986.

Computer-Aided Genealogy

Clifford, Karen. *The Complete Beginner's Guide to Genealogy, the Internet and Your Genealogy Computer Program.* Baltimore: Genealogical Publishing, 2001.

_____. *Genealogy and Computers for the Advanced Researcher: Featuring Trade Secrets of Professional Genealogists, Pre-1850 Primary Sources (Census, Probate, Vital, Land, Passenger Lists, Military, Other Records), New PAF 2.31 Techniques for Expanding Your Family Lines.* Baltimore: Printed for Clearfield by Genealogical Publishing, 1997.

_____. *Genealogy and Computers for the Complete Beginner: The PAF Computer Program, Automated Data Bases, Family History Centers, Local Sources.* Baltimore: Reprinted for Clearfield by Genealogical Publishing, 1995.

_____. *Genealogy and Computers for the Determined Researcher.* Baltimore: Printed for Clearfield by Genealogical Publishing, 1995.

Cosgriff, John Cornelius. *Turbo Genealogy: The Computer-Enhanced "How to Find Your Roots" Handbook.* Christianburg, VA: Progenesys Press, 1987.

Crowe, Elizabeth Powell. *Genealogy Online: Researching Your Roots.* New York: McGraw Hill, 1996.

Eastman, Richard. *Your Roots: Total Genealogy Planning on Your Computer.* Emeryville, CA: Ziff-Davis Press, 1995.

Helm, Matthew, and April Leigh. *Genealogy Online for Dummies.* Foster City, CA: IDG Books Worldwide, 1998.

Howells, Cyndi. *Netting Your Ancestors: Genealogical Research on the Internet.* Baltimore: Genealogical Publishing, 1997.

Kemp, Thomas Jay. *Virtual Roots: A Guide to Genealogy and Local History on the World Wide Web.* Wilmington, DE: Scholarly Resources, 1997.

Nichols, Elizabeth L. *Understanding Family Search; Personal Ancestral File (PAF), Family History Library Catalog, More Resource Files, and Using Them All in Harmony.* Vol. 2 of *Genealogy in the Computer Age.* Salt Lake City: Family History Educators, 1997.

Przecha, Donna. *Guide to Genealogy Software.* Baltimore: Genealogical Publishing, 1993.

1. "How to Search for Your Roots" comprises several articles including Sandra Lee Jamison, "For African Americans: Uncovering a Painful Past," *Time* 153 (April 19, 1999).

Photographs of individuals and groups can provide useful context when conducting historical research. Above, Arthur Jr. and Fairy Mae Smith and their daughters rest in their living room. Their house, located at 571 Ransom Street, was one of many that were built as part of the Flanner House Homes Project. Utilizing a sweat equity concept, residents helped build their houses on the West Side of Indianapolis during the 1950s. (O. James Fox Collection, P 0266, IHS)

Native American Research

M. TERESA BAER

In the 2000 federal census, more than 15,000 Hoosiers claimed Native American ancestry. According to Jeannie Regan-Dinius, who in 2000 was the Executive Director of Historic Forks of the Wabash in Huntington, Indiana, being an Indian was a popular aspiration at the turn of the millennium. Many people cherish stories that depict an Indian as part of their ancestors' families and hope that the stories are true, even though the details have been lost over time. There is something at once romantic and noble about Native Americans. Their belief in the spiritual nature of all life beckons to folks in this supertechnical age. Ironically, many Americans want to recapture the meaningful culture that their government tried to supplant.

Regan-Dinius and Nick Clark, who at the time of the 2000 census was the Executive Director of the Museums at Prophetstown in Lafayette, Indiana, caution that Native American genealogy research must start at the same place all other such research starts—with what a person knows about today's generation. Researchers should work their way back with documented proof of each predecessor's birth date and place, marital information, and so forth, until they come to the ancestor who united with an Amer-

ican Indian. At this point, the researcher might find an Indian ancestor on a tribal roll—if the researcher knows the ancestor's tribal affiliation. An understanding of the migratory history of Native Americans in Indiana since the late 1700s will help to determine the tribal group to which the native ancestor likely belonged.

During the 1790s the U.S. government began using military tactics to acquire land in the Old Northwest Territory. Several groups of native people lived in the region that would become the state of Indiana. Elizabeth Glenn and Stewart Rafert locate various groups in their chapter of the book *Peopling Indiana: The Ethnic Experience.* The Miami, Delaware, and Shawnee had villages in the area of Kekionga (near Fort Wayne); the Wea and Kickapoo, which absorbed the remnants of the Mascoutens at this time, resided at Ouiatenon (near Lafayette); and the Piankashaw and some Kickapoo lived near Vincennes. The Potawatomi were expanding out from their villages in the north near the St. Joseph and Kankakee rivers trading posts. Concentrations of Potawatomi and Wea resided in the regions near the mouths of the Tippecanoe and Eel rivers, respectively. New groups migrated to Indiana at this time.

Howard Chandler Christy's *Signing of the Treaty of Green Ville* was commissioned by the state of Ohio, and the final version hangs in the Ohio statehouse. The treaty of Greenville, signed in 1795, secured for the United States south-central Ohio and a small portion of what would become southeastern Indiana. (Image from IHS collections; information from "Ohio Memory: An Online Scrapbook of Ohio History [Columbus, OH: Ohio Historical Society and participating institutions, n.d., online at www.ohiomemory.org/index.html {accessed October 17, 2006}])

Among these were bands of Delaware, including the Munsee, a small group of Nanticoke from the eastern United States, and Wyandot and Ottawa from the northern Great Lakes area. Summarizing several county histories' reports about Native Americans, archaeologists Ellen Sieber and Cheryl Ann Munson in *Looking at History: Indiana's Hoosier National Forest Region, 1600–1950* locate several native groups in the Hoosier National Forest region for a few short decades after 1770. Piankashaw and Delaware groups reportedly lived in what are now Jackson, Lawrence, Monroe, and Orange counties. Shawnee resided in Jackson, Lawrence, and Orange counties. Potawatomi lived in Lawrence and Monroe counties. Bands of Wyandot resided in Jackson, Orange, Perry, and Crawford counties, and some Miami lived in Monroe and Perry counties.

After glorious victories led by Miami Chief Little Turtle and the Shawnee war leader Blue Jacket, the Indians, who had lost British support, were defeated by Gen. Anthony Wayne in 1795. Subsequently, indigenous leaders signed the Treaty of Greenville, and the tribes began dispersing—the Shawnee to Ohio and what is now southeastern Missouri, the Delaware to the White River, and the Miami to the upper Wabash. From 1803 to 1809, territorial governor William Henry Harrison signed treaties with tribal leaders that garnered the southern third of Indiana and portions of east and west-central Indiana for the United States. In the War of 1812, Harrison and his troops destroyed at least twenty-five Indian villages in Indiana. After the war, the Piankashaw and the majority of the Wea and Kickapoo settled in Illinois or Missouri, but the rest of Indiana's indigenous populations remained.

The United States moved rapidly after the War of 1812 to obtain the rest of the Indian-held lands in Indiana. In the New Purchase Treaty of 1818, the Indians ceded all lands south of the Wabash River except the Big Miami Reserve and smaller Potawatomi reserves adjacent to it in north-central Indiana. In subsequent treaties between 1821 and 1832 the Potawatomi and Miami Indians relinquished land north and west of the Wabash and Miami rivers. Two years later, the Miami reserve shrunk. The Potawatomi gave up their reserves, and many of them moved west. The federal government forcibly removed the rest to Kansas in 1838. By 1840 the Miami owned only a small reserve named for Miami Chief Meshingomesia and several individual allotments.

All but a few of the Miami moved to Kansas. Those who stayed were the families of chiefs Jean Baptiste Richardville, Francis Godfroy, Metocina (father of Meshingomesia), and white captive Frances Slocum and her Miami husband Shepaconah. Other Miami soon returned to Indiana. By 1850 approximately two hundred fifty lived in Indiana, and as many lived in Kansas. They resided in Miami, Wabash, and Grant counties and near the cities of Fort Wayne, Huntington, and Lafayette. Living near rivers, this small group of Indiana natives resumed their traditional lifestyle of hunting, fishing, horticulture, and gathering edible and medicinal plants.

Regan-Dinius and Clark depict the time of removal as a time of widespread dispersal of Indians. While thousands of natives marched the trails of tears and death to western places such as Oklahoma and Kansas, many escaped by running in every direction, hiding among other tribal groups or posing as white or black people. Therefore, tracing an Indian ancestor from the mid-nineteenth century can be difficult. Although individuals had always traveled, migrated, and intermarried with other tribes, before the 1830s

Indians most likely lived among their own people, and their tribes' descendants may have recorded their membership. During the removals, however, any native from a traditionally eastern or southern tribe might be found anywhere—or not be found if the native's true ethnicity was never recorded on a government document, such as a census or marriage record.

Indians who moved to reservations or stayed in Indiana were not included in federal censuses because they were not American citizens. However, in order to determine which individual natives were to be given annual allotments to fulfill the terms of the numerous Indian treaties, the U.S. government documented tribal membership on tribal rolls. The annual allotments stretched thinly over the tribal populations. Thus, when the government took a roll of the Miami Tribe of Indiana for an 1854 treaty, the tribal council insisted that an individual or group could only be included on the roll by consent of the council. Two groups that the Indiana Miami refused to add to their tribal rolls were Miami who had moved to the Indian village Papakeechi in Michigan in order to avoid removal in 1840 and the family of Richardville's half-sister, Josetta Beaubien.

During the ensuing one hundred fifty years, numerous groups, some like these displaced Miami and others with less substantial claims, tried and failed to prove their kinship with one of the federally recognized tribes or petitioned the government to recognize them. The tribal rolls for the years 1885–1940 can be found on National Archives and Records Administration (NARA) microfilm record group M 595, which is available by interlibrary loan through most public libraries or directly from the NARA—Great Lakes Region in Chicago. The data on the rolls varies but usually includes the English and/or Indian name, age or date of birth, gender, and relationship to the head of the family. The rolls taken after 1930 include degree of Indian blood, marital status, place of residence, and other information. The NARA also has tribal school and allotment records.

After the time of the removals, the most important migration by Native Americans to Indiana occurred after World War II. Native Americans, similar to other Americans, moved to industrialized cities in order to secure jobs. Thus, there are Native Americans in Indiana from every national region, although individuals from tribes originally from the eastern United States comprise the bulk of the state's native population. People who claim American Indian ethnicity are spread around the state evenly at a rate of approximately 0.2 percent except in the northern third of Indiana where they represent from 0.3 to 0.4 percent of the population. Cherokee, concentrated in east-central Indiana, are now the largest indigenous group; the Miami are second. Another important group is the Pokagon Potawatomi in the South Bend area, which is currently the only group in Indiana with federal recognition.

Present Localities of the Indian Tribes West of the Mississippi: Showing the Boundaries of the Indian Tribes in 1843 ([Philadelphia]: J. T. Bowen, [1843-4]; in IHS collections; courtesy of Leigh Darbee)

In 1992 Gov. Evan Bayh created a state Indian Commission to address Native American concerns and to raise public awareness about the state's indigenous population. Several American Indian organizations arose in the last two and a half decades as well to foster intertribal communication and to rejuvenate native culture. These groups sponsor powwows to celebrate and teach their culture. Notices of upcoming powwows appear on Native American Internet sites, for instance, at www.powwows.com or at the Web site for the Museums at Prophetstown listed below. The latter organization also publishes a free, intertribal Internet newsletter as do numerous North American Indian groups. The Eiteljorg Museum in downtown Indianapolis also hosts and sponsors Native American cultural events.

As Regan-Dinius and Clark state, the best way to research a native ancestor is to determine who in the family partnered with one, at what time, and in what place. If the research does not indicate the tribal affiliation of the native ancestor, determine which native groups lived in the area at the time. Then search the tribal rolls for those groups. Once the research has progressed this far—and only at this point—can federally recognized tribes assist in the search. Contact information for Indiana's indigenous groups (supplied by Clark) and for the federally recognized Cherokee tribes are listed below. For a list of all recognized tribes, see the *Federal Register* 65, no. 49 (March 13, 2000): 13298–13303, or visit the Bureau of Indian Affairs Web site at www.doi.gov/leaders.pdf. Clark also supplies a list of useful sources for researching Indiana natives, and excerpts from it are reproduced at the end of the chapter. The IHS library has extensive collections, too. A quick search using the keyword "Indian" produces a list of more than six hundred entries, including manuscripts, rare books, maps, references, and visual sources.

Cherokee Nation of Oklahoma
PO Box 948
Tahlequah, OK 74465
918-456-5000; 800-256-0671

Eastern Band of Cherokee Indians
PO Box 455
Cherokee, NC 28719
828-497-7000

United Keetoowah Band of Cherokee Indians (UKB)
PO Box 746
Tahlequah, OK 74465
918-456-6533; fax 918-453-9345

Delaware Tribal Headquarters
220 NW Virginia Avenue
Bartlesville, OK 74003
918-336-5272

Munsee Delaware
289 Jubilee Road
Muncey, Ontario N0L 1Y0
Canada
519-289-5156

Kickapoo Tribe of Kansas
1107 Goldfinch Road
Horton, KS 66439
785-486-2131; fax 785-486-2801

Miami Nation of Indians of Indiana
80 West 6th Street
PO Box 41
Peru, IN 46970
765-473-9631
800-253-3578; fax 765-472-4162

Miami Nation of Oklahoma
202 South Eight Tribes Trail
Miami, OK 74354
918-542-1445

Peoria Nation of Oklahoma
PO Box 1527
Miami, OK 74355
918-540-2535; fax 918-540-2538

Pokagon Band of Potawatomi Indians
58620 Sink Road
Dowagiac, MI 49047
269-782-6323; 888-376-9988

Absentee Shawnee Tribe of Oklahoma
2025 South Gordon Cooper Drive
Shawnee, OK 74801
405-275-4030

Eastern Shawnee Tribe
PO Box 350
Seneca, MO 64865
918-666-2435; fax 918-666-3325

Loyal Band Shawnee Nation
PO Box 149
Miami, OK 74355
918-542-7006

Historic Forks of the Wabash
PO Box 261
Huntington, IN 46750
260-356-1903

Museums at Prophetstown
PO Box 331
Battle Ground, IN 47920

Selected Bibliography: Clark, Nicholas L. "Casual Reading List, Native Americans: Their History in the Wabash Valley" (paper for the Museums at Prophetstown, Lafayette, June 17, 1999); Glenn, Elizabeth, and Stewart Rafert. "Native Americans." In *Peopling Indiana: The Ethnic Experience*, Robert M. Taylor Jr. and Connie McBirney, eds. Indianapolis: Indiana Historical Society, 1996, 392–418; McPherson, Alan. *Indian Names in Indiana*. Kewanna, IN: Alan McPherson, 1993; National Archives Web site: www.archives.gov/genealogy/heritage/native-american/; Rafert, Stewart. *The Miami Indians of Indiana*. Indianapolis: Indiana Historical Society, 1996; Sieber, Ellen, and Cheryl Ann Munson. "Cultures in Transition: Native Americans, 1600–1800." In *Looking at History: Indiana's Hoosier National Forest Region, 1600–1950*. Washington, DC: U.S. Department of Agriculture, Forest Service, 1992; Bloomington: Indiana University Press, 1994, 16–24; *The Papers of William Henry Harrison, 1800–1815*, edited by Douglas E. Clanin et al. Indianapolis: Indiana Historical Society, 1999; U.S. Census Bureau. "United States Census 2000." Calculations by Indiana business Research Center, IU Kelley School of Business. On the Internet at http://www.stats.indiana.edu/c2k/c2kframe.html (accessed December 13, 2006); The author interviewed Nick Clark and Jeannie Regan-Dinius in 2000 in preparation for the original version of this chapter, which appeared in *The Hoosier Genealogist* 40 (June 2000): 2:73–78.

Indiana's Native Americans: Excerpts from a "Casual Reading List"

Compiled by Nicholas L. Clark

Alley, D. Peorias: A History of the Peoria Indian Tribe of Oklahoma. Peoria Nation of Oklahoma, 1991.

Always a People: Oral Histories of Contemporary Woodland Indians. Rita Kohn and Lynwood Montell, eds. Indiana University Press, 1997.

Anson, Bert. The Miami Indians. University of Oklahoma Press, 1970.

Atlas of Great Lakes Indian History. Helen H. Tanner et al., eds. University of Oklahoma Press, 1987.

Clifton, James A. The Pokagons, 1683–1983: Catholic Potawatomi. University Press of America, 1984.

———. The Potawatomi. Chelsea House Publishers, 1987.

Edmunds, R. David. Potawatomis: Keepers of the Fire. University of Oklahoma Press, 1978.

Gipson, Lawrence H. The Moravian Indian Mission on White River. Indiana Historical Bureau, 1938.

Grumet, Robert S. The Lenapes. Chelsea House, 1989.

Howard, James. Shawnee! The Ceremonialism of a Native American Tribe and Its Cultural Background. University of Oklahoma Press, 1981.

Johnston, Basil. Indian School Days. University of Oklahoma Press, 1988.

Kinietz, W. Vernon. The Indians of the Western Great Lakes: 1615–1760. University of Michigan Press, 1940, reprint, 1996.

Lurie, Nancy O. Wisconsin Indians. State Historical Society of Wisconsin, 1980.

Ourada, Patricia K. The Menominee Indians: A History. University of Oklahoma Press, 1979.

Sugden, John. Tecumseh: A Life. Henry Holt and Company, 1997.

Tanner, Helen H. The Ojibwa. Chelsea House, 1992.

Weatherford, Jack. Native Roots: How the Indians Enriched America. Crown, 1991.

White, Richard. The Middle Ground: Indians, Empires, and Republics in the Great Lakes Region, 1650–1815. Cambridge University Press, 1991.

Inclusion and Exclusion
Indiana's Chinese Community

DAN CARPENTER

I
t was a Who's Who of Indianapolis's extended Chinese American family that browsed the hors d'oeuvres tables and posed for snapshots in the gleaming, cavernous banquet room of the Scottish Rite Cathedral in celebration of Phoebe Jung's ninetieth birthday. There was Phylis Lan Lin, the pioneering University of Indianapolis sociology professor, for whom the university's baccalaureate program

in social work is named; Glen Kwok, executive director of the International Violin Competition of Indianapolis; Amy Cheung, member of an old-line restaurateur family and a noted pediatrician who has served thousands of poor youngsters through her free clinic; biochemist David Wong, codiscoverer of the blockbuster antidepression drug Prozac and president of the Indiana Chinese-American Professional Association; Caterina Blitzer, executive director of the International Center of Indianapolis and one of Sino-Hoosierdom's many distinguished friends.

The degrees, professional laurels, entrepreneurial success, and civic contributions of these couple of hundred guests seemed capable of fueling a fair-

sized city by itself; but the collective résumé has long since ceased to be news. Achievement is widely taken for granted, like so much else about Indiana's Chinese Americans. Assumptions, however, can be deceiving. "We're supposed to be such a patriarchal society," quipped Alfred Tsang, himself an engineer turned lawyer and deputy state attorney general, now retired. "And so how do we have these women who are civil engineers and doctors?"

Both in spite and because of its reluctance to blow its own horn, not only about its successes but also about its benefits to the larger society, this far-from-homogeneous group wears the mantle "model minority." Nothing at the blithe reception for Jung contradicted that image—or bespoke the irony it carries in light of the checkered history of America's receptivity toward Chinese and other Asian immigrants and their descendants.

Few attendees at that elegant event on August 18, 2001, were more quietly accomplished than Benny Ko, M.D., husband of Jung's daughter Vicky. A specialist in nuclear med-

Phoebe and David Jung, ca. 1937 (Photo courtesy of Benny and Vicky [Jung] Ko)

icine, radiology, and radiation oncology, Ko has volunteered for medical missions in needy areas around the world. He is also an avid amateur historian. It devolved upon Ko to deliver the formal tribute, also described as a roast, for the widow Jung, who sat smiling upon a table laden with roses and graced with traditional gold pictographs signifying longevity and happiness. Enthroned alongside her was a family friend of many years, 104-year-old Gus Streeter, a prominent veteran of World War I.

As Ko rendered his lighthearted, poignant eulogy to his mother-in-law, the audience felt the sensation of reading a living history book. She was born in 1911 in China, the year in which four thousand years of emperors were overthrown in a bloody revolution. She took advantage of the break in tradition to pursue education, study English, and remain single until her mid-twenties, all radical departures for a female. She escaped the Japanese horrors known in infamy as the Rape of Nanking by grudgingly accepting an uncle's advice to leave her job in Nanking in 1937. She escaped the maelstrom of the Communist Cultural Revolution by fleeing with her husband and children to America in the early 1960s. Most, if not all, of this amazing résumé might have been different, Ko pointed out, had it not been for U.S. laws and regulations that prevented her grandfather and father from bringing their families to this country late in the nineteenth or early twentieth centuries while they worked as laborers, then merchants, in the land known to the Chinese as the Golden Mountain. The

most prominent and noxious of these prohibitions was the federal Chinese Exclusion Act of 1882.

Aside from those such as Ko who have taken a scholarly interest, there appear to be few among Indianapolis's 12,500 residents of Chinese descent (year 2000 census figures) who are conscious of the exclusion act. Extended and modified several times before its repeal in 1943, it is the experience of a dying generation, the contemporaries and near-contemporaries of Jung. Yet the impact of this unprecedented and sweeping restriction on the size, development, and accommodation of Indianapolis's Chinese American community cannot be dismissed any more than it can be measured. Steve Tuchman, an Indianapolis immigration lawyer who knows the Chinese American community well, brands it "the first and ultimate example of our reactionary, highly politically charged immigration policy." Ironically, it targeted an ethnic group whose members mostly intended not to stay and raise families and compete for resources indefinitely, but rather, as was the case with Jung's grandfather and father, to earn some money and return to their homeland.

While there is some scholarly disagreement as to the social and political roots of this nation's original immigration barrier, the consensus attributes it to the hot-and-cold diplomatic and trade relationship between the United States and China, coupled with nativist bigotry and fear for jobs in the Western states, where the great midcentury need for hardworking "Chinamen" in railroad building and gold mining had diminished. The act suspended immigration of Chinese laborers for ten years (later extended); allowed those residing here as of 1880 to stay, travel abroad, and return; forbade further naturalization; and established exemptions for teachers, students, merchants, and travelers. Women, already tending to stay behind in China for economic reasons, felt the effects of exclusion laws more than the men; intermarriage between Chinese men and white women was, of course, taboo.

As a secondary destination for Chinese pilgrims, Indiana played a relatively small part in the causes and effects of the exclusion act or of a series of prior and subsequent federal measures that affected the Chinese. The 1880 census, the first to mention the Chinese in Indiana, counts 13, all males. By the 1940s, there were fewer than 500, concentrated in laundry and restaurant businesses in Indianapolis. As special restrictions against "Eastern Hemisphere" visitors and immigrants have been lifted over the past generation, the Indiana population of ancestral Chinese has risen from 986 in 1960 to 5,212 in 1980, to 7,371 in 1990, to more than 12,500 in 2000. At Indiana and Purdue Universities and the University of Notre Dame, enrollment of students from the People's Republic of China has grown from 3 in 1970 to 1,265 in 2000; and of Taiwanese students, from 79 in 1970 to 462 in 2000 (although the latter figure has fallen in recent years). An urban/suburban people, Indiana residents of Chinese descent are found in most of the state's ninety-two counties. They have not lived free of prejudice. But as a rule, the professionals and students who are predominant among the contemporary arrivals are welcomed by an Indiana establishment that covets their skills and nurtures its own trade and diplomatic relations with a Chinese sister state, Zhejiang Province.

It used to be more complicated. Generally benign, patronizing accounts from the daily newspapers of the first half of the twentieth century indicate that the Chinese, known for keeping to themselves and for their widespread intention to return to their homeland, never attained the status of a threat as they did in the West. There were pejorative references, to be sure, citing the "strangeness" and "mystery" of the isolated people and the small-scale operation of the criminal-protection underworld known as the tong. But the Chinese, particularly the more affluent and Western-savvy as opposed to the obscure laborers, also came in for blandishments and political defense. Indeed, in the view of Jack Chen, author of *The Chinese of America*, this state distinguished itself during

a peak time of discrimination and brutality: "Senator Oliver P. Morton of Indiana, who served as chairman of the Joint Special Committee to Investigate Chinese Immigration in 1877, wrote a minority report declaring that if the Chinese had been white no such outcry would have been raised against them."

In a book bristling with passionate accounts of anti-Chinese racism, Chen goes on to praise various other Caucasian groups and individuals who were moved to speak out against the oppression of this singled-out minority. But if Chinese subjects of the laws were themselves outraged, they tended not to show it publicly. Caution is one readily inferred reason. Another is pride. As Ko put it in an interview, "It *was* an insult—but to them, things only smart when you have self-doubt as to who you are. When in your heart you were born as a Chinese and will die as a Chinese, it doesn't affect you so much, what others may think of you."

So the Chinese in America endured and coped. One way of coping was the so-called "slot racket," in which a U.S. citizen of Chinese lineage would visit his ancestral homeland and tell the U.S. government he had a new son or daughter—usually son, in keeping with the desire to carry on the family name. That "offspring" would be classified as a U.S. citizen under the law, and a certificate would be issued to the father accordingly. The paper, entitling a young person to a "slot" in the United States, would then be given or sold under the table to an otherwise ineligible young person in China.

That is how David Jung, Phoebe's future husband, made it to this country in about 1915 from Canton in southern China. That is why he claimed a relative named Lee. David Jung began life on the Golden Mountain ironing clothes sixteen hours a day in Chicago and then moved to Indianapolis to take a waiter's job at the Bamboo Inn, a second-story establishment on Monument Circle considered to have been the city's first Chinese restaurant. A Christian, he expanded and polished his English through his attendance at a local church, where he developed an invaluable friendship with a couple he met there, a dentist named Glenn Pell and his wife, Ruth. With the Pells' encouragement, he pursued English and

Jong Mea Chow Mein was among Indiana's oldest Chinese restaurants. (Photo courtesy of Frances Chen Russell)

Lion Dance performed by the Indiana Association of Chinese Americans at the third annual Carmel International Art Festival, 2000 (Photo by James Yee, *Daily Ledger*, Hamilton County, Indiana)

education, to the point of earning a doctorate in chemistry from Indiana University in 1936. The following year, when he was thirty-six, he returned to China to teach.

"The people who came in the early part of the century were sojourners," Ko notes. "They wanted to make money and move back. Those who came in the '50s and '60s and beyond were immigrants, intending to stay." The Chinese political system and economy have done much to influence the pattern of intention of Chinese immigrants. They changed the plans of the Jungs, who eventually lost hope that they could live and work as Chinese apart from the subjugation of the Chinese government. When they placed themselves among the tens of thousands of would-be refugees in Hong Kong in 1962, they still faced frustration. While the Chinese Exclusion Act had been dead two decades, the McCarran-Walter Act of 1952 still imposed minuscule quotas for Asian immigration to the United States, and the "national origins" language of entry policy would not be expunged until the Immigration Act of 1965.

But David Jung had friends here—Mary and Eric Wadleigh, daughter and son-in-law of the late Pells. The Wadleighs apprised Indiana University of Jung's credentials and secured his employment under

Tai chi demonstration at the International Festival in Indianapolis (Photo courtesy of Frances Chen Russell)

the law's allowances for needed skills. When he died in 1989 at age eighty-nine, he held several patents in medical technology and was professor emeritus of the clinical pathology department.

Thus did frustrated sojourners become valued immigrants. So thoroughly Chinese that their children arrived here not knowing English, they lived to see them reach success along paths of astonishing variety. Daughter Becky obtained a master's degree in piano performance, son Corky became a banker in Hong Kong, and son Jackie became an aerospace engineer. Daughter Vicky holds a master's degree in fine arts and a PhD in education administration and has worked as a flight attendant since shortly after getting her bachelor's degree in mathematics from Indiana University in 1969. Son Dicky started the Hong Kong Inn on Indianapolis's far east side in 1969, knowing virtually no English. Today his place of business is Yummy on the northwest side, a mecca of authentic Chinese cuisine. Though he is an eminent part of a still-thriving restaurateur class in the Indianapolis community, he regrets not having had a chance to earn a college degree, as each of his children has.

Lum Lee shares that feeling; but unlike Dicky Jung, who came here as an adult and had to pursue a living, Lee arrived at sixteen in 1950 and later was able to enroll in Butler University. He chose not to stay there, notwithstanding the wishes of his father, Daniel, who had become owner of the Mandarin Inn at 38th Street and College Avenue after years of sixteen-hour days and seven-day weeks toiling in restaurants and laundries. Lum Lee was born in 1934 in Canton after one of his father's visits home and came to Indiana under a provision of the law that granted automatic citizenship to offspring only until their sixteenth birthday. With immigration authorities' suspicions about the slot rackets, "Even I had to face challenges to make sure I was the real one."

Lee did not find college to his liking and, taking care not to mention it to his father, purposely neglected to apply for his student deferment and let the Army draft him. After a two-year hitch and a few years of working on his own, he joined his father, who had started the Lotus Garden on the east side. Four years later, in 1964, Lum Lee started a second Lotus Garden in Greenwood, operating it until his retirement in 1997. He and his wife, Bik Chan Lee, have reared five children—three engineers, an architect, and a urologist. "Chinese life is simple here," Lee says. "All they do is develop their kids for higher education, because the parents didn't have it."

A bridge between the tireless entrepreneurs who jumped through hoops to work in America and the professional classes who are welcomed and recruited today by hospitals, universities, and corporations, Lum Lee views racial history through a positive but clear lens. "Life here is a lot better now. There are better opportunities than there used to be. A lot of equal opportunity. My dad taught me a lot about their life. He lived to see the prosperity. He and my grandfather, we have more than they ever dreamed of. If you're under forty or fifty years old, you have no idea what we're talking about."

It wasn't just poverty and a language barrier, Lee acknowledges. It was discrimination: denial of hotel accommodations and jobs in factories; laws against coming to this country in the first place. Yet he insists "America is open to those who are willing to work," and he remembers being embraced by the Caucasian Hoosiers with whom he went to school. "The first I learned the American way was through those kids. They helped me a lot."

More than a generation after the Chinese Exclusion Act and the McCarran-Walter Act, discrimination and assimilation remain issues in the Chinese American community. To promote both intragroup solidarity and fellowship with the rest of a diversifying city and state, several organizations have been formed since the early 1970s: the Indianapolis Association of Chinese Americans, Taiwanese American Association, Indiana Chinese-American Professional Association, and Asian-American Alliance of Indiana. No less a refuge and resource for this predominantly Christian group is the Chinese Community Church, formed in the early 1970s on the north side of Indianapolis and relocated to Carmel in keeping with the housing preferences of many Chinese American professionals in Indianapolis. Part of its ministry is teaching English to newcomers who may be far down the socioeconomic scale from residents of that prestigious suburb, the Golden Mountain's local putative Gold Coast.

Carmel resident Frances Chen Russell, a pianist and retired college music teacher, who has been active formally and informally in Chinese American affairs and overall race relations, submits that assimilation has become a given to the educated younger generation but remains problematic to the many immigrants on the other end of the economic scale who come without English and find subsistence work in restaurants. While the history of explicit discrimination is "beyond my memory and practically beyond my consciousness, except for reading about it," Russell finds it naive to deem the "model minority" fully integrated. "We are an odd lot," she says, "in that we realize we're minorities only when it is to our disadvantage. For example, we were excluded from Ivy League schools because too many of us were qualifying." As to the complimentary clichés about the Chinese as industrious, honest, clean, and scholarly, regardless of their factual basis, "It is annoying to be stereotyped. In this town I would still describe us as a silent, invisible group. We don't speak up. People don't hear our voices. That's why we founded the pan-Asian group (Asian-American Alliance)."

Contemporary race relation problems recounted by Chinese Americans can be as serious as obstacles to obtaining licensing for a business, or as nettlesome as the common assumption by strangers that one is a foreigner. Vicky Ko says her son and daughter, now in their twenties and born and reared in Terre Haute, wearied of being asked their nationality. Yet there is debate among Chinese Americans as to how much to be bothered by such neutral or well-meaning provincialism. "I'd rather have somebody at least try to chitchat than to worry about being politically correct," Benny Ko declares.

When Russell says her people need to assert their identity, she speaks from a larger perspective. Born in Malaysia in 1940 to Pearl Liu, who held a doctorate in biology from the University of Michigan, Russell was living in southern China in 1949 and fled with her mother and sister "literally on the last boat, two weeks before the Communist takeover." Her father? "He was a Chinese who said no matter what happens in his country, a man doesn't leave." A college professor, John Ren Bing stayed

United States airman Alfred Tsang, age 21 (Photo courtesy of Alfred Tsang)

and despite constant pressure from the party never became a Communist.

After living in Malaysia and Singapore, Bing's wife and daughters came to Michigan in 1956 "under some sort of immigration quota," Russell recalls. "Maybe it was through the Methodist church in Ann Arbor." She eventually studied two years at tiny Albion College, where her mother was a professor, but felt "I was in a fishbowl" because of her family tie and her ethnicity. She transferred to the University of Michigan, where she earned bachelor's and master's degrees in music.

Before undertaking doctoral work in ethnomusicology at Brown University, Russell took a job at Tougaloo College in Mississippi, where she met her future husband, David Russell, a Woodrow Wilson Fellow who was part of a team of newly minted MBAs sent South to help black colleges. This was 1965, a key moment in another American racial struggle. The couple—she Asian, he white—was conspicuous. "Some restaurants wouldn't admit us. We were 'others.' We had no identity of our own. We associated with blacks so we were considered black. I was too naive; I didn't know about civil rights problems. I went down there to teach music. I learned a lot. It was a wonderful six years. It opened my eyes. I'm a little different from other Chinese people. I had an opportunity to live among people not common to immigrants, who mainly find themselves with the population that is not the minority."

Alfred Tsang, who was born in New York but lived in China from age three to fourteen, describes his people as "a community in diaspora" that has never attained integration outside its ancestral land despite its success, perseverance, and adoptive patriotism. Tsang's father, Tsang Kwong Bo, came here as the son of a treaty merchant and was denied citizenship under the Exclusion Act, yet he gave consent to have his son enlist in the U.S. Army Air Corps before finishing high school during World War II. His wife back in China, Chan Miew Yee, reared Alfred under Confucian ideals that deemed it shameful to avoid serving and allow another mother's son to fight in his place. Alfred Tsang flew bombing missions over Japan, sorties that devastated civilian populations and were, he is bitterly convinced, unjustified morally or militarily. Even as he celebrates a long life of fulfilled American dreams— he has mastered two professions and reared three happy achievers with his wife, Buzzy—Tsang says his story cannot exclude sorrow—"about not realizing until after his death how my father endured his humiliation in silence while signing off his son to harm's way to serve the country that denied him; and the pain inflicted upon my conscience in having participated in the firebombing of urban areas in Japan described by a career general on [Gen. Douglas] MacArthur's staff as barbaric." When he dies, Tsang intends for his ashes to be mixed with soil from mainland China and Taiwan (to transcend division), from Iwo Jima (in affinity with the 7,000 Marines who died preparing his B-29's landing strip), and from Japan (as his "symbolic reconciliation with the innocent people who suffered"). He wants some of the mixture to be buried in Arlington National Cemetery and some scattered over the Pacific.

For Alfred Tsang, as for Frances Chen Russell and many others of their ethnicity, the thirst for social justice was born in the personal and grew to embrace the universal, including people under the flag of China's old adversary, Japan, and the African Americans who have often been pitted against ethnic Asians. The lesson, as enunciated pointedly by Jack

Lion statues at the Indianapolis Zoo were donated to Indiana from its Chinese sister state, Zhejiang Province. (Photo courtesy of Dan Carpenter)

Chen in *The Chinese of America*, is that a "model minority" remains a minority:

The anti-Chinese atrocities of the 1870s and 1880s were paid for and are still being paid for in the social distress of other ethnic minorities, in the social disturbances of the civil rights movement of the 1960s and 1970s, and in the catastrophic results of unwise foreign policy decisions inspired by racist attitudes rather than by prudent assessments of the nation's best interests. Who knows if the bill has yet been paid in full? America is a nation of nations. Shackling the creative activities of any of its constituent peoples is a loss to all the others.

Selected Bibliography: Blitzer, Caterina Cregor. "Images of Chinese Americans in Central Indiana." Paper presented at "Myths and Realities—Perceptions and Questions for Community 2000." ICPA–IACA–AAAI Joint Annual Meeting, November 18, 2000; Brownstone, David M. *The Chinese-American Heritage*. New York: Facts on File, 1988; Chen, Jack. *The Chinese of America: From the Beginnings to the Present*. New York: Harper and Row, 1981; Chin, Tung Pok. *Paper Son: One Man's Story*. Philadelphia: Temple University Press, 2000; Ling, Huping. *Surviving on the Gold Mountain: A History of Chinese American Women and Their Lives*. Albany: State University of New York Press, 1998; McCunn, Ruthanne Lum. *Chinese American Portraits: Personal Histories, 1828–1988*. San Francisco: Chronicle Books, 1988; Miscevic, Dusanka. *Chinese Americans: The Immigrant Experience*. Southport, CT: Hugh Lauter Levin, 2000; Su, Julie Tao. *Indiana Chinese American Resources Directory*. Indianapolis: InfoNet, 1992; Taylor, Robert M. Jr., and Connie A. McBirney, eds. *Peopling Indiana: The Ethnic Experience*. Indianapolis: Indiana Historical Society, 1996.

Part 6
Providing Context and Accuracy

Cover and page from the diary of S. Jennie (Pardun) Vawter, b. 1847, Manchester, Indiana (Jennie Vawter Papers, SC 2444, IHS)

17 ½

goes to ploughing in the garden &c So begins the affairs of my new home — and so I expect things will progress very pleasantly. I like my home very much.

Sept. The first Sunday in May. 1868. To day &c, Lizzie my husband and I are making preparations to go to Liberty Church and hear Bro Lanham. we all go. there is a large congregation assembled. perhaps to heare the gospel — perhaps to to See the newly married pare as this is the first Sunday we go to church. well I have enjoyed my self very well to day. I was dressed in my infare suit.

The first Sunday in June/68. well to day — Lizzie, my husband, and I start to Liberty to church — we are going to have a basket dinner we Girls have our's very nicely spread some four or five eat dinner with us we then clear away our dinner and while Lizzie walks around with her young associates my husband and I get into our carrige and sit and converse very pleasantly through intermission. the hour for service has arriven the ministers Bros Land and Lanham ascend the pulpit and we have a very good meeting and dismiss and go home. I'll tell you journal as I just think of it — my husband and I went to madison yesterday (Sat, and had our photo: draw no more this time.

Vawter Diary, 1869–1879

GEORGE R. HANLIN

———————————————•———————————————

When researching family history, it is good practice to use primary sources—documents such as letters, diaries, court records, and contemporary newspaper accounts—to gain an understanding of the subject at hand. Secondary sources, which consist of interpretations of history (usually after the fact), are also valuable tools. But reviewing and studying documents directly related to a subject add the firsthand details and provide the insight essential to understanding it.

The Indiana Historical Society's library is an excellent source of primary materials. It holds a variety of papers relating to individuals, families, businesses, and other organizations, all providing important data about life in Indiana. One small but notable IHS library collection contains just two items: the diary of Jennie Vawter and an accompanying typescript. While the diary is rather brief, it nonetheless serves as important documentation of family history and nineteenth-century social life in Ripley and Jefferson counties, Indiana.[1]

Jennie Vawter was born Sarah J. Pardun on April 18, 1847, the daughter of Abraham Pardun of Shelby Township, Ripley County. Though Jennie writes that she began keeping a diary at age seventeen, the volume the IHS holds begins later, running from January 1, 1869, to August 20, 1879, and focusing heavily on 1869–1870. Among other things, it discusses Jennie's marriage to John M. Vawter (the son of Beverly and Elizabeth Vawter of Monroe Township, Jefferson County) on April 15, 1869; the establishment of their home in Smyrna Township, Jefferson County; and the births of two children, a daughter, Minnie, on April 13, 1870, and a son on August 11, 1875. Much of the diary centers on social activities, such as Fourth of July and Christmas celebrations, and religious life, including events at churches in Hopewell and Shelby. The diary also frequently mentions trips to places such as Dupont, Lancaster, Madison, and Wirt in Jefferson County and New Marion and Rexville in Ripley County.

Perhaps of most interest to genealogists are Jennie's references to friends and neighbors in the areas of southwestern Ripley County and northwestern Jefferson County. She mentions some forty family names, including Pickett, Adam, Spears, Earhart, Grooms, Breeden, and Toph. However, she usually refers to individuals only by the titles of Mr., Mrs., or Miss, without a first name. For only about a dozen people does she mention full names. Those include

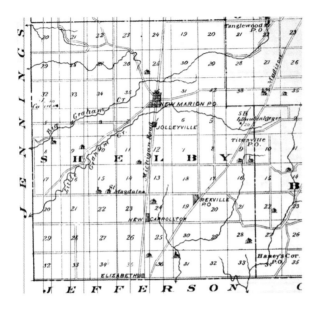

The southwest portion of this Ripley County map of 1876 shows New Marion and Rexville, two of the towns named in the Vawter diary. (*Maps of Indiana Counties in 1876* [Indianapolis: Indiana Historical Society, 1968, 1999]; repr. from *Illustrated Historical Atlas of the State of Indiana* [Chicago: Baskin, Forster and Co., 1876])

John Surber, Mollie Bienfiel, Mary Caplinger, Ann Hartsock, Joe Lawler, Mrs. Em Castner, Milt West, Hattie Boyer, Alice Hyatt, Selema Cooper, Lucinda Spears, Israel Robbins, Israel Noyes, and J. M. Morss (who married Jennie's sister Ann).

As Jennie's diary illustrates, one problem with using primary sources is that they often create as many questions as they answer. Who were these friends and neighbors? Where did they live, and how did they know the Vawters and Parduns? The genealogist uses many tools to help answer these questions, such as deed records and county histories. In this case the 1870 census index confirmed that many of these families lived in Ripley and Jefferson counties, but other mysteries remain. Another problem using primary sources is that the people recording the information make mistakes. They misremember events, apply their own worldviews to the details, spell names inconsistently, and incorrectly record data. Many times in her diary, for example, Jennie misspells the names of neighbors and nearby towns, and no doubt she makes factual errors as well. Still, the valuable information found in primary sources and the details they provide make them a vital part of research.

One item in Vawter's diary that genealogists will find especially helpful is an attendance record for students. At the top of the record is a title that reads "School commenced Oct 1863." Below it is a grid with dates running across the top, beginning on Monday, the nineteenth, and ending the next month on Tuesday, the twenty-fourth. Running along the left-hand side of the grid are the names of students and their ages. To the right of each student's name is an attendance record. Below is a re-creation of the students listed on the first page of the record and their ages:

Lewis B Roice	6
Henry Caldwell	12
Sarah A Gollay	9
Elizie Caldwell	9
Kannie[?] Caldwell	6
Filomea Roice	9
Lewis H Humphries	12
Edgar Humphries	9
Albert H Humphries	7
William Golaspie	4
Mary Humph[ries?]	15
Nancy C Brokaw	10
Wm C Golay	14
George W Dohoney	11
Alexander Caldwe[ll?]	15
John Thomas Roice	16
Charles Roice	14
George Golay	12
James Edwards	14
John Green[?]	11
James H Humphries	15

At this point the page ends, and the school record starts again two pages later. One can assume it is for the same session because the dates on this page correspond with those on the first, but run from October 27 to November 24.[2] The list of students continues:

William Dohoney	8
Martha E Dohoney	5
Mary F Dohoney	9
Albrado Dohoney	5

Whitley Dohoney	8
John Brokaw	16
Louisa Dohoney	12
Charly Humph[ries?]	17
Humphrey Roice	5
Burdit Golay	6
David Caldwell	6

The school records raise additional questions. First, who kept the records? The heading is dated 1863, long before Jennie began this diary. The name of her husband is handwritten in the front of the book, and the writing in the school records appears to match the handwriting in John's name. It is possible that the book belonged originally to him and that Jennie wrote in it later. (Indeed, her writing surrounds the school records, making this theory seem plausible.) Then one wonders who the students were and what school they attended. Research reveals that many of the children's surnames are listed in southern Monroe and northern Madison townships in Jefferson County in the 1870 census index. In addition, an 1859 Jefferson County directory places many of these families in that region, several near the now-defunct post offices of Mud Lick and Stony Point, on the southeastern boundary of what is now the Jefferson Proving Grounds. It should be pointed out that variations of the family names appear in these two sources. For example, the name Humphries also appears as Humphrey, and the name Roice appears elsewhere as Royce and Royse. Because the census and the directory indicate that John Vawter's father lived in Monroe Township, one can surmise that John grew up there. It is possible, therefore, that John was once a teacher in the vicinity and that the list of students belonged to him.

After exploring the Vawter diary in depth, one easily realizes the value of such primary sources. They are rich in history and are often colored with invaluable detail. As shown by some of the questions posed above, however, they are not without their flaws. No matter how diligently one digs, the search often leaves mys-

Northwest portion of an 1876 Jefferson County map, showing Dupont, Lancaster, Madison, Mud Lick, Stony Point, and Wirt (*Maps of Indiana Counties in 1876* [Indianapolis: Indiana Historical Society, 1968, 1999]; repr. from *Illustrated Historical Atlas of the State of Indiana* [Chicago: Baskin, Forster and Co., 1876])

teries that can be solved only by educated guesses. The key is to mine primary sources with care, sorting out the nuggets of good information and further exploring those that are questionable. In the end, the time and energy spent exploring primary sources, gleaning facts, and then trying to address the questions they raise will lead researchers to a precious wealth of knowledge and understanding about the lives of their ancestors.

●

1. Jennie Vawter Diary, 1868–1879, SC 2444, Indiana Historical Society. Some of the information in this chapter comes from the collection guide, written by Alexandra S. Gressitt, September 28, 1994.

2. All dates in the school records correspond to October and November 1863 dates in "The Perpetual," a historic calendar tool created in 1985 by Columbian Art-Works in Milwaukee.

Benjamin Harrison Flag Quilt

RAYMOND M. FEATHERSTONE JR.

●

The following narrative describes the sources used to research a signature quilt that was probably presented to Benjamin Harrison after the Civil War and before his inauguration as president of the United States. The research focus was not on the famous recipient of the quilt, but on the quilt—its age and why it was made, on the individuals, approximately 250 in all, whose names appear on it, and on how and when the quilt came to belong to the First-Meridian Heights Presbyterian Church of Indianapolis.

Often overlooked in family history research projects, signature quilts typically were made as fund-raising projects or for special occasion presentations. They were most popular from the 1830s to the early 1900s, although they are still being made today. Fund-raising quilts were often prepared by church organizations, especially ladies aid and foreign missionary societies. A quilt top was pieced together, and members of the congregation donated a small sum to sign their names. It was not unusual for several hundred names to be written on a single quilt. The names were usually written in India ink or pencil, and the latter were embroidered as time permitted. Once the quilt was completed, it was auctioned to the highest

bidder, thereby producing even more revenue. The presentation quilt was also signed by individuals with a common bond. However, the objective was to mark a special occasion such as a minister's retirement or a young woman's wedding.[1]

Signature quilts may be the only surviving written record for many of the women who signed them. Women's names did not appear in U.S. census records prior to 1850 unless a woman was the head of a household, and no birth or death records were kept by the state of Indiana prior to the 1880s.

In most communities, there are several potential sources to search for signature quilts of a bygone era. County and town historical societies, local churches, museums and historic home museums, antique shows and shops, quilt shows, and county fairs are all possibilities.

In 1988 an old quilt was discovered in the closet of the church I attended on the north side of Indianapolis. It had been stored away several years before and forgotten. Knowing nothing about the quilt, the recently arrived minister asked the congregation for help. A few of the longtime members remembered that the quilt had been included with other archival items moved from the former First Presbyterian

The Benjamin Harrison flag quilt is now the property of the President Benjamin Harrison Home in Indianapolis. (Photo by Raymond M. Featherstone Jr.)

Church when it merged with the Meridian Heights Presbyterian Church in 1970.

I was an antiques dealer and quilt collector and previously had done some amateur genealogy research on my family in New York State in the early 1800s; therefore, I volunteered to research the quilt's history. Fortunately, I was able to take the quilt home for an extended period and examine it in detail.

The quilt design is of four American flags sewn together, each with an unusual circular arrangement of the star field. The quilt exhibits exceptionally fine handiwork of twelve to thirteen stitches to the inch. Besides the names of approximately 250 individuals, it carries a center presentation inscription: "Presented by the Women's Missionary Society of the Elizaville Presbyterian Church to Genl. Benjamin Harrison and to wife." In addition, there is an inscription that I could read only partially: "[Old Waters ?] 36th and 40th," which was situated among the names.[2] This led me to believe it was possible that some of the quilt "signers" were veterans who had served under Harrison during the Civil War, although none of the names were prefixed with a military rank.

The "signatures" appeared to be written by one person in a uniform and legible script. Unfortunately, they were written in indelible purple pencil that had faded greatly, and some of them were too faint to read. In some instances signatures with a common surname were grouped together as if they depicted family members.

Congregants were questioned for additional clues about the quilt's history. A couple of members remembered that it had been displayed at the merged church in 1976 in conjunction with the national bicentennial celebration. One member produced a photograph of the quilt taken at the church during the celebration. No one remembered it having been displayed at any other time at either church, but one member thought that the quilt had been donated to the old First church in the 1930s by William Henry Harrison III, grandson of Benjamin Harrison.

Since the quilt was not dated, a logical first step was to establish the approximate date when it was made and presumably presented to the Harrisons. Once the date was established, other resources, such as newspaper articles, government and private documents, and church records, could be searched.

These sources in turn could give answers about who donated the quilt and why and about how and when the quilt arrived at my church.

Unfortunately, Mrs. Harrison's first name was not given—as was often the case with nineteenth-century signature quilts. This was an important omission since Harrison married twice, and the inclusion of his wife's first name would have narrowed the time frame. Based on the use of the title "Genl." for Harrison in the inscription, the quilt might have dated from between January 1865 when Harrison was promoted to brigadier general and 1888 when Harrison was elected president, a span of twenty-three years. During all this time, he was married to his first wife, Caroline, who died in 1892. It was possible that the quilt was presented in honor of a special occasion such as an anniversary of the Civil War's end, a wedding anniversary, or Harrison's inauguration.

The next focus in dating the quilt was on the thirty-eight stars displayed on each flag. Traditionally, each star on the American flag represents one of the states in the union at the time the flag was made. The thirty-eighth state admitted to the union was Colorado on August 1, 1876, while the thirty-ninth state was North Dakota admitted on November 2, 1889, during Harrison's presidency. It seemed reasonable that the quilt was made in the intervening thirteen-year period. At first I thought the time span could be compressed slightly more since the center

inscription was to "Genl.," not President Harrison, and he was inaugurated in February 1889. But this was put in doubt when I learned that Harrison was commonly referred to as general even during and after his presidency.[3]

The quilt signature for the Rev. D. B. Banta appeared to yield a more precise clue about when the quilt was made. Since the center inscription mentioned the Elizaville Presbyterian Church, Banta might have been pastor there at the time the quilt was made. Elizaville was a community approximately twenty miles northwest of Indianapolis in Boone County. The Indianapolis–Marion County Public Library carries an extensive collection of current telephone directories for small Indiana towns, but the church was not included in the Elizaville telephone listings. On a driving tour of Elizaville I could not locate the church in question. However, one of the older citizens said that it had been abandoned around 1920 and torn down in the 1970s after a tornado destroyed its roof.

Next the national headquarters of the Presbyterian Church USA, Department of History, located in Louisville, Kentucky, and the Christian Theological Seminary (CTS) in Indianapolis were contacted. Historians at both organizations provided similar information—that the Elizaville church was organized in October 1875 and closed in 1914 due to declining membership. According to the book *Early Life and Times in Boone County, Indiana,* by Samuel Harden (1887), the church had only eighty-three members in 1887. Thus, it is doubtful that church membership was the single common bond for the 250 quilt signers. CTS records indicate that Banta served the Elizaville church between 1888 and 1890. Therefore, it is probable that the quilt was made in 1888 and presented to Benjamin and Caroline Harrison after Benjamin's election to the presidency in November and before November 1889 when North Dakota became a state.

The quilt presentation would have been a major event in Elizaville, a small, rural town. Newspapers from the 1880s in the Lebanon

Elizaville Presbyterian Church, 1970 (Photo by Ralph W. Stark, courtesy of Lebanon Public Library Archives)

President Benjamin Harrison and his first wife, Caroline Lavinia (Scott) Harrison (W. H. Bass Company Collections, P 0130, IHS)

(Boone County) Public Library covered Elizaville happenings. Two articles in 1881 issues of the *Lebanon Patriot* and the *Boone County Pioneer* were about the church group that later made the Harrison quilt: "The Good Ladies of the Presbyterian Missionary Society Are Putting the Names on the Nickel Quilt This Week. Come Boys, Shake Up Your Weasel Skins" and "The Presbyterian Missionary Society Is Piecing a Quilt for the Heathen. Your Name Will Be Beautifully Stitched Upon the Quilt and Sent Directly to the Hindoo for Five Cents." Unfortunately, no information was found in the 1880s newspapers about the quilt's presentation to the Harrisons.[4]

At this point I began researching the quilt's signers at the Lebanon Public Library, which, like many other city and county libraries, has a large collection of local and county history books, documents, and photographs. A cursory search of these resources did not locate any additional information. Next I went to the Patrick Henry Sullivan Museum and Genealogy Library in nearby Zionsville. It, too, has an extensive collection, including the book *Soldiers Buried in Boone County, Indiana.* This book lists veterans' names, units and wars fought, and cemeteries and townships where buried—information abstracted

from the *Lebanon Reporter* of May 27, 1927. Several of the soldiers listed who were buried locally had served in the 40th Indiana Regiment during the Civil War. However, none of the names of these soldiers were included in the list of names on the quilt. This seemed to lessen the possibility that the "40" in the "Old Waters" inscription referred to a Civil War regiment. Conversely, the names of several other veterans in the book were on the quilt, but they had not served in the 40th Regiment. An on-site survey of the nearby Mud Creek Cemetery revealed some grave markers with names that matched some on the quilt, indicating that these individuals had lived in the locale. But it was still impossible to make a definitive conclusion about the common bonds among the quilt signers beyond the church tie.

The quilt was then examined again for other clues about who made it. The focus was on the unusual arrangement of the stars in the four identical American flags that composed the quilt. Instead of the typical arrangement of stars in rows, they were displayed in two circles with a single star in the center and one at each corner. Although it had not been established that many of the quilt signers were former soldiers, perhaps the flag design was taken from

During the Civil War, military units on both sides of the conflict usually unfurled flags before proceeding into battle, typically distinctive regimental banners and the U.S. colors. Several flag designs were used by the military, the most common one with the traditional "stars in rows" pattern, each star representing one state. Sometimes the star field was arranged in a circular fashion as was found on the Harrison flag quilt. Approximately 20 percent of the Indiana regiments carried national colors with such a star pattern. These photos give two such examples. Note how the 40th's regimental flag has a star pattern that appears to be half of the pattern used in the Harrison flag quilt. The flag for the 121st Regiment has a similar pattern with thirty-five stars. (*Indiana Battle Flags and a Record of Indiana Organizations in the Mexican, Civil and Spanish-American Wars* [Indianapolis: Indiana Battle Flag Commission, 1929]; photo from the Indiana Battle Flag Collection, courtesy of the Indiana War Memorial Commission)

a military unit. *The Official Military Atlas of the Civil War* (1978) contains illustrations of flags carried by Union and Confederate regimental units during the war. One flag illustration, similar in design to the quilt flags, showed a thirty-six-star flag carried by Union cavalry and light artillery units. Apparently during the Civil War, President Abraham Lincoln refused to have any stars removed from the national colors, hence the stars represented the full union.

Military units that served under Harrison during the Civil War were researched at the Indiana Historical Society library while I was seeking any connection between Harrison and the 36th and 40th regiments or any cavalry or light artillery units. Two Civil War dictionaries did not reveal any military ties from these groups to Harrison, who was commanding officer of the 70th Indiana Regiment throughout the war. Regimental rosters of men who served in the Civil War were researched in Glenda K. Trapp's eight-volume set of Civil War records titled *Index to the Report of the Adjutant General of the State of Indiana* (1986). The rosters include name; rank; company and regiment; place, date, and cause of death; and where buried and by whom. A few of the quilt names appeared in these records, but the soldiers' hometowns were scattered throughout Indiana. There was not enough evidence

to support the theory that many of the quilt signers were former soldiers from the Boone County area or were soldiers who had served under Harrison.

I next turned to the questions of how and when the quilt arrived at the First Presbyterian Church. Since a church member thought that Harrison's grandson may have donated the quilt to the church, the life of William Henry Harrison III was researched in the Indiana Division of the Indiana State Library in downtown Indianapolis. Its Indiana newspaper-clipping file, organized alphabetically by subject, produced no leads. However, its newspaper index card file contained subject heading references for many Indiana newspapers dating between 1898 and 1991. Under William Henry Harrison III, there were references to several articles in Indianapolis newspapers from 1926 to 1956. Microfilm of these newspapers showed that he had served several terms as a representative in the Indiana General Assembly. After losing elections in Indiana in 1934 and 1936, he moved his family to Sheridan, Wyoming, where he hoped to run for U.S. Congress. A more recent article stated that William Henry Harrison III served five terms in the U.S. House of Representatives as a Republican from Wyoming. Unfortunately, when contacted at his retirement home in

Florida in 1988, he was too ill to talk on the telephone, and he died two years later.

It is not unreasonable to think that William Henry Harrison III donated the Harrison flag quilt to the church prior to his moving west in late 1936. First Presbyterian Church was a logical choice as a permanent repository since his grandfather, Benjamin Harrison, had been a very active member of the Presbyterian Church both in his youth and in later life and was a member of old First upon his death in 1901. Caroline Harrison was also an active member of old First. In addition, the Harrisons' daughter "Mamie" was married at old First in 1884 according to the pamphlet *Ben Harrison's Children: A Family Album* published by the President Benjamin Harrison Home. Session minutes of the First Presbyterian Church for the 1930s were reviewed in hopes that the gift of the Harrison quilt would be recorded, but the minutes for the ten-year period did not yield any mention of the quilt.[5]

In 1996 the officers of the First-Meridian Heights Presbyterian Church decided the quilt should be housed with temperature and humidity controls to preserve it from further deterioration. The logical repository was the President Benjamin Harrison Home at 1230 North Delaware Street, Indianapolis, just three blocks from the old First church. The home is furnished with many Harrison family artifacts and is open to the public for guided tours. The flag quilt is displayed from time to time along with several other quilts of the time and place. I am indebted to Harrison Home curator Jennifer Capps and intern Catherine Hatcher in particular for providing an updated transcription of Harrison quilt signers.[6]

The Harrison quilt is still a mystery. Today, the best estimate of its date is 1888–1889, but other research might produce a more specific answer. Resources for additional research include vital records for individuals whose names are on the quilt, which can be found at the Indiana State Library, Genealogy Division. This division has indexes for birth and death records covering the period from 1882 through 1920 and indexes for marriage records from 1850 through 1920, compiled by the Works Progress Administration from 1939 to 1941. The indexes cover about two-thirds of the Indiana counties including Boone

and the surrounding counties.[7] From these records, death dates for some of the quilt signers might be established, and the earliest death could put an outer limit on when the quilt was made. For instance, if the first of the quilt signers died in 1889, the quilt would probably have been made in 1889 or before.

Other resources not yet researched include the Indiana State Archives in Indianapolis, the Allen County Public Library in Fort Wayne, the Boone County Historical Society in Lebanon, and the Internet, which was not available at the time of my research in 1988.[8] Additionally, the reference materials that I used can often be found around the state at more than one Indiana repository. With the evidence presented here, a willing and dedicated researcher could readily continue the investigation of the Benjamin Harrison flag quilt.

———————————•———————————

1. Linda Otto Lipsett, *Remember Me: Women and Their Friendship Quilts* (San Francisco: Quilt Digest Press, 1985), 15–34.

2. In the transcription of the names on the quilt by Catherine Hatcher, intern, President Benjamin Harrison Home, made in 2003, this entry is interpreted as "Olda Waters 36 of 40."

3. Harry Joseph Sievers, *Hoosier President: The White House and After*, vol. 3 of *Benjamin Harrison* (Indianapolis: Bobbs–Merrill, 1968), 123, 147n19, 169n26, 261n53, 263, 265n67, 275n106. Staff at the President Benjamin Harrison Home in Indianapolis confirmed that Harrison was often referred to as General.

4. The two newspaper articles mentioned might have been published for the purpose of advertising the quilts to obtain donations; whereas the Harrison quilt may have been made as a gift and therefore was not "advertised" in the papers.

5. It is possible that William Henry Harrison III donated the quilt prior to or after the 1930s.

6. The complete list of names on the quilt was published in *The Hoosier Genealogist* 43 (fall 2003): 3:145–47. Using a magnifying tool, Catherine Hatcher transcribed more than half the names on the quilt. The rest of the names were too faded to read. Hatcher's list was alphabetized by the author.

7. Randy Bixby, "Genealogy Division of the Indiana State Library," *The Hoosier Genealogist* 40 (December 2000): 4:200.

8. Indeed, the Internet supports the author's research. Members of the 36th and 40th Indiana regiments may have had their names placed on the Harrison quilt—not because they fought *under* Harrison, but rather, because they fought *alongside* him. During the Atlanta Campaign in spring and summer 1864, the 36th, 40th, and 70th Indiana regiments served together as part of the Army of the Cumberland, participating in the following engagements: Battle of Resaca, May 14–15; near Cassville, May 19; operations on line of Pumpkin Vine Creek and battles about Dallas, New Hope Church, and Allatoona Hills, May 25–June 5; operations about Marietta and against Kenesaw Mountain, June 10–July 2; Pine Hill/Mountain, June 11–14; Lost Mountain, June 15–17; Assault on Kenesaw, June 27; Ruff's Station, Smyrna Camp Ground, July 4; Chattahoochie River, July 5–17; Peach Tree Creek, July 19–20; and Siege of Atlanta, July 22–August 25. (Mike Northway, "Regimental Index," on the Web site "The Civil War Archive" at www.civilwararchive.com/regim.htm [accessed May 18, 2006], compiled from Frederick H. Dyer's, *A Compendium of the War of the Rebellion*, 1908).

Selected Bibliography: Clark, Ricky. "Quilts of the Western Reserve." *Timeline* (July/August 2003): 35–41.3.

Diseases and Treatments in the Nineteenth Century

PAMELA J. HEATH

Searching the Internet can be efficient and rewarding for genealogists; however, the results yielded are often unexpected and confusing. Such was the case in February 2002. While I was sifting through scores of nineteenth-century Indiana census records, something unfamiliar and interesting appeared: the "Tippecanoe County 1850 Mortality Schedule."[1] It lists name, age, gender, birthplace, month of death, and cause of death for each person who died in Tippecanoe County in 1850. While mortality schedules are available for other Indiana counties, they were compiled supplemental to the four censuses taken from 1850 to 1880.[2] The entire mortality schedule was fascinating reading. Because there were no familiar diseases listed, the causes of death were somewhat confusing. What were these peculiar-sounding ailments?

An important aspect to appreciating the daily lives of our ancestors is understanding the diseases from which they suffered—how the diseases spread, what if anything was used to treat them, and ultimately what the causes of death were. A lack of knowledge of nineteenth-century definitions for illnesses and a question as to whether each definition translates the same in modern terminology led to further research. Arguably, it is impossible to view the meaning of anything through another person's eyes, especially 152-year-old eyes, but it is possible to gain a working knowledge of old medical terms by using available sources. The Internet is a valuable tool for searching local public and university libraries to learn where such resources are located and information for accessing them. Library Web pages also give days and hours of operation, whether interlibrary loan is an option, and whether there are any restrictions on using the sources. The Internet can also provide access to resources and information across the globe through foreign college and university libraries and archives.

Indiana University, home to Lilly Library, contains many rare books dating back hundreds of years and has proven valuable in researching the meanings of the diseases listed on the 1850 mortality schedule. A three-volume medical dictionary published in 1743 was the starting point in discovering the diseases' meanings.[3] A particular benefit of this dictionary is the accompanying list of treatments available at that time, which from a twenty-first century perspective, often seem worse than the actual disease. Lilly Library also houses a general-use dictionary published in New York in 1846.[4] The publication of these two sources one hundred years apart became the foundation for comparing definitions. The absence of some diseases from either one or both of the dictionaries was also noteworthy.

The research at Lilly Library was followed by a search of the 1913 edition of *Webster's Dictionary* via the Internet.[5] The same diseases and definitions were referenced there and in the 1977 edition of *Webster's New Collegiate Dictionary*.[6] Two final questions remained: Do these diseases and ailments still exist? If so, what are their modern names?

Checking through more recently published sources proved more challenging than first imagined because most of the diseases are presently called by other names or in some cases have been eradicated through vaccination and/or medical chemical advancement over the past century. Research will continue as sources are found and made available, but presently, there is enough information to form a basic understanding of our ancestors' illnesses and perhaps to provide a glimpse into the fear and helplessness they must have experienced.

Common Diseases and Medical Terms of the Nineteenth Century

CHOLERA: From Latin word *choler* meaning bile.

1. An immoderate perturbation of the Belly attended with a discharge of Bile upwards and downwards and proceeding from a continual indigestion ailment. (1743)

2. *Cholera Morbus*: a sudden evacuation of the bile both upwards and downwards. (1846)

3. *Cholera Infantum*: is also referred to as "summer complaint" in children.[7]

4. One of several diseases affecting the digestive and intestinal tract and more or less dangerous to life, esp. the one commonly called *Asiatic cholera*. It is characterized by diarrhea, rice-water evacuations, vomiting, cramps. (1913)

5. Any of several diseases of man and domestic animals usually marked by severe gastrointestinal symptoms. (1977)

CHRONIC: A disease, which is inveterate, of long continuance or progresses slowly. (1913)

CONFINEMENT: Death occurring during or as a result of childbirth.

CONGESTIVE FEVER: A fever depending upon internal congestions. (1857)

CONSUMPTION:

1. A progressive wasting away of the body; esp., that form of wasting, attendant upon pulmonary phthisis and associated with cough, spitting of blood, hectic fever, etc. (1913)

2. *Consumption of the bowels*: inflammation and ulceration of the intestines from tubercular disease. (1913)

3. A progressive wasting away of the body esp. from pulmonary tuberculosis. (1977)

(Consumption is the equivalent of tuberculosis. It is questionable if and/or how nineteenth-century Americans differentiated the pulmonary disease from the intestinal disease, but the common phrase in both illnesses was a "wasting away.")

CROUP:

1. An inflammatory affection of the larynx or trachea, accompanied by a hoarse, ringing cough and stridulous, difficult breathing. (1913)

2. A spasmodic laryngitis esp. of infants marked by episodes of difficult breathing and hoarse metallic cough. (1977)

DROPSY: Thirteenth century shortening of *hydropsy*.

1. Listed as hydropsy. (1743)

2. An unnatural collection of water in any part of the boby [body], proceeding from a greater effusion of serum by the exhalent arteries, than the absorbents take up. (1846)

3. An unnatural collection of serous fluid in any serous cavity of the body or in the subcutaneous cellular tissue. (1913)

4. Edema. (1977–present)

ERYSIPELAS: Fourteenth century

1. Also known as "St. Anthony's Fire." (1743)

2. Quotes Galen [Greek physician and writer {129–ca. 199 A.D.}]: "'If a Fluxion, says He, be

mixed of Blood, and Yellow Bile, immoderately hot, or only of fervid and Very thin blood, the Affection is called Erysipelas.'" (1743)

3. A disease called St. Anthony's Fire; an eruption of a fiery acrid humor, on some part of the body, but chiefly on the face. (1846)

4. St. Anthony's Fire; a febrile disease accompanied with a diffused inflammation of the skin, which, starting usually from a single point, spreads gradually over its surface. It is usually regarded as contagious, and often occurs epidemically. (1913)

5. An acute febrile disease associated with intense edematous local inflammation of the skin and subcutaneous tissues caused by a hemolytic streptococcus. (1977–present)

(Current medical doctors refer to this as *cellulitis*.)[8]

FLUX: Fourteenth century—from Medieval Latin word *fluxus*.

1. Excrements are rendered very like water. (1743)

2. An extraordinary issue or evacuation. (1846)

3. A fluid discharge from the bowels or other part; especially, an excessive and morbid discharge; as, the bloody flux or dysentery. (1913)

4. A flowing of fluid from the body; esp. an excessive abnormal discharge from the bowels. (1977–present)

INFLAMMATION: Fifteenth century

1. A local response to cellular injury that is marked by capillary dilatation, leukocytic infiltration, redness, heat, and pain and that serves as a mechanism initiating the elimination of noxious agents and of damaged tissue. (2002)

(Eighteenth- and nineteenth-century language was not found in the sources used for this research.)

MALARIA: 1740 Italian words *mala aria* for "bad air." There was no listing for malaria in the 1743 *Medicinal Dictionary* or in the 1846 *Webster's Dictionary*.

1. Air infected with a noxious substance capable of causing disease. (Archaic definition listed by *Merriam-Webster's Collegiate Dictionary*, 2002)

2. Air infected with some noxious substance capable of engendering disease; esp., an unhealthy exhalation from certain soils, as marshy or wet lands, producing fevers. (1913)

3. A morbid condition produced by exhalations from decaying vegetable matter in contact with moisture, giving rise to fever and ague and many other symptoms characterized by their tendency to recur at definite and usually uniform intervals. (1913)

4. A human disease that is caused by sporozoan parasites in the red blood cells, is transmitted by the bite of anopheline mosquitoes, and is characterized by periodic attacks of chills and fever. (2002)

(During the Civil War, doctors used quinine to treat malaria and malarial fevers.)[9]

MILK SICKNESS: Defined only in the *On-Line Medical Dictionary*.

1. An acute, often fatal disease caused by the ingestion of milk from an animal having a disease known as trembles. It is marked by weakness, vomiting, constipation, and sometimes muscular tremors. It is caused by poisoning by white snakeroot and the rayless goldenrod.

2. Mentioned as "the trembles." (1857)

MORTIFICATION: Fourteenth century.

1. Influx of the vital Humours into the Arteries and their return through the veins being prevented. (1743)

2. Also listed under Gangrene and quotation by Galen: "'A mortification not yet formed but will afterwards be formed.'" (1743)

3. Listed under Gangrene—a mortification of living flesh; to become mortified. (1846)

4. The death of one part of an animal body, while the rest continues to live; loss of vitality in some part of a living animal; gangrene. (1913)

5. Necrosis; gangrene. (1977)

PUERPERAL: 1768—from Latin *puerperal*—a woman in childbirth; *puer* is child, and *parere* is to give birth to.

1. Of, relating to, occurs during, or immediately following childbirth. (1913, 2002)

2. *Puerperal fever.* An abnormal condition that results from infection of the placental site following delivery or abortion and is characterized in mild form by fever but in serious cases the infection may be spread through the uterine wall or pass into the bloodstream—called also *childbed fever, puerperal sepsis.* (2002)

RICKETS: 1634. Not listed in 1743 dictionary.

1. A disease which affects children in which their joints become knotted and their legs and spine grow crooked. (1846)

2. A disease which affects children, and which is characterized by a bulky head, crooked spine and limbs, depressed ribs, enlarged and spongy articular epiphyses, tumid abdomen, and short stature, together with clear and often premature mental faculties. (1913)

(Doctors currently know it is caused by a deficiency of Vitamin D.)

SCARLET FEVER: 1676. Not listed in 1913 dictionary.

1. An acute contagious febrile disease caused by hemolytic streptococci . . . and characterized by inflammation of the nose, throat, and mouth, generalized toxemia, and a red rash. (2002)

SCROFULA: *Merriam-Webster's Collegiate Dictionary* of 2002 lists 1791 as the origin of scrofula; however, the origin is listed in volume 3 of James's *Medicinal Dictionary* as 1745.

1. "The King's Evil" much related to Swine. Usually appears at ages 3, 4, and 5, but disappears by manhood. Similar to the Gout. (1745)

2. "The King's Evil" Characterized by hard and scirrous tumors in the glands of the neck. (1846)

3. A constitutional disease, generally hereditary, especially manifested by chronic enlargement and cheesy degeneration of the lymphatic glands, particularly those of the neck, and marked by a tendency to the development of chronic intractable inflammations of the skin, mucous membrane, bones, joints, and other parts, and by a diminution in the power of resistance to disease or injury and the capacity for recovery. Scrofula is now gen-

An understanding of the nutritional elements contained in foods was all that was needed to prevent rickets. The young child shown here contracted the disease, which resulted from a severe deficiency of Vitamin D. Thanks to vitamin fortification of many food products we consume, rickets is uncommon in many parts of the world today. (L. Emmett Hold, *Diseases of Infancy and Childhood* [New York: D. Appleton and Co., 1898], plate v)

erally held to be tuberculous in character, and may develop into general or local tuberculosis (consumption). (1913)

4. Swellings of the lymph glands in the neck; tuberculosis of the lymph glands in the neck. (1977)

SMALLPOX: 1518. Not listed in 1743.

1. Variolous disease. (1846)

2. A contagious, constitutional, febrile disease characterized by a peculiar eruption; variola. (1913)

(By the Civil War, Americans knew smallpox could be prevented by a vaccination; however, serums were often improperly prepared. This disease was eradicated in all human carriers by 1995.) [10]

TYPHOID: 1845.

1. Resembling typhus; weak, low. (1846)

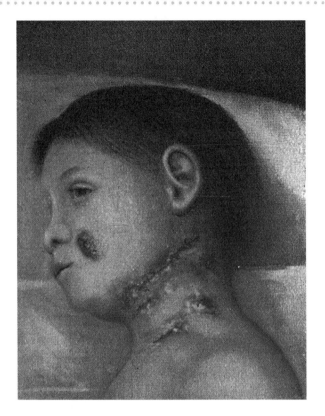

The young child depicted in this photograph suffers from scrofula. The sores on his neck are agonizing and will spread to his face and perhaps down his chest—if he survives long enough. Before the advent of antibiotics, the disease was nearly unstoppable. Mothers could only comfort their sick children and often watched them die slowly. (L. Emmett Hold, *Diseases of Infancy and Childhood* [New York: D. Appleton & Co., 1898], 828)

2. Of or pertaining to typhus; resembling typhus. (1913)

3. Typhoid Fever, a disease formerly confounded with typhus, but essentially different from the latter. It is characterized by fever, lasting usually three or more weeks, diarrhea with evacuations resembling pea soup in appearance, and prostration and muscular debility, gradually increasing and often becoming profound at the acme of the disease. Its local lesions are a scanty eruption of spots, resembling flea bites, on the belly, enlargement of the spleen, and ulceration of the intestines over the areas occupied by Peyer's glands. (1913)

(Doctors currently know the bacteria causing typhoid fever to be salmonella typhosa and is usually ingested by drinking contaminated water.)

TYPHUS: 1785.

1. Fever accompanied with great debility. (1846)

2. A contagious continued fever lasting from two to three weeks, attended with great prostration and cerebral disorder, and marked by a copious eruption of red spots upon the body. (1913)

3. Caused by the Rickettsial organism. Difficult to differentiate from typhoid fever and was clinically separated only a few decades before the Civil War. Spread via body lice.[11]

4. Any of various bacterial diseases caused by rickettsias—a severe human febrile disease that is . . . transmitted esp. by body lice and is marked by high fever, stupor alternating with delirium, intense headache, and a dark red rash. (2002)

Clear and precise definitions of the following illnesses have not yet been found in the sources used in this research: Sinking Chills, Delirium Fever, Lung Fever, Winter Fever, and Bold Hives.

Common Medical Treatments of the Nineteenth Century

The nineteenth century was an incredible era in America—synonymous with revolutionary cultural alterations. Americans experienced rapid and intense changes in the world around them. Medical science was just one, albeit an important, aspect of society undergoing massive and widespread transformations. Yet amidst historic economic, social, and industrial changes, many family and community traditions in Indiana remained constant. This resistance to the surrounding upheaval is apparent in the medical field. Doctors and midwives who used herbal remedies and medical treatments—some that sound barbaric today—rendered valuable services to rural Hoosiers throughout the opening years of the twentieth century.[12]

In Stockton Township, Greene County, Indiana, Edward Joseph Wautelet was an alternative medical source, and more important, a loyal and caring friend.[13] Wautelet arrived in Greene County, circa 1894, from Belgium, a trained and licensed physician. However, Wautelet's Belgian credentials did not

Wautelet farmhouse, ca. 1909 (Courtesy of George Wautelet)

qualify him for an Indiana medical license. Nevertheless, Wautelet did not let the licensure issue stand in the way of helping his family and, occasionally, his friends and neighbors, too.

Wautelet earned a living the same way many men in southwestern Indiana did—he farmed and worked in a coal mine.[14] He and his wife, Susan Wautelet, owned their farm. The Wautelets raised fruits, vegetables, and livestock, supporting themselves and their two children and aiding extended family members who lived in the area. Susan supplemented the family income by selling eggs, butter, and surplus vegetables. Edward cultivated grape arbors from which he made wine, which he regularly mixed with his food, eating them in one dish. Edward also had a special garden where he grew medicinal plants and herbs that are still mentioned by his son and nephew.[15]

Shortly after the end of World War I, a diphtheria outbreak took the lives of many children in and around Greene and Clay counties.[16] Family stories relate that Wautelet knew how to treat and cure diphtheria long before any of the local licensed doctors. One story tells that Wautelet was summoned late at night to a neighbor's home, where a small boy was near death. Arriving in short order, he directed the child's father to close and lock all the windows and doors, and then throw away the medicine given by the local doctor. Wautelet further insisted that the family members keep his visit and treatment a complete secret. Once the child's father agreed, Wautelet carried his satchel of home-brewed herbal medicines and salves into the child's room, closed the door behind him, and locked it. He stayed with the child through the night, never coming out or requesting anything from the child's parents. Just as the sun came up, Wautelet opened the door and invited the parents in to see their son sitting on the floor, playing cheerfully, as though he had never been ill.

Later that day, the doctor returned to check on the young boy, only to find him completely cured. The doctor inquired whether Wautelet had been present, but the parents kept their vow of secrecy. The doctor was not fooled. He tried to find out what Wautelet had used to cure the child, but no one had been in the room except Wautelet and his patient. The doctor and local sheriff were frustrated—this was not the first time Wautelet had illegally saved the life of a person stricken with diphtheria, nor would it be the last. Eventually, Wautelet was offered a medical license in exchange for his cure, but he declined it. Instead, Wautelet continued to farm his land in Greene County, raising medicinal herbs to care for his family, friends, and neighbors, until the end of his life.

Although many diseases and illnesses that once plagued our ancestors have been remedied by modern medicine, in nineteenth-century Indiana the success of available medicines and treatments was a matter of trial and error. There were five main classifications of drugs and medicines: *haematics*, which produce changes in the blood; *neurotics*, which target the nervous system; *eliminatives*, also known as purgatives, which were supposed to rid the body of disease by purging; *astringents*, which were supposed to cause muscular contractions, thus preventing hemorrhaging, diminishing secretions, and giving tone to the muscular system, capillary vessels, glands, ducts, stomach, and intestines; and *topicals*, which were ointments or salves absorbed through the skin to treat specific ailments.[17]

Haematics were used for diseases believed to originate in the blood such as erysipelas, mortification, puerperal fever, scarlet fever, and countless others. The favorite haematic of the period was quinine. Sarsaparilla was an herb first used by the Spaniards in 1563 as a cure for venereal disease, but Americans found that its effects were multipurpose. It was successful in cleansing the blood, it counteracted the effects of mercury, it cured scrofulous sores, and, acting as an antacid, it eased dyspepsia.[18]

Neurotics were drugs and herbs that passed through the blood to the nerves or nerve centers.[19] Patients quickly felt the effects. Neurotics included stimulants, narcotics, and sedatives. Stimulants were used for many things, but inducing patients to perspire excessively was the recommended treatment for nearly all fevers, various forms of dropsy, erysipelas, inflammations, and malaria. Boneset (Indian sage, cross wort, thorough wort), button snakeroot, common sage, rue, balm, and spicewood were all used to stimulate the body to sweat.[20] Belladonna, hop, and foxglove were common sedatives, while opium-based compounds such as morphine and laudanum were used for pain. Doctors did not understand the addictive qualities of narcotics. Thus, the number of drug addicts was epidemic among Civil War casualties.[21]

Eliminatives were the most frequently used herbs and drugs during the nineteenth century even though they yielded horrible side effects. Their purpose was to rid the body of disease through vomiting and/or evacuating the bowels. Some doctors used purgatives to induce excessive salivation and found mercury as well as iodine to be very successful. Apomorphia, common blackberry bush, and ipecacuanha were used to induce vomiting. Mayapple root, cod liver oil, castor oil, common blackberry bush, and foxglove were used to evacuate the bowels.[22] Ammonia, turpentine, and camphor were the most common expectorants used in ailments of the lungs, throat, and chest including consumption. Seneka snakeroot was used to treat rattlesnake bites, and it was believed to be a cure for pleurisy. Cathartics were used to accomplish an overall cleansing of the body from illness and disease. The side effects were extreme and often fatal. Commonly dispensed cathartics were acetates of magnesium and potassium, calomel, sulphur, and mercurial chalk.[23]

Astringents were used primarily to prevent hemorrhaging. Tobacco leaf poultices were frequently used to treat gunshot wounds. Pennyroyal, spicewood (fever bush, allspice bush, spice berry), chamomile, chinquapin (dwarf chestnut), and common tansy were believed to strengthen the stomach and intestines.[24]

Topical medications were ointments or salves absorbed through the skin and were classified as either an antiseptic—oxygen, chlorine, bromine, creosote, carbolic acid, and benzoic acids—or as a rubefacient, such as white and black mustard, burgundy pitch, and camphor. The latter group produced redness of the skin.[25]

Some physicians developed routine treatments for frequently encountered illnesses. Scarlet fever was treated with aconite for the fever, bitartrate of potassium as a diuretic, belladonna as a sedative, chlorine water for sloughing the throat, and carbonate of ammonium, cold affusions, cathartics, chlorate of potassium, mercury, a mustard bath, quinine, and sharp purging. If smallpox was diagnosed, the treatment was cold baths, carbonate of ammonium, and quinine. Women who developed puerperal fever within days of giving birth were treated with a

Three herbs used as neurotics (left to right): boneset, button-snakeroot, and foxglove (A. F. Sievers, *The Herb Hunters Guide: American Medicinal Plants of Commercial Importance*. Misc. Pub. No. 77 [Washington, DC: U.S. Department of Agriculture, 1930], published on the Internet by Purdue University, Center for New Crops and Plant Products, www.hort.purdue.edu/newcrop)

tartar emetic, bromide of potassium, bleeding, a chlorine solution for vaginal washings, leeches, mercury, opiates, and hot poultices. Scores of women died.[26] A person diagnosed with consumption received arsenic for fever reduction, atropia for night sweats, alcoholic drinks and belladonna for sedation, bismuth and coto bark for diarrhea, brandy or rum mixed with milk and an egg for breakfast (if the individual survived through the night), chloral, creosote, and cod liver oil, and places on their skin were blistered to release poisons from their body.[27]

Nineteenth-century medical treatments may seem primitive and even barbaric to readers in the twenty-first century, but they were usually administered with the best of intentions: the desire to ease discomfort and make people well. Many medical practitioners such as Edward Wautelet helped family and neighbors without interest in material gain. In fact, in Wautelet's case, his personal risks exceeded any profits. While modern medicine has improved beyond any nineteenth-century imagining, the personal care by family and friends that was once commonplace is now, sadly, rare.

———————————————•———————————————

1. Adina Dyer, "Tippecanoe County 1850 Mortality Schedule," 1998, RootsWeb.com, at http://ftp.rootsweb.com/pub/usgenweb/in/tippecan/vitals/1850mort.txt (accessed March 20, 2006).

2. There are many ways to gain access to mortality schedules on the Internet; use a search engine and type "indiana mortality schedules."

3. Robert James, *A Medicinal Dictionary*, 3 vols. (London: T. Osborne, 1743–45).

4. Noah Webster, *An American Dictionary of the English Language . . . Abridged from the Quatro Ed. of the Author, to which Are Added a Synopsis of Words Differently Pronounced by Different Orthoëpists; and Walker's Key to the Classical Pronunciation of Greek, Latin, and Scripture Proper Names* (New York: Harper and Brothers, 1846). Webster first published his dictionary in 1828.

5. Noah Webster, *Webster's Revised Unabridged Dictionary of the English Language; the Dictionary Proper Being the Authentic Ed. of Webster's International Dictionary of One Thousand Eight Hundred and Ninety*, edited by Noah Porter (Springfield, MA: G. and C. Merriam, 1913), accessed online through the Web site for the Project for American and French Research on the Treasury of the French Language by the University of Chicago at http://humanities.uchicago.edu/orgs/ARTFL/ (accessed March 20, 2006).

6. *Webster's New Collegiate Dictionary* (Springfield, MA: G. and C. Merriam, ca. 1977).

7. Charles H. Cleaveland, *Pronouncing Medical Lexicon* (Cincinnati: Longely Brothers, 1857).

8. Frank R. Freemon, *Gangrene and Glory: Medical Care During the American Civil War* (Urbana: University of Illinois Press, 2001), 212.

9. Ibid., 207–8.

10. Ibid., 209.

11. Ibid., 205.

12. The professionalization of American medicine was a social phenomenon that started during the 1820s but did not gain full momentum until after the Civil War when significant advancements were made in both science and technology. For a discussion on the professionalization of medicine in Indiana, see Clifton J. Phillips, "Public Health, Welfare, and Social Reforms," in *Indiana in Transition: The Emergence of an Industrial Commonwealth, 1880–1920* (Indianapolis: Indiana Historical Bureau and Indiana Historical Society, 1968), 469–502.

13. 1930 U.S. Federal Census (Washington, DC: U.S. Bureau of the Census).

14. Edward Wautelet worked in an underground mine called Twin Mine, probably located near the borders between Greene and Clay counties.

15. George Wautelet, oral interview with author, Linton, IN, May 2, 2002; Victor Wautelet, telephone interview with author, Belleville, FL, July 27, 2002.

16. George Wautelet interview.

17. Morse Stewart Jr., *Pocket Therapeutics and Dose Book* (Detroit: Geo. D. Stewart, 1878), 11.

18. John C. Gunn, *Gunn's Domestic Medicine; or, Poor Man's Friend* (Knoxville, TN: F. S. Keiskell, 1833), 349.

19. Stewart, *Pocket Therapeutics and Dose Book*, 11.

20. Gunn, *Gunn's Domestic Medicine*, 375–81.

21. Freemon, *Gangrene and Glory*; Thomas Lowry, *The Story the Soldiers Wouldn't Tell: Sex in the Civil War* (Mechanicsburg, PA: Stackpole Books, ca. 1994); and W. J. Rorabaugh, *The Alcoholic Republic: An American Tradition* (New York: Oxford University Press, 1979).

22. Gunn, *Gunn's Domestic Medicine*, 356–78.

23. Stewart, *Pocket Therapeutics and Dose Book*, 11.

24. Gunn, *Gunn's Domestic Medicine*, 371–80.

25. Stewart, *Pocket Therapeutics and Dose Book*, 11.

26. Gunn, *Gunn's Domestic Medicine*, 366.

27. Marc McCutcheon, *A Writers Guide to Everyday Life in the 1800s* (Cincinnati: Writer's Digest Books, ca. 1993), 159.

Selected Bibliography: *Encarta® World English Dictionary*. North American ed. For Microsoft Corporation by Bloomsbury Publishing P.L.C., 2002, at http://dictionary.msn.com (accessed March 20, 2006); *Merriam-Webster OnLine*. Merriam-Webster, 2002, at www.m-w.com (accessed March 20, 2006); *On-Line Medical Dictionary*. Department of Medical Oncology, University of Newcastle upon Tyne, 1997–2002, at http://cancerweb.ncl.ac.uk/omd/ (accessed March 20, 2006); Tyler, Varro E. *Hoosier Home Remedies*. West Lafayette, IN: Purdue University Press, 1985.

Coal Mining in Indiana

JUDITH Q. MCMULLEN

*"Indiana coal goes on for what seems to be forever! Total estimated reserve is
51 billion tons which, at the present rate of usage, should last for about 2,000 years."*
—Indiana Coal *(Indianapolis: Public Service Company of Indiana, 1945)*

C oal mining is one of Indiana's oldest and most important industries. Bituminous coal was first discovered in Indiana along the Wabash River in 1763. In 1804 coal was first reported in land surveys and on maps. In 1837 American Cannel Coal, located at Coal Haven (later renamed Cannelton) became the first coal company to be officially granted a charter by the state of Indiana. In 1850 John Hutchinson developed the first underground shaft coal mine at Newburgh, Indiana.[1] *The Coal Map of Indiana*, on the opposite page, shows twenty-five Indiana counties that had active coal mines and/or coal deposits evident underground in 1938 (see inset map, top right).

According to Thomas Neil Wynne, by 1924 "Indiana was the sixth coal producing state with an annual production of 22,340,000 tons." Production had quadrupled since 1898 due to the depletion of the natural gas supply. Coal was considered a "cheap fuel," and it had increasing value for steam purposes.[2] Before the 1920s underground mining was the primary method of extracting coal in Indiana. However, by 1926 much of the coal was being produced by strip mines because the operating costs were lower, which reduced the price to consumers. James Madison states that surface mining "permitted mechaniza-

tion that . . . contributed to the concentration of a very small number of large coal companies." Early Indiana companies that "helped develop the massive earth-moving equipment commonly seen today in . . . the Midwest" included Ayrshire Collieries, Enos Coal Mining, Maumee Collieries, and Sherwood-Templeton Coal.[3]

However, Madison states that strip-mining "turned a bucolic countryside into a scarred landscape of little practical value."[4] Indiana passed legislation in 1941 requiring the planting of trees and grass to restore strip-mined land (the second state to require such reclamation), including reforestation and the creation of small lakes and streams. There are many success stories about reclaimed Indiana lands. Ed Kluemper, president, Pike County Commissioners, states that "coal companies have made great strides in reclaiming" land in his county, turning it into "game-filled acres."[5]

A list of fatal coal-mining accidents in 1908 shows the many groups represented in Indiana's mines: "Negro," white, "Scotch," French, English, Russian, German, Polish, and Australian.[6] The number of miners employed in Indiana coal mines has fluctuated over time—from fewer than 3,500 in 1879 to more than 31,000 in 1923 (the state's most productive period) to fewer than 3,000 in 2003.[7]

Nevertheless, the future for the Indiana coal industry looks bright. In 2003 there were thirteen coal-producing companies in the state. Indiana ranked eighth nationally in coal production as of April 2004, showing a 2.5 percent annual increase.[8] In addition, the National Mining Association forecasted the second highest national coal production in recorded history for 2004.

●

1. *Indiana Surface Mining: Past, Present, Future*, Indiana Department of Natural Resources, Division of Reclamation, 1977.

2. Thomas Neil Wynne, *Facts on Indiana Coal* (Indianapolis: W. K. Steward, 1926), 7.

3. "Methods of Mining Coal," *Our Hoosier State Beneath Us* (Bloomington, IN: Indiana Department of Natural Resources and Indiana Geological Survey, 198-), online at www.indiana.edu/~librcsd/etext/hoosier/ CO-12.html (accessed March 28, 2006).

4. James Madison, *The Indiana Way: A State History* (Indianapolis: Indiana University Press and the Indiana Historical Society, 1986), 283–84.

5. "Village Profile, Pike County, Indiana," online at www.villageprofile.com/indiana/pikecounty/pike county.html (accessed March 28, 2006). See also *The Coal Miner's Cry: Coal Mining in Pike County, Indiana, from 1835 to 1999*, Beth Bohnert and Dixie Cooper, eds. (Vincennes, IN: Vincennes University, 1999).

6. Kathryn D. Schakel, "Some Aspects of Coal Mining in Indiana" (master's thesis, Butler University, 1934).

7. *Coal: Mining and Use in Indiana*, vol. 2 (Terre Haute, IN: Rose-Hulman Institute of Technology, Center for Technology Assessment and Policy Studies, 1977), 42–43.

8. Kathryn R. Shaffer, *Indiana Mineral Industry News* (Bloomington, IN: Indiana Geological Survey, first quarter 2004), online at http://igs.indiana.edu/ geology/minRes/m&findustry/2004q1.pdf (accessed March 28, 2006).

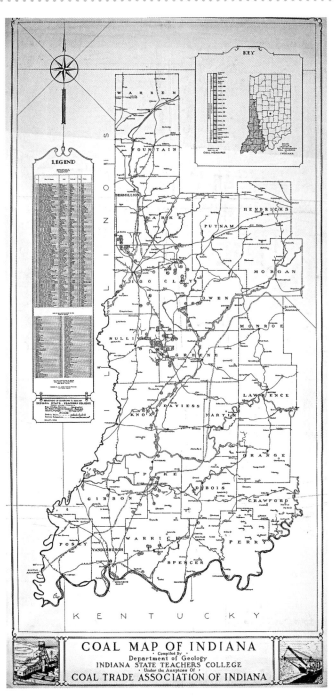

Coal Map of Indiana, Department of Geology, Indiana State Teachers College, 1938 (IHS collections)

Indiana Cotton Mills
1850–1954

M. TERESA BAER AND LEIGH DARBEE

———————————— • ————————————

From 1850 until 1954, the Indiana Cotton Mills at Cannelton, Indiana, processed raw cotton from southern cotton plantations into thread and a coarse, brown muslin. By 1885 Cannelton was producing six million yards of cloth per year. During the Civil War, the mill also manufactured uniforms for Union soldiers. Perry County Historian Michael F. Rutherford writes that the Indiana Cotton Mills "made goods for the automobile industry, [and] clothing, shoes, mattresses, rubber tires, asbestos and cloth bag companies."

Cannelton's Transformation from Village to Industrial Town

The cotton mill at Cannelton was an impressive enterprise during the nineteenth century. It was the largest of twenty-four cotton mills in operation in the Ohio River Valley, and at its inception it was the largest industry in Indiana. A paper by Leigh Darbee describes the building as "five stories high, 280 feet long and 60 feet wide, with twin towers approximately 100 feet tall. It was built of sandstone, with stone gutters and a tin roof." The mill "incorporated features devised to promote the safety and comfort of workers. The large windows let in light and air. One

tower contained stairways connecting to all floors, while the other housed water closets. A ventilation system was also built into this latter tower; a draft created down through the tower, to the base of the chimney, and then up the chimney, carried away the airborne cotton particles which were an unavoidable byproduct of all the production processes. In addition," Darbee states, "the towers housed five fire hoses for each floor. In the event of fire, the hoses could be quickly connected to an engine and huge cisterns in back of the building."

The Cannelton Cotton Mill was started by a group of investors—southern cotton plantation owners and northern businessmen. Nearly one-third of the group also owned stock in coal companies as coal was planned as the source of energy for the mills. In 1853 the original investors sold the company to a small group of the original owners, and the company was thereafter known as the Indiana Cotton Mills. Some form of the partnership lasted until after the Civil War when the Newcombs, a southern plantation-owning family, gained an 80 percent share in the company.

Cannelton's cotton mills heralded the transition of Indiana's economy from primarily agricultural to primarily industrial. Advancing on eastern manufacturing practices, Cannelton's founders infused the mills with large capital outlays and used the investment to centralize the production of cloth in one manufacturing unit—from raw cotton to finished product. This was an important step in the evolution of U.S. industry and in the American capitalist system. The Indiana Cotton Mills soon became an important link in the growing network of goods and services nationwide. Cloth from the Indiana Cotton Mills was distributed in Cannelton, Cincinnati, Louisville, Chicago, and St. Louis.

The owners of the cotton mill planned a community in which their operatives were to reside. They set aside land and paid for the building of a public school and supplied two lots for each religious society. They built boardinghouses for the single employees and planned rental houses that would accommodate four families. They also sold lots to their employees so that the latter could build their own houses. To encourage the growth of local businesses, the mill owners offered lots for sale and built a fire department.

The creation of the Indiana Cotton Mills rapidly transformed Cannelton from a small rural village to a fair-size industrial town. Numerous businesses developed after 1850 that depended on the mill for their existence. Among these were saw and grist mills; manufacturers of shingles and tin and iron sheets; dry goods, apothecaries, and grocery stores; seamstress, shoemaking, butcher, and bakery shops; artisan shops for blacksmithing, cabinetry, printing, and wagon making; churches, hotels, and saloons; and hundreds of houses.

The Creation of Cloth

The cotton that was used to make Cannelton's muslin came from the southern states. Before the Civil War, slaves grew and harvested most of this cotton. The cotton came to Cannelton in four-hundred-pound bales toted on barges along the Ohio River. It

Undated photograph of the Indiana Cotton Mills with the company name and logo, which advertises Hoosier Sheetings, the textiles made at Cannelton[1]

had already been ginned, which means that the seeds had been removed. On the day before processing was to begin, less than a dozen workers, usually men and boys, opened a dozen or more cotton bales on the main floor of the Picker Building, allowing the cotton to expand overnight.

The next day, approximately sixty-five men and boys using a series of machines with rollers of spikes and needles began combing the cotton fibers to separate them into small fluffy masses. The machines with the largest spikes and needles were called breakers and openers. As the cotton became fluffy and more workable, the laborers sent it to the basement through a chute where men and boys using picker machines with smaller spikes and needles continued the process. The picker machines forced air through the cotton, blowing unwanted debris through ducts into the dust room in the basement. Picker Room workers took the cleaner, finely separated fibers to the main floor where laborers formed it into rolls of crude batting called laps using lap winders. Next, carders, who were usually males, ran the batting through a series of small-toothed rollers in carding machines. At this point, the cotton was forming into loose ropes called slivers, which were coiled into tall round cans. Children collected loose fibers and took them to the Picker Building to use again. Meanwhile, men and

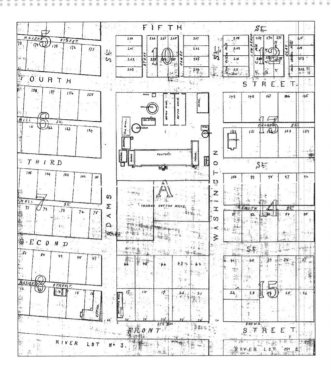

(Above) Milne and Bruder, *Plan of Lots in Cannelton*, lithograph (Louisville, KY, n.d.)

(Right) Recruitment poster for German workers, 1852

boys ran several coiled slivers through drawing frames at one time. The drawing frames pulled several fibers together and ran them through even smaller teeth on faster rollers, producing even smaller, tighter slivers that the workers coiled into cans.

The next step took place on both the first and third floors. Men and boys worked the second set of slivers through roving frames called slubbers. Slubbers formed the rope of slivers into a yet smaller, weaker "rove" while applying a slight twist (slub) to strengthen it. Slubbers produced cotton yarn, which was wound on spools.

The spools of yarn were ready for the spinning frames, which were located on the third floor and in the attic. Most of the 123 workers in the spinning rooms were women and girls. Using spinning wheels, they stretched and spun the yarn into two sizes of thread. Workers in the attic wound the larger size thread, #14, onto large reels called warps.

Warps could weigh as much as five hundred pounds after they were filled with thread. Thus, one warper machine in the attic was enough to keep the 440 looms supplied with thread. The smaller thread, #24, served as the cross-thread (woof) in the woven cloth. Spinners filled bobbins with this smaller thread, which was then ready for use on the looms.

The attic was a busy area. Approximately twenty-one workers passed the warp threads through the "slasher" and steam-heated starch on this floor. Then they quickly dried and rewound the threads on smaller loom warps and drew each thread through heddles, which guided the warp threads in the looms. About 115 women and girls performed the bulk of the weaving on up to 450 looms on the second floor and in the basement. After the weavers wove the two thread sizes into the brown muslin cloth, about half a dozen men and boys in the cloth room trimmed, folded, and packed it for shipping.

The Lives of Cannelton's Workers

The owners of the Indiana Cotton Mills advertised heavily for workers as the need arose—in newspapers and with broadsides and pamphlets. The core of their original workforce was 250 experienced mill workers from the eastern seaboard, most of them young girls between the ages of 15 and 30. The workers were attracted by promises of better pay and greater opportunity in the West. These promises attracted an increasing number of families and foreign immigrants. By 1860 nearly 60 percent of the workforce was comprised of equal numbers of Germans, English, and Irish. Cannelton residents composed most of the rest of the workers. Also by 1860, half of all the operatives were men. The 1870 census shows that large southern families moved to Cannelton after the Civil War. In his Perry County history, Michael F. Rutherford states that "Superintendent Wilber on 1 August 1890 gave the number of employees as '309—78 of them men.' The 231 remainder was made up of women and children. Boys and girls from the age of 12 were regularly employed for full shifts until child labor laws in the 1920s ended the age-old practice."

Records compiled for several family groups at Cannelton by historian Anita Ashendel show the strategy that many mill families developed to try to build better lives for themselves. Most adults and children down to the age of ten worked in the mill unless a male head of household worked as a craftsman, such as a blacksmith or shoemaker, or as a miner in the nearby coal mines. At the mills, women and girls worked in the lower-paying jobs of spinning and weaving to which the mill restricted them. The men worked in the higher-paying processing jobs and also in jobs related to fueling the mills and performing maintenance on the machines. Many boys advanced into these positions as they became adults. Experienced men were also promoted into the overseer jobs in each room of the mill.

If a household had young children, the mother or an older daughter generally stayed home to care

Unidentified workers and machinery at the Indiana Cotton Mills

for them. Youngsters attended school until they were old enough to work in the mill, or sometimes they did both since schools were in session less than six months each year. Some families with female heads of households lived together and divided work into a similar pattern. Most single workers roomed in one of the company-owned tenements, in boardinghouses, or with mill families. Using these strategies some mill workers were so impoverished that they barely eked out an existence. Others, however, either saved money to buy land in the western territories or built homes on company-owned lots or in the outlying country-side and laid down roots in the Cannelton area.

The story of the Indiana Cotton Mills at Cannelton is the story of the American textile industry in a nutshell. Like the industry in general, the Indiana Cotton Mills arose out of the evolution of the western industrial age. They flourished for approximately one hundred years, enduring extensive technological and social changes. Worker unrest existed from the beginning and included a three-day strike in 1851 when the wages were adjusted to match those in the eastern textile mills. The Civil War and its aftermath forced the cotton mills' owners to stop production for months-long stretches or to run the mills for nine-hour days instead of the usual twelve. The Indiana Cotton Mills survived the early-twentieth-century floods of the Ohio River Valley. Even the Great Depression did not destroy them. Instead, the mills staffed two eight-hour shifts in compliance with the cotton textile manufacturing code of the day.

The company's failure in 1954 appears to be due to the globalization of the world's economy. Most of Cannelton's machinery was sold to textile manufacturers in Cuba and South America, suggesting that the Indiana Cotton Mills, like America's textile industry, suffered from production costs that were not competitive in a global marketplace.

As the underdeveloped countries around the world began the process of industrialization after World War II, they produced goods with labor that was cheap compared to American or western-European labor. The term "sweatshop" became notorious, associated with textile mills in places such as Central and South America and Asia. Like nineteenth-century Americans, mill workers in these regions are working long hours for low pay.

————————————————————— • —————————————————————

1. The illustrations for this chapter come from Indiana Cotton Mills Records, 1849–1948, M 0156 and OM 0125, Indiana Historical Society.

Selected Bibliography: Ashendel, Anita. "Fabricating Independence: Industrial Labor in Antebellum Indiana." *Michigan Historical Review* 23 (fall 1997): 1–24; Darbee, Leigh. "Adaptation on the Industrial Frontier: Worker Recruitment at the Indiana Cotton Mills, 1850–1860." Indiana Historical Society, n.d. (copy in possession of the Indiana Historical Society Press); De la Hunt, Thomas James. "Manufacturing Enterprises at Cannelton." Chap. 15 in *Perry County: A History*. Indianapolis: W. K. Stewart, 1916; Fletcher, Stephen J. "The Business of Exposure: Lewis Hine and Child Labor Reform." *Traces of Indiana and Midwestern History* 4 (spring 1992): 2:12–23; Historic Landmarks Foundation of Indiana Headquarters. Files for Indiana Cotton Mills and Cannelton Historic District. Indianapolis; Indiana Cotton Mills Records, 1849–1948, M 0156, OM 0125. Indiana Historical Society; Indiana 15 Regional Planning Commission and Historic Cannelton. Cannelton Historic District Nomination for the National Register of Historic Places, 1986; Rutherford, Michael F. "The Cotton Mill." Chap. 8 in *Perry County, Indiana—Then and Now*. Paducah, KY: Turner Publishing and Mark A. Thompson, 2000; Torrey, Kate Douglas. "Visions of a Western Lowell: Cannelton, Indiana, 1847–1851." *Indiana Magazine of History* 73 (December 1977): 4:276–304; Wilson, Harold S. "The Indiana Cotton Mills: An Experiment in North–South Cooperation." *Indiana History Bulletin* 35 (May 1965): 75–83.

Analyzing the Accuracy
of Research Material

RICHARD A. ENOCHS

———————————————— • ————————————————

nformation extracted from a source can be no better than the source itself. Asking "How good is your source?" is another way of asking how well qualified is the source. Is it original evidence or a later layer placed over the original? A later layer could be an index of topics and/or names from the original, an abstract or summary of the original, or selected extracts from or a verbatim transcript of the original. Any of these layers can serve a good purpose. The indexer's contribution allows the researcher quicker access to passages of interest. Abstractors and extractors select what they believe to be the salient points from original texts and compress the material into less space. Less space permits commercial publication that provides broader distribution of the condensed material. The original evidence may be difficult to read due to an older script style, paper deterioration, fading ink, or bleeds through from the reverse page. In addition, the custodial repository's security policy or geographic location may restrict accessibility. Therefore, extracts and verbatim transcripts increase legibility and provide greater access.

Indexes

While the researcher is indebted to any individual who has contributed a layer that improves legibility and access, he or she must judge the risk of error in each layer of human involvement. To qualify a given source, peel back one layer at a time and analyze each layer for accuracy and authenticity. The top layer is usually the index, which is published at the back of a publication, in back of each volume of a publication, or in a separate book. Consider who created the index. Was it the compiler or an associate, or someone working independently at a later time? The greater the distance between compiler and indexer, the greater the chance for error. A cross-referenced index suggests greater effort by the indexer than one without. Even when alternative spellings are provided, the researcher is ultimately responsible for considering all possible variations. In addition, the researcher needs to ascertain how the index treats the material. Is it indexed by pagination of the abstract, of selected extracts, of the verbatim transcript, of the original source, or by another system such as assigning entry or case numbers as in land or probate records? A good index provides an explanation of the pagination at the beginning of the index section and also establishes the time frame of the source that is indexed.

Abstracts

Many published sources contain only portions of the original text, called *abstracts* if the original text is paraphrased or summarized, or called *extracts* if the original material is transcribed verbatim. These types of layers are often identified in the book's title, by words such as "Abstracts of" or "Extracts from." Either should specify the source that was abstracted, extracted, and/or transcribed. When this information is not given in the title, it should be included in the introduction.

An abstract has the greatest latitude in varying from the original; therefore, abstracts require the greatest scrutiny. An abstractor of local records who is unfamiliar with family names of the subject area is likely to commit errors in spelling those names. To evaluate a source, consider how it was created. For instance, an abstractor of recorded wills scans each will for the name of the testator (person who left the will) and his or her beneficiaries. The abstractor may overlook information that falls outside of these parameters even though some of it might be unique to the will and would be of importance to a researcher.

Consider an example that occurred in research conducted on a client's behalf. In one book of abstracts of an Indiana county's will book, the abstractor faithfully reported two sons named in a will. The research subject, a third son, Alexander, was not mentioned. Rather than stop the inquiry at this point, the researcher proceeded to qualify the source by accessing the will book that was abstracted, which was on microfilm. The abstract was compared with the will book—not only for what it documented but also for what it did not document. In this case, the name of the testator and those of the beneficiaries matched. The latter included three named daughters and the two named sons, a predeceased son David and a surviving son Gideon. But the will also provided for the balance of the testator's personal estate "to be divided

equally between my three sons and three daughters." Analyze what this means. The testator had a third son who was mentioned but not named in the will. So, the researcher thought, "Might there be a corroborative source that names the third son?"

A published history of the county provided several references to the testator. The history revealed that his sons David and Alexander scouted the county prior to their family's move. The testator and a neighbor set out for their new home with the testator's sons Alexander and Gideon. During this trip, Alexander axed a way through the forest and brush for the wagons. The testator left his son Alexander in the new county while he returned to his former home for his wife and other family members. When Indians stole the testator's dog, Alexander and Gideon found it. Thus the research subject, Alexander, was established as both the son of the testator and the brother of the two sons named in the will. The information that the testator had a son not mentioned in the abstract became known only by examining the actual will. And the identity of the son unnamed in the will became known by seeking a corroborative source that named him.

Extracts and Transcripts

As opposed to an abstractor, an extractor or a transcriber has no latitude in varying from the original source. Paraphrasing is not allowed. Any interpretive statement or annotation should be separated from the transcript's text and so identified. For the researcher, qualifying extracts or transcripts is the same procedure as qualifying abstracts. The original source should be accessed and compared with the extracts or transcript. However, as the following narrative relates, finding an original source is not always simple.

The September 2000 through June 2001 issues of *The Hoosier Genealogist* published an every-name index of volume 1 in a series of early Knox County, Indiana, court records. Although the series starts with the county's formation in 1790, events prior to 1790 are mentioned, and, except for one interruption from February 1792 to January 1796, this series of county court records runs through November

1813. Due to the absence of marriage records prior to 1807 and deed records prior to 1814 in Knox County, this series may provide a researcher with the earliest extant evidence to establish a person in the county during the preterritorial period.

The *original* court records were transcribed as a part of the 1940–1942 Indiana Historical Records Survey conducted by the Works Project Administration (WPA). Copies of all transcripts, except the 1790–1792 record, are available in seven volumes at the IHS's William Henry Smith Memorial Library. Because of their size, several of the volumes have been divided and bound separately, accounting for the series of seven volumes appearing in eleven books or parts. It is not known if the 1790–1792 record was transcribed, but the original was included in a WPA microfilming project. A copy of the microfilm is available at the Indiana State Archives.

The 1940–1942 transcription is labeled as the <u>unproofed</u> *transcript* of the *Common Pleas Court Minutes, Knox County, <u>Indiana</u>, 1796–1799*. Examine the two underlined words. The transcript is honestly labeled as <u>unproofed</u>. There has been no attempt to remove any accidental errors of omission or commission from the layer of transcription. The second key word, <u>*Indiana*</u>, shows a lack of historical perspective in the Indiana Historical Records Survey. Knox County was a part of the Northwest Territory during the 1796–1799 period. Indiana did not become a territory until 1800, nor a state until 1816. Another reason for caution appears on page 222 of volume 1 of the transcript, in the case of Pierre Lafure vs. Luke Decker in the May 1799 court term. Only eight names are given for a jury of "twelve good and lawful men." The researcher realized from these clues that the transcript might contain serious errors and determined to *examine* the original record. (Incidentally, volume 1 is one of the volumes that was bound in two books, titled "Part 1" and "Part 2"; however, the pagination from Part 1 to Part 2 is continuous.)

Initially, a microfilm of the original was thought to be at the Indiana State Archives. But the microfilm titled "Knox Co., IN, reel no. 60, Item No. 7" proved to have different pagination than volume 1 of the transcript at the Smith Library. For example,

page 21 of the transcript corresponded to page 15 of the microfilmed version of the record, and yet the microfilm contained a paraphrase of the same court case on its page 6.

It was then noted that the title of the microfilmed version was *Minutes of the Common Pleas Court, 1796–1801, Knox Co.* However, the title of volume 1 of the transcripts at IHS was *Common Pleas Court Minutes, 1796–1799, Knox Co.* Notice the differences between the two titles. Not only are they worded differently, the time covered in the microfilmed version is two years longer than that covered in volume 1 of the transcript version. Returning to the IHS's library, it was discovered that the microfilm title matched the title for volume 2 of the transcript series, and that the microfilmed version matched the pagination and the text of the transcript in volume 2. In fact, a search of the microfilmed series showed that the filmed version matched the transcript version for all but the 1796–1799 record as transcribed in volume 1 of the IHS version. At this point, Alan January, the head of the Indiana State Archives, suggested contacting the Knox County Records Library in Vincennes for help in locating the original record for volume 1 of the transcript.

Brian Spangle of the Knox County Records Library explained that the *original* court record books had been transferred from the Knox County Courthouse to his library where each book was stored in a separate archival box. He furnished a list of the original record books in his possession from the labels on each box. Unfortunately, the desired title was not included. Upon requesting suggestions of a possible alternative location for this original, Spangle noticed an archival box that was not labeled. Investigating the contents of that box, Spangle found the original record for volume 1 of the transcripts. Spangle photocopied requested pages from the original 1796–1799 record, which the researcher checked against corresponding pages in the transcript. In this manner, it was verified that the original record book that was transcribed for volume 1 of the series by the Indiana Historical Records Survey is housed and may be accessed at the Knox County Records Library.

Remember the concern about serious errors in the <u>unproofed</u> transcript of volume 1? Compare the following two listings of the same jury:

From *transcript*, volume 1, part one, page 222: *"a jury to wit, Claudius Coupin, Joseph, Borries, Jacques Cardinal, Daniel Smith, Lognor, James Black, and Elias Biddle twelve good and lawful men."*

From *original* at Knox County Records Library, 1796–1799, page 184: *"a jury to wit: Claudius Coupin, Michel Joseph, Lambert Borrois, Jean Bet. Bonham, Alexander Vallie, Gabriel Hurst, Lorient Bazadone, Jacque Cardinal, Daniel Smith, Francois Lognor, James Black, & Elias Biddle twelve Good and lawful men."*

One immediately notices that the latter provides the names of four jurors omitted in the transcript: Bonham, Vallie, Hurst, and Bazadone, as well as first names for some of the jurors that volume 1 of the transcript overlooked.

Short of accessing the original record in person or by photocopy, a minor sticking point may be resolved by correlating the text of volume 1 with that of volume 2, which was found upon inspection to probably be a transcript of an *abstract* of the original that remains in Knox County. Volume 1 contains a run of two less years and yet has 130 more pages than volume 2. As logic dictates the greater likelihood of material being deleted rather than added in a later version, volume 1 is judged to be the older, thus more accurate and complete version. But although the trustworthiness of volume 2 is qualified because it represents a transcriber's interpretation of a summarized version of the original text, it is nevertheless a viable, although lesser, source.

Both "original" records, those in Knox County and the abstracted version on microfilm at the Indiana State Archives, and hence both transcript volumes—volume 1 that is an unproofed transcript of the *original* and volume 2 that is a transcript of the microfilmed *abstract* of the original—follow the chronological order of the court's business. Thus the report of the court's business on a given day in volume 1 is also reported as being on the same given day in volume 2. The exact correlation of dates is useful when trying to determine the likely correct spelling of a name that appears in several variations. For instance, in the court case of Robert Johnston vs. William Linn in February 1799, in volume 1, page 352, a juryman is given as <u>T</u>ebulon Hogue. Within volume 1, the researcher sees that some of the other references to this man vary in the spelling of Hogue, but all agree that Hogue's first name was <u>Z</u>ebulon. Correlating this information with references to the same man in volume 2, the researcher finds Hogue listed in the same jury of the same date in the same case on page 143. This listing confirms the first name should be <u>Z</u>ebulon, not <u>T</u>ebulon.

Checking both transcript volumes also provides more complete information even though not all passages of volume 1 are replicated in volume 2. For example, the shortened jury list in the case of Pierre Lafure vs. Luke Decker in the May 1799 court term reported in volume 1, page 222, is also reported in volume 2, page 72. The latter source, however, provides the complete jury list, as verified above by the original in Knox County.

Many late-eighteenth-century residents of Knox County were French. Often an English-speaking scribe or a later American transcriber would have difficulty spelling or reading a French name. In such instances, additional external sources may be required to fully verify and correctly spell names. Some suggestions of useful sources in these cases follow: Albert G. Overton, "Census of Post Vincennes, 1787," *Midwestern Genealogy* 1, no. 3: 10–14, and 2, no. 4: 7; *Land Claims Vincennes District* (Indianapolis: Indiana Historical Society, 1983); and Knox Co. Probate Records, reel no. 1, 1790–1813. The last source is abstracted and indexed in *The Northwest Trail Tracer*, volumes 10–12, 17, and 18, published by The Northwest Trail Genealogical Society, Lewis Historical Library LRC 22, Vincennes University, Vincennes, IN 47591. All of the suggested sources are available at the Indiana State Library, Genealogy Division.

The Historical Collections Department of the Knox County Public Library (KCPL) holds all records formerly housed at the Knox County Records Library. The Historical Collections Department is located directly across the street from the main KCPL building at 502 North 7th Street, Vincennes, Indiana; phone: 812-886-4380. For further information or to see the library's hours of operation, visit the KCPL's Web site at www.kcpl.lib.in.us/kclib.

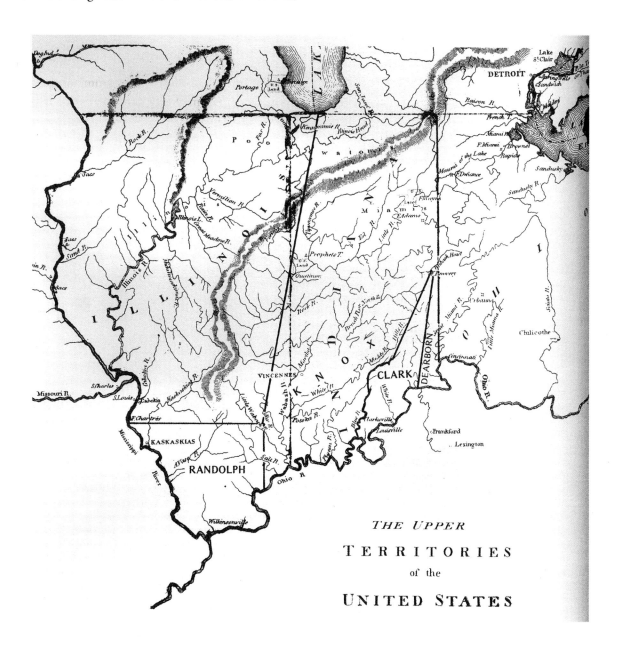

Frontispiece, *Census of Indiana Territory for 1807*, ed. Rebah M. Fraustein (Indianapolis: Indiana Historical Society, 1980; repr., 1990). This map was apparently adapted from Kneass and Delleker, *The Upper Territories of the United States*, map, published in Mathew Carey, *Carey's General Atlas* (Philadelphia: M[athew] Carey, 1814).

World War I Letters to the Sammy Girls of Henry County

M. TERESA BAER

I f you dig through archival material for the world wars of the early twentieth century, you are likely to run across manuscripts for local and national women's organizations that supported hometown troops by writing letters and sending everything from hand-knitted sweaters to candy. "Sammy Girls" was one such group from Lewisville, Franklin Township, Henry County, Indiana.

In1986 the Henry County Historical Society favored the Smith Memorial Library with a gift of the Sammy Girls' correspondence. The oldest letter in the collection indicates that the group may have been formed and functioning in 1914; however, the majority of the correspondence dates from 1918 through the summer of 1919 when the troops were arriving home. The collection is also limited in that it contains letters written by men in response to the women's letters and care packages, but it contains few samples of the women's letters. Therefore, the Sammy Girls Collection, while telling us little about the Lewisville organization, tells us a lot about the lives of the soldiers and sailors whom the women were supporting.

The letters from Henry County's young men praised the members of the Sammy Girls for "doing their bit" to win the war. They overflowed with warm thank-yous, telling the volunteers that nothing was better to them than letters from home. From more than one hundred letters we can glean that the women were sending socks, sweaters, lots of candy, handkerchiefs, shoe polish, and so forth. Some of the responses show the ever-present humor of camp life. Writing from Camp Taylor, Kentucky, on November 30, 1918, Earl Hayes thanks the girls for the toothpaste they had sent, stating that Orville Morgan, his hometown buddy, was so happy to receive his toothpaste that "he washes his teeth all the time now. . . .

He acts like a little kid with an 'all day Sucker.'" Morgan's letter, dated the next day, responds to Hayes's jest, "That's nothing; [Hayes] didn't even know that it was tooth-paste until I told him."

Just like a *MASH* episode, however, this humor coexisted with the sobering facts of life and war. Hayes's letter also states that 806 people in Camp Taylor, Kentucky, had died from the flu. Earlier letters from several stateside sources describe the Spanish influenza outbreak of the fall of 1918 when thousands of Americans died, and towns and cities were placed under quarantines. Stateside hospital personnel also write about the wounded men they were tending,

and the tediousness of military service—constant rounds of eight- to twelve-hour work shifts plus hour upon hour of training, drills, exercises, and lectures. While the continual activity apparently kept fearful thoughts of going overseas at bay, it did not alleviate the perpetual loneliness that the men expressed in many of their letters. Writing from Camp McClellan, Alabama, October 13, 1918, Aaron Ayres closes: "To a lonesome little Sammy Girl from a lonesome Sammy." The men missed home, and they missed their buddies. Often they asked for news of particular friends, and at other times, they supplied word about a fellow Henry Countyite for the Sammy Girls

American Troops in Parade — PARIS - 1918 4th of July   A. P.

Postcard from Wm. Emerson Jones to the Sammy Girls, November 1918, depicting American troops on parade in France on July 14, 1918—Bastille Day, France's independence day

An undated postcard from folder 12 of the Sammy Girls Collection shows a portion of the Loire River, which runs north from the Cévanne Mountain Range in southeastern France, then west to the Bay of Biscay. The Loire River valley in northeastern France is famous for its castles and vineyards.

to pass along. In this way, the women helped keep information flowing about and among their hometown troops. In a letter from Pvt. Walter E. Fowler of the 118th Engineers, France, dated December 17, 1918, we learn that Oscar H. Bills, who had written to the Sammy Girls from Camp Gordon, Georgia, in May 1918, was probably dead. Fowler states that he is "so sorry" about Bills when referring to Bills's brother, Capt. Floyd Duffy Robert.

The letters from overseas do not mention battles or casualties until well after the war is over. Each is marked for censorship, signed and dated by United States military personnel, and some parts of letters are marked through or cut away. We learn the types of jobs different men performed and where they have been, but not specifically where they are. In fact, many of the letters' openings show the place as "somewhere in France." Some letters read like travelogues, providing vivid descriptions of topography, cityscapes, historic sites, and the British and French people. An undated letter from Lt. Ralph W. Test indicates how American troops were greeted overseas. Writing about traveling by train through northern England, Test states, "At every stop the children from the schools were at the station with flags to greet us. A division of Yankees meant lots to them." At war's end, Test, who was a gas officer for the 155th Brigade, supplies details about one of the worst battles Americans fought—at the Argonne. Test states that the last fifteen miles to the front was an area that "was checkered with shell holes and trenches. Barb wire was everywhere. There was not a single house standing. . . . My brigade started with over 10,000 men and came out at the end of that month of terror . . . with but 4000." Of the "thirty days under fire" he reports "Shells screeching

Postcard from Wm. Emerson Jones to the Sammy Girls, November 1918

Postcard of a French train station from Pvt. Walter E. Fowler to the Sammy Girls, March 1919

thru the air[.] the zip of bullets. The whole was deafening. The dead everywhere. The mangled forms of Germans and Americans scattered everywhere. The moans of the wounded. . . . In no mans land the snipers hit all about one but not a bullet touched me. . . . Signing the letter as "a Franklin Twp. Boy," Test mourns his experience, "O if I could but forget the fiendish destruction of that month in the Argonne."

The end of the battle at the Argonne signaled the end of the war. Letter after letter breathes a huge sigh of relief. Speaking of the Armistice celebration in a letter dated November 16, 1918, Pvt. George Martin of the air service exclaims about "such crowds as were there" in Paris. "We sure did do some celebrating, every body was just simply wild." Reacting more soberly about war's end, Clyde E. Rogers with the motor ambulance in France muses in correspondence from January 13, 1918, "I dont think that we will ever see any more war In our time or at Least I hope not. for I think this has took the fight out of the most of the countrys."

Sadly, of course, Rogers was mistaken. But, many soldiers probably echoed this sentiment internally as they began the long wait to come home. Gunney Gray of the Field Hospital at Camp Custer, [Michigan?], writes on December 16, 1918, about the troops who "are comming in here every day from over Seas and from other camps to be mustered out," but he doesn't know when he and the others at his camp will be allowed to go home. Fred Bunker of the 339th Infantry writes morosely from the "rain deer pasture" of Archangel, Russia, on Christmas Day 1918, wondering how the end of the war will affect him and the other men stuck on the bewildering Russian front. Pvt. George N. Showalter was working on the roads in Blondefontaine, France, in February 1919, hoping that rumors he had heard were untrue—that the Americans had to stay in France until all the roads were fixed. Pvt. Fowler had "just returned from Tours, France, with a colored American Troop Train" on December 17, 1918, and was running the trains at Le Mans, France, in March 1919. In April 1919 Pvt.

Marvin G. Showalter in Gondercourt, France, "saw the King and Queen of Belgium and General Perishing [sic] at [a] football game." Finally the long wait, like the war, came to an end. A postcard of June 12, 1919, from Pvt. Clark S. Dishman, formerly with a supply company in France, states that he arrived in New York via the transport *Leviathan* and that he was going to Camp Merritt. In two of the last letters in the collection dated July 1919, Roy Warring to his aunt Erie B. Ross and Ross to the Sammy Girls, we learn that Warring, who had been at a ground school for aviators in August 1918, had been discharged and was living in Chicago.

The Sammy Girls Collection depicts military life during World War I as only firsthand documents can— with immediate impressions, personal insights, raw humor, and unguarded emotions. The letters share the deep attachment young men felt for their hometowns, fellow soldiers, and the wonderful women they had left behind. They remind us of the vital importance of organizations like the Sammy Girls which "did their part" to win the war. The collection also serves genealogists with a harvest of names from nearly ninety years ago.

Photograph of an unidentified soldier from folder 10 of the Sammy Girls Collection. In the summer and fall of 1918, the Sammy Girls were apparently asking their correspondents to send photographs. This may be one of the photographs they received as a result of their request.

Bibliographic Note: Sammy Girls Collection, 1914–1926, M 0453, Indiana Historical Society. Information for this chapter comes from the collection guide, written by Kim Rivers, June 1986, and from the letters in the collection. All the postcards featured in this chapter come from the Sammy Girls Collection.

A PUBLICATION OF THE GENEALOGY SECTION
INDIANA HISTORICAL SOCIETY

HUSBAND

Family Name _____

Generation _____

Born	Place
Chr.	Place
Marr.	Place
Died	Place
Bur.	Place

HUSBAND'S FATHER _____ HUSBAND'S MOTHER _____

HUSBAND'S OTHER WIVES

WIFE

Born	Place
Chr.	Place
Died	Place
Bur.	Place

WIFE'S FATHER _____ WIFE'S MOTHER _____

WIFE'S OTHER HUSBANDS

CHILDREN List each child (whether living or dead) in order of birth Given Names / SURNAME	SEX M F	WHEN BORN			WHERE BORN			DATE OF FIRST MARRIAGE TO WHOM	WHEN DIED		
		YEAR	MONTH	DAY	TOWN	COUNTY	STATE OR COUNTRY		DAY	MONTH	YEAR
1											
2											
3											
4											
5											
6											
7											
8											
9											
10											
11											
12											
13											
14											

PEDIGREE CHART

DATE

NAME

STREET ADDRESS

CITY   STATE

1
BORN
WHERE
WHEN MARRIED
DIED
WHERE

NAME OF HUSBAND OR WIFE

2
Father
BORN
WHERE
WHEN MARRIED
DIED
WHERE

3
Mother
BORN
WHERE
DIED
WHERE

4
Paternal Grandfather
BORN
WHERE
WHEN MARRIED
DIED
WHERE

5
Paternal Grandmother
BORN
WHERE
DIED
WHERE

6
Maternal Grandfather
BORN
WHERE
WHEN MARRIED
DIED
WHERE

7
Maternal Grandmother
BORN
WHERE
DIED
WHERE

8
Great Grandfather
BORN
WHERE
WHEN MARRIED
DIED
WHERE

9
Great Grandmother
BORN
WHERE
DIED
WHERE

10
Great Grandfather
BORN
WHERE
WHEN MARRIED
DIED
WHERE

11
Great Grandmother
BORN
WHERE
DIED
WHERE

12
Great Grandfather
BORN
WHERE
WHEN MARRIED
DIED
WHERE

13
Great Grandmother
BORN
WHERE
DIED
WHERE

14
Great Grandfather
BORN
WHERE
WHEN MARRIED
DIED
WHERE

15
Great Grandmother
BORN
WHERE
DIED
WHERE

16
Gt. Gt. Grandfather

17
Gt. Gt. Grandmother

18
Gt. Gt. Grandfather

19
Gt. Gt. Grandmother

20
Gt. Gt. Grandfather

21
Gt. Gt. Grandmother

22
Gt. Gt. Grandfather

23
Gt. Gt. Grandmother

24
Gt. Gt. Grandfather

25
Gt. Gt. Grandmother

26
Gt. Gt. Grandfather

27
Gt. Gt. Grandmother

28
Gt. Gt. Grandfather

29
Gt. Gt. Grandmother

30
Gt. Gt. Grandfather

31
Gt. Gt. Grandmother

A PUBLICATION OF THE GENEALOGY SECTION
INDIANA HISTORICAL SOCIETY

Contributors: Authors

Randy Bixby grew up surrounded by four generations of her mother's family and was introduced to genealogical research by a co-worker in 1976. She first noticed the strong relationship between Indiana and her home county in Wisconsin while looking for an Irish immigrant ancestor's land records. Bixby abstracted the complete census of Columbia County and neighboring Adams County in *1850 Federal Census of Adams and Columbia Counties, Wisconsin* (Indianapolis, 2002). Copies of the book are available at the Indiana State Library, the Wisconsin Historical Society, and the Library of Congress, among other places, and can be purchased from the author. Bixby is the manuscripts curator/archivist at Southern Illinois University at Carbondale.

Richard L. Bland has a PhD in anthropology (archaeology) from the University of Oregon. He presently works as an archaeologist for the Oregon State Museum of Anthropology, the research division of the Museum of Natural History at the University of Oregon. He spent many years working as an archaeologist in Alaska and maintains his connection with that state by translating Russian archaeological texts into English for the National Park Service and other organizations.

Carolyn M. Brady does freelance local historical and genealogical research in southeastern Wisconsin. She has also worked for museums and historical sites, including Chinqua-Penn Plantation in North Carolina and the Morris-Butler House Museum in Indianapolis. She has a master's degree in public history from Indiana University in Indianapolis. She can be reached through her Web site, www.carolynbrady. com.

Dan Carpenter is an editorial columnist for the *Indianapolis Star* and author of *Hard Pieces: Dan Carpenter's Indiana* (Bloomington: Indiana University Press, 1993).

Douglas E. Clanin earned an MA in history from Indiana University and worked on the Documentary History of the Ratification of the Constitution project at the University of Wisconsin, 1970–1980. Clanin came to the Indiana Historical Society (IHS) in 1980 to serve as editor of the Harrison project, which culminated in a microfilm publication, *The Papers of William Henry Harrison, 1800–1815* (Indianapolis: Indiana Historical Society, 1999). Clanin also served as a book editor and an author who published articles in IHS Press periodicals and in other historical publications. After serving for several years as an editor on the documentary project, the Papers of Lew and Susan Wallace, Clanin retired from the Society in 2005.

Amy Johnson Crow is a certified genealogist, a prolific author and speaker, and the coauthor of *Online Roots: How to Discover Your Family's History and Heritage with the Power of the Internet* (National Genealogical Society Guides Series, 2003). Crow serves as an officer of numerous Ohio historical and genealogical organizations, is a delegate to the Federation of Genealogical Societies, and became the president of the International Society of Family History Writers and Editors in 2006.

Leigh Darbee worked at the Indiana Historical Society for nearly twenty-five years, for most of that time as the library's curator of printed collections. In 2004 she moved into the for-profit sector, becoming assistant to the president of The Indiana Rail Road Company.

William DuBois Jr. is a former managing editor of the *Muncie (IN) Star* and editor of the *Portland (IN) Commercial-Review*. He was an executive assistant to governors Otis R. Bowen and Robert D. Orr, ran a state agency for Gov. Orr, and spent more than a decade in higher education, retiring in 1998 from Ivy Tech State College, where he was executive director of marketing and public relations. He has authored corporate histories, family genealogies, and articles for *The Hoosier Genealogist* and coauthored Gov. Bowen's autobiography *Doc: Memories from a Life in Public Service* (Bloomington: Indiana University Press, 2000).

A native of the Hoosier State, **Richard A. Enochs** worked for twenty years as a genealogical researcher. He was active in numerous historical and genealogical associations and served on the board of the Indiana Genealogical Society. Enochs wrote several articles regarding research and compiled transcriptions of original sources for the *Indiana Genealogist*, *The Hoosier Genealogist*, and other publications. He also authored two books: *Rowan County, NC, Vacant*

Land Entries, 1778–1789 (1988) and *From A to B: Migration Research* (1994). Enochs passed away in 2006.

Raymond M. Featherstone Jr. is a freelance writer living in Indianapolis. He has done volunteer work for the Indiana Historical Society, and his article "The King of Speed: Erwin G. 'Cannon Ball' Baker" appeared in the winter 2003 issue of *Traces of Indiana and Midwestern History*.

James R. Feit is the past president and a current board member of the Indiana chapter of Palatines to America. He is also the former chair of the Indiana Historical Society Genealogy Programs Advisory Board. He is a member of the Indiana German Heritage Society and is a frequent lecturer on researching German ancestry.

Laurann Gilbertson holds a bachelor's degree in anthropology and a master's degree in textiles and clothing from Iowa State University. She has been textile curator at the Vesterheim Norwegian-American Museum in Decorah, Iowa, since 1991. Her current research projects include *Kvinden og Hjemmet*, a Norwegian-language magazine for women published in Cedar Rapids, Iowa, and quilt-making among Norwegian immigrants.

Suzanne Hahn is the director of reference services at the William Henry Smith Memorial Library at the Indiana Historical Society (IHS). She received her master's degree from the Indiana University School of Library Science in 1996. Prior to joining the staff at the IHS in 2000, she worked at the Library of Congress and the Center for Naval Analyses in Washington, DC.

George R. Hanlin formerly served as assistant editor at the Indiana Historical Society, where he helped publish the Society's popular history magazine, *Traces of Indiana and Midwestern History*, and several books, including *Indiana in Stereo: Three-Dimensional Views of the Heartland*. He holds a bachelor's degree in journalism and a master's degree in nonprofit management from Indiana University.

The mother of four children, **Pamela J. Heath** obtained a master's degree in nineteenth-century American history from the University of Indianapolis in 2003.

Andrea Bean Hough holds two master's degrees from Indiana University, in American history and library science. She has worked with the historical collections in libraries at Indiana University, the University of Houston, and the Indiana State Library, where she served as head of the Indiana Division and then as associate director. She was awarded a Fulbright Fellowship in England for 2001–2002. She has served on the boards of the Friends of the Indiana State Archives, the Indiana Online Users Group, the Marion County Historical Society, and the Society of Southwest Archivists.

Giles R. Hoyt is professor of German and Philanthropic Studies at Indiana University-Purdue University at Indianapolis (IUPUI), director of the IUPUI Max Kade German-American Center, president of the Indiana German Heritage Society, board member of the Society for German-American Studies, and coeditor of the International Bibliography of German-American Studies.

Alan January is the program director of the Indiana State Archives. He holds a PhD in American history from the University of Iowa.

Patricia K. Johnson retired in 1992 after thirty-four years as a research scientist. She has been doing genealogical research for thirty-five years. Johnson has authored or coauthored ten books on Elkhart County records and has also authored a Steele family genealogy. She was the quarterly editor for the Elkhart County Genealogical Society for eight years and is currently the publication chair for that society. Johnson was the Northeast District director of the Indiana Genealogical Society for six years and is currently on the advisory board for Family History Publications at the Indiana Historical Society.

A graduate of Indiana University and Harvard Law School, **Tanya D. Marsh** is senior counsel for Kite Realty Group. A genealogical hobbyist for more than a decade, she also serves on the genealogical programs advisory board for the Indiana Historical Society. Marsh lives with her husband and sons in Indianapolis.

A retired journalist, **Chris McHenry** is staff genealogist at the Lawrenceburg, Indiana, Public Library; Dearborn County historian; member of the Dearborn County Cemetery Commission; and Dearborn County Historical Society secretary. She also serves on the advisory board for the Indiana Historical Society's genealogy programs.

A professor of social sciences at Oakland City University in Indiana, **Randy K. Mills** has authored numerous articles and books on midwestern history, including *Jonathan Jennings: Indiana's First Governor* (Indianapolis: Indiana Historical Society Press, 2005).

Gregory Hunter Mobley is an archives specialist in the Ruth Lilly Special Collections and Archives in the University Library at Indiana University-Purdue University at Indianapolis (IUPUI). He received a BA in history from Indiana University in Indianapolis in 1993. His research interests include IUPUI history and genealogy.

An experienced historical author, Rev. **Timothy Mohon** MDiv, is pastor of Grand Prairie Baptist Church in Marion, Ohio. Mohon has published articles about Baptist and Southern Methodist records in Indiana in *The Hoosier Genealogist*.

Ernie (Ernest D.) Moore grew up in Waynetown, Montgomery County, Indiana. After serving two years in the army, he attended Eastern Kentucky State College, graduating with a BS in accounting in 1960. Moore worked fifteen years with the U.S. General Accounting Office and seventeen years with the Department of Energy, retiring as the assistant regional manager of the department's Inspector General Office in New Mexico. He and his wife, JoAnne, live in Danville, Kentucky.

Wilma L. Moore is senior archivist, African American History, Indiana Historical Society. Moore may be contacted for questions regarding African American genealogical research and the study of the history of blacks in Indiana by e-mail, wmoore@indiana history.org, or by phone, 317-234-0049.

A retired healthcare executive, **Leigh E. Morris** is the mayor of La Porte, Indiana. He has been a member of the Society of Indiana Pioneers for almost twenty-five years and is the immediate past president of the society. The late Indiana governor Frank O'Bannon awarded him the Sagamore of the Wabash in 1999.

Patricia Shires Orr became interested in genealogy when she and her husband inherited family documents and photographs. A member of several local and state genealogical and historical societies, she was a volunteer for *The Hoosier Genealogist* from 2003 to 2006 and wrote articles for the publication. Orr holds a master's degree in library and information science from Simmons College, Boston, Massachusetts, and worked as a corporate librarian.

Jeannie Regan-Dinius has been the cemetery registry coordinator for the Indiana Division of Historic Preservation and Archaeology since 2001. She has a BA in history and an MS in information management and urban planning. Before working for the State, she worked as the executive director of Historic Forks of the Wabash in Huntington, Indiana.

Ruth Reichmann, PhD, is an adjunct professor of German at Indiana University-Purdue University at Indianapolis; program director, Max Kade German-American Center; and president emerita, Indiana German Heritage Society.

Elaine G. Rosa is the Indiana Historical Society's (IHS) director of education. She holds a BS in business and an MA in history, both from Indiana University. Rosa joined the staff of the IHS in 2000. Since 2003 she has managed the activities of the IHS Education Department and is responsible for the implementation of statewide educational programming for adult,

family, and student audiences. Previously, she coordinated IHS public educational programs for adults and families. Prior to joining the IHS, she was director of marketing and public relations for a historic house museum in Indianapolis and has more than seventeen years experience in corporate marketing.

Linda Herrick Swisher is the public information coordinator at the Hammond (Indiana) Public Library. She has spoken at local and national genealogy conferences and has authored genealogy columns in *Ancestry Magazine* and for local newspapers. She is the editor of *TWIGS*, the Northwest Indiana Genealogical Society's newsletter. She was a former officer for the Indiana Genealogical Society, the South Suburban [Chicago] Genealogical and Historical Society, and the International Society of Family History Writers and Editors.

Stephen E. Towne is assistant university archivist at Indiana University-Purdue University at Indianapolis. He conducts research on the American Civil War and has authored articles and edited works on Indiana and the Civil War.

Barbara Truesdell, PhD, is the assistant director of the Center for the Study of History and Memory at Indiana University, Bloomington, Indiana. A shorter version of her chapter in this book appears as an introduction to the children's book *Casper and Catherine Move to America*, published in July 2003 by the Indiana Historical Society Press.

Martin Tuohy has served on the staff of the National Archives and Records Administration-Great Lakes Region in Chicago since 1992. He has an AB in history from Wabash College and an MA in U.S. history from the University of Illinois at Chicago. He is currently writing several articles on various topics about railroad workers during the first half of the twentieth century and a book about African American coal miners in the 1870s Midwest. Tuohy serves on the Illinois State Historical Records Advisory Board and the Illinois State Archives Advisory Board through 2008.

The current president of the Indiana Genealogical Society, **Betty L. Warren** has been hooked on genealogy since the age of nine. She earned professional certification as a genealogist from Brigham Young University and owns the family research business Be It Remembered. A long-standing member of the Indiana Historical Society, Warren sits on its genealogy programs advisory board and has taught several of its basic genealogy workshops.

Elizabeth Wilkinson received a BA in history from Indiana University, Bloomington, Indiana, and an MA in history as well as an MLS from Indiana University in Indianapolis. Currently, she is head of the Manuscript Section at the Indiana State Library. She serves on the board of the Society of Indiana Archivists.

Curt B. Witcher, MLS, FUGA, IGSF, is the department manager of the Historical Genealogy Department of the Allen County Public Library and curator of the library's Rare Book Collection. He is a past president of both the National Genealogical Society and the Federation of Genealogical Societies as well as the founding president of the Indiana Genealogical Society. Witcher is also a prolific state and national author and speaker.

Contributors: Editors

———————————●———————————

M. Teresa Baer is the editor, Family History Publications, at the Indiana Historical Society (IHS) Press. She has a BA in history, an international studies certificate, and an MA in comparative history from Indiana University in Indianapolis. Baer has published a number of historical and genealogical essays in books and periodicals and served as the editor for a variety of IHS Press book projects.

Kathleen M. Breen is an editor with the Indiana Historical Society Press. She is a coeditor of the family history publication *Centennial Farms of Indiana.*

Geneil Breeze is the editorial assistant, Family History Publications, at the Indiana Historical Society Press. She has found her Indiana ancestors dating back to the 1840s in Daviess and Monroe counties.

Evan M. Gaughan is the graduate intern for the Indiana Historical Society Press, 2006–2007. After receiving a BA in journalism and history from Indiana University, Bloomington, she moved to the East Coast where she worked in publishing and education. Gaughan is currently pursuing a master's degree in early modern European history at Indiana University in Indianapolis.

Intern for Family History Publications at the Indiana Historical Society Press, 2004–2005, **Amanda C. Jones** is currently the survey coordinator for Historic Landmarks Foundation of Indiana. Jones is a graduate student in the public history program at Indiana University in Indianapolis. She frequently assists her parents in their genealogical quests.

Doria Lynch is currently a candidate for a master's degree in the public history program at Indiana University in Indianapolis and was an intern at the Indiana Historical Society Press, January to May 2006. Doria is currently employed as a historian at the United States District Court for the Southern District of Indiana.

Formerly the assistant editor, Family History Publications, Indiana Historical Society Press, **Judith Q. McMullen** now lives in San Antonio where she is a copy editor for Educational Testing Service.

Bethany Natali completed her master's degree in the public history program at Indiana University in Indianapolis in 2006. While a graduate student she served as the Family History Publications intern for the Indiana Historical Society Press, 2005–2006.

Index